THEORETICAL PRINCIPLES OF PSYCHOSOMATIC MEDICINE

I. T. Kurtsin

THEORETICAL PRINCIPLES OF PSYCHOSOMATIC MEDICINE

Translated from Russian by N. Kaner
Translation edited by Dr. E. Lieber

A HALSTED PRESS BOOK

JOHN WILEY & SONS, New York · Toronto

ISRAEL PROGRAM FOR SCIENTIFIC TRANSLATIONS, Jerusalem

©1976 Keter Publishing House Jerusalem Ltd.

Sole distributors for the Western Hemisphere
HALSTED PRESS, a division of
JOHN WILEY & SONS, INC., NEW YORK

Library of Congress Cataloging in Publication Data

Kurtŝin, Ivan Terent'evich.
    Theoretical principles of psychosomatic medicine.

    Translation of *Teoreticheskie osnovy psikhosomatiche-skoĭ meditŝiny.*
    "A Halsted Press book."
    Bibliography: p.
    1. Medicine, Psychosomatic. 2. Psychology, Physio-logical. I. Title. [DNLM: 1. Psychosomatic medicine. WM90 K964t]
RC49.K8313   616.08   75-5587
ISBN 0-470-51100-1

Distributors for the U.K., Europe, Africa and the Middle East
JOHN WILEY & SONS, LTD., CHICHESTER

Distributors for Japan, Southeast Asia and India
TOPPAN COMPANY LTD., TOKYO AND SINGAPORE

Distributed in the rest of the world by
KETER PUBLISHING HOUSE JERUSALEM LTD.
ISBN 0 7065 1510 2
IPST cat.no.22132 1

This book is a translation from Russian of
TEORETICHESKIE OSNOVY PSIKHOSOMATICHESKOI MEDITSINY
Izdatel'stvo "Nauka"
Leningrad, 1973

Printed and bound by Keterpress Enterprises, Jerusalem
Printed in Israel

CONTENTS

PREFACE

At the beginning of the twentieth century two major trends emerged in the study of human and animal physiology, which continued to develop along parallel lines for several decades without fusing or even drawing together, despite the fact that the climate was favorable for such an outcome.

The first of these trends sprang from Sechenov's concept of the reflex nature of psychic [sic] activity, which led to studies of the physiology of the brain, culminating in Pavlov's theory of higher nervous activity. Pavlov's general theoretical principles, based on a vast quantity of material obtained from the experimental study of conditioned reflexes, have revolutionized medical thinking with regard to the causation of disease and have thus affected every aspect of medical practice, whether curative or preventive. Moreover, the application of his teachings to the field of cortical physiopathology has led to the solution of certain basic problems of neuropathology and psychiatry in the Soviet Union. Pavlov's theories have now become the cornerstone of both the theory and practice of medicine.

The other trend had its source in the ideas of the French physiologist Bichat (1801) who divided all bodily activity into animal functions — those involved in the interaction of the body with the external environment — and vegetative functions which reflect the activity of the internal organs. The distinctive feature of this theory lies in its concern with the physiology of the autonomic nervous system. It was based on the ideas of the British physiologist Langley (1903), regarding the physiological, pharmacological and morphological aspects of the nervous structures involved in the regulation of autonomic activity in the body. These structures play a part in the regulation of such functions as digestion, the circulation of the blood, respiration, nutrition [sic], metabolism, urine formation, endocrine activity and reproduction and they also affect the chemical composition and physicochemical properties of the body fluids.

Langley's theory rests on three main points: a) the efferent nature of the vegetative nervous system; b) the antagonism between its sympathetic and parasympathetic divisions; c) the autonomy of the vegetative nervous system which acts independently of the cerebral hemispheres.

Langley's ideas had a far-reaching influence on medicine, particularly in regard to the diagnosis and treatment of a number of internal diseases. Moreover, the pathological process itself came to be regarded as a disturbance of the normal equilibrium between sympathetic and parasympathetic tone. The terms sympathicotonia and vagotonia were coined to denote an increase in sympathetic or parasympathetic tone, respectively. This theory was used to explain the etiology of many conditions, including hypertension, peptic ulcer, bronchial asthma and cardiac and vascular neuroses. Clinicians began to talk of "vegetatics," "vegetology," and "vegetopathology," and to classify patients as vagotonic or sympathicotonic. Clinical laboratories devised a variety of tests of autonomic function, while clinical syndromes were given names such as vegetative cardiac neurosis, vegetative vascular neurosis, secretory and motor gastric and intestinal neuroses, vegetopathy, vegetoneurosis, vegetative dystonia, vegetative stigmatization, vegetosis and sympathosis. The treatment of these conditions was obviously based on their presumed etiology.

It is not known how long scientific thought would have continued to develop along these separate lines and how long physiology and medicine would have adhered to these two trends — which artificially divided the integrated nervous system of animals, separating its higher nervous activity from visceral reactions and somatic from autonomic functions — had it not been for two fundamental investigations by Bykov and his colleagues, which put an end to this dichotomy.

The first of these studies, by Bykov and Alekseev-Berkman (1926), showed that a conditioned reflex may be involved in urine formation: an internal activity which had hitherto been thought by many workers to be controlled exclusively by autonomic and endocrine mechanisms. The other study (Bykov et al., 1928), demonstrated the existence of an interoceptive conditioned reflex. A temporary connection was formed between the activity of an internal organ (in this case, the kidney) and that of the cerebral cortex, through the stimulation of sensory endings, or interoceptors, lying in the tissues of the internal organs themselves and in the walls of the blood vessels.

It became clear that the Pavlovian principle regarding the formation of temporary connections was also applicable to the activity of the internal organs and to the biochemical processes taking place in the cells of the body. Intensive experimental studies of these aspects led to the conclusion that conditioned reflexes could modify any autonomic process, including the activity of the heart, blood vessels, stomach, pancreas, liver and gallbladder; the permeability of cell membranes; metabolism; thermoregulation, and the periodicity of physiological activities.

These findings vindicated Pavlov who had insisted that all the functions of the body are under the authority of the higher division of the central nervous system. His principle of the integrity of the organism was now given concrete expression, for studies of higher nervous activity began to be merged with investigations of the vegetative processes involved in the digestive, cardiovascular, respiratory and other physiological systems. The animal organism was now regarded as an integral and indivisible entity. The problem of interoception which, like that of the corticalization of autonomic functions, had been studied for several decades with somewhat conflicting results, was now imbued with new meaning. It became clear that the corticalization of autonomic activity constitutes a normal stage in the physiological development of the nervous system. The mechanism regulating autonomic activities is shifted from the lower neural structures to the cerebral cortex, to which all the lower autonomic centers are now subordinated. It was also found that all the internal organs and the blood vessels which supply them, are richly provided with mechano-, chemo-, thermo-, and osmoreceptors. These have been described in detail by Soviet neurohistologists, in particular by members of the Kazan school (Dogel' et al., Lavrent'ev et al., Kolosov et al.) who played a leading part in their discovery. The physiological literature became inundated with papers confirming that the stimulation of interoceptors could produce various visceral and somatic effects (Cherni-govskii et al.) and under certain conditions could also modify higher nervous activity (Bykov et al.). As the structure and function of the interoceptive analyzers became clear, the mechanism of the corticovisceral reflex arcs began to be understood (Chernigovskii et al.). The following aspects in particular were investigated: the specific features of interoceptive conditioned reflexes and the common nature of irradiation, concentration and reciprocal induction of excitation and inhibition for both exteroceptive and interoceptive conditioned reflexes (Airapet'yants et al.); the significance of interoception in the regulatory activity of the higher divisions of the CNS (Gal'perin et al.); certain patterns and mechanisms of interoceptive conditioned reflexes: the closure and receptor mechanisms of the autonomic ganglia, the multistage nature of the afferent connections of internal organs, the principal and collateral interoceptive pathways (Bulygin et al.); the electrophysiological characteristics of the internal analyzers of both peripheral and central structures (Anokhin et al., Delov et al., Chernigovskii et al., Budylin et al., Raitses et al., Tolmasskaya et al.); various intrasystemic, interorgan viscerovisceral reflexes (Parin et al., Rikkl' et al., Solov'ev et al., Polosukhin et al., Poltyrev et al.), and the interoceptive metabolic reflexes (Karaev et al.).

It became evident that feedback plays an essential role both in autoregulation of the activity of the cerebral centers and in the cortical regulation of optimal visceral activity.

Bykov's theory of the relationships between the activity of the cerebral cortex and that of the internal organs (corticovisceral physiology) was based on three principles: a) the corticalization of all the autonomic processes of the body, that is, the functional subordination of the autonomic nervous system and endocrine glands to the cerebral cortex; b) the existence of interoceptive connections between the internal organs and the cerebral cortex, not only through innate, unconditioned reflexes, but also through temporary conditioned reflexes. These latter ensure the optimal activity not only of the organ itself but also of the brain centers which govern the entire "internal economy" of the organism; c) the participation of afferent signals in the maintenance of homeostasis, in higher nervous activity and in the general behavioral reactions of the animal to external agents and in man also to social factors.

The next stage in the development of this theory was based on the study of the vegetative changes which were found to accompany pathological conditions of the cerebral cortex in animals, particularly experimental neurosis (Petrova et al., Usievich et al., Dolin et al., Prikhod'kova et al., Apter et al., Kurtsin et al.).

These investigations clearly demonstrated that a pathological condition of the cerebral cortex is soon followed by significant changes in the autonomic activity of the viscera. While Pavlov and his school had shown that neuroses involved disturbances of normal higher nervous activity, lasting for weeks, months or even years, it now appeared that similar prolonged changes may occur with regard to gastrointestinal secretion and motility, vascular tone, cardiac contraction, urine formation, respiration and endocrine and metabolic reactions. Thus corticovisceral pathology obtained a place within the field of general pathology. It is concerned with the corticovisceral origin of

a large group of human disorders belonging to the category of psychosomatic medicine (Bykov and Kurtsin, 1948, 1949, 1951, 1954, 1959, 1960,
1962, 1963, 1966a, 1966b, 1968; Kurtsin, 1965b, 1971a).

The theoretical interest of this field of study lies in the fact that the experimental neuroses which precede these conditions and lie on the borderline between physiology and pathology, represent the preclinical stage of the
psychosomatic disorder. This stage rarely comes to the attention of the
clinician who is generally only called in to deal with the full-blown pathological syndrome.

The corticovisceral theory was not confined to disorders of visceral
activity, such as secretory disorders of the stomach, liver, pancreas and
intestine; neurogenic polyurias [sic]; endocrine disturbances such as diabetes, thyrotoxicosis and sexual impotence and certain metabolic conditions.
It was also found to play a part in such organic disorders as gastric and duodenal ulcer, hypertension and hypotension, stenocardia [angina
pectoris] and myocardial infarction, bronchial asthma and atherosclerosis.

As a result of these new views a number of experimental models of psychosomatic disorders were created and methods were developed for the treatment and prevention of such conditions. Nevertheless, many essential
aspects of the theory and principles of corticovisceral disturbances were
neglected by both laboratory workers and clinicians, so that the underlying
principles remained imperfectly understood. However, in the last few
years attempts have been made in many countries to determine the central
and peripheral mechanisms, both nervous and endocrine, of corticovisceral
integration and to clarify the role of these mechanisms in the formation of
corticovisceral relationships and in their breakdown. Particular attention
has been paid to the trigger mechanisms of psychogenic stress, the levels
at which corticovisceral and viscerocortical reflexes occur and the pathways
which they follow. Much attention has also been paid to the humoral (hormonal) link in the neuroendocrine mechanisms of corticovisceral disturbances
and the structure and function of the visceral analyzer and the other interoceptive mechanisms of these disorders. Studies have also been carried out
on the various forms of autonomic disturbance which follow the primary
breakdown of the cortical mechanisms governing the "internal economy" of
the organism, as well as on the mechanism of production of specific lesions
of internal organs, as part of the general neurosis which underlies many
diseases. Other investigations have dealt with the role played in the development of such functional disturbances by vascular mechanisms, not only of
the brain itself (and of the cerebral cortex in particular) but also of the
viscera, including the blood-brain and blood-visceral barriers. Nor have
the role and significance of metabolic processes at the cellular and subcellular levels been forgotten, including disturbances of synthesis or activity
of enzymes, hormones and other mediator systems.

My colleagues in my own laboratory of corticovisceral physiology and
pathology at the Pavlov Institute of Physiology of the Academy of Sciences
of the USSR have also taken part in many of these investigations and this
monograph will include our experimental findings, in addition to a review of
the world literature on the subject. Our studies have been stressed, since
they consist of long-term experiments using Pavlovian techniques. These

include the simultaneous or parallel control of the state of the cortex (higher nervous activity) and of internal organs, such as the heart, blood vessels, stomach, liver, pancreas, intestine, kidneys and endocrine glands, using uniform experimental schedules (normal state, experimental neurosis, period of convalescence) and the same animals (mainly dogs) over many months or even years.

It is my pleasant duty to offer my sincere gratitude to the colleagues V.A. Andreeva, V.L. Balakshina, K.F. Britikova, N.K. Gaza, L.N. Gulyaeva, E.K. Kuznetsova, V.K. Bolondinskii, V.B. Zakharzhevskii, I.V. Sergeeva, N.M. Rybnikova, N.F. Suvorov, and V.V. Nikolaeva, with whom I have worked for many years and who have helped in the investigation of a number of highly complex problems, to which they have contributed their knowledge, efforts, and talents.

INTRODUCTION

The mechanisms of corticovisceral disturbances occurring as a result of psychic trauma or emotional stress, or under the influence of unusually powerful stimuli, or stimuli which are biologically and socially incompatible, are no less complex and diverse than those responsible for the normal interactions between the cerebral cortex and the internal organs and autonomic nervous system. This is particularly true of the central mechanisms associated with the neocortical, paleocortical and subcortical structures, which constitute the main foci of disturbance in psychic and emotional stress, psychosis and neurosis in the subclinical forms of corticovisceral disturbances and in the psychosomatic disorders which have of late become widespread throughout the world. Unfortunately, our knowledge in this field is still very limited. It is dependent not only on the results of experimental and clinical studies concerning the part played by various nervous structures of the cerebral cortex and infracortical formations in the etiology, manifestations and outcome of corticovisceral disturbances, but also on the extent of our knowledge of the normal activity of the cerebral centers: their interrelationships, reciprocal influences and, above all, the part they play in the regulation of the autonomic processes of the body. Although these cortical-subcortical interrelationships are of primary importance in the study of higher nervous activity and have been investigated for decades in many countries, much remains unclear, with conflicting and debatable results, while certain aspects have been totally ignored.

Suffice it to say that no consensus has yet been reached on such a cardinal point in the Pavlovian theory of higher nervous activity as whether the closure of conditioned reflexes takes place in the cerebral cortex (Pavlov, 1951; Voronin, 1965; Asratyan, 1970; Ivanov-Smolenskii, 1971), in subcortical nervous structures, such as the reticular formation of the brain stem (Fessard, 1960; Gastaut and Roger, 1960; Doty, 1963), in the mesencephalic region (Penfield and Jasper, 1954); or possibly in all these areas, if the problem is considered from the point of view of integrative cerebral activity (Khananashvili, 1970).

The role of the cerebral hemispheres in closure of the conditioned autonomic and interoceptive reflexes is a still more controversial issue. Certain authors (Bykov, 1942; Airapet'yants, 1952, 1962, 1971; Sager, 1960; Gasanov, 1970; Ivanov-Smolenskii, 1971), maintain that closure takes place in the cortex, while according to others (Belenkov, 1965; Sosenkov, 1965; Karamyan, 1970), it occurs at the level of subcortical neural structures. Even if one accepts the first view, shared by the majority of those belonging to the Pavlovian school, the particular region and cortical layers in which it occurs are still unknown. It may take place in the analyzer nucleus, or in the projection fields of the unconditioned reflex with which the conditioned reflex excitation is associated, or between them, along the intercortical and intracortical paths of confluence of the excitation waves; or, finally, in the dorsolatera areas of the frontal cortex, since after lobotomy monkeys were found to hav lost all the conditioned reflexes which had been systematically established i them over several years (Lagutina et al., 1970). The association areas of th cortex are yet another possibility to be considered.

The mechanism of short-term and long-term memory, a problem closely related to the question of the closure of temporary connections, is similarl obscure. It may be based on the RNA code, on extension of the neuronal processes and filaments, or on the establishment of new interneuronal connections (contacts), or on all these factors. Experiments are continuing to determine the cause of the trace reactions produced in the nervous system under the influence of external (exteroceptive) and internal (interoceptive) stimuli (Sokolov, 1969; Firsov, 1972; Il'yuchenok, 1972). An understanding o the mechanism by which information is acquired, fixed, stored, and "playec back" would also make an important contribution to our knowledge concerning the pathology of memory, particularly the mechanisms underlying the breakdown of memory, as well as the nature of chronic psychosomatic disorders.

Furthermore, despite the considerable advances made in neurophysiolog we do not yet have a clear picture of the localization of the afferent, efferen and coordinating (associative) mechanisms in the brain. Not enough is know about the way in which the autonomic and somatic pathways overlap at differ ent levels of the CNS, particularly in the cerebral cortex and in the subcortical formations of the brain stem. Yet such knowledge is the key to an understanding of the integrated adaptive reaction of the body to environmental factors, in which an important part is played by the autonomic component (Orlov, 1971a; Dolin and Dolina, 1972).

Another controversial question concerns the area in the cortex where the impulse is switched over from an afferent to an efferent pathway and the structures by which this is effected. Interoceptive stimulation from organs in the abdominal and thoracic cavities appears to modify the bioelectric activity of certain zones in the limbic cortex (Delov et al., 1961; Petrova, 1966), while the stimulation of certain points in that area of the cortex gives rise to autonomic effects (Chernigovskii, 1967; Beller, 1971; Orlov, 1971a). It may thus be assumed that in the cerebral cortex and particularly in the limbic area, the apparatus processing the interoceptive impulsation is in close proximity to that which produces the efferent "command" impulse (Kurtsin, 1960). Certain findings also suggest that the cells of the upper (outer) layers of the cerebral cortex (layers I—IV) belong mainly to the afferent system, while those of the lower (inner) layers, especially V and VI, belong to the efferent system, as is the case with somatic innervation in the sensorimotor area of the cortex (Ivanov-Smolenskii, 1971). From histological data it is assumed that closure of the temporary connection takes place in the upper (outer) layers of the cerebral cortex. Yet, such information is clearly insufficient to solve this cardinal problem in the phys iology of higher nervous activity. Nor is any conclusive answer available as to whether the cerebral cortex should be regarded merely as the seat of "closure mechanisms for temporary connections" and of those "analyzer mechanisms" which have been adapted to deal with the interactions between the environmental factors, according to Pavlov's theory of higher nervous

activity (Pavlov, 1951). However, according to Bykov's theory of the corticalization of the functions of the internal organs (1954), the cortex also
governs visceral and autonomic activity and thereby the internal environment
of the body. Still another question concerns the relationship of these mechanisms to the physiological basis of psychic and emotional reactions which so
often lead to corticovisceral disturbances and psychosomatic disorders in
man (Kurtsin, 1965g, 1968a, 1968b, 1970a, 1970b, 1971a; Dolin and Dolina,
1972).

Only concrete facts based on precise experimental investigations, particularly regarding the integration of cortical and subcortical regulatory mechanisms, can provide the answers to all these fundamental questions.

Chapter 1

THE MECHANISM OF CORTICO-SUBCORTICAL INTEGRATION

The new developments in neurophysiology are based on a great variety of research techniques, ranging from stimulation or extirpation to the administration or application of hormonal, mediator, or pharmacological substances and on steadily improving methods of electrographic recording of the primary response. Together with conditioned reflex studies and with the wide use of such techniques as strychnine neuronography and retrograde degeneration of the conducting paths, they have shed new light on certain aspects of cerebral integration. It is now possible to focus on functions of the brain in relation to its structure and specifically on the varying involvement of certain cortical and subcortical formations in the mechanisms regulating viscero-autonomic and endocrine reactions. An impressive body of experimental data has been amassed in this field (see the reviews by MacLean, 1955, 1959; Anokhin, 1958, 1964, 1971; Anand, 1963; Gellhorn and Loofbourrow, 1963; Nauta, 1960, 1963, 1968; Voronin, 1965; Suvorov, 1967, 1971; Khananashvili, 1968, 1970; Ivanov-Smolenskii, 1971; Makarchenko and Dinaburg, 1971). At this point we shall limit ourselves to an examination of the findings and inferences regarding the corticalization of autonomic activity and the central mechanisms of corticovisceral disturbances, both matters of fundamental importance.

The nervous formations and cerebral structures which are of interest in this connection are the limbic system, thalamus, reticular formation, hypothalamus and the cerebellum.

Limbic system. The structure and functions of the limbic system have lately been subjected to detailed study by neurohistologists and neurophysiologists in many parts of the world, as can be seen from the considerable volume of literature on the subject (see the reviews by Kaada, 1951; Fulton, 1953; MacLean, 1955, 1959; Barraquer-Bordas, 1958; Airapet'yants and Sotnichenko, 1967; Orlov, 1969; Makarchenko and Dinaburg, 1971; Zambrzhitskii, 1972), in addition to a number of symposia and conferences on the subject (Montpellier, 1962; Tokyo, 1965; Washington, 1968; Lyons, 1968). The advances in this field have added a new chapter to modern physiology: the neurophysiology of the limbic system. Detailed studies (Kaada, 1951, 1960; MacLean, 1955, 1959; Sakai et al., 1960; Nauta, 1963) have shown that the limbic system is deeply involved in the behavioral, emotional, and olfactory reactions of the organism and in the regulation of its autonomic visceral activity, so that it has come to be referred to as the visceral brain

Structurally, the limbic system consists of a fairly large complex of neural formations, situated at various levels of the cortex and subcortex. It comprises the limbic, temporal and orbital areas of the cerebral cortex, the hippocampus, amygdaloid nucleus, septum, olfactory bulb, fornix, anterior thalamus, and hypothalamus. Its limits are becoming increasingly well-defined as research on the subject progresses. Certain authors (Barraquer-Bordas, 1958; Kaada, 1960) consider the limbic system to consist of the piriform area, posterior orbital cortex and central rhinencephalon (the cingulate gyrus, hippocampal gyrus, uncus, dentate and splenial gyri, hippocampus, piriform gyrus, septal nuclei, fornix, amygdaloid nucleus, and the insula); while according to others (Nauta, 1963; Ban, 1965) it is made up of the following three complexes: 1) cingulate gyrus, hippocampus, hypothalamus, anterior thalamus, central gray matter and mesencephalic tectum; 2) orbital-insular-temporal area with the amygdaloid nucleus; 3) the medial forebrain bundle which is connected with the hypothalamus, septum lucidum, hippocampus and mesencephalon. Others do not include the hypothalamus in the limbic system, although they do not deny that it bears a close structural and functional relationship to it. Many of the above formations have nothing in common with each other, either anatomically or phylogenetically; on the contrary, they are quite heterogeneous, and the reason they are grouped together is that they help to maintain the homeostasis of the internal environment of the organism and play a part in the formation of emotional-behavioral reactions. The limbic system is regarded from a basically different point of view by Airapet'yants and Sotnichenko (1967) who visualize the visceral brain as an aggregate of analyzer apparatuses situated at various levels of the CNS and connected with the viscera independently of emotional and behavioral reactions. All this shows that our knowledge of its structure and function is far from complete.

A fundamental component of the limbic system is the limbic cortex, or cingulate gyrus, situated on the medial surface of the hemisphere. Lying above the corpus callosum it commences posteriorly at the isthmus, where it is directly continuous with the hippocampal gyrus. According to some authors (Fulton, 1953; Portis, 1953), it is derived from the mesocortex, occupying an intermediate position between the archicortex and neocortex (Figure 1), but others (Adrianov and Mering, 1959; Zambrzhitskii, 1972) place it directly in the neocortex, although with certain reservations. This diversity of opinion is due to the very complex and peculiar cytoarchitectonics of the cerebral cortex, which have been described by the Institute of the Brain of the Academy of Medical Sciences of the USSR. The outer surface is derived mainly from the neocortex, while the inner surface represents the archicortex which is separated from the neocortex by the periarchicortex. The base of the brain originates from the paleocortex which is separated from the neocortex by the peripaleocortex. Thus, the cerebral cortex can be divided into five zones. In man, 95.6% of the entire surface of the cerebral hemispheres is taken up by structures originating in the neocortex, 2.2% by those from the archicortex, 1.3% come from the periarchicortex, 0.6% from the paleocortex and 0.3% from the peripaleocortex. The limbic cortex accounts for 4% of the entire neocortex, which is more than the area of the insula (1.8%), but less than that of the postcentral (5.4%) and precentral (9.3%) areas, not to speak of the frontal and temporal areas, each of which accounts for 23.5% of the entire neocortex.

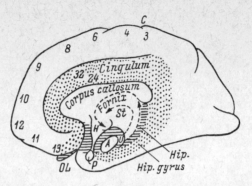

FIGURE 1. Location of the archi-, meso- and neocortex (after Portis, 1953).

Hatched area marks the archicortex, stippled area the mesocortex, blank area the neocortex; 3—13: cortical areas; 32 and 24: anterior limbic areas; H: hypothalamus; A: amygdaloid nucleus; OL: olfactory bulb; U: uncus; C: central sulcus; St: stria terminalis; P: pituitary; Hip.: hippocampus; Hip. gyrus: hippocampal gyrus.

According to the architectonic map of the cortex in dogs drawn by Gurevich and Bykhovskaya (1927), the anterior part of the limbic cortex of the dog consists of areas 24 and 32 and in the posterior part, of areas 23 and 31 (Figure 2), while according to others (Adrianov and Mering, 1959), it is made up of two large areas L_I and L_{II}. It has numerous efferent and afferent connections with various cortical and subcortical structures. For instance, in monkeys it has been found to be connected with areas 8 and 46, in the center of the frontal region; with areas 2, 4, 6 and 45, in the posterior frontal gyrus; with areas 11 to 13 and 15, in the orbital region; with areas 1, 2, 5 and 7, in the posterior parietal gyrus; with area 19 in the occipital region; with areas of the archicortex (hippocampus) and mesocortex (presubicular and entorhinal areas), with the prefrontal cortex (areas 8, 10 and 12), and with the nuclei of the hippocampus, of the reticular formation of the brain stem and of the striopallidal system. In monkeys, cats and rabbits the limbic cortex is known to be connected with the mediodorsal and anterior thalamic nuclei, infralimbic field, reunial nucleus, caudate nucleus, intralaminar nuclei, subthalamus, and with the nuclei of the pons, central gray matter, mesencephalic tectum, preoptic region and hypothalamus. Direct descending pathways have been described from the anterior limbic cortex via the fornix to the posterior hypothalamus, as well as to the outer nuclei of the mammillary bodies and from the posterior limbic cortex to the caudate nucleus, putamen, exterior geniculate body and reticular formation of the thalamus and medulla oblongata. Areas 24 and 32 are connected by associative fibers with one of the areas of representation of the splanchnic nerve in the region of the ansiform (horizontal) fissure (Ermolaeva, 1969).

Experimental studies have been made of the trigger and corrective effects of the limbic cortex on respiration, blood pressure, cardiac rhythm and contraction, salivation, gastric and intestinal secretion and motility, micturition, and the contraction of the urinary bladder (MacLean, 1955, 1959; Delgado, 1967; Devyatkina, 1971). Stimulation of the limbic cortex modifies

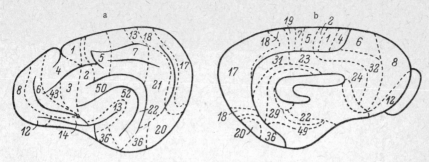

FIGURE 2. Cytoarchitectonic fields (numbers) of the cerebral cortex of the dog (after Gurevich and Bykhovskaya, 1927):

a) lateral surface; b) medial surface.

the interoceptive conditioned reflexes, and the concentration of 11-hydroxycorticosteroids in the blood (Gasanov, 1970), the rate of intestinal absorption and of cellular respiration of the intestinal mucosa, and the movements of the gallbladder and of the intestinal villi. In Chernigovskii's laboratory it has been shown that the stimulation of certain zones increases intestinal motility, stimulation of other zones inhibits it, while in yet other zones both effects are produced, moreover, there exist areas of maximum activity (Beller, 1971). Significant autonomic changes also result from the extirpation of various portions of the limbic cortex. For example, in Anokhin's laboratory extirpation of the posterior part in dogs caused disturbances in conditioned and unconditioned salivation (Kas'yanov, 1949); in Airapet'yants' laboratory excision of the posterior and anterior portions in dogs produced changes in conditioned viscerochemical and visceromechanical reflexes (Vasilevskaya, 1967), micturition reflexes (Airapet'yants, 1962, 1971) and interoceptive glycemic reflexes (Gasanov, 1970). In our laboratory destruction of the anterior and posterior parts of the limbic cortex in dogs modified conditioned and unconditioned salivation to exteroceptive and interoceptive stimuli, as well as gastric and hepatic secretion, micturition and vascular tone (Gulyaeva, 1962; Gaza, 1965a; Bakhtadze, 1967). Many autonomic effects have also been produced in human subjects during surgical operations.

There are a good number of experimental findings which indicate that the orbital cortex (areas 3 and 43) is another important region regulating visceroautonomic activity. According to Kaada (1960), it is even more closely connected with these processes than the posterior limbic cortex and the hippocampal-fornix complex. Of late, the orbital cortex has come to be regarded as a component of the integrated "orbital-temporal-limbic cortex" including the insular and entorhinal formations. Stimulation of the orbital cortex in dogs produces changes in respiration, vascular tone, gastrointestinal motility and salivation (Suvorov, 1967). The vagus and splanchnic nerves are projected on the orbital cortex and it is through them that many autonomic activities are regulated. This significantly extends the range of influence of the orbital cortex on visceral function, possibly to the paraventricular and ventromedial hypothalamic nuclei and from them to the internal organs along the autonomic nerves.

An equally important division of the visceral brain is the premotor corte
(areas 4 and 6) which possesses nervous connections with the limbic cortex
Electrical or chemical stimulation, especially of area 6, produces various
vascular effects, affects gastrointestinal motility, the heart rate and
respiration, and causes the blood pressure to fluctuate. Extirpation
of this area leads to changes in gastrointestinal motility, in metabolic
activity, in exteroceptive conditioned and unconditioned salivary reflexes and in conditioned reflexes involving the liver and kidneys (Bykov's
school). However, extirpation of area 6 does not abolish cortical regulation
of such autonomic activity, which merely functions at a somewhat more
primitive level. Moreover, normal autonomic activity gradually becomes
restored after the operation.

The efferent pathways from the premotor cortex to the internal organs
may use the ordinary pyramidal tracts. The axons of the Betz cells, which
conduct the impulse between the motor analyzer of the cortex and the motor
neurons of the anterior horn of the spinal cord, occupy a relatively small
part of the pyramidal tract. Since both hemispheres together contain only
about 70,000 Betz cells, while each of these tracts contains about a million
fibers at the level of the medulla oblongata, some of these fibers must constitute the axons of the cortical cells which regulate autonomic activity.
They are, however, not the only and probably not the main connection betwee
the premotor area of the cortex and the internal organs. The main connection apparently passes along autonomic pathways in the extrapyramidal system: the thalamus, corpus striatum, substantia nigra, red nucleus and body
of Luys (subthalamic nucleus). The system transmits both excitatory and
inhibitory influences, while stimulation of the internal organs, or of the
afferent nerves connected with them, modifies the spontaneous bioelectrical
activity of the premotor cortex.

In man and higher animals the premotor areas, like the orbital and limbic areas of the neocortex, are probably the seat of the cortical nuclei of the
visceral autonomic analyzer, since, if these areas are removed, the connection between the brain centers and the information system of the internal
organs remains severed for several months. In the period immediately following the extirpation, previously formed interoceptive (visceromechanical,
viscerochemical, etc.) conditioned reflexes disappear and no new reflexes
can be established (Airapet'yants, 1962; Gaza, 1962; Gulyaeva, 1962; Vasilevskaya, 1967; Gasanov, 1970). Evidently, these regions of the cortex also
constitute the site at which afferent impulses are switched over or rather,
transformed into efferent impulses. On passing through the infracortical
formations, including the hypothalamus, the impulses are switched over to
the cholinergic or adrenergic conduction within the autonomic nervous system. However, the fact that the disturbances in conditioned reflex activity
caused by extirpation of the above-mentioned parts of the cortex disappear
after a few months and that normal activity of the cerebral cortex is restored, raises the question as to which of the remaining fields of the cerebral
cortex compensate for this loss of function. Do certain brain centers undergo a process of "reeducation" and "training"? At any rate, the cortical component of the central mechanism governing autonomic activity does not appear to be localized in specific, permanently fixed sites, but is capable of
great functional lability. However, the cortex itself may already contain

certain main nerve centers and others which serve in an auxiliary or reserve capacity, in order to make the cortical system regulating autonomic activity as durable and reliable as possible.

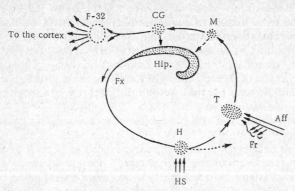

FIGURE 3. Relationships between the cerebral cortex and subcortex — the "hippocampal chain" (after Anokhin, 1958):

Aff: influx of afferent impulsation from the periphery via the lemniscal system; Fr: reticular formation; T: thalamus; H: hypothalamus; HS: humoral stimulation of hypothalamic centers; Fx: fornix; F-32: limbic area 32; Hip.: hippocampus; CG: cingulate gyrus; M: marginal gyrus.

A vital constituent of the limbic system, which MacLean (1955) has aptly termed its "heart," is the hippocampus, considered by different authors to belong to the neocortical or to the paleocortical structures. Like the limbic cortex, it has numerous afferent and efferent nervous connections. The afferent connections come from the hippocampus of the opposite side, from the septal region, presubiculum, entorhinal region and possibly from the cingulate gyrus. The efferent connections pass to the medial and periventricular regions and the hypothalamic mammillary bodies and hence to the rostral, medial and intralaminar regions of the thalamus; in addition, some of the fibers from the hippocampus join the medial forebrain bundle and then proceed to the lateral division of the preoptic area. It is to be stressed that there are connections between the hippocampus and neocortex via the temporo-hippocampal tracts, which connect the entorhinal cortex with the hippocampus. The latter forms part of the excitatory circuit within the limbic system (Figure 3). This circuit, regarded by Papez (1937, 1962) as the nervous seat of the emotions, includes, in addition to the hippocampus, the fornix, hypothalamic mammillary bodies, thalamus, limbic cortex and the cingulate gyrus (Figure 4). Impulses arising in the hippocampus pass upward to affect the bioelectrical activity of the neocortex and downward to stimulate the anteromedial, anteroventral, mediodorsal, central, centrolateral, and dorsolateral thalamic nuclei and the neurons of the anteroventral, dorsolateral, and dorsomedial nuclei of the reticular formation of the brain stem.

Mention must also be made of the connections of the hippocampus with the nuclei of the striopallidal system and of the functional relationships within

the hippocampus itself, such as between its dorsal and ventral divisions.
the basis of experiments on primates, the hippocampus is considered to b
specifically responsible for bringing together exteroceptive and interocep
information within the complex structure of the cerebral formations. Stir
lation of the hippocampus may elicit various kinds of autonomic reaction,
including changes in gastrointestinal motility and secretion, vascular ton
cardiac function and respiration, as well as in the work of the lymphatic
system, in endocrine function and in metabolism. Injury to the hippocamp
disturbs protein formation by the liver, thus altering the serum protein
ratio. It also prevents the establishment of interoceptive conditioned reflexes (Sitdikova, 1970; Chintaeva, 1971). The hippocampus affects the int
nal environment of the body through the hypothalamus and brain stem, wit
both of which it is connected, both structurally and functionally.

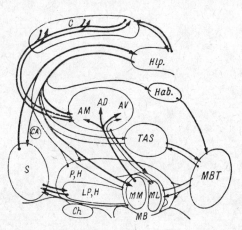

FIGURE 4. Connections between the "Papez circuit" and the hypothalamus
(after Sakai et al., 1960):

AD: anterodorsal nucleus; AM: anteromedial nucleus; AV: anteroventral
nucleus; C: cingulate tract; CA: anterior commissure; Ch: chiasma; Hab.:
habenula; Hip.: hippocampal formation; LP, H: lateral preoptic and hypothalamic areas; P, H: preoptic and hypothalamic areas; MB: mammillary
body; TM: tectum; ML: lateral mammillary nucleus; MM: medial mammillary nucleus; S: septum; TAS: thalamic activating system.

Both the piriform gyrus and the amygdaloid nucleus help to regulate au
nomic activity. Bilateral damage to these structures, or to the ventral pa
of the hippocampus, gives rise to a chronic disturbance of bile formation
and of the sensitivity and motility of the gallbladder. On stimulation they
may inhibit or activate respiration, cardiac function, gastrointestinal mot
ity (Bogach, 1971) and contraction of the gallbladder (Danilova and Klimov
1967). Although many aspects of the afferent and efferent connections of t
amygdaloid nucleus are still obscure, it is definitely known that it contain
projections from the reticular formation of the brain stem, the intralamin
nuclei of the thalamus, the hippocampus and the corpus striatum, as well

from the septum lucidum, cerebellum and the anterior piriform area of the cortex via Broca's band. Afferent fibers also reach the amygdaloid nucleus from the neocortex, namely, from the temporal, central and orbital areas. The efferent connections of the amygdaloid nucleus are represented by two bundles: ventral (assumed also to contain afferent fibers) and dorsal. The dorsal bundle terminates in the anterior commissure, in the preoptic hypothalamic region near the septum lucidum. The projection area of the ventral bundle is broadly overlapped by the dorsal bundle; the ventral efferent pathway has been much less studied. An amygdalo-thalamic pathway is thought to exist. The efferent connections of the amygdaloid nucleus with the piriform cortex and with the temporal and cingulate gyri are well known.

Even less is known about the septum lucidum than about the amygdaloid nucleus. By virtue of its situation, it is considered to be the anatomical center of the entire limbic system. It receives afferent fibers from the amygdaloid nucleus, the hippocampus, and the olfactory bulb. Its efferent fibers form part of the medial forebrain bundle and provide a connection with the hypothalamus, preoptic region, and tegmentum. Functional relationships have been determined between the septum lucidum and the thalamus: water and salt metabolism, vascular tone, and the circulatory system are known to be influenced by the septal nuclei.

In concluding this survey of our present state of knowledge of the structure and function of the limbic system, the following three points must be stressed:

1. The two-way connections between the components of the limbic system itself and between this system and other cerebral structures and formations permit the wide integration of incoming stimuli and exert a regulatory influence on various visceral and autonomic mechanisms. This arrangement in no way restricts the functions of the limbic system which governs even such vital visceral mechanisms as defense and sexual reactions, and visual and auditory sensory responses. It is now clear that the brain reacts to stimulation of an autonomic activity in a complex manner: calling many cortical and subcortical formations into play, some of which are excited, while others are inhibited. These then interact among themselves, producing an efferent excitation of the systems and organs that require to take part in the complex response to the stimulus. However, before starting on its way to the effector organs, the excitation must pass round the closed minor or major hippocampal circuit until it attains a supraliminal (critical) intensity.

2. Excitation of limbic structures produces dramatic behavioral and emotional autonomic reactions on the part of the cardiovascular, respiratory and digestive systems, as well as significant endocrine changes, particularly in the pituitary and adrenals, the hormones of which play an important part in the reaction to stress (see Chapter 6).

3. The fact that the limbic system exerts both excitatory and inhibitory influences on autonomic activity makes for more highly differentiated and often even selective control over the internal environment of the body. Of particular importance is the inhibitory autonomic effect on the circulation, digestion and respiration produced by stimulation of the limbic cortex, especially area 24. The hippocampus takes an active part in inhibition; on electrical stimulation it inhibits alimentary, defense, and motor reflexes in many animal species. It is thought that the impulses flowing from the hippocampus to the reticular formation block the excitation waves radiating from

the brain stem to the thalamus. These mainly produce a theta rhythm which is characteristic for the hippocampus, but which can be synchronized with the bioelectrical activity not only of the thalamus but also of the neocortex. The pacemaker* of the theta rhythm is thought to be located in the septum. The amygdaloid nucleus is considered to be mainly responsible for produci the inhibitory effects of the limbic cortex and other limbic structures on th nuclei and tracts of the brain stem. It also plays a part in generalized acti vation of the cerebral cortex. The amygdaloid nucleus thus appears to serv as a kind of relay station for the entire limbic system.

The striopallidal system. This plays a most intimate and activ part in cortico-subcortical integration. It consists of the two corpora stria ta, each of which is made up of two subcortical nervous formations: the caudate nucleus and the lenticular nucleus. The latter is subdivided into th putamen and globus pallidus. These components are not phylogenetically similar; the caudate nucleus and putamen are more recent and consequentl more sophisticated structures, while the others are old formations. In ani mals with a less well-developed cortex, the striopallidal system and the optic thalamus together constitute the highest division of the CNS. In the higher mammals and man, the striopallidal system is very closely related t the neocortex, especially the premotor area which is part of the extrapyra midal system (Figure 5). The caudate nucleus and putamen are the highest subcortical centers for the regulation of motor function, but their activity, together with that of the diencephalon, red nucleus, cerebellum and the oth formations of the extrapyramidal system, is under the control of the motor area of the cerebral cortex (the pyramidal system).

Like the neocortex, the striopallidal system lacks any clearly defined, le alone direct, connections with the internal organs and blood vessels. Never theless, physiological experiments have shown that this system too may exert a regulatory influence on the viscera. For example, stimulation of th caudate or lenticular nucleus, or injury to these bodies, is followed by changes in cardiovascular and respiratory activation, in salivation and intesti nal motility and in the formed elements of the blood; there are temperature changes and in some animals growth is arrested. Working with dogs in our laboratory, Suvorov (1967, 1971) demonstrated that stimulation of the caudat nucleus with an electric current of 1—3 V causes vasoconstriction, increase pulse and respiratory rates, a rise in blood pressure of 15 to 20 mm Hg or more, and sometimes increased salivation. These effects are accompanied by inhibition of unconditioned reflex salivation, distortion of the vascular reaction to conditioned and unconditioned stimuli, and inhibition of the vas- cular reaction to direct stimulation of the premotor zone of the cerebral cortex. Efferent pathways from the striopallidal system to the hypothalamu mesencephalon and spinal nuclei may play a part in transmitting the cortica influences on visceral activity.

According to many investigators the caudate nucleus plays an active role in complex behavioral manifestations, including conditioned reflex acts. It also exerts an inhibitory effect on many cerebral structures, including the

---

* Pacemaker — a technical term used in biology. It signifies a special internal device controlling the level and changes in activity of certain living organs, as well as their metabolism and function. The pacemaker is usually endogenously regulated (Adolph, 1968).

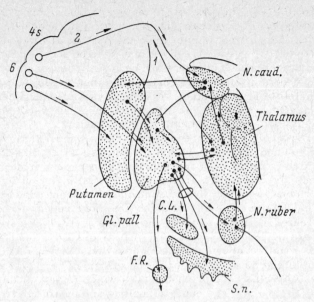

FIGURE 5. Connections of the striopallidal and extrapyramidal systems:

6 and 4s: premotor and motor areas of the cerebral cortex; 1: ascending thalamocortical fibers; 2: pathway from the "inhibitory" areas of
area 4 to the caudate nucleus (N.caud.); Gl.pall.: globus pallidus;
C.L.: body of Luys; N.ruber: red nucleus; S.n.: substantia nigra;
F.R.: reticular formation of medulla oblongata. Arrows indicate the
directions or destinations of impulses.

cortex, counteracting the excitatory effects of the reticular formation of the
brain stem. The striopallidal system is also important in that it inhibits
autonomic visceral activity. It must not be thought, however, that only the
striopallidal and hypothalamic systems can call forth such inhibitory autonomic effects. These may also be produced at other levels of the central
nervous system, down to and including the spinal cord. It cannot be excluded
that in both central and peripheral structures similar effects may be mediated by the interaction of cholinergic and adrenergic innervation: the nervous
stimulus being transmitted by chemical mediators. The action of the cerebellum must also be taken into account among the central inhibitory mechanisms (see below).

    The optic thalamus. The thalamus plays an important part in
cortico-subcortical integration. It is the main subcortical sensory center
in which terminate almost all the afferent pathways leading to the cortical
part of the external and internal analyzers (the thalamocortical pathway or
the specific thalamocortical projection system). The thalamus is connected
with all parts of the cerebral cortex. The fibers spread out from the thalamus toward the cortex as the corona radiata. Impulses of all kinds reach the
thalamus by numerous pathways, such as the bulbothalamic fibers from the
nuclei of the posterior funiculi of the medulla oblongata, the rubrothalamic

pathway from the red nucleus and the lateral spinothalamic tract from the spinal cord (exteroceptive). Fibers of the trigeminal, glossopharyngeal, vagus, splanchnic and pelvic nerves terminate in the thalamus (Durinyan, 1965). The pulvinar receives some of the fibers from the visual tract, wh then make for the visual cortex, within the bundle of Gratiolet. In additio the thalamocortical tract contains sensory fibers of the third cranial nerv on their way to the central and superior parietal gyri. In turn, the above-mentioned areas of the cortex send impulses to the thalamus via the corti thalamic tract. The thalamus is also connected to the frontal cortex by a ferent and efferent pathways. The projections of these cortical pathways mainly located in the somatosensory zones, the removal of which leads to degeneration of the thalamic nuclei. The sensorimotor area of Roland ser for the representation of autonomic respiratory and digestive activity.

The thalamus also makes ample connection with subcortical structures in particular, the reticular formation of the brain stem, the nuclei of the striopallidal and limbic systems, the hypothalamus and the cerebellum. I forms part of the connections of the spinal cord and brain stem with the cerebral cortex. It is connected to the extrapyramidal system through the ansa lenticularis, with the mammillary bodies via the bundle of Vicq d'Az which also contains fibers passing in the opposite direction, and with the ol and the superior colliculus.

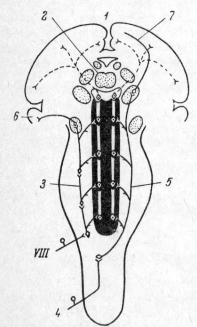

FIGURE 6. Specific and nonspecific afferent pathways (after Magoun, 1958):

1) cerebral hemispheres; 2) thalamic nuclei; 3) lateral lemniscus; 4) sciatic nerve; 5) medial lemniscus; 6) auditory area of the cerebral cortex; 7) specific thalamocortical projection system. Dark area shows the reticular formation of the brain stem receiving collaterals from the lemniscal fibers; the white strips inside the reticular formation indicate the multineuronal path of propagation of nonspecific impulses.

Besides specific nuclei which send somatosensory, proprioceptive and vi ceral stimuli to the cerebral cortex, the thalamus also contains nonspecifi nuclei, belonging to the nonspecific projectional thalamocortical system which exert a diffuse activating effect on the cerebral cortex (Figure 6

The effects of these two kinds of nuclei on the cortex are reciprocal. The abundant structural connections of the thalamus enable it to participate in numerous cerebral functions, including the mechanisms governing autonomic reactions. Some thalamic nuclei, especially the postventral nucleus, are the last precortical relay station for the main stream of afferent impulses from the viscera. The switching of impulse transmission from autonomic to somatic systems also takes place at the level of these nuclei, under the control of the somatosensory area of the cerebral cortex (Durinyan, 1965), the cortex here exerting trigger, corrective, and inhibitory effects (Tolmaskaya, 1964; Il'yuchenok and Gilinskii, 1971).

The reticular formation. Besides the specific projection system, the subcortical centers are also connected with the cerebral cortex by a nonspecific, diffuse projection system, the ascending and activating reticular formation (Moruzzi and Magoun, 1949; Brodal, 1958; Rossi and Zanchetti, 1957; Magoun, 1963; Shelikhov, 1962; Il'yuchenok, 1965). It consists of the reticular nuclei of the medulla oblongata, pons and mesencephalon, the basal part of the diencephalon (subthalamus and posterior hypothalamus) and the intralaminar and reticular thalamic nuclei, with numerous interconnections so that the excitation of any one nucleus is immediately transmitted to all the others and the entire system reacts as an integrated unit. A distinction must be made between the nonspecific projection systems of the thalamus and of the brain stem. Both exert a diffuse activating influence over the cerebral cortex. However, they act reciprocally and this at times results not in activation but in diffuse or selective inhibition of cortical activity. Some authors tend to regard them as a single system, both structurally and functionally, a view which may well be valid, since they are connected by three pathways: the reticulothalamic, the tegmentothalamic and the tectothalamic tracts, while the nonspecific thalamic system acts as the connecting link between the ascending, activating, reticular system and the neocortex. Among the numerous pathways from the reticular formation to the cortex, the most important are those proceeding from the medial and ventral thalamic structures across the ventromedial margin of the internal capsule to the frontal motor, sensory, and limbic areas of the cerebral cortex and from the lateral and dorsal nuclei across the dorsolateral margin of the internal capsule to the parietal, visual and auditory regions of the cortex. Excitation is transmitted via the medial lemniscus and the intraseptal nuclei, which act as relay stations. Through the reticulocortical and corticoreticular connections the reticular formation can become involved in the process of excitation generated in the cortex by impulses arriving via the specific, lemniscal pathways. On the other hand, these connections also enable the cerebral cortex to utilize the reticular formation for autoregulation and for the regulation of activity of the autonomic nervous system with which the reticular formation is connected.

Stimulation or destruction of the reticular formation affects thyroid activity and the rate at which oxidative processes proceed in the body; gastric secretion and intestinal motility give rise to respiratory and circulatory changes. Blockage of the adrenergic structures of the reticular formation by chlorpromazine inhibits the activity of the hypothalamic-pituitary-adrenal system, causing first bradycardia and then tachycardia, with slowing of the respiratory rate and a fall in the rectal temperature (Uspenskii et al., 1964). If the body is excessively hydrated, chlorpromazine exerts an antidiuretic effect by increasing the reabsorption of water and lowering the filtration rate, while at the same time bile formation falls some 30—37% below the initial level (Balakshina et al., 1967). The reticular structures of the bra also exert a regulatory effect on certain autonomic activities, such as the interoceptive metabolic reflexes from the rectum, gallbladder and stoma to the vascular and respiratory systems, and the automatic pressor and c pressor reflexes from the area of the carotid sinus. The cholinergic stru tures of the reticular formation also play a part in the mediation of condition reflexes. These findings indicate that the reticular formation plays an im portant part in the central regulation of autonomic activity. The excitatio generated in it by impulses arriving from the periphery along nerve fiber and by means of chemical mediators in the blood, such as adrenalin and carbon dioxide, radiates in two directions: along the caudal and the rostr projection fibers. In the first case, the excitation passes along the reticu bulbo-spinal pathways and autonomic nerves to the internal organs, promc or modifying their activity; in the second case, it proceeds to the cortex a subcortical formations. The reticular formation also makes a two-way co nection with the cerebellum by means of reticulo-cerebellar and cerebell reticular pathways.

At this juncture it should be noted that the stream of impulses entering the cortex from the receptors in the viscera, blood vessels and endocrine glands, like that from the sensors of the external analyzers, splits in two reaching the brain stem. Some of these impulses are channeled along spe cific pathways through the thalamus into strictly localized zones (the EEG "primary response"; latent period 8—10 msec). The remainder first ente the reticular formation (the nonspecific pathway), where they are probabl delayed for a time on account of the multiple synaptic switches effected by means of chemical mediators (acetylcholine or noradrenalin) and then dis perse to various cortical zones on a broad front (the EEG "secondary res ponse"; latent period 30—80 msec), giving rise to an effect of generalized excitation.

The nerve fibers of the specific pathway terminate actually on the bodi of the cortical cells, ensuring a rapid local effect, whereas those of the n specific pathway terminate on dendrites. Activation of the dendrites genera a more persistent excitation of the cell; this may be necessary to promote the circulation of nerve impulses along reverberating circuits, that is, fo maintaining the excitation after stimulation has ceased (Gaito, 1966). The axonal-cell body endings of the specific fibers are projected mostly onto layer IV of the cortex, whereas the axonal-dendritic endings of the nonspe cific fibers are projected onto all the layers. Since the reticular formatio receives multiple collaterals from all the specific systems, it plays an im portant part in cerebral integration. On electrical or chemical stimulatio it inhibits the bioelectrical activity of the hippocampus and of the caudate, amygdaloid and septal nuclei (Borodkin, 1971), and these limbic formations, in their turn, inhibit the bioelectrical activity of the reticular formation. This is a further example illustrating the fundamental conclusion that all t components of the limbic system are functionally interrelated, with the re that they are continually interacting and influencing one another. This is made possible by the reciprocal nervous connections, including multineu ronal circuits whose main relay stations lie in the hypothalamus and the preoptic zone.

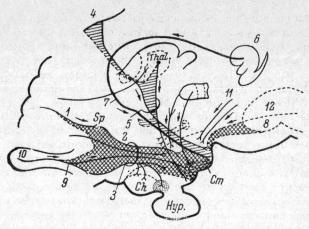

FIGURE 7. Main afferent pathways of the hypothalamic region (after Kozlovskaya and Val'dman, 1963):

1) corticoseptal hypothalamic pathway; 2) septohypothalamic pathway; 3) medial forebrain bundle; 4) corticothalamic pathway; 5) hypothalamic-thalamic pathway (descending fibers); 6) hippocampus; 7) fornix; 8) reticular formation; 9) bundle of Edinger; 10) olfactory bulb; 11) bundle of Schütz (ascending fibers); 12) vago-supraoptic pathway. Cm: nuclei of mammillary bodies; Ch: chiasma; Hyp.: pituitary; Sp: septum pellucidum; Thal.: anterior thalamic nuclei.

Hypothalamus. This takes a central position among the many cerebral neural formations which play an active part in governing the activity of the internal organs. It is closely connected with structures of the brain stem, limbic system, striopallidal formations, thalamus and cortical areas of the forebrain (Lissak and Endröczi, 1965) (Figures 7 and 8). According to the voluminous literature on the physiology of the hypothalamus, as regards corticovisceral relationships this gland acts as a kind of railroad junction which provides trains and despatches them to the center (subcortical and cortical formations) and to the periphery (the organs and tissues throughout the body). However, it also provides transit facilities for the cortical stimulation of various autonomic and metabolic processes, as well as for any cortical correction of the integration of autonomic and metabolic activity required to prevent homeostatic changes, which takes place at the hypothalamic level. Pavlov (1951) compared the hypothalamus to a crossroads on which the stimuli converge from the internal world, that is, from the organs of the body. With its destruction, communications are cut between the cerebral hemispheres and this internal world: the total activity of the organs of the body. The importance of the hypothalamus was considered by Orbeli (1962) to lie in the fact that it is the highest center of autonomic innervation, exerting an adaptive and trophic influence on all the organs and tissues. Many paired nuclei have been identified in the hypothalamus by Grashchenkov (1965) who divided them into three major groups: anterior, medial, and posterior. All of them are closely interlinked and connected with other brain formations by associative, efferent, and afferent fibers. The hypothalamus plays a part in

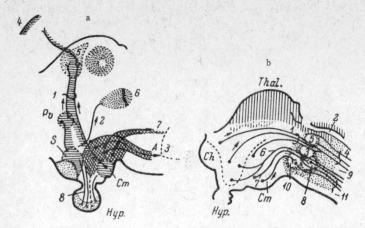

FIGURE 8. Main efferent pathways of the hypothalamic region (after Kozlovskaya and Val'dman, 1963):

a: 1) mammillothalamic tract (bundle of Vicq d'Azyr); 2) pallidohypothalamic pathway (ascending fibers); 3) brain stem; 4) cingulate gyrus; 5) anterior thalamic nuclei; 6) globus pallidus; 7) descending efferent pathways to brain stem and spinal cord; 8) pituitary stalk; b: descending hypothalamic pathways: 1) bundle of Schütz; 2) aqueduct of Sylvius; 3) red nucleus; 4) posterior longitudinal bundle; 5) nucleus of posterior commissure; 6) dorsal hypothalamotegmental bundle; 7) mammillotegmental bundle; 8) central tegmental nucleus; 9) mesencephalic reticular formation; 10) interpeduncular ganglion; 11) reticulospinal pathway. S: supraoptic nucleus; Pv: paraventricular nucleus; Cm: nuclei of mammillary bodies; Hyp.: pituitary; Thal.: thalamus; Ch: chiasma.

the following vital functions: 1) regulation of the blood circulation, digestic respiration, urine formation and body temperature; 2) control of the metabolism of carbohydrates, fats and proteins, as well as of nuclear and other types of metabolism; 3) regulation of the ionic environment within the body (homeostasis); 4) autonomic integration of somatic activity. It is also very closely associated with the regulation of the endocrine system which plays an important part in all cellular and tissue activity. Selye's concept of the general adaptation syndrome (Selye, 1952, 1972), widely accepted in physiology and in clinical practice, assigns to the hypothalamus the leading part i triggering the pituitary-adrenal hormone system (see Chapter 6). Accordin to current views, the hypothalamus also plays a key part in the neurohumo regulation of water and salt metabolism. Of particular importance is the neurosecretory activity of the hypothalamus (Polenov, 1968; Voitkevich, 197 The presence of groups of neurosecretory cells and numerous nuclei regul ing diverse autonomic and somatic functions creates a peculiar mosaic of excitatory and inhibitory processes in the hypothalamus (Voitkevich and Dedov, 1972).

Hess (1956) concluded that the hypothalamus contains two antagonistic zones: ergotropic, or sympathetic, and trophotropic, or parasympathetic, with reciprocal functions. The reciprocal influences of different zones of the hypothalamus are clearly displayed in the regulation of certain gastrointestinal activities (Bogach, 1971; Kosenko, 1971). For example, in dogs t rate of absorption of glucose and chlorides in the intestine is increased by stimulation of the medial part of the hypothalamus and decreased by stimu tion of the posterior part. The stimulus is transmitted to the intestine alor the splanchnic nerves and partly in the vagosympathetic trunks, but also along humoral pathways, by means of adrenalin from the adrenal cortex and of ACTH from the anterior lobe of the pituitary (Dobrovol'skaya, 1969). However, local microelectrode stimulation of individual neurons of the lateral hypothalamic nucleus has revealed the presence of both pressor and depressor neurons in the same, rather than in different zones. A revision of ideas concerning the principle of reciprocal innervation of the hypothalamus may be necessary (Tonkikh, 1968), although this principle certainly plays an important part in the activity of the CNS, including conditioned-reflex mechanisms (Ivanov-Smolenskii, 1971).

The hypothalamus exerts a stimulatory effect on the cortex. Its posterior portion and the mammillary bodies appear to act selectively, since on stimulation they inhibit alimentary but intensify defense conditioned reflexes. Destruction of these formations seriously impairs the analytical and synthesizing activity of the cerebral cortex (Chereshnev, 1971). The two conducting paths from the sub- and hypothalamus to the cortex pass through the internal capsule. One of these connects the hypothalamus with areas 24 and 32 of the limbic cortex; the other connects it with the frontal and orbital cortical areas. They act reciprocally, giving rise to a circular flow of impulses with the participation of areas 4 and 6 of the premotor cortex, hippocampus and other cerebral structures, in addition to the limbic cortex and the hypothalamic mammillary bodies (Makarchenko and Dinaburg, 1971).

Cerebellum. Our survey of the central regulation of autonomic activity would be incomplete without mention of the cerebellum which has long been known as the organ which regulates and coordinates motor activity. It is also involved in the regulation of autonomic processes. Like the cerebral cortex, the cerebellum can be divided into a phylogenetically old, or paleocerebellum, and a new, or neocerebellum. The first includes the vermis and flocculus, the second, the cerebellar hemispheres. While the cerebral cortex is made up of six layers of nerve cells (molecular, outer granular, pyramidal, inner granular, ganglionic, polymorphous), the cerebellar cortex possesses only three such layers: molecular, ganglionic and granular. The ganglionic layer contains large Purkinje cells which provide both afferent and efferent connections between the cortex and the central nuclei: the nucleus deutatus, nucleus emboliformis, nucleus globosus and nucleus fastigii, located in the white matter of the cerebellum. Both the afferent and efferent fibers pass through the three pairs of cerebellar peduncles which connect the cerebellum with other divisions of the CNS. The vermis is connected with the spinal cord and medulla oblongata via the inferior peduncles, forming the cerebellospinal system, whereas the cerebellar cortex is connected with the cerebrum by fibers from the middle and superior peduncles, forming the cerebrocerebellar system.

The two nerve tracts which are of interest here are: 1) the tract running to the reticular formation of the medulla oblongata, from which excitation can be transmitted to the nuclei of the cranial nerves and via the reticulospinal tract to the nuclei of the segmental apparatus of the spinal cord; 2) the cerebello-thalamic tract passing from the cells of the nucleus dentatus, nucleus globosus and nucleus emboliformis of the cerebellum to the thalamus. In addition the cerebellum is connected with the cerebral cortex by the corticopontocerebellar tract. The first neuron of this tract originates in cells of the motor, premotor and temporal zones of the cerebral cortex, passes through the internal capsule, and terminates in the gray matter, where the second neuron takes over, which passes through the middle cerebellar peduncles into the cerebellar cortex (neocerebellum). The nuclei of the pons constitute one of the important links between the cerebral cortex of the same side and the cerebellar cortex of the opposite side; together with the middle peduncles they participate in the pyramidocerebellar and fronto-temporo-occipito-pontocerebellar systems. Still another connecting system passes through the olive. It consists of three sections: 1) fibers connecting the cerebral cortex with the thalamus (corticothalamic fibers), 2) fibers connecting the thalamus with the inferior olive (thalamo-olivary tract), and 3) fibers connecting the olive with the cerebellum (olivocerebellar tract). Extirpation of the cerebral cortex alters the bioelectrical activity of the cerebellum: the slow potentials becoming weaker or even disappearing. However, the connections between the cerebral cortex and the cerebellum are bilateral (Papoyan, 1971) and pass through the pons and thalamus.

Participation of the cerebellum in the regulation of autonomic activity has been demonstrated by many investigators (see the review by Bratus', 1969) notably by Orbeli (1962) and his colleagues. Recently, a short-term experiment in Chernigovskii's laboratory (Talan, 1970) has shown this to be the case with regard to the digestive and urinary tracts and the cardiovascular system. Electrical stimulation of areas IV, V, VIIA, VIIB, VIII, and IX of the cortex of the vermis elicited predominantly inhibitory motor reactions in the urinary bladder and tended to lower the blood pressure, while duodenal peristalsis was sometimes excited and sometimes inhibited. The effects were strictly specific: stimulation of certain points (excitatory zone) always produced excitation, stimulation of others (inhibitory zone) produced inhibition while stimulation of still other points gave rise to both effects (mixed zone). It was found that stimulation of the cerebellar nuclei: the nucleus fastigii, the nucleus interpositus and the dentate nucleus, likewise elicited these autonomic effects. An excitatory, an inhibitory, and a mixed zone were identified in the nucleus fastigii, two excitatory zones and one mixed zone the nucleus interpositus, an excitatory and a mixed zone in the nucleus dentatus. The activity of the subcortical nuclei depends on the cerebellar cortex which permanently exerts an inhibitory effect on them. This inhibitory system is probably reciprocally connected with similar systems in the neocortex, caudate body and hippocampus, through the thalamus and pons and through the corticospinocerebellar and frontal-temporal-occipitocerebellar pathways. It is also connected with the inhibitory system of the medulla oblongata and spinal cord, through the cerebellospinal pathways.

We have thus reviewed the structural and functional connections of many of the infracortical formations, all of which are to some degree connected with the cerebral cortex. They all evidently take part in the general cerebral integration of the mechanisms which govern autonomic processes and visceral activity. The question now arises as to whether the leading part in the integration is played by the cerebral cortex or by the subcortical formations of the brain stem.

Chapter 2

INTERACTION OF THE CEREBRAL CORTEX
WITH INFRACORTICAL CEREBRAL STRUCTURES
AND THE CONVERGENCE OF IMPULSES

It is exceedingly difficult to decide what constitutes the leading factor in cortico-subcortical integration and in the mechanisms governing autonomic visceral activity in the animal organism. Many aspects of this problem have not yet been adequately studied and the results obtained so far do not always lend themselves to comparison. Recently, certain workers outside the USSR have tended to ascribe such activities as integration and coordination, not to the cerebral cortex but to the reticular formation (Gastaut and Roger, 1962), the mesencephalic region (Penfield and Jasper, 1954), or the hypothalamus (Hess, 1956; Gellhorn and Loofbourrow, 1963), mainly on the strength of electrophysiological data. There has also been a revival of the idea that the autonomic nervous system is truly autonomous and acts independently of the neocortex.

Among the infracortical formations, the role is usually assigned to the hypothalamus. This, according to Vogralik (1965), is the principal "coordination center of the organism," responsible for adaptation to the external environment and for the coordination of vital processes and other activities, so that "the cerebral cortex is only involved in the case of so-called behavioral acts, such as the satisfaction of hunger, thirst and other natural needs" (p. 3). According to Sudakov (1970), "the central role in alimentary motivation and in the integration, by the motivation of hunger, of all the other divisions of the brain, up to and including the cortical elements, is played by the alimentary centers of the hypothalamic region; these centers act as a 'pacemaker' for all activity due to alimentary motivated excitation" (p. 188).

The concept regarding the leading significance of the hypothalamus in behavioral and autonomic visceral reactions is also found in a number of other physiological and clinical studies (Makarchenko and Dinaburg, 1971). At first sight, there would seem to be nothing surprising in this, since the hypothalamus occupies a central position among all the subcortical formations concerned with the regulation of the autonomic functions and metabolic processes. It is regarded by Nauta (1960) as a "focal point of the extensive nervous mechanism" connecting the fore- and midbrain. Indeed, every autonomic function in the animal body is affected by stimulation or destruction of the hypothalamic nuclei. Even such general states as hunger and satiety are wholly related to excitation of the so-called "satiety center" in the medial part of the hypothalamic region and of the "hunger center" in its lateral part (Anand, 1963; Delgado, 1967, 1969). The hypothalamus is also said to play a leading role in emotional reactions (Sudakov, 1971).

Yet, these authors who ascribe a role of the first importance to the hypothalamus have not produced any convincing evidence that in man the hypothalamus alone, without the cerebral cortex, would be capable of the high degree of adaptation achieved in persons with a normally functioning cerebral cortex. They tend to underestimate the fact that any emotion, together with its motor, autonomic, and speech reactions, can be elicited in a human subject without implanting electrodes in the brain, but solely by means of the spoken or written word. This vital word acts through the second signal system, that is, through the higher cortical mechanisms. We may recall the reaction of the eminent American scientist Jefferson (1958). After listening to a paper in which all the major activities of the cerebral cortex were attributed to the subcortical formations, he was led to exclaim "Poor cortex! You have come down so low that now you are only used as a suitable spot for the implantation of electrodes." (p. 637). Most worker do not, of course, go to quite such extremes in their theories. They reserve for the cortex the role of the "poor relation." It can be connected to the hypothalamus when required for the satisfaction of thirst, hunger or sexual desire, or in order to evoke a state of aggression or of passive defense.

The facts, however, do not support this view. In the first place, the deni of direct nervous connections between the cerebral cortex and hypothalamu (Szentogathai et al., 1968) is a very moot point. Such connections do exist and they have been histologically demonstrated (Nauta, 1963, 1968; Ermolaeva, 1969; Samoilov, 1971). Those who deny their existence failed take into account the fact that the processes of phylogenesis and ontogenesis, especially at the mammalian level, involve not only progressive increase in the complexity of hypothalamic function and structure, but also the formation of new nervous connections (Karamyan, 1970). Because of their small size, these connections have not always shown up, unless highly sophisticated techniques were used. It has now been demonstrated, for example, that the hippocampus is connected by descending fibers with the mammillary bodies and the tuber cinereum of the hypothalamus (Nauta, 1963; Szentagothai et al., 1968), while the prepiriform region and olfactory bulb are connected with the lateral part of the hypothalamus. Direct pathways connect the frontal cortex with the mammillary bodies and also with the lateral and posterior hypothalamus, and there are projections from certain areas of the frontal and orbital cortex to the supraoptic and paraventricula nuclei of the hypothalamus.

The hypothalamic nuclei are thought to be closely connected with areas 1 to 4 and 6, as well as with the occipital and temporal areas of the cerebra cortex. There are connections between areas 6, 8, and 9 of the cerebral cortex and the posterior and ventromedial parts of the hypothalamus.

A recent neurohistological study on predators (cats) (Samoilov, 1971) has been carried out with the help of modern impregnation techniques in V. N. Maiorov's laboratory and of electron microscopy in A. S. Iontov's laboratory. Both the projection areas (sensorimotor areas S_1 and S_2) and the association areas (parietal areas 5 and 7) of the neocortex have been shown to possess direct efferent (corticofugal) connections with subthalami and hypothalamic formations. The conducting paths pass mainly through the internal capsule, corpus callosum, anterior commissure and the bundle of Vicq d'Azyr (mammillothalamic tract). In addition, the neocortex is connected with the hypothalamus via the paleocortex and archicortex, especially through the hippocampus, retrosplenial region and presubiculum, which are directly connected with the hypothalamus, since it has been demonstrated that their destruction leads to the degeneration of certain nerve fibers in the mammillary bodies. Most of the connections between the cerebral cortex and the hypothalamus are bilateral. Direct connections of the hypothalamus with the neocortex were discovered by Motorina (1966) and confirmed by Makarchenko and Dinaburg (1971).

The nervous connections, moreover, are not confined to direct pathways. There are also indirect functional connections between the cerebral cortex and hypothalamus via a number of subcortical structures, particularly the thalamus, and the existence of such corticothalamic and thalamo-hypothalamic fibers cannot be denied. Moreover, apart from the morphological findings, there is much physiological evidence that the hypothalamic mechanisms regulating autonomic activity in the intact organism are under the control of the cerebral cortex (Anokhin, 1964; Rosin, 1965; Kharchenko and Myznikov, 1967; Bogach, 1969; Kosenko, 1971). For example, the frontal cortex exerts an inhibitory effect on hypothalamic excitation of the salivary and gastric glands (Bogach, 1971). "Liberation" of the hypothalamus from the inhibitory influence of the cortex plays an important part in intensifying autonomic reactions which are generated by emotional excitement (Gellhorn and Loofbourrow, 1963) or by electrical stimulation of the hypothalamus itself (Bogach, 1969; Kosenko, 1971).

Stimulation of the cerebral cortex increases the neurosecretion of the cells of the supraoptic hypothalamic nucleus and simultaneously increases thyroid activity. The excitability of the hypothalamic structures is enhanced in conditioned-reflex alimentary stimuli. Lagutina et al. (1964) found a relationship between hypothalamic reactions and the activity of the limbic cortex; this was most clearly manifested during the formation of highly complex behavioral acts which included autonomic components. Suvorov, working with dogs in our laboratory, observed (1967) that stimulation of the orbital area of the cerebral cortex 2 min before stimulation of the anterolateral hypothalamus completely altered the autonomic response. A pressor vascular reaction with a rise in the respiratory rate occurred instead of a depressor vascular reaction with a reduced respiratory rate. Many other findings of this kind could be cited. Here it is important to emphasize the fundamental point that the activity of the hypothalamic autonomic centers can be triggered or modified by the conditioned-reflex mechanism. In dogs, for example, after 15—20 applications of a sound signal combined with electrical stimulation of the hypothalamus, the application of the sound signal alone produced whining, convulsions, pupillary dilatation, defecation, micturition and other reactions arising from hypothalamic stimulation (Kharchenko and Myzinkov, 1967). A salivatory conditioned reflex can also be established in this manner (Bogach, 1971).

A vascular conditioned reflex to exteroceptive stimuli together with direct stimulation of the hypothalamus is quickly established (Tuge et al., 1964). Reflexes to interoceptive stimuli are similarly formed. Suvorov (1967) succeeded in establishing a conditioned reflex to stimulation of the gastric mechanoreceptors combined with electrical stimulation of the hypothalamu which produced a pressor reaction. The combination of electrical stimula tion of the hypothalamus with a conditioned signal produces a second-order defense reaction with an accompanying conditioned-reflex respiratory re- action (Fedorovich, 1970). Farm animals quite readily develop a condition reflex based on a conditioned lactatory reflex that is closed at the hypo- thalamic level.

Finally, it has been shown in animals that the frontal cortex plays a part in determining the feeling of satiety on eating. In this connection I would recall the experiments I conducted on dogs in Bykov's laboratory, using an established stereotype of conditioned alimentary reflexes (after Pavlov). It was found that a feeling of satiety could be produced either by inflating a rubber balloon in the animal's stomach prior to the experiment in the con- ditioned-reflex chamber, or by combining sham feeding with the balloon technique (Table 1).

TABLE 1. Production of alimentary conditioned reflexes in dogs on sham feeding (after Kurtsin, 1938)

Stimulus	Magnitude of conditioned reflex, drops of saliva			
	hungry (controls)	after sham feeding	stomach stretched by a balloon	sham feeding combined with stretching of stomach
Metronome (+)	16	13	8	2
Light (+)	10	6	8	4
Metronome (-)	0	2	1	0
Light (+)	3	9	2	0
Touch stick (+)	7	5	7	0
Metronome (+)	8	7	5	0
Light (+)	5	4	4	0

Note: Period of application of each stimulus alone — 25 sec; metronome rate (+) 120 per min; metronome rate (-) 60 per min.

Consequently, alimentary satiety in the animal is regulated not by the hypothalamus alone, but also by the cortical centers. These centers may in fact play the leading part because, judging by the magnitude of the con- ditioned reflexes, the normal and often somewhat increased alimentary excit- ability of the cells of the cerebral cortex is almost instantaneously restore when stimulation of the gastric receptors is discontinued.

The cerebral cortex evidently makes extensive use of the hypothalamus in its connections with the internal milieu of the organism, in regulating the functions of internal organs, endocrine glands and the vascular system, and also for emotional-behavioral reactions. Apart from the influence of impulses, the hypothalamus is also subjected to the tonic inhibitory influence of the cortex, particularly the frontal cortex. There are grounds for regarding the hypothalamus not only as playing an important part in the integration of visceral and somatic autonomic activity at the subcortical level of the brain stem, but also as an executive organ which serves to

implement the higher regulatory influences of the neocortex in general
and of the limbic system in particular. Thus, in our opinion, all claims
that the hypothalamus is independent of cortical influence and plays the
leading role in the control of autonomic visceral activity are unfounded,
since it has been shown that though the hypothalamic centers are very important biologically, in higher animals and man they are regulated, coordinated and generally controlled by the higher cerebral centers at the
level of the cerebral cortex.

We fully agree with those who consider that the hypothalamus, like the
other infracortical formations, is part of the integral cortico-limbic-
reticular complex which adapts all the autonomic and visceral systems to
changes in the external and internal environment (Speranskaya, 1961;
Tonkikh, 1968).

Much that has been stated concerning the hypothalamus also applies to
the reticular formation, but with regard to the latter the following must
be emphasized. On the basis of electrophysiological studies, during the last
fifteen or twenty years, the reticular formation of the brain stem, rather than the
cerebral cortex, has come to be widely regarded as the highest organ for the
integration and regulation of somato-autonomic activity. The task of
closure of the conditioned reflex in the brain has also been ascribed to it.
Indeed, judging from the electrophysiological parameters (findings such as the
activation or desynchronization reaction, modification of the EEG frequency
and amplitude, rhythm assimilation, evoked potentials, epileptiform discharges, action potentials or firing of individual neurons), a change occurs
in the biopotentials in the reticular formation of the brain stem and thalamus
even before the appearance of the conditioned reflex somato-autonomic reaction (Fessard, 1962; Gastaut and Roger, 1962; Doty, 1963).

However, such an electrical outburst does not yet constitute a conditioned
reflex. It is rather the reflection of the highly complex interactions which
exist in general between the cerebral cortex and the reticular formation.
The EEG phenomena are usually diffuse and generalized and involve extensive cortical and subcortical areas. In this form they resemble the
phenomenon of Bahnung or the summation reflex, more than a conditioned
reflex (Asratyan, 1970). Nor should it be forgotten that the electrophysiological findings show that only certain cortico-subcortical formations are
involved, whereas the conditioned reflex is a complex phenomenon in which
numerous, though selectively chosen neural structures take part, under the
decisive and controlling influence of the cerebral cortex. This was also
Pavlov's view when he wrote that in the formation of a new nervous connection, the process of closure takes place entirely in the cerebral hemispheres (1951, Vol. 3, book 2, p. 92). At the same time, he did not categoric-
ally deny the possibility that subcortical nervous formations might affect
the closure of a true conditioned-reflex connection.

What is important here is quite a different matter: the phenomenon of sudden closure of conditioned connections which have formed
spontaneously without preliminary training. This is often encountered not
only in the laboratory (Ivanov-Smolenskii, 1971) but also in man, in everyday life. A conditioned reflex is often formed after a single association of
an indifferent stimulus with an innate response, especially when the unconditioned stimulus is of importance for the organism. A word can serve as
a genuine stimulus which elicits a conditioned-reflex response to some

phenomenon, object or person the very first time it is experienced. In
such cases which are encountered at every turn, there are no valid grounds
for assuming that the reflex is first closed in the reticular formation of
the brain stem and that this rudimentary type of conditioned reflex then
gradually assumes its completed form in the cerebral cortex, as would follow from the convergence-projection theory of Gastaut and Roger (1962).
However, the reticular formation participates in the establishment of any
temporary connection by dispatching activating and inhibiting impulses to
the cortex (Voronin, 1965). Now that physiology has recovered from its
attack of "reticular fever" and few workers inside or outside the Soviet
Union insist on crediting the reticular formation with higher cerebral
functions, it has become obvious that the reticular formation of the brain
stem, belonging to the subcortical part of the brain, plays an essential part
in the activity of the cerebral cortex and in the maintenance of its tone.
At the same time, it is subordinate to the cerebral cortex which utilizes
the nuclei and mechanisms of the reticular formation in governing autonomi
and visceral activity (Karaev, 1971).

The strongest connections of the reticular formation are with the
anterior limbic areas of the neocortex (Tolmasskaya, 1964; Borodkin, 1965,
1971; Sokolov, 1969).

It has been experimentally shown that the cortex can also exert a
facilitating or blocking influence on the same neurons of the reticular formation which are activated by afferent stimuli; but it also affects those
reticular neurons which do not respond to afferent impulses. The convergence zones of the cortical projections are the mesencephalic reticular
formation, the nonspecific (medial) thalamic nuclei and the subthalamic
region. By controlling the level of excitability of the reticular formation,
the cerebral cortex apparently controls its own excitability. The existence
of the so-called corticofugal "valve effect," based on filtration of the
ascending flow of sensory impulses at different "switching-over"levels,
must also be taken into consideration. It should be stressed that the
reticular formation acts as an intermediate link in the very complex adaptive reactions of the cerebral cortex. A significant part in the interaction
between the cortex and the subcortical reticular formation of the brain
stem is played by the hypothalamus which is linked to them by numerous
bilateral connections (Shelikhov, 1962; Il'yuchenok and Gilinskii, 1971;
Samoilov, 1971).

Recent electrophysiological studies in the Soviet Union and elsewhere
have led to a clearer and more specific understanding of the influence
exerted by the cerebral cortex on the functions of the reticular formation.
For example, it is now known that the stimulation of various loci on the
sensorimotor, frontal, orbital, temporal and cingulate areas of the cortex
induces electrical effects in the reticular formation, as well as simultaneous changes in bioelectrical activity in the subthalamus, hypothalamus and
nonspecific thalamic nuclei. The majority of the corticoreticular pathways
originate in areas 4 and 6 of the premotor region of the cerebral cortex.
Mention should also be made of the internal capsule through which pass all
the projectional fibers connecting the cerebral cortex with the underlying
cerebral centers and divisions of the central nervous system, as well as of
such connecting pathways as the corticobulbar, corticospinal and corticopontine (frontopontine and occipito-temporopontine) tracts. The principal

pathway for impulses proceeding from the cortex to the reticular formation is the pyramidal tract. Cortical impulses originating mainly in the frontal area either inhibit or promote the activity of the reticular formation, depending on whether they arrive via direct or indirect pathways. As a result of the interplay between the excitatory and inhibitory mechanisms, this activity is either intensified or blocked. A particularly important activity of the cerebral cortex is maintenance of the tone of the inhibitory mechanisms of the medulla oblongata, as is seen from the fact that the medullary inhibitory structures become strongly excited on stimulation of the specific cortical areas, 4s and 19s. Decerebration at the level of the brain stem releases the medullary inhibitory mechanisms from these cortical influences.

The frontal areas of the cerebral cortex are thought by some to play the decisive part in the integration of both behavioral acts and autonomic reactions. It is they which are able to inhibit the subcortical neural structures down to and including the reticular formation, as well as the spinal conducting paths and autonomic centers. In short-term experiments on cats, Ermolaeva (1969), using the method of evoked potentials, detected a change in the bioelectrical activity of groups of neurons in the mesencephalic reticular complex on interruption of the corticoreticular connections. This change is evidence of the elimination of the postsynaptic cortical inhibitory influences. At the same time, the reticular formation generates new biopotentials which did not previously exist, indicating disinhibition of the pathways conducting visceral impulses which do not function when the corticoreticular connections are intact. In man this activating function of the reticular formation is dependent on influences from the limbic area of the cerebral cortex. The great majority of corticofugal pathways are in contact with those areas of the reticular formation which connect the cerebral cortex with lower nervous structures, down to the peripheral nerves (Iontov et al. 1972).

Histological studies (Brodal, 1956) have demonstrated the presence of descending, conducting pathways from all areas and loci of the cerebral cortex to all the components of the reticular formation. The only possible physiological significance of such a connection is that it assists the cerebral cortex to incorporate the most diverse somatoautonomic complexes into an integrated adaptive reaction, while receiving comprehensive information and activating impulses from many points of the reticular formation. This possibly explains the fact that not only the subcortex and cortex, but also many of the internal organs and systems are involved in the pathological process resulting from a disturbance of higher nervous activity, that is, on the breakdown of the complex mechanism of cortical-subcortical interaction.

The descending connections between the cerebral cortex and the striopallidal nuclei include corticofugal fibers from the frontal and temporal areas of the cortex. Impulses pass to the globus pallidus from the precentral and postcentral gyri and to the corpus striatum from areas 2 to 4 and 8 of the cortex. The impulses from the cerebral cortex pass to the subcortical autonomic centers mainly in the corticopallidal or striopallidal structures of the extrapyramidal system. For example, the efferent pathway from the limbic cortex probably proceeds to the hypothalamus via the supraoptic and paraventricular nuclei, and via the thalamic nuclei and the mammillary bodies in the posterior part of the hypothalamus, since destruction of these formations somewhat diminishes the visceral effects produced by stimulation of the limbic cortex (Chernigovskii, 1967). The pathway continues through the nucleus alae cinereae of the medulla oblongata and then along the vagus and sympathetic nerves to the effector organs such as the stomach (Kosenko, 1971). In the cardiovascular system these pathways have been described in detail in monographs by Suvorov (1967) and by Makarchenko and Dinaburg (1971). The pyramidal tract may contain direct pathways from the cerebral cortex to parasympathetic and sympathetic nerves, since it is now known that this tract contains non-medullated autonomic fibers. In the pyramidal tract they reach the nerve cells in the lateral horns of the spinal cord, where the impulses are then switched to other pathways.

It must also be emphasized that the reticular formation may be involved in cortical conditioned-reflex control mechanisms. This vital activity is demonstrated by the following experiments. In rats and rabbits the reticular formation was stimulated with a weak electric current which did not elicit any perceptible reactions. This stimulation was then combined with feeding, so that ultimately the weak electrical stimulation of the reticular formation became a conditioned signal for an alimentary reaction (Tuge et al., 1964). A conditioned reflex of this kind can be established in response to the stimulation of a particular part of the reticular formation, while stimulation of other areas that are not reinforced by the alimentary reaction serves as the differentiation. It would seem that the conditioned reflex produced as a result of direct stimulation of the reticular formation of the brain stem can be elicited by the stimulation of any area in the cerebral hemispheres (John et al., 1965). The following experiments were carried out in Zubkov's laboratory on dogs in whom electrodes had been implanted in the region of the reticular formation of the brain stem. Alimentary conditioned reflexes were then established in one chamber and defense reflexes in another, the reticular formation center being stimulated identically in each chamber. Yet, despite the identical stimulation, the reaction in each chamber was determined by the specific conditioned factors of the surroundings of the animals, so that the dogs salivated in the "alimentary" chamber but displayed a defense reaction in the "defense" chamber. A number of such experiments have been performed, and they all point to the same conclusion: that the reticular formation, like the other subcortical formations, is functionally subordinate to the cerebral cortex which utilizes it whenever necessary for the maintenance of its own tone (the principle of self-regulation), as well as for its connections with viscerosomatic formations via both innate and acquired reactions (Kostenetskaya, 1965; Ivanov-Muromskii, 1971).

The cerebral cortex also exerts a regulatory influence on the nuclei of the striopallidal system. For example, corticofugal fibers from the frontal and temporal areas of the cortex convey impulses from the precentral and postcentral gyri to the globus pallidus and from areas 2 to 4 and area 8 to the corpus striatum. In man the cortical-striopallidal connections are particularly complex and involve a number of levels (Puchkova, 1968).

These pathways and connections are now being determined with greater accuracy, despite the welter of conflicting findings, which arises from the fact that the same cortical and subcortical nervous structures may participate in the control of many autonomic-visceral activities and at the same time serve for their autonomic-somatic projection (Kassil', 1968; Val'dman, 1971; Makarchenko and Dinaburg, 1971; Mogendovich and Temkin, 1971). Nevertheless the following findings seem to have been firmly established: 1) stimulation of the limbic and reticular nuclei, the striopallidal and thalamo-hypothalamic regions, the cerebellum and certain areas of the medulla oblongata and spinal cord produces visceral-autonomic effects; 2) the various nuclei of the subcortical neural structures are morphologically and functionally interconnected, so that they may be consecutively or simultaneously switched into the mechanisms of corticovisceral interactions; 3) the neocortex constitutes the highest cerebral center for the integration and coordination not only of all somatic but also of all autonomic-visceral functions. In other words, it serves as an analyzing and synthesizing center which exerts excitatory and inhibitory influences over all the cells of the body, through a system of sub-cortical nervous formations and structures, peripheral nerves and ganglia and endocrine glands. For this it makes extensive use, via a feedback mechanism, of the general and specialized receptors and of the afferent signals which reach the external and internal analyzers along specific and nonspecific channels; 4) by making wide use of the descending and ascend-ing pathways of the subcortical structures, the neocortex is able to establish contact with various subcortical centers, not only by means of phylogenetic-ally established innate connections but also through ontogenetically acquired temporary connections. As a result the cortical-subcortical relationships and interactions are extremely stereoscopic as well as highly dynamic and reliable.

All these findings are in accord with the principle that the organism is an integrated whole. This principle forms a cornerstone of the dialectical-materialist view of the ceaseless interaction of the life and activities of the animal organism with the constantly fluctuating conditions of the environ-ment; an interaction which is mainly mediated through the cerebral cortex.

To ascribe to subcortical structures the dominant role in the integration of somatic-autonomic and mental-emotional activity, is to deny the evolution-ary development of the living organism in general and of the central nervous system in particular. It means that one ignores the enormous body of evidence testifying that the human cerebral cortex is not only the organ of mental activity, but also the supreme nervous center for analysis and synthesis, which integrates, coordinates, and regulates the condition and activity of all the internal organs, endocrine glands and blood vessels and of all somatic-autonomic activity.

This is why it is impossible to agree with those who assign the cerebral cortex a secondary, auxiliary role in the mechanism of integration and control of autonomic-visceral activity and in the regulation of such bio-logical states as thirst, hunger, and libido. While this point of view em-phasizes the dominant role of the cerebral cortex in the central mechan-isms regulating autonomic-visceral activity, it by no means detracts from the importance of the subcortical stem formations which constitute a "functional unit" with the cerebral cortex (Anokhin, 1971). According to Pavlov, the cerebral cortex analyzes and synthesizes all external and in-ternal stimuli which have previously passed through the subcortical forma-tions, where they are significantly modified and to some extent integrated. In other words, in Pavlov's view the subcortical centers provide a back-ground for the cerebral cortex which imprints on it, as it were, an intricate

pattern of movement of nervous activity, which ensures the highest possible
degree of attunement to both the external and internal environment. Such
an arrangement serves to express the level of sophistication attained by
this division of the central nervous system in the course of its long evolution. Thus, the subcortex with its numerous, structurally and functionally
diverse nerve centers should be regarded as the main intermediate link in
the system of corticovisceral relationships. This does not mean, however,
that it remains passive in relation to the functional state and activity of the
cortex. The subcortex in its turn affects the cortex, constituting, as Pavlov
says, its source of strength. Its influence is exerted in two ways, specific
and nonspecific, represented by the two interrelated thalamocortical projection systems, about which much still needs to be learned (Narikashvili,
1962; Sudakov, 1971; Zambrzhitskii, 1972).

Thus, the cerebral cortex serves to regulate the activity of the infracortical formations, of their "blind strength," to use Pavlov's words,
providing sophisticated guidance and control. In its turn the subcortex
acts as a source of energy for cortical tone stimulating its activity. The
pattern of cortical-subcortical interactions, especially those of the stimulatory and inhibitory systems, determines the condition of the internal organs
and of all autonomic and somatic activity, as well as the general homeostasis
of the body. It must also be remembered that, besides its short-term, rapid
effects, the cerebral cortex also exerts a long-term, prolonged, tonic influence
on the internal organs and activities. These influences are transmitted
through the same subcortical nervous centers which continuously maintain
the tone of the cerebral cortex itself. The result is a constant interaction
between the cortical and subcortical structures, which determines the state
of activity of both the cerebral cortex and the autonomically innervated
organs. In this way the autonomic centers exert a continuous nervous control over the activity of the internal organs (Kibyakov, 1964). Fresh neurophysiological evidence is increasingly confirming that nearly all the
cortical areas are diffusely connected with various subcortical structures,
combining with them to form cyclic excitatory and inhibitory systems. In
his last years Pavlov repeatedly emphasized his belief in the existence of
dynamic systems of conditioned and unconditioned reflexes, including the
important reticulocortical, hypothalamocortical, thalamocortical and strio-
pallidocortical excitatory systems. Their purpose is to maintain a steady
level of excitation in the cortical-subcortical-cortical complex. There
also seem to be interactions between the individual cyclic excitatory
systems. Thus, for example, as soon as the reticular formation begins to
exert an activating (promoting) effect on the neocortex, the reciprocal inhibitory corticoreticular mechanism also comes into play. Numerous findings have also been reported regarding the mechanism of consecutive and
simultaneous, positive and negative induction. For example, reciprocal
relationships have often been detected between the hippocampus and nonspecific diencephalic structures, or between the mesencephalic reticular
formation and the limbic area of the cerebral cortex.

There is reason to assume, however, that in the formation of integrated
adaptive acts the cerebral cortex also exerts a specific influence on the
subcortical centers. This specificity is closely related to ascending
activating influences, as well as to specific subcortical effects. According
to Anokhin (1968, 1971) and to Ivanov-Smolenskii (1971), these latter effects

are dependent on the quality of the biological reactions.   The question of
the form taken by cyclic cortico-subcortical mechanisms was first raised
by Barenne and McCulloch (1938), with regard to corticothalamic interactions, and their findings have subsequently been corroborated by a number
of other electrophysiological studies. It has become clear that the mechanisms of cortical-subcortical reverberation of excitation are not governed
by bilateral corticothalamic connections alone, but that others also exist,
as in the case, for example, of the Papez circuit (1962) involving the limbic
system of the brain.   The physiological significance of such cortical-subcortical reverberations appears to lie in the establishment of stable cyclic
interactions that are specific for reactions of a definite biological quality,
the reverberation allowing a prolonged, tonic state of tension to be maintained in the cortex (Figure 9).   It is also thought to play an important part
in the mechanism of formation of action acceptors (Anokhin, 1971).

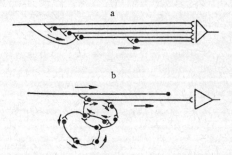

FIGURE 9. Two basic forms of circuit in the CNS
(after Gellhorn and Loofbourrow, 1963):

a) open (multiple) circuit; b) closed (reverberating)
circuit in which a number of circuits interact, thus
allowing activity to be maintained over a prolonged
period.

However, the above approach and the results obtained do not cover all
aspects of the complex problem of cortical-subcortical integration. There
is no doubt that the effect of simultaneous stimuli on various receptive zones of
the body results in the arrival of numerous impulse fluxes in various cerebral
formations. Yet Sherrington (1906) already considered that the convergence of impulses which he himself had discovered was the result of the
spatial and temporal interaction (occlusion and facilitation) of afferent and
efferent conducting paths and formulated the principle of a "final common
path." Subsequently, the principle of convergence was shown to be of the
first importance by the numerous investigations carried out by the Pavlov
school into the closure of temporary connections in the brain. It became
clear that impulse convergence may take two forms: permanent, structurally consolidated and genetically determined, and dynamic, or functional
convergence formed during the life of the organism as a result of external
stimuli on the nervous system. The theory of convergence was put on a
qualitatively new and decisive basis when it was found to take place on

neurons. The multisensory convergence of impulses on neurons of different cerebral formations is also a phenomenon of major importance in the integrative activity of the cortex and subcortex. Studies on neurons not only confirmed the existence of convergence but also determined its various forms. They demonstrated that the convergence on a neuron of multisensory impulses was produced by the interaction of two or more afferent signals of different sensory modalities. Visceral, somatic, visual, auditory and vestibular stimuli were found to cause convergence, with interaction of their impulses, on neurons of different parts of the brain, including the mesencephalic and pontine reticular formations, nonspecific thalamic nuclei, and the limbic system (Anokhin, 1968, and others). This interaction is seen at its most intensive on the neurons of the neocortex, especially in the motor area. Here the pyramidal cells provide the necessary background for the integration of the excitatory process in the brain, since they are particularly suitable for extensive multisensory convergence. Furthermore, it must be borne in mind that the cerebral cortex contains not only afferent and efferent neurons, but also numerous intercalary or associative neurons. Sometimes these latter form entire fields, as in the parietal assocation region, which contains a zone in which the cortical representations of all the analyzers overlap. In such a field the terminals of the analyzers in the different parts of the cortex can connect and interact with one another. Above all, such phenomena occur here as closure of conditional reflexes, switching of the excitation from afferent to efferent paths and overlapping of autonomic and somatic projections. Multisensory convergence and interaction of impulses are also widely represented on the neurons of the association zones of the cerebral cortex.

Besides these multisensory neurons, the cerebral cortex also contains polyvalent (monomodal) neurons, on which only a single type of stimulus converges. The convergence and interaction of impulses on neurons in various parts of the brain can be brought about not only by stimulation of the different analyzer systems of the body, but also by the stimulation of individual cortical and subcortical structures. This has been clearly demonstrated, for example, in the case of hypothalamic neurons which react sensitively to stimulation of the sensorimotor cortex, the mesencephalic and pontine reticular formations and various limbic formations (Baklavadzhyan, 1970; Zilov, 1971). The afferent projections of the visceral systems are organized in a manner which ensures the convergence of signals of different modalities on the same neurons at all levels of the CNS (Kullanda, 1970).

Thus, a knowledge of the convergence and interaction of impulses on neurons is essential for an understanding of the very complex mechanisms of cortical-subcortical integration. In the first place the findings show that the neurons themselves constitute the elementary mechanism of integration, which assumes more sophisticated and certainly more extensive and complex forms at higher levels of the CNS. The highest and most complete degree of integration takes place at the level of the cerebral cortex, which carries out the final processing and the most sensitive analysis of the information reaching the brain and produces the integral behavioral-autonomic reaction. The following analogy might be drawn. The cerebral cortex, acting through the pyramidal system, exerts a refining influence on the tone and contractions of striped muscle which is under the control of the voluntary nerves. In the same way, the neocortex may control autonomic activity via the archicortex, paleocortex and infracortical formations. In this case it would stimulate or inhibit the limbic, striopallidal, reticulothalamic and cerebellar control systems which are directly connected with the viscera, and in particular the hypothalamic centers of the parasympathetic (cholinergic) and sympathetic (adrenergic) innervation. By stimulating different centers, the cerebral cortex can exert a regulatory, excitatory or inhibitory influence on the activities of the internal organs, including the metabolic processes which are taking place in their cells and tissues. It must be strongly emphasized, however, that the corticovisceral regulatory mechanisms are basically synergistic rather than antagonistic. Shortly before his death, Bykov stated (1959, pp. 1019–1020) that "the activity of the cerebral cortex is inseparable from that of the lower divisions of the brain (subcortex), with which the cortex maintains permanent, dynamic relationships. It is the cortex, however, which plays the leading role." This view, expressed by the initiator of the theory of cortical-subcortical relationships, has been fully confirmed by experimental studies of the mechanisms of cortical-subcortical integration, which have been carried out in many countries over the past 10 to 15 years and which have been briefly reviewed in this chapter.

Chapter 3

THE CORTICALIZATION OF AUTONOMIC VISCERAL ACTIVITY AND THE SELF-REGULATION OF THE INTERNAL ORGANS

The thesis of the dominance of the cerebral cortex in the central mechanisms governing autonomic visceral activity is mainly based on evolutionary and developmental data and on studies of corticovisceral physiology.

CORTICALIZATION OF AUTONOMIC VISCERAL ACTIVITY ACCORDING TO PHYLO- AND ONTOGENETIC DATA AND STUDIES OF CORTICOVISCERAL PHYSIOLOGY

In the evolution of the central nervous system the phylogenetically newer formations have not replaced the ancient or older structures but coexist with them, though acquiring a functionally dominant position. Thus it is only natural that though the cerebral cortex (neocortex), the supraseg- mental division of the cerebrum lacks direct connections with the internal organs, it makes contact with them by way of subcortical structures, the brain stem, medulla oblongata and spinal cord, as well as the cerebellum. In the course of phylogenetic development, the neocortex not only becomes larger but also acquires a more complex structure and more complex reciprocal connections with other brain formations: differentiation of the cortical areas and layers takes place, and the analytic and synthetic func- tions of the cells and nuclei become more sophisticated. In this way there arises a part of the brain in which both structure and function are exceed- ingly complex yet highly integrated. In higher mammals it becomes the dominant part of the brain (Shevchenko, 1972) and it is, moreover, endowed with higher mental functions found in no other nervous structures.

It can now be seen why a discussion of the corticalization of autonomic- visceral activity must start out from the fact that the cerebral cortex, the youngest yet most differentiated and sophisticated part of the brain, has taken over all the functions of integration, coordination, and regulation in the broadest sense of the term, that is, the functions not only of the central nervous system, but also of the autonomic (vegetative) nervous system which were previously carried out in a primitive manner by what are now the lower cerebral centers. This is a fundamental premise and, as a re- sult, in describing the subcortical formations the stress has been laid here not on their structural isolation and functional autonomy, but rather on their morphological and functional connections with the cerebral cortex.

In the early stages of postnatal life the cerebral cortex already lays claim to predominance, first through the use of innate, unconditioned-reflex mechanisms and then also through acquired, conditioned reflexes. Onto-genetic studies have shown that in rabbits and puppies, for example, adap-tive behavior in the first two weeks of postnatal life is mainly achieved through a complex of unconditioned reflexes, while after this period, con-ditioned reflex mechanisms begin to gain in importance (Obraztsova, 1964). The autonomic response (intestinal motility) to direct stimulation of the cerebral cortex also arises in the first few days after birth and is similarly taken over by conditioned reflex mechanisms by the 4th week of postnatal life. On the other hand, an alimentary conditioned reflex can be detected in puppies immediately after birth. Interesting findings in this connection have been reported by Volokhov (1964) who claims that the integration of various adaptive reactions in the early stage of postnatal development is mainly carried out by subcortical nervous formations, including the reticular formation. However, once all the connections between the reticular forma-tion and the neocortex and subcortical centers have been established in the animals, integration of the components of the integrated adaptive reaction is carried out at the level of the cerebral cortex. A newborn baby possesses only subcortical, innate connections and the most complex of these, such as thalamic-hypothalamic-stripopallidal connections, are formed in the first few weeks or months after birth. However, the simplest, conditioned and un-conditioned, cortical-extrapyramidal connections arise in the very first months of life, while the first, most primitive, conditioned-conditioned con-nections, such as the cortico-pyramidal connections, start to appear in the 4th to 6th month after birth (Ivanov-Smolenskii, 1971). Verbal conditioned connections become established later (Delgado, 1971).

This sequence of development with age provides evidence that the con-ditioned-reflex mechanism already becomes superimposed on the inborn cortical regulation of autonomic activity in the earliest weeks of postnatal development. This mechanism becomes supreme in the adult state, especi-ally in man, on account of his unique second-signal system, whereby the first system receives verbal signals, through words uttered, heard or seen. Another characteristic of humans is the dominance of the cerebral cortex over the activity of the lower divisions of the brain (Ivanov-Smolenskii, 1971). The influence of the cortex on the subcortical formations may be diffuse or local and thus selective. It takes place by the irradiation and reciprocal induction of excitation and inhibition. The latter may be either unconditioned and phylogenetically determined or conditioned and thus arising ontogenetically. The cerebral cortex, acting through the sub-cortical and other lower centers, integrates the entire external and internal activity of the body and brings it into equilibrium with the external environ-ment, thus providing the optimal conditions for existence.

This concept of predominance of the cerebral cortex has also been sub-stantiated by numerous experimental findings obtained by the following methods: a) direct stimulation of the cortex, b) total or partial extirpation of the cortex, and c) conditioned reflex techniques.

That cortical unconditioned reflexes stimulate the motility and secretion of the viscera was already known in the 19th century, mainly through the well-known experiments by Danilevskii, Bekhterev and Mislavskii, who applied electrical stimuli directly to various areas of the cerebral cortex. Recent experiments using a modification of this same method have demonstrated the importance of the limbic, premotor and orbital areas of the cortex in the mechanism governing autonomic activity, while the topography of these cortical mechanisms was more accurately delineated. It was found that the circulation of the blood was affected by stimulation of the orbital, piriform and anterior sylvian gyri and of the anterior part of the limbic area; respiration by stimulation of the anterior sigmoid, anterior suprasylvian and orbital gyri and of the anterior limbic area; digestion by stimulation of the anterior sygmoid and orbital gyri and the limbic region; while micturition and defecation were affected by stimulation of the limbic area and the piriform gyrus.

The excision of various areas of the cerebral cortex also produced important results, similar on the whole to those elicited by electrophysiological techniques. These also accorded with clinical observations on human subjects with damage to the cerebral cortex from wounds, tumors, or surgery, which produced significant changes in cardiovascular, digestive, metabolic, endocrine and other activities dependent on autonomic innervation. However, the Pavlovian technique of using conditioned reflexes (Bykov's school) has proved to be the most valuable method of demonstrating the principle of corticalization of the autonomic activity of the viscera. By this means an enormous number of experiments performed without the need for vivisection or anesthesia have led to the cardinal conclusion in the theory of corticovisceral relationships: that the cerebral cortex is capable of exercising a trigger or corrective action on any autonomic activity or on any process taking place in the cells and tissues of an internal organ. By this method, conditioned reactions of internal organs and visceral systems, down to such cellular processes as gas-exchange and various metabolic activities, have been reproduced in human subjects, both in the laboratory and under the conditions of everyday life.

Further important evidence regarding the dominance of the cerebral cortex has been provided by numerous reports from the Soviet Union and elsewhere, that in man the conditioned-reflex production of autonomic changes, even at a pathological level, by the suggestion of various emotional, mental, behavioral, or merely viscero-autonomic states can be induced by the suggestion under hypnosis of various emotional, cerebral, behavioral, or merely viscero-autonomic conditions. Thus, there are reports of cardiovascular and respiratory changes induced by the suggestion of fear and pain, heavy physical work, or complete rest. The suggestion of a meal evoked salivation and the secretion of gastric and pancreatic juices qualitatively conforming to the kind of food suggested, while the suggestion of a drink of water or sweet tea induced micturition, hemoconcentration and hyperglycemia. Clinicians and physiologists testify that the word as a stimulus can call forth profound physiological and biochemical changes which are capable of suppressing and even altering innate, unconditioned autonomic reactions. Such findings would seem to confirm and consolidate the idea of the predominance of the cerebral cortex in the central mechanisms governing autonomic visceral activity. Yet, this thesis has recently become the subject of controversy, partly on terminological grounds and partly on account of other differences of opinion resulting from the lack of concrete facts on the subject. The latter is to some extent attributable to methodological shortcomings, that is, to experimental error. On the whole, however, it would appear that the controversy mainly involves a fundamental principle: the relationship between the cerebral cortex and the internal organs. This matter therefore requires to be discussed further here, not least on account of the polemical nature of certain publications by opponents of the theory of cortical dominance. For example, in the recent monograph by Orlov (1971a), the author openly states: "One of the purposes of this work is to counter the widespread opinion that the cerebral cortex plays a dominant and ubiquitous part in the regulation of all types of cardiovascular activity, both normal and pathological" (p. 7). Again, in a paper delivered to the All-Union Conference on Problems of Corticovisceral Physiology, Konradi (1971) declared: "The dogmatic notion, commonly encountered in the literature, that the cerebral cortex plays a 'leading' part in the regulation of autonomic activity, needs to be revised" (p. 117).

Any discussion of these different points of view must begin with the question of terminology, which inevitably affects the experimental aspects.

SOME TERMINOLOGICAL AND METHODOLOGICAL ASPECTS OF THE THEORY OF CORTICO-VISCERAL RELATIONSHIPS

Expressions such as "the cerebral cortex influences the activity of the internal organs" or "the cerebral cortex regulates the functions of the internal organs" have long been freely used in the physiological and clinical literature. It has been claimed (Orlov, 1968; Chernigovskii, 1969) that the terms "influence" and "regulate" do not mean the same thing and that Bykov tended to use the former term, especially in his early works. It is true that cortical influences need not necessarily be regulatory, as, for example, in neurotic states of the cerebral cortex. However, under normal conditions, by influencing the activity of the internal organs, the cerebral cortex thereby regulates their functions. For its part, regulation cannot occur without an influence being exerted. This question was not discussed by Bykov and his colleagues and the two terms were often used indiscriminately. For example, in his paper "The Influence of the Cerebral Cortex on the Activity of the Internal Organs and Tissues (Results and Prospects)," Bykov (1937) stated "Even this very incomplete list demonstrates the profound effects of cerebral influences and shows that processes assumed to be 'unconscious' can be regulated by stimuli from the higher division of the CNS" (p. 143). In some of the titles of his papers the two terms appear on an equal footing as, for example: "The influence of the cerebral cortex on tissue processes" and "Cortical regulation of the activity of internal organs." Bykov ascribed more importance to the term "regulation," especially when discussing the fundamental question whether the cerebral cortex influences visceral activity and the chemical processes in the cells and whether such influence would be of a general or of a specific nature. Thus, in the introductory pages of his book: "The Cerebral Cortex and the Internal Organs" he outlined a scheme for "determining the patterns of cortical regulation of all activities" (Bykov, 1942, p. 30). It may be more convenient to unite these terms and to speak of "regulatory influences," as did Chernigovskii (1969), or of "cortical regulatory activity" after

Airapet'yants (1971), or else of cortical mechanisms for the regulation of processes, as follows from the concept of the development of physiological regulation elaborated by Adolph,(1968),or possibly to replace them altogether by the single word "control"*. According to Dali's dictionary Pavlov uses an equivalent term in his well-known aphorism (1951): "The higher [nervous] division wields authority over all the phenomena occurring in the body" (Vol. 3, book 2, p. 410). However, all these difficulties can be overcome by regarding this as a purely terminological controversy, so that from the semantic point of view, each of the above terms differs slightly from the others, they all indicate the identical phenomenon: the regulation of processes and activities, and may therefore be used interchangeably.

Furthermore, it seems to us that whenever the adjective "corticovisceral" is attached to terms such as "physiology," "theory," or "relationships," it quite unambiguously emphasizes the specific role and significance of the cerebral cortex, rather than of the higher nervous system in general, in relation to the activity of the internal organ. For the influence of different parts of the CNS was and often still is studied apart from the cerebral cortical mechanisms. It certainly never occurred to us that just this term would serve to distort the matter, puzzling certain authors and moving them to rebuke the proponents of the corticovisceral theory for establishing a direct connection between the cerebral cortex and the internal organs (Nikulin, 1954). It was also claimed that the corticovisceral theory failed to account for the complex, highly ramified chain of reflexes (Davydovskii, 1954), or "for the mechanisms which serve to connect the cortical and autonomic reactions" (Myasnikov, 1958, p. 32) and that it would be more correct to represent these relationships as cortical-subcortical-ganglio-visceral (Asratyan and Simonov, 1965), that is, to incorporate in the name the intermediate stages between which impulses travel from the cerebral cortex to the internal organs. In recent years Soviet physiologists, in both official statements and private conversations about corticovisceral matters have often been heard to substitute the term "cerebrovisceral" for "cortico-visceral." In this they were quite correctly guided by the consideration that the entire cerebrum, that is, the subcortex in addition to the cortex, takes part in the regulation of visceral activity. For the same reason, a few years ago the American scientist S. A. Corson called his laboratory at the Institute of Psychiatry at Columbus, the laboratory of cerebrovisceral physiology.

It has also been proposed that the corticovisceral theory should be renamed the "cortical-subcortical-thalamic-hypothalamic, medulla oblongata choline-adrenergic, humoral-hormonal theory." The name of any theory dealing with relationships and mechanisms of interaction may, if so desired incorporate the names of all the nervous and endocrine formations and all the chemical and physical substances which play any part in them. Such a device might satisfy those who suffer from scientific myopia and regard the concise term "corticovisceral relationships" as a "black box" and nothing more. Yet, how can any connection between the cerebral cortex and the viscera be conceived without the intermediate nervous formations?

---

* [The Russian term used here is "upravlenie" which itself has at least 2 meanings and can equally well be translated as "govern." The 2 terms are used more or less interchangeably in this translation, unless the context seems to favor one over the other.]

The limbic system would be missing, with its cortical and subcortical nervous structures, as well as the striopallidal and thalamic-hypothalamic regions, the reticular formation of the brain stem, the specific and non-specific thalamic systems, the medulla oblongata and the spinal cord and, finally, there would be an absence of the peripheral autonomic nerves and ganglia which transmit a continuous flow of impulses of descending "command" and of ascending visceral information. At the present stage of knowledge, the corticovisceral connection cannot be envisaged without the participation of the endocrine system and other biologically active sub-stances, particularly the central and peripheral mediators of nervous ex-citation. Yet, what is the point of including in the overall appellation all those stations, main and intermediate, all the halts and sidings, which make up the corticovisceral system of communication and all the different routes taken by the "commands" and "responses"? Science normally aims at the concise formulation of ideas, assuming a certain level of education and of knowledge of the subject.

None of the adherents of the theory of corticovisceral physiology and pathology have implied that direct connections exist between the cerebral cortex and internal organs, if for no other reason than because the cortico-visceral and viscerocortical reflex mechanisms, like so many other bio-logical mechanisms of an adaptive nature, consist of innumerable neural and humoral components whose activity takes the form of chain reactions. Such reactions incorporate numerous short and long reflex arcs which originate in different receptor fields and are closed at different levels of the nervous system. The trigger mechanisms may be nervous impulses or hormonal, mediator or metabolic substances, which determine the volume, ramifications, extent and depth of the reactions (Bykov, 1942; Anokhin, 1958, 1971; Bykov and Kurtsin, 1960; Kurtsin, 1960, 1965i, 1968c; Voronin, 1965; Tonkikh, 1968; Beritov, 1969; Asratyan, 1970; Bulygin, 1970, 1971; Ivanov-Smolenskii, 1971). In short, we are in favor of retaining the traditional terms "corticovisceral theory" and "corticovisceral physiology and pathology" first used in Soviet medicine and accepted by progressive scientists in many countries.

A different attitude toward these terms has been adopted by Pshonik (1970). According to him, the existing demonstrations of the formation of visceral conditioned reflexes do not mirror reality, since laboratory experi-ments are artificial models created by the experimenter and the findings obtained in animal experiments of this kind under abnormal conditions can-not be extrapolated to natural conditions. His view is apparently shared by Konradi (1971), who writes: "The suggestion that interoceptive conditioned reflexes may exist in the internal organs is of great theoretical interest. It must, however, remain almost entirely within the framework of laboratory findings until it can be shown that interoceptive conditioned (and for that matter, even unconditioned reflexes) play a part in the normal activity of the organs whose receptors have been shown to be capable of taking part in such reflexes" (p. 118).

This point of view is not essentially new if regarded in the framework of the history of the theory of conditioned reflexes (Maiorov, 1949, 1954). In the 1920s and 1930s when Pavlov's dialectical-materialist theory of higher nervous activity began to gain ground in other countries, certain Western scientists claimed that, being based on experiments performed in soundproof chambers, it could have no validity for real life. Yet, even then, it became obvious to many that this criticism was groundless, since life itself furnished the decisive arguments in this respect. In the Soviet Union and elsewhere it was repeatedly shown that the principle of temporar connection was valid for man as well as for animals.

Similar objections, albeit in a more up-to-date form, are now again being voiced, this time with reference to the cortical regulation of the activity of internal organs, which is an outcome of Pavlovian teachings. The views of Pshonik and of Konradi intentionally or unintentionally cast doubt on the whole of experimental physiology, whose significance for the solution of many problems concerning the nature and activity of man has repeatedly been demonstrated and is now generally recognized throughout the world. Furthermore, this criticism is also based on incorrect premises, since the production of autonomic effects by conditioned reflex mechanisms under laboratory (i. e. artificial) conditions has been repeatedly confirmed in studies on animals and man under normal conditions (Ol'nyanskaya and Slonim, 1971). The following examples will suffice: in man, gastric and pancreatic secretion occurs in response to the sight and smell of food (a natural conditioned reflex); tachycardia or bradycardia, vasodilatation or vaso-constriction occur in response to verbal stimulation of an emotional nature. A increase was noted in the respiratory rate of a man traveling in winter on the platform of a freight car from Leningrad to his work in Lyuban', knowing that h would have to spend 24 hours there in a cold, uncomfortable office, while there was a fall in the respiratory rate on the way back to Leningrad, when he was look ing forward to returning to his family in their warm, comfortable apartment. Similar findings were noted in sheep moved from pen to pasture on perceiving vast, sunlit green fields with the anticipation of grazing and exercise, and on their return to the pen for the night, with the prospect of immobility and hunger. The regulatory influence of the cerebral cortex on such internal processes as carbohydrate and gas-exchange metabolism has been demonstrated in laboratory animals by Ol'nyanskaya (1964) and in farm animals by Soldatenkov (1956) and by Berkovich et al. (1967b). The possibility of the voluntary, conscious (i. e. conditioned-reflex) regulation by healthy persons of reactions which are usually involuntary, has often been discussed (Valueva, 1967). Investigations in the field of occupational physiology and sport medicine have also shown that the cerebral cortex programs the autonomic infrastructure of human muscular activity by means of condi-tioned-reflex mechanisms (Antal, 1962; Ol'nyanskaya, 1964; Dan'ko, 1967).

To support his views Pshonik (1970) quotes a passage taken from Bykov (1942): "... it would be mental laziness on our part were we not to make use of our work to explain the principles underlying the harmony of the dif-ferent parts of the body and the preservation of the integrity of the organism in its natural surroundings" (p. 31). Here Pshonik lays emphasis on the phrase "its natural surroundings," which he takes to mean that all results obtained in laboratory experiments must be tested under natural conditions. This reading, however, would appear to be Pshonik's own interpretation, as can be seen if the beginning of the sentence is supplied: "The method employed by us (the method of conditioned reflexes — I. K.) has taught us to perceive the regulatory adaptations of the organism in their highest manifestations." Now it is quite obvious that Bykov's meaning was quite different from that ascribed to him by Pshonik. Bykov was discussing the act that he had very successfully applied the method of conditioned reflexes to the study of the regulatory mechanisms of the body, which had not previously lent themselves to investigation by other techniques. He was saying that these studies of the adaptative mechanisms responsible for the harmony of the different parts of the body and the preservation of its integrity within the external environment should be continued and on a wider scale. Thus, the point of view which we have just criticized can hardly be upheld even by those who opposed the corticovisceral theory of physiology and pathology from its inception, or who began to oppose it after the death of its initiator. Yet, one must not pass over the element of truth that is present in Pshonik's assertion. A fundamental study of the question of corticovisceral interactions certainly constitutes one of the most important tasks of present-day physiological research. Nobody will deny that the concept of conditioned-reflex activity, as handed down to us by Bykov, is insufficiently developed (Konradi, 1968) and is therefore in need of a great deal of further study, especially in the context of animal and human ecology. Physiological experiments still constitute a very important tool for research into cortico-visceral pathology, although it must be noted that the objections advanced by Pshonik and Konradi are echoed by some clinicians. For example, it has been claimed that isochemic heart disease is specific to man (Ganelina, 1968; Kruchinina and Kraevskii, 1971), so that animal experimentation is invalid, and the subject can only be studied from the clinical aspect and in human subjects.

Similarly, the study of the emotional conflicts which underly most psychosomatic disorders are sometimes held to be the exclusive province of clinical medicine, so that physiological experiment can have no bearing on this problem (Wittkower and Solyom, 1964). Those who make such allegations seem to have forgotten the following words of Pavlov, which have become a motto of contemporary clinical medicine: "only by passing through the fire of experiment will medicine as a whole become what it should be, that is, always consciously moving forward" (Pavlov, 1951, Vol. II, book 2, p. 297). Another of Pavlov's generalizations that has been forgotten but which is borne out in practice is that "since the general principles of higher nervous activity, located in the cerebral hemispheres, are the same for higher animals and man, the basic manifestations of this activity, both normal and pathological, must also be the same" (1951, Vol. 4, p. 415). Consequently, the physiological basis of emotional conflict and the effect of extremely powerful stimuli on the cerebral cortex are common to man and higher animals. The differences lie only in the etiological aspects and in the psychoemotional coloring of the reaction. Although in man the dominant role is played by words and their meaning, any emotional conflict is ultimately based on a material cause (see Chapter 4). Its initial stage consists of an excessive strain on the strength and mobility of the excitatory and inhibitory processes, not only in the subcortical (mainly diencephalic) region, but also in the cerebral cortex, and it is this which tends to give rise to neurosis and corticovisceral disturbances. Hence the justification of the laboratory investigation of the emotions and experimental models of emotional conflicts.

Incidentally, the classical treatise by the eminent American biologist Cannon (1953) "Bodily Changes in Pain, Hunger, Fear and Rage: Account Recent Researches into the Function of Emotional Excitement," which is so frequently referred to in western studies of psychosomatic medicine, represents the results of experiments performed chiefly on animals. Mor over, our present-day knowledge of the emotions has been considerably ex tended by the remarkable studies by the American physiologists Olds (1958 and Delgado (1966, 1967, 1969), on animals with electrodes implanted in the brain.

We therefore cannot agree with the statement that human emotional conflict can only be studied in man. Experimental physiology supplies much valuable information that is essential to an understanding of the natu of conflict and above all, of the nervous structures that are involved in the initiation of a conflict and of the neurohumoral pathways which mediate the aut nomic, somatic and mental effects of an emotional conflict (see Chapters 4 and

By making extensive use of the Pavlovian technique of experimental in jury to the cortical mechanisms regulating higher nervous activity and the activity of the internal organs, a number of original models of neuroses an psychosomatic conditions have recently been constructed. Experimental models have even been devised for such purely human diseases as gastric and duodenal ulcer (Shvalev et al., 1963; Baladzhaeva, 1968; Kurtsin, 1968 Chumburidze, 1970; Startsev, 1971) and ischemic heart disease (Teplov, 1962; Zakharzhevskii, 1966a, 1966b; Bugaev, 1971; Startsev, 1971; Tsvetkova, 1971).

SOME CONTROVERSIAL ASPECTS OF THE
THEORY OF CORTICOVISCERAL RELATIONSHIPS

Other authors hold different views. Thus, Ivanov-Smolenskii (1971), emphasizing the well-known Pavlovian principle that "the power of the cortex over the subcortex increases with age," as well as his own findings concerning the regulatory influences of the cortex on highly complex un- conditioned reflexes such as the instincts, writes as follows: "However, it would be a serious mistake to assume that autonomic visceral activity, the internal secretions and the general metabolism are usually brought about by means of cortical regulation" (p. 419). In his opinion, the auto- nomic visceral and metabolic reactions, including endocrine activity, de- pend mainly on the hypothalamus and the limbic system. However, by deny ing the dependence of the autonomic visceral activities of internal secretion and of metabolism on cortical regulation, while acknowledging their dependence on the hypothalamus and the limbic system, Ivanov-Smolenskii puts his opponents in a quandary, since hypothalamic activity is under the control of the cerebral cortex, and the components of the limbic system which are most closely connected with the regulation of autonomic viscer mechanisms are the limbic, temporal, orbital and premotor cortical areas all of which belong to the neocortex (Adrianov and Mering, 1959; Airapet'yants and Sotnichenko, 1967; Orlov, 1971a).

The same difficulty is encountered in opposing Bogach (1968) who main tains that the claim that the cortex plays an exclusive and all-important role in the regulation of gastric secretion and in other autonomic process of the body is unsubstantiated (p. 4). This dogmatic statement is complete at odds with reality. Moreover, it even clashes with the author's own declaration that his laboratory and others in the Soviet Union and elsewhere have demonstrated the part played by the limbic cortex, the amygdaloid nuclei and the hippocampus in the regulation of gastric secretion and that the regulatory influences of these formations of the neocortex, archicortex and paleocortex are mediated by the hypothalamus.   We may add for our part that gastric secretion and other secretory and motor activities of the digestive tract, as well as the autonomic processes of the cardiovascular, respiratory, urinary and other systems, are similarly implemented by the cerebral cortex (that is, by the neocortex, paleocortex and archicortex), and mainly through hypothalamic mechanisms which play a coordinating role in the corticalization of autonomic activity.

The situation becomes more complicated when an investigator is unable to reproduce, for example, a conditioned-reflex phenomenon that has been repeatedly demonstrated by others.   In such cases, the disagreement is no longer a question of terminology, but of experimental technique; for example, workers in Gantt's laboratory (1964) were unable to induce hyperglycemia, changes in the secretion of gastric juice, bradycardia and tachycardia, as conditioned-reflex responses to the intravenous administration of adrenalin, histamine, acetylcholine and atropine, respectively.   Yet, under different experimental conditions, this same laboratory clearly succeeded in evoking these autonomic activities in the form of a conditioned reflex.   This means that in the first case the investigators failed to take into account all the details necessary to the experiment; a point emphasized by the fact that in other laboratories conditioned reflexes have been established to the administration of histamine (Bakhtadze, 1967; Kohout and Korobová, 1969), adrenalin (Makarychev and Kurtsin, 1951; Mityushov, 1964), acetylcholine (Makarychev and Kurtsin, 1951) and atropine (Bykov, 1942; Bykov and Kurtsin, 1960).   The conditioned reflex is more difficult to achieve with large doses of these substances or with highly toxic substances which induce a parabiotic state in the nerve cells (Gantt, 1957).

Doubt has also been cast on the influence of the cortex on reabsorption by the renal tubules, on account of the conflicting results reported at different times and by different researchers.   For example, the schools of Bykov and of Orbeli have shown that urine formation can be increased or inhibited by means of conditioned reflexes.   Balakshina and other associates of Bykov (1942) demonstrated the two pathways, neuro-conductor and neuro-humoral, along which cortical influences on the kidney are transmitted. The important part played by the antidiuretic hormone was established in experiments on dogs with completely denervated kidneys.   However, in Ginetsinskii's laboratory the antidiuretic conditioned reflex was not achieved on dogs on the administration of pituitrin, although a stable state of conditioned-reflex hydration and polyuria was produced (Ginetsinkii et al., 1961).   Gantt (Gantt et al., 1965) could not produce a conditioned reflex to an auditory stimulus (tone), reinforced by 1,300 ml milk in two dogs, from each of whom one kidney had been removed and the other transplated on to the neck, even after 200 combined presentations.   On the other hand, Corson (1966) produced an antidiuretic conditioned reflex in dogs by combining a sound with the electrodermal stimulation of a paw.   The decisive part here is played by the actual conditions of the experiment, as noted by Corson himself, particularly observance of the time factor, the period of hormonal administration playing an important part in the development of the complex reflex reaction. This aspect was also emphasized in a special study that was carried out in our laboratory (Balakshina et al., 1966). Also of importance are the general condition of the animal, in particular the state of the system under investigation, and the hormone dosage. It is evident that the negative reports regarding the possibility of inducing conditioned reflexes to the action of humoral agents cannot be regarded as conclusive and further studies are needed on the subject.

Another questionable and somewhat dogmatic concept has been put forward by Konradi (1968, 1971) and by Orlov (1968, 1971a). These authors maintain that the notion of the dominant (leading) and universal role of the cerebral cortex in regulating the activity of the internal organs should be critically examined and radically revised. In their opinion, by no means all cardiovascular activity, let alone every autonomic reaction, can be elicited or modified by means of conditioned reflexes or by direct stimulation of the cortex. Moreover, the degree of cortical influence and the physiological role of the cortex differ markedly in different forms of autonomic reaction. This conclusion is based on experiments with rabbits, in which these authors were unable to produce a conditioned reflex based on an unconditioned depressor reflex, notwithstanding a large number of presentations. They also failed to establish a conditioned reflex to stimulation of the aortic nerve [sic] reinforced by an unconditioned defense reflex. In human subjects they were unable to produce a vasodilatatory conditioned reflex based on hyperemia due to muscular activity and on vasodilatation caused by the application of heat to the skin. In general, the vascular effects resulting from reactive hyperemia, Valsalva's experiment and venous occlusion could not be reproduced by means of conditioned reflexes, whereas a conditioned reflex could be established by reinforcement with vasoconstrictor stimuli. These findings led to the following conclusions: a) the influence of the cerebral cortex on vascular reactions varies with their biological significance; its involvement in the regulation of vascular reactions taking part in complex behavioral acts is beyond doubt, but its participation in self-regulatory reactions of local significance remains obscure; b) vascular sensitivity and the vasomotor centers are not represented on the cerebral cortex, while cortical influence on the circulation is not exercised directly but is related to the formation of motor, defense, alimentary, thermoregulatory, and other complex conditioned reflexes, or else takes place by some kind of subordinate mechanism.

Certainly, a vascular reaction, by virtue of its biological purpose, must always accompany any adaptive reaction of the organism, including conditioned reflexes. According to Anokhin (1958, 1971), the separate effector components of a conditioned reflex reaction are generally not isolated reflexes, but themselves represent the results of a central integrative process, thus ensuring the unified nature of the reaction. One can hardly dispute this conclusion, especially since it has been repeatedly demonstrated by many investigators (Jacobson, 1967; Danilov and Makarovskaya, 1969). We have ourselves shown, for example, that in dogs the offer, or even the sight of food evokes vascular as well as secretory reactions in the digestive organs: the salivary glands, stomach, pancreas and intestines (Golovskii and Kurtsin, 1960; Pastukhov, 1970; Kuznetsova, 1971).

It would be a mistake, however, to consider that a vascular reaction must always be "tied" to adaptive conditioned-reflex reactions, since pure, conditioned-reflex cardiovascular effects have also been demonstrated. For example, the cardiac component of alimentary and defense conditioned reflexes is liable to persist for some two years after the conditioned motor reaction has disappeared (Gantt, 1953). Clinical pathology provides innumerable examples of isolated cardiac and vascular damage of cortical (psychogenic [sic]) origin. It is also possible to elicit a conditioned vascular reaction and to study it experimentally, including a vasodilatory reaction which, in the isolated state, can often be clearly differentiated from the conditioned vasoconstrictor reaction. The phenomenon has been reproduced plethysmographically by a number of physiologists, including Rogov (1951) and Pshonik (1952), in both animals and man.

The conclusions of Konradi and Orlov concerning the absence of cortical vasomotor centers patently contradict many firmly established physiological findings, such as the following: a) stimulation of the vascular and lymphatic baroreceptors modifies the bioelectrical activity of the premotor, sigmoid, suprasylvian, temporal and limbic areas of the cerebral cortex, but not of the occipital and parietal areas (Bulekbaeva, 1967; Chernigovskii, 1967); b) the cortical loci which on stimulation give rise to the maximum vascular effects, both pressor and depressor, do not coincide with the loci which, when stimulated, affect gastric and intestinal motility (Beller, 1971); c) electrical stimulation of motor points in the cerebral cortex alters the blood flow in the corresponding muscles of the limbs, although the systemic blood pressure is hardly affected; d) vascular conditioned reflexes can be elicited on direct stimulation of certain cortical areas (Suvorov, 1967; Orlov, 1971a).

One should also mention the experimental production of conditioned reflex hypotension after a number of combinations of the conditioned signal with injections of acetylcholine (Makarychev and Kurtsin', 1951), chlorpromazine (Aliev, 1967), or histamine (Bakhtadze, 1967). Working in our laboratory, Bakhtadze (1967) succeeded in producing a persistent hypotensive state in rabbits after excision of the frontal cortex. This explains our cautious attitude to the experimental findings reported by the associates of Orlov and Konradi, who did not succeed in producing a conditioned fall in blood pressure despite 200 to 250 attempts at combining an indifferent stimulus with stimulation of the depressor or the aortic nerves. It may be that the sharp drop in blood pressure caused by stimulation of these nerves gives rise to cerebral anemia, leading to a diminished excitability of the cortical cells which prevents the formation of any temporary connections. Unfortunately, these authors do not report the oxygen tension in the cerebral cortex or in the blood leaving the brain, at the moment of stimulation of the depressor or aortic nerves. It would be very important to know these data before any final conclusion is reached concerning the impossibility of producing a depressor conditioned reflex. Incidentally, this methodological finding is also omitted in the reports of Odinets (1965) who, working with dogs, repeatedly combined a conditioned signal with electrical stimulation of the vagus nerve attached to a skin flap on the neck, but was on the whole unable to demonstrate any conditioned-reflex excitation of the liver cells. Conditioned reflex biliary secretion occasionally occurred, but only after some 100 to 120 combinations. The nerve was stimulated with an electrical current of such a strength that the depth and rate of respiration rose to twice or 2.5 times their previous values, while the heart rate was markedly slowed.

For 5 to 7 sec the heart even stopped entirely, this being accompanied by involuntary defecation and micturition, that is, by manifestations of shock. Stimulation of the vagus was only followed by an unconditioned-reflex rise in bile secretion in 30 to 50% of cases, according to the author. Under such conditions it seems hardly possible to seriously think or say that a conditioned reflex has been established.

Clearly, however, methodology is not all. It has come to be held that a conditioned signal must always produce an action identical with the unconditioned reaction with which it was combined. However, this rule, established by Pavlov, only applies to reactions which are useful to the organism from the evolutionary point of view. In other cases the signal seems to evoke a defense-adaptation reaction, although this is not always very apparent. Other authors (Denisenko, 1960; Kozenko, 1961; Serdyuchenko, 1962) have also attempted to produce conditioned-reflex circulatory arrest by combining an indifferent stimulus with stimulation of the vagus nerve. However, at the 35th to 50th presentation, instead of circulatory arrest, a very persistent conditioned-reflex pressor reaction was evoked, which was difficult to extinguish. Hence, it would appear that a temporary conditioned reflex connection will be neither established nor consolidated if it gives rise to conditions detrimental to the organism and particularly if it threatens life. Such conditions undoubtedly include a severe depressor reaction and circulatory arrest. Instead, an inhibitory reaction is developed as a defense measure and this too is a reflection of the conditioned-reflex mechanisms of the cerebral cortex. Denisenko, Kozenko and Serdyuchenko are all inclined to such a conclusion. The possibility that conditioned reflexes may be evoked to serve as active compensatory mechanisms, is also not denied by Orlov (1971a, p. 188), even though he takes a critical attitude to the experimental findings of these authors.

STIMULATORY AND INHIBITORY MECHANISMS OF THE CEREBRAL CORTEX

Cerebral anoxia, which tends to occur on stimulation of the depressor system, may lead to parabiosis of the brain cells and result in paradoxical responses, with inhibition of the conditioned reaction rather than excitation. This phenomenon is readily reproduced under experimental conditions by the administration of certain toxic substances or powerful drugs. Deeper and faster breathing can be rapidly induced in human subjects as a conditioned reflex response to muscular activity signals, but this is soon inhibited and is liable to undergo inversion (Antal, 1962). The phenomenon of a conditioned reflex with the opposite sign has also been observed in experiments attempting to produce conditioned reflex hydremia. According to Ginetsinskii and his colleagues (1961), this type of reaction is more or less the rule when homeostatic changes are used to reinforce conditioned reflexes. In their opinion such reflexes are of a compensatory nature, and even if they cannot always be directly demonstrated in the course of the experiment, they can be revealed by careful analysis of the data. This matter is mentioned here because the activity of the vasomotor centers in the course of an experiment is clearly of the greatest importance and cannot be ignored by those who only produce conditioned reflex reactions by purely Pavlovian techniques. In such cases, as pointed out by Ivanov-Smolenskii (1971), it is also desirable to take note of other conditions which are liable to produce temporary connections: for example, the indifferent stimulus should not previously have been associated with any activity, nor should it be too strong, as otherwise it is very difficult for the conditioned connection to be formed. According to Pavlov, a conditioned reflex will be formed without fail provided all the rules are strictly followed. Ivanov-Smolenskii (1971) concluded that failure to produce a new conditioned connection must be attributed not to the method itself, but to the disregard of some condition essential for connection formation, due to the fact that the experimenter possesses only a superficial and inadequate knowledge of the principles of the theory of higher nervous activity (p. 56).

It is difficult to apply this criterion to the results reported by the above investigators who, to our own knowledge, are highly experienced and conscientious workers. It seems that other factors must also be involved. However, the above statements can hardly be reconciled with the assertions that cortical vasomotor centers do not exist and that vascular conditioned reflexes cannot be elicited. In fact, it tends to corroborate their existence in the physiological if not necessarily in the anatomical sense. At the same time, it must be admitted that both the mechanism of vascular reflexes (which are mainly of a depressor nature) and their relationship to the level of excitation of the corresponding neurons in the cerebral cortex, are still largely obscure and therefore require more detailed investigation (Konradi, 1971; Orlov, 1971a).

In our opinion, the inhibitory system of the neocortex (Figure 10) deserves special attention, and not solely in its relation to the operation of the vasomotor centers. To ignore it when interpreting experimental findings leads to erroneous conclusions. It results, for example, in denial of the flow of bile into the intestine in the sham-fed dog, on the sight and smell of food. Yet, a dog is sham-fed with lumps of sugar which not only constitute an inadequate alimentary stimulus but, as we have ourselves shown, even exert an inhibitory effect on the digestive activity. A dog gnawing for an hour on a bone without any meat on it provides another example of experimental conditions under which the stimulatory influence of the cerebral cortex on the biliary mechanism can hardly be expected. Yet, such negative findings are used as examples of the alleged weakness of the thesis of dominance of the cerebral cortex and the principle of corticalization of autonomic functions.

During a discussion at the All-Union symposium on bile physiology and pathology (Kurtsin, 1965c), the radiologists asked why the sight of food which stimulates contractions of the gallbladder in animal experiments, does not do so in man (Kurtsin, 1952; Gorshkova and Kurtsin, 1967a, 1967b; Klimov, 1969). Moreover, in man gallbladder contractions are not stimulated by the suggestion of food (Preobrazhenskaya and Bul', 1959), nor even on holding a cream cake or the yolk of an egg in the mouth for 15 minutes without swallowing it (Lindenbraten, 1965).

Although the sensitivity of radiological techniques is insufficient to detect the initial phase of gallbladder contraction, the reaction of the gallbladder can be observed by this method as early as 10 to 30 seconds after

the introduction of 50 g yolk (Klimov, 1969). However, the entire phenomen
is probably dependent on conditioned-reflex inhibition of the alimentary re
action. As is known from practical experience in the laboratory, a cat car
sit for hours by a hole waiting for a mouse to appear without salivating
(inhibitory phase), until the prey has actually been caught. When a feast is
shown on the stage and the actors, attempting to give a lifelike performanc
try to work up an appetite in themselves and the spectators, hungry membe
of the audience do not start to salivate, for the conditioned reflexes of their
cerebral centers are differently attuned, the spiritual "food" here inhibiti
the natural alimentary reaction. Thus one should not expect alimentary
contractions of the gallbladder even in a subject who, under the same kind
of conditions as in the theater, watches the professor sit down at the table in
the presence of his assistants to eat an attractively served steak with a
hearty appetite. Of course, the alimentary reactions of the subject will be
sharply inhibited, just as in the case of the audience at the play; the more
so that this is probably his first experience of such theatricals in an X-ray
department.

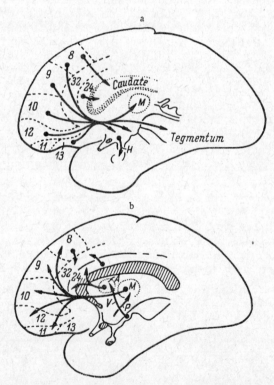

FIGURE 10. Cortico-subcortical connections directly involved in the inhibitory action of the cerebral cortex
on subcortical formations, particularly the hypothalamus (after Anokhin, 1958):

a) frontal-hypothalamic connections; b) hypothalamic-frontal connections; M: medial thalamic nucleus;
H: conducting pathway connecting the hypothalamus and pituitary; A: anterior thalamic nucleus; P: periventricular tract between the hypothalamus and the thalamus; V: bundle of Vicq d'Azyr connecting the
mammillary bodies and the thalamus. Numbers indicate the cortical areas.

Filatov (1964) has specially studied the possibility of establishing conditioned-reflex connections in previously prepared human subjects and has
found that although such connections can be formed if the subject has
mentally processed the incoming information and is aware of the forth-
coming procedure, they are likely to be weak. Consequently, the frequent
inability to produce positive conditioned-reflex reactions in animals and
man must be attributed to the mechanism of cortical inhibition, apart from
any technical errors and deficiences. It may be based on the same neural
structures which, according to Vvedenskii (1901), alter their activity in
relation to the strength and frequency of the stimulus (optimal or minimal
state, summation or blockage of stimuli, or refractory state). Possibly it
is due to different structures, with some part being played by Renshaw-type
neurons or to specific inhibitory synapses (Eccles, 1964). It may also involve "inhibitory cortical zones" (4s, 19s), the experimental stimulation of
which markedly affects the inhibitory structures of the medulla oblongata
and correspondingly inhibits cardiovascular, digestive and other autonomic
activity.

Possibly the cerebellar inhibitory system also plays a part, in addition
to the neocortex and paleocortex and the hippocampal, striopallidal and
thalamic-hypothalamic inhibitory systems. The inhibitory reaction taking
place in the central nervous formations probably proceeds with the aid of
γ-aminobutyric acid as the inhibitory mediator. This substance is thought
to affect the chemical reactions occurring in the postsynaptic membrane,
thus raising the excitation threshold and consequently lowering the potential
of the dendrites and neuron body (Gaito, 1966).

Thus, the ultimate autonomic effect is the result of highly complex cortical-
subcortical integration, in which a significant part is played not only by
stimulatory (facilitatory) but also by the inhibitory (blocking) mechanisms
of the cerebral cortex. The numerous feedbacks transmit both stimulatory
and inhibitory influences from the neocortex and limbic cortex to the meso-
diencephalic system and then to the internal organs.

LEVELS OF CORTICAL INFLUENCE AND SELF-REGULATORY ACTIVITY OF ORGANS AND VISCERAL SYSTEMS

Recognition of the dominance of the cerebral cortex in the mechanisms
regulating the internal milieu of the animal body immediately raises the
question of the level at which it exerts its influence. In fact, we are becoming more and more convinced with each experiment that the cerebral
cortex regulates autonomic functions and biochemical processes at various
levels of cellular organization. Two mechanisms for the implementation
of cortical influences have so far been discovered and their action has
been corroborated by extensive experimental findings and numerous
clinical observations. A trigger mechanism acts when a cortical impulse
initiates activity in an organ which has been in a state of physiological rest
and a corrective mechanism is brought into play when the activity of an
organ is modified (intensified or weakened) by a cortical impulse. However,

this thesis immediately raises a number of new questions: 1) Do the cortical impulses actually reach the cells of the organ and can the changes in cellular activity be attributed to the influence of the cortical impulse? 2) May the cerebral cortical influences not be mediated by the vascular and endocrine systems?   3) May the highly evolved animal organism not posses an indirect system of control over autonomic activity, basically analogous to the automatic control systems now widely used in industrial processes? These questions have only arisen gradually and recently since at first it was hoped to demonstrate the existence of some fairly simple, although fundamentally important form of conditioned reflex to an internal activity or biochemical process, at the cellular or even at the subcellular level.

In 1965, at an All-Union symposium on bile physiology and pathology, I was the first to suggest that a conditioned-reflex change in the continuous process of bile formation might be due not to cortical impulses acting directly upon the liver cells, as was claimed, but to their indirect effect via vascular mechanisms or hormones such as secretin, and that if this were the case it was questionable whether one could speak of direct cortical influences on the liver. The same considerations apply to the influence of the cerebral cortex on the secretory cells of the stomach, pancreas and intestine, where an important role is ascribed to local hormones such as gastrogastrin, gastrogastrone, secretin and pancreozymin, as well as to hemodynamic changes occurring during secretory activity. Obviously, according to this point of view, the problem also involves a large group of endocrine glands. Can it be assumed, in fact, that there exists a direct, specific nervous influence on the hormone production of glands outside the brain? As yet, no findings have been reported to directly support such an assumption (Voitkevich, 1970). There is no doubt that the autonomic nervous system can affect vascular tone and endothelial permeability and thereby the osmotic properties of the blood, in this way influencing the formation of hormones and their passage into the blood. Understandably, the problem became especially acute when the discussion turned to cortical influences on basal and other forms of metabolism, not to speak of thermoregulatory mechanisms and the rhythms of vital processes. At a later date, Konradi (1968) made a similar suggestion regarding intestinal absorption and tissue respiration. In his opinion, cortical regulation of these activities may also be due to changes in blood supply and in the discharge of hormones into the blood.

The subject has been approached differently by other authors, who have claimed that all autonomic activity, metabolic processes, cell nutrition, and in general, the entire "internal economy" of the body at both cellular and subcellular levels, are self-regulated, so that there is no necessity for continuous control or for it to be continuously governed by the cerebral cortex (Davydovskii, 1954; Nikulin, 1954; Kositskii and Chervova, 1968; Pshonik, 1970).

In his study of this fundamental problem, Chernigovskii (1969) doubts the ability of the cerebral cortex to "directly influence processes occurring at the cellular level and even less so those at the subcellular level" (p. 907) Here he is speaking of such processes as the transport of various substances an ions, the metabolism and energetics [sic] of the cells, cell division and the synthesis and utilization of biologically active substances. In Chernigovskii' opinion, processes of this kind are all fully autonomic, self-regulating, self-organizing and most likely very "rigidly" coded. This is a new idea, apparently inspired by the fact that the concept of the corticalization of autonomic activity has itself transgressed the boundaries of the regulation of the specific activities of an organ and has embraced the "deeper" biochemical processes taking place at the cellular and subcellular levels. However, the general acceptance of this novel thesis is hindered by not being in accord with the facts. Indeed, according to Bykov (1952, p. 150) "the influence of the cerebral cortex extends to the most fundamental manifestations of vital activity, such as tissue oxidation, or changes in membranes in connection with the diffusion of substances through them. Again, the duration of cerebral influence is striking. A brief stimulus reaching the brain is capable of causing prolonged changes in the state of various mechanisms (which cannot be more closely specified in our present state of knowledge), manifesting themselves in metabolic changes in this ultimate vital activity, which may last for many days." With regard to the assertion concerning the "rigid" coding of biochemical processes, one must bear in mind the series of investigations which demonstrated the possibility of conditioned-reflex modification of gas exchange mechanisms (Bykov, 1942; Soldatenkov, 1956; Ol'nyanskaya, 1964) and of hormone synthesis (Eskin et al., 1959) and the numerous observations concerning long-term changes in gas exchange mechanisms (Nikolaeva, 1965, 1966, 1967, 1971; Ovcharova, 1966), and in the metabolism of carbohydrates, phosphorus, proteins and lipids (Andreeva, 1955; Khaikina, 1958; Bykov and Kurtsin, 1960, 1966a; Kurtsin, 1960, 1968b; Volynskii, 1971) and of other substances, in the cells and tissues of the internal organs, when the cerebral cortex is in a state of neurosis (Figure 11).

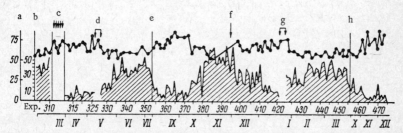

FIGURE 11. Changes in higher nervous activity and basal metabolism in a dog with experimental neurosis (after Kurtsin, 1965b):

Upper curve — oxygen intake (cm^3/min), lower curve summation of positive salivary conditioned reflexes during the experiment (scale divisions); a) amount of oxygen absorbed; b) magnitude of reflexes; c) conflicts of cortical processes lasting a number of days; d, g) rejection of food; e, h) experiment interrupted; f) administration of caffeine. Roman numerals — months.

Again, one must recall the possibility of changes in the absorptive properties of cells in conditioned-reflex excitation (Romanov, 1956), of changes in animal viscera in the course of oxidation processes (Bykov and Kurtsin, 1960; Korobkina and Kurtsin, 1960), and in the metabolism of macroergic phosphorus compounds (Dmitrieva and Kurtsin, 1960) when the brain is

subjected to extremely powerful sonic stimulation. It has also been show
that the permeability of cell membranes is dependent on changes in cerebr
cortical activity, both short-term (Chernigovskii, 1938; Bykov, 1942;
Berkovich et al., 1967b) and prolonged (Rybnikova, 1955; Hua Kuang, 1955;
Kurtsin and Kuzovkov, 1961; Sultanov, 1967; Kurtsin, 1968b; Kuzovkov,
1971a; Faitel'berg, 1971).

Findings of this kind in the field of corticovisceral biochemistry (Kurts
and Bolondinskii, 1967) are daily becoming more numerous. It has recent
been shown in our laboratory that prolonged suppression of cerebral
cortical activity alters the nucleic acid content of the digestive organs
(Table 2).

TABLE 2. Nucleic acid content of the digestive organs of dogs in normal state and in experimental neurosis
(after Bolondinskii and Gaza,1967; Kurtsin and Bolondinskii,1967; Bolondinskii and Gulyaeva,1971)

	Intestinal mucosa		Liver		Gastric mucosa	
	RNA	DNA	RNA	DNA	RNA	DNA
Normal ...	52.6±1.8	40.0±1.3	37.2±0.6	16.1±0.4	39.2±1.4	29.4±1.1
Neurosis ..	46.8±2.0	40.2±1.7	30.8±1.6	14.5±0.8	47.5±3.1	30.4±2.1
Change ...	-11.0%	Absent	-18.0%	Absent	+21.0%	Absent

Note: The RNA and DNA content of the intestine, stomach and liver were determined in 3, 4, and 5 dogs
respectively.

The experiments also showed that in neurotic animals a decrease in the
ribonucleic acid content of the mitochondria of the liver cells is accompanied by a rise of about 10% in the content of nucleases, that is, of the RNA-
splitting enzymes (Gaza and Nechaeva, 1970). This means that variations
in cerebral cortical activity may significantly affect the enzymatic activity
of the cells of the viscera.

All these changes in metabolic, enzymatic and other activity, which
occur when the higher divisions of the central nervous system are in a
state of neurosis, are accompanied by prolonged ultrastructural alterations
in the visceral cells, as has been shown by electron microscope studies
carried out by our laboratory, together with the laboratory of electron
microscopy of the Institute of Experimental Medicine of the Academy of
Medical Sciences of the USSR (Manina et al., 1968) and with the laboratory
of the Narimanov Medical Institute of Azerbaidzhan (Guseinov and Kurtsin,
1971). Long-term studies of visceral activity in dogs were carried out
under normal conditions and in neurotic states. Periodic electron microscopic examination of biopsy material showed the following features in the
secretory glands of the stomach: a varying degree of destructive changes
of the secretory granules, in some places lowered reactivity of the mitochondrial apparatus with enlargement and increased density of the endoplasmal reticulum and in other places its destruction, with concomitant
enlargment of the ribonucleoprotein (RNP) granules; a diminution in the
number of glycogen granules which, like the RNP granules, are scattered,
sometimes singly, sometimes in groups; excessive accumulation of the
RNP granules in the endoplasmic reticular membranes; marked

constriction of the intracellular canaliculi in delomorphous cells, and marked dilatation of the canaliculi, vacuoles, and vesicles of the Golgi apparatus. All such ultrastructural changes in the secretory cells must of necessity affect their activity (Gulyaeva et al., 1971b). The following changes were found in the liver: widening of the sinusoids and contraction of the spaces between the endothelium and the sinusoid-facing surface of the parenchymal cells (Disse's spaces) in some areas of the liver lobule, while other areas on the contrary showed contraction of the sinusoids and widening of Disse's spaces; on account of their high electron density, the nuclei and nucleoli of the liver cells stood out sharply, as did the mitochondria which appeared, scattered, or in clusters, against a background of apparently amorphous cytoplasm; fat droplets collected in the cytoplasm at the vascular end of the liver cell; the rough endoplasmic reticulum was altered in places and showed dissociating RNP granules; the mitochondria here also had a high electron density and in places adhered closely to one another; the bile canaliculi were dilated, their diameter reaching $2-4\mu$. All these ultrastructural alterations must give rise to metabolic and other changes in the activity of the liver cells (Gaza and Guseinova, 1971). In the kidney changes were observed in all parts of the nephron, but were more marked in the glomerulus, mainly in Bowman's capsule, in the visceral epithelium, and in the capillary endothelium; the epithelial and endothelial basement membranes and the capsule were thickened in places, obliterated, and the electron density was low, especially in the inner and outer layers; the cytoplasm of the cells of the visceral epithelium and of their trabeculae, together with the pedicles, were swollen in places and shrunken in others; occasional small mitochondria were observed here, with dense granules and the Golgi apparatus was enlarged on account of vacuolization; there were distinct changes in the endothelial cells which were either widened or thickened, with widening of the endoplasmal reticulum, vacuolization of the Golgi apparatus, and numerous vesicles of various sizes with transparent contents; the mesangium cells stood out sharply with their ultraparticles, in contrast to their normal state. Such ultrastructural changes must inevitably affect glomerular filtration and capillary reabsorption (Guseinova and Sergeeva, 1971). In addition to these intracellular changes, these electron microscopic studies in neurotic states have revealed a significant degree of mucosal hyperemia due to marked dilatation of the capillary bed which was packed with erythrocytes (Gulyaeva and Agadzhanova, 1968). These intracellular and extracellular changes cannot be considered to be specific to the neurotic state. In the first place they are reversible and do not show signs of degeneration (Manina et al., 1968), secondly, they somewhat resemble the phenomena described by other investigators as occurring in other cells in a variety of pathological states, such as acute hypoxia.

The histological findings including the results of electron microscopic studies, as well as physiological and biochemical data regarding the conditioned-reflex and nervous changes in cell respiration and cellular enzymatic activity, in the metabolism of proteins, nucleic acids, carbohydrates, lipids, water and salts and in the permeability of cell membranes, all testify to the existence in the animal organism of cerebrocortical influence, not only at the cellular, but also at the subcellular level of self-regulation and activity. This is also indicated by conditioned-reflex changes in hemopoiesis (Chernigovskii et al., 1967), the recurrence of anemia after conflicts of nervous processes (Kan, 1971) and disturbances of erythrocyte maturation and cell regeneration in bony, muscular, epithelial, connective and other tissues in prolonged pathological conditions of the cerebral cortex (Guseva, 1953; Bykov and Kurtsin, 1960; Chachanidze, 1965; Kuznetsov, 1966; Kurtsin, 1968b, 1971d). In general there would be little reason to expect biochemical changes in the visceral cells accompanying disturbances of cortical activity due to psychotropic substances, extremely powerful sound or light stimuli, or the excision of cortical areas, or from other damage to the cortex, if the cortical regulatory mechanisms were totally unrelated to cellular and subcellular activity, and if all the processes taking place at those levels were absolutely autonomic, adhered to a rigid genetic code and were independent of the cerebral cortex. In fact, however the opposite is true. In cases of this kind the changes involve such specifically cellular and intracellular processes as oxidation and the transformation of various types of chemical energy into the energy of macroergic phosphate compounds: that is, processes which are now believed to take place mainly in the cell mitochondria.

All these facts reaffirm the existence of cortical control, not only over autonomic activity but also over "deeper" cellular and subcellular metabolic and energy processes, and cellular growth and compensatory mechanisms. In fact, if it is admitted that the cerebral cortex influences cellular activity, it can hardly be denied that it influences the underlying metabolic processes. In our opinion, the cortical influences penetrate to the level at which changes are effected in cell metabolism and in other cellular activities including the permeability of cell and subcellular membranes, the ionic ratios and the activity of enzyme systems. On the other hand, these influences are incapable of altering the specific nature of an activity: for example, they cannot transform the secretory function of a cell into a motor function, or vice versa. The functional specialization of cells is indeed "rigidly" fixed by the molecular genetic code.

Here my own view is identical with that of Chernigovskii (1971), as state in his brief review of the life and work of Academician Bykov: "In his monograph* Bykov brilliantly presents proof of the effect of nervous influences on the most intimate aspects of the vital activity of the organism. An activity as generalized as metabolism is subjected to regulatory influences from the higher divisions of the CNS — the cerebral cortex. The nervous system affects not only the specific activity of an organ, but also its metabolism and blood supply, that is, its trophism." (p. 13).

Acknowledgement of the far-reaching influence of the cerebral cortex on the internal organs immediately raises the question of the nature of this influence and the way in which this cortical control is actually exerted. It is obvious that it is indirect and mediated through neurohormonal and neuroconductor pathways (see Chapters 1, 6 and 7). In the first case it is exerted through the hormones of the endocrine glands (Selye, 1952, 1971) which the cortical impulses reach by nervous pathways. In the second case the cortical excitation is transmitted by mediators from neuron to neuron and from the terminal neuron to the effector cell (Bykov et al., 1937; Turpaev, 1962; Kibyakov, 1964; Clegg and Clegg, 1969; Naumenko, 1971).

---

* "The Cerebral Cortex and the Internal Organs." 1942. (Russian)

This concept accords with the view that the cerebral cortex appears to be capable of influencing processes occurring at a deep level, although this only takes place indirectly, through one or more series of intermediate links (Chernigovskii, 1969, p. 909). These links include the endocrine glands and vascular mechanisms, but a major part in the cortical control of autonomic visceral innervation is played by lower control mechanisms situated at various levels of the central and peripheral nervous apparatus. This is especially apparent when the corticovisceral relationships and interactions are regarded in the light of automatic control theory. It has repeatedly been noted in biological studies that autonomic activity in man and higher animals is a most rewarding field for the application of the principles of this theory (Drischel, 1960; Grodins, 1963; Adolph, 1968).

The fact that certain resemblances exist between the activity of the autonomic nervous system and the operation of a mechanical control system has frequently been emphasized. The latter produces and maintains a physical or chemical characteristic at a certain predetermined level just as the autonomic nervous system produces and maintains the constancy of the internal environment (homeostasis). In a technical system of this kind any disturbance or other change in the variables automatically switches on special integrators which prevent any deviation from the preset optimal level of activity of the system. Similarly, deviations from the norm in the animal organism automatically arouse "controlling" and, in particular, disturbing factors and these, aided by the information system (the analyzers and the nervous and humoral feedback mechanisms), activate the "neural integrator" (the autonomic nervous system) and the "humoral integrator" (the endocrine glands), to produce a defense-adaptation reaction that is biologically aimed at restoring to normal the level of the activity of the cells, organs, and systems of organs. The result is a "closed chain of causation" of biological effects that is analogous to the closed circuit control of technical processes. Such closed circuits may be constructed in different ways and involve a larger or smaller number of organs.

The fact that cells removed from the organism can live and even multiply on an artificial culture medium at an artificially maintained temperature for many days and weeks, suggests that a self-regulatory mechanism must exist at the cellular, subcellular and possibly even the molecular level. In itself it demonstrates the strength and potential of the genetic code, but nothing more. Again, the fact that isolated organs, such as the heart, intestine, liver, kidney, lung and uterus, can fulfil their specific functions in the presence of an artificial circulation, or on perfusion with a nutrient fluid, suggests that a self-regulatory mechanism exists at the organ level. Similarly, the ability of a group of organs belonging to a particular system, such as the cardiovascular or digestive systems, to function for several hours under artificial conditions outside the body, suggests that a self-regulatory mechanism may exist at the systemic level. Finally, the fact that in decorticate animals the processes of digestion, circulation, respiration, urine formation and many other complex activities, including pregnancy, fetal development, and parturition, continue to take place, suggests that a self-regulatory mechanism exists at the intersystemic level.

Nevertheless, the ability of biochemical and physicochemical processes of various degrees of complexity to proceed outside the organism by no means signifies that they will take place exactly as in the intact organism which possesses special neurohumoral regulatory mechanisms. This is indicated by numerous observations on decorticate animals. Extirpation of the cerebral cortex is known to impair the secretory activity of the digestive glands, to deprive the cells of the vital ability to adapt themselves to different nutritional factors and to diminish the reactivity and adaptivity of the cardiovascular system and the blood. According to Sergievskii (195? in decerebrate animals the adaptive mechanisms of the respiratory system are seriously affected, just as in oligophrenic [sic] patients. In birds, there is a marked disturbance of nitrogen metabolism in the pituitary, thyroid and reproductive organs (Nazaryan, 1964). In general, in decorticat animals the autonomic visceral component in such activities as circulation respiration, digestion, urine formation and lactation, functions in a weaker, simpler, less perfect and more primitive manner (Belenkov, 1965; Lobanov 1965; Cherkes, 1968; Asratyan, 1970, and many others). This is accompanied by various trophic changes in the cells and tissues (Bayandurov, 1949; Popov, 1953), including dystrophic changes in the cells of the myocardium and the endocrine glands. Significant disturbances also appear in the reproductive organs and total cessation of reproduction has been noted in poultry (Karapetyan, 1964). According to Mikaelyan's comparative studies (1964), decerebration in vertebrates and reptiles disturbs reproductive activity: decerebrate turtles did not lay eggs for a year. Bilateral decerebration of birds destroys their reproductive function completely and irreversibly. In mammals decortication was found to inhibit reproduction. Decorticate dogs (with histologically confirmed complete extirpation of the cerebral cortex) lost their conditioned reflexes and did not develop new ones, nor even autonomic mechanisms (Sager, 1960; Lobanova, 1965; Airapet'yants, 1971). Such animals are complete invalids, capable of existing only under laboratory conditions with continuous human assistance If such an animal is set free, it will soon die of hunger and thirst even if surrounded by food and water; or else it will be destroyed by predators, against whom it no longer possesses either inborn defense-adaptation reactions or the conditioned reflexes acquired before the operation.

The autonomic activity of animals and man is also affected by "functiona decortication" as, for example, in neurosis (Bykov, 1942; Usievich, 1953; Bykov and Kurtsin, 1960, 1968; Kurtsin, 1960; 1965b; Dolin, 1962; Gorshkova and Kurtsin, 1967b; Suvorov, 1967, 1971; Lagutina et al., 1970) and even in physiological sleep (Kurtsin, 1952; Komarov, 1953; Peleshchuk, 1962; Vein, 1970).

However, having applied the automatic control theory of technology to co? ticovisceral physiology and pathology, and admitting that such self-regulatory mechanisms exist at a variety of levels in highly-evolved animals, including man, how is one to understand the principle of the unity of the organism? According to Pavlov, "Man is certainly a system, but a unique one, in the supremacy of its self-regulation" (1951, Vol. 3, book 2, p. 187). He also emphasized that our system is highly self-regulatory, self-maintaining, self-restoring, self-repairing and even self-improving (ibid., p. 188).

This concept was based on Pavlov's idea of the important part played by the central nervous system in the human body, as well as by the mechanisms which connect the living organism with the external environment, which were discovered by him and his colleagues.

Obviously, in the case of multicircuit systems such as the animal body, all the "closed" minor circuits and systems must be subordinated to a single, regulatory control center. At the level of man and the higher animals, the central control organ is the cerebral cortex and the adjacent subcortex which, through the "main switchboard" represented by the limbic system, the thalamo-hypothalamic region, and the reticular formation of the brain stem, exert their regulatory influence on the "nervous" and "humoral" integrators and through them, on all the autonomic processes in the cells and tissues. It seems that one must also recognize the principle that as the level of activity rises from the lowest molecular and possibly submolecular level to the highest level of the cortex, throughout the entire organism, the lower level becomes subordinated to the higher one. More-over, the features of the higher control mechanisms are not limited to the arithmetical sum of the properties of the lower ones. The autonomy dis-played by the latter outside the organism is relinquished by them in the intact animal.

On the other hand, as the structural and organization level rises and be-comes more complex, the higher systems which control the organism as a whole become increasingly more important than the lower systems of partial control. This principle acquires special significance in man, whose inter-actions with the environment are primarily governed by social factors, for these mainly exercise their biological effects at the cortical level which controls all parts of the organism. It seems that the existence of well-adjusted self-regulatory mechanisms must be recognized not only at the cellular, subcellular and molecular levels (as has been confirmed by a number of examples from the fields of physiology and molecular biology), but also at the level of organs and systems of the body, and since self-regulation is even a feature of higher nervous activity (Anokhin, 1958, 1971; Krauklis, 1964; Syrenskii, 1970), it may be justified to regard this as a biological law. On the other hand, the principle of hierarchical control of activity at all the above levels and within the CNS itself, must also be acknowledged. Feedback mechanisms which supply the higher centers with information about all events taking place on the periphery and at the inter-mediate stages are widely employed to ensure optimum performance. It is also indisputable that the automatism found in the cells, organs and lower nervous centers is subordinated in higher animals to the general neuro-humoral adaptation mechanisms, thereby acquiring new qualitative character-istics in conformance with the principle of the unity of the organism. This system of coordination apparently ensures the precise and harmonious activity of all the lower self-regulatory mechanisms, as well as the reliable performance of the organism as a whole and, of course, of the actual ef-fector organs (Kurtsin, 1969d). The cerebral cortex is able to exert its influence on autonomic activity at the intersystemic, systemic, and organ levels with the help of vascular and trophic nerves.

However, the activity of the cerebral cortex, its blood supply and the metabolic processes of its cells and glia, themselves require a certain amount of regulation which does indeed exist. The specific activity of the cortex is determined by the degree and nature of exteroceptive and intero-ceptive impulses arriving via specific, thalamocortical and other pathways. The cortical blood supply is mainly regulated by sympathetic innervation from the hypothalamus, while the ascending activating system of the brain stem and the nonspecific thalamic system serve its trophic branches (see Chapter 2). However, the cerebral cortex also has jurisdiction over the activity of all these nervous systems of both the proximal and distal formations, including the corticothalamic and corticoreticular connections, which mediate the self-regulation not only of their own specific activities, but also of the blood supply and metabolic processes of the nerve cells and glia.

In concluding this discussion of the criticisms leveled at the thesis of the dominance of the cerebral cortex in the central mechanism governing corticovisceral activity, attention should be drawn to Orlov's suggestion that the regulatory activity of the cerebral cortex is restricted to triggering and implementing the most complex biological reflexes, including their cardiovascular elements. This idea must be given particular consideration since it accords with many findings established in various laboratories in the USSR and elsewhere. However, Orlov's prejudices and his belief in the infalli bility of his concept have moved him to make use of certain arguments which undermine rather than bolster its foundations. For example, in discussing the structure of the cortical and subcortical mechanisms regulating unconditioned-reflex vascular reactions, he claims that the cortical and subcortical pathways are not equivalent: exclusion of the cortical pathways merely modifies the reaction, whereas exclusion of the subcortical pathways eliminates it (Orlov, 1971a). This brings him to the truly astonishing conclusion that "it is therefore impossible to speak of a leading or dominant role of the cerebral cortex, even in the implementation of these unconditionec reflex vascular reactions" (p. 198). This reminds one of the story of a scientist who was trying to locate the organ of hearing in an insect. He laid the insect on the bench and fired a pistol; the insect naturally ran away. Its legs were then removed and the experiment was repeated; this time, the insect stayed put. Comparing the results, the investigator came to the conclusion that the organ of hearing was situated in the insect's legs.

How is it possible to seriously claim that the cortex does not influence the vascular system, when all the pathways leading from the cortex to the blood vessels via the subcortex have been destroyed? It is just as well that Orlov also uses other findings and arguments which serve to extend and deepen the role of corticovisceral relationships as related to cardiovascular physiology. On the other hand, Simonyan (1968), a Moscow surgeon, seems to be totally at a loss regarding the corticovisceral theory. He writes: ". . . Physiology, in a noisy tussle with itself, resembling the wrestling of Nanaian boys, has produced a cut-and-dried theory regarding the all-encompassing dominance of the cerebral cortex and has presented it to the clinicians in a black box. Surgery, which has acquired a modern, but modest apartment, does not know where to put the gift or what to do with it" (p. 120). A surprising statement, to put it mildly! An acquaintanceship with the surgical literature does not give one such an impression. On the contrary, Pavlovian ideas on higher nervous activity and corticovisceral relationships have deeply influenced the theory and practice of modern surgery, particularly as regards the cardiovascular, digestive, respiratory and central nervous systems, as can be seen from the writings of such outstanding Soviet surgeons as I. I. Grekov, S. S. Yudin, A. V. and A. A. Vishnevskii, V. N. Shamov and B. V. Petrovskii, A. A. Busalov,

P. N. Napalkov and many others. However, Simonyan still found a use for the "gift" of the physiologists. He writes: "We know a female patient who hated enemas, but willingly filled her rectum with water from a basin, in which she sat and sucked up the water through the anus." (1968, p. 124). She had mastered the technique by practice and through her desire to wash out her rectum. So much for practice. Now for Simonyan's theory: "Thus, when the reflexes from the interoceptors prove inadequate, the cerebral cortex intervenes by compensating on its own level" (p. 124). It is only a step, however, from the sublime to the ridiculous. The external anal sphincter which attracted Simonyan's attention and on which his concept is based, is voluntary, being one of the striped muscles of the perineum, and is innervated by the interior hemorrhoidal nerve, a lateral branch of the pudendal nerve. Consequently, this case has no bearing on cortico-visceral or autonomic connections.

In conclusion, I would like to say that I fully share Orlov's opinion (1971a, 1971b) that the correctness of a theory is tested both by experiment and by practice. New findings correct the theory and shape it more clearly — unless they reveal the shakiness of its foundations. In such a case, the theory dies, however dear it may be to its author, giving way to new theories which correspond more closely with reality (p. 18). Yet, I am confident that the "new" findings and hypotheses presented above will not shake the foundations of the cortiovisceral theory, nor will they destroy the thesis of the dominant (leading) role of the cerebral cortex in the central mechanisms governing the autonomic-visceral activity of the organism. This thesis has already been substantiated by evolutionary and developmental evidence, as well as by the findings of corticovisceral physiology. However, a wealth of experimental and clinical data accumulated over the last twenty years has shown beyond doubt that a brief or prolonged change in the activity of the cerebral cortex elicits a correspondingly brief or prolonged change in the autonomic processes and in the activity of the visceral systems. Thus, the thesis of the dominance of the cerebral cortex is also supported by the evidence of corticovisceral pathology.

Chapter 4

THE CENTRAL MECHANISMS OF CORTICO-VISCERAL DISTURBANCES

Among the numerous unsolved problems of corticovisceral pathology, probably none is more complex and still so obscure as the question of the central mechanisms of corticovisceral disturbances. The foundations of the corticovisceral theory of pathology were laid at a time when the present-day neurophysiological methods of studying cerebral structure were still in their infancy. These methods have since yielded a wealth of information on cortical-subcortical integration, which has naturally affected the development of corticovisceral pathology. Even so, Pavlov's conditioned-reflex techniques which for many years were practically the only means of studying experimental neurosis, allowed objective and accurate measurements to be made, which have helped to solve the basic problem concerning pathological cerebral function. The problem concerns the nature of neurosis and of the visceral disturbances which often accompany it. Prolonged deviation from the norm of both higher nervous activity and visceral activity were found to occur when the cerebral cortex was subjected to any of the following procedures: a) an extremely powerful stimulus; b) frequent and finely-differentiated inhibitory conditioned signals; c) successive positive and inhibitory stimuli, without an interval between them; d) simultaneous stimuli of entirel dissimilar biological significance (alimentary, defense, sexual, herd). Such stimuli put too great a strain on the strength and mobility of the excitatory and inhibitory processes of the cells of the cerebral cortex, finally leading to exhaustion of the cortex and to a chronic disturbance of the normal cortical-subcortical relationships.

This concept is in complete accord with the principles of Pavlov's theory of higher nervous activity (1951), such as the closing and the analytico-synthetic functions of the cortex; the dominance of the cortex in the interaction of the body with the external and internal environments; the dynamics and mutual induction of excitatory and inhibitory processes; and the limits of th working capacity of cortical cells and the parabiotic state which results from their overstimulation. Moreover, it has been supported by abundant evidence which has been reviewed and analyzed in a number of physiological monographs (Gnatt, 1944; Masserman, 1944; Petrova, 1946; Bykov and Kurtsin, 1949, 1952, 1955, 1960, 1962, 1963, 1966a, 1966b, 1968; Usievich, 1953; Chernigovskii and Yaroshevskii, 1953; Kurtsin, 1954, 1960, 1961, 1962, 1965b, 1968b, 1971b, 1971d; Kakhana, 1960, 1970; Chernigovskii, 1960; Dolin, 1962; Poltyrev, 1962; Havlíček, 1962; Teplov, 1962; Gellhorn and Loofbourrow, 1963; Mityushov, 1964; Kurtsin and Nikolov, 1966; Gorshkova and Kurtsin, 1967; Suvorov, 1967; Yakovleva, 1967; Klimov, 1969; Nichkov

and Krivitskaya, 1969; Pastukhov, 1970; Startsev, 1971) and clinical publications (Lang, 1950; Chernorutskii, 1952; Bochorishvili, 1958; Istamanova,
1958; Davidenkov, 1963; Uspenskii et al., 1964; Chachanidze, 1965; Vilyavin
and Nazarenko, 1966; Kosenko and Paramonova, 1967; Pressman and
Pressman, 1968; Ivanov-Smolenskii, 1971).

The essential aspects of these studies, based on Pavlovian theory, may
be summarized as follows: a) the development of experimental models of
such human diseases [sic] as general and visceral neuroses, secretory
disorders of the stomach, liver, pancreas, intestine and endocrine glands,
disorders of gastrointestinal and biliary mobility, vascular neuroses,
stenocardia [sic] [angina pectoris] and coronary insufficiency, hypertension and hypotension, gastric and duodenal ulcer, amenorrhea and
diabetes; b) a completely new approach to the etiology, pathogenesis,
diagnosis, treatment and prevention of psychosomatic diseases.   Moreover,
the pathological process itself could be experimentally reproduced at will,
essentially by the "breakdown" of cortical regulation; more specifically,
of the conditioned reflex mechanism.   At the same time, diminution of
cortical tone was very soon shown to be one of the centrally acting factors
in the pathogenesis of corticovisceral disturbance.   This was supported
by the finding that in neurotic animals and in patients suffering from various
forms of neurosis and mental disorder, once cortical tone improved
and cortical activity returned to normal, autonomic activity did, too. However,
despite the fact that an important role was assigned to the cerebral cortex
in the initial phase of neurosis and corticovisceral pathology, this did not
mean that the whole problem was solved.   It was still necessary to find
the answers to many vital questions regarding these pathological processes;
above all, their starting point within the cerebral cortex, their method of
spread to the subcortical centers and their primary manifestations.

THE ROLE OF DIFFERENT CEREBRAL STRUCTURES
IN THE MECHANISMS OF CORTICO-
VISCERAL DISTURBANCES

Where in fact do the excitatory and inhibitory processes come into
conflict, with resultant neurosis and pathological manifestations in the
viscera? Where is the epicenter of the neurotic conflict and what receives
the impact of the extremely powerful stimulus which overtaxes the nervous
mechanisms? Pavlov's writings on the physiology and pathology of the higher
nervous system and the studies in corticovisceral physiology and pathology
discussed above do not supply an answer to these particular questions.
They only tell us that all stimuli, according to their nature, are transmitted
to specific cortical terminals of the analyzers, where they undergo highly
sophisticated analysis, so that the initial neurotic process may be assumed
to take place in the nuclei of these analyzers.   We know, however, that the
analysis is followed by a synthetic reaction related to the efferent nervous
mechanism, which the stimulus may reach by irradiation.   Consequently,
the central structures of the efferent system are not exempt from the
neurotic process.   However, between the analyzing and synthesizing components of the integrated analytical-synthetic center, there are intercalary

associative conductors, centers and subcortical fields, in which the neurotic process may be concentrated. In short, it can be seen that it is not so easy to answer these seemingly simple questions, unless one gives free rein to one's fancy and indulges in speculation. According to Suvorov and Danilova (1966), the conflict of positive and inhibitory conditioned reflexes takes place in the cortical areas of representation of those unconditioned reflexes from which the conflicting conditioned reflexes are derived. Although their opinion is not supported by direct evidence, it appears to conform with the theories concerning the central mechanisms underlying angioneuroses [sic] and hypertensive states (Suvorov, 1967, 1971). It has also been found that higher nervous activity is usually disrupted more rapidly by the simultaneous appearance of competing foci of excitation in the cortical areas of representation of unconditioned reflexes, than by the conditioned alimentary excitation and inhibition (Startsev, 1971).

According to Grushevskii (1969) who has also taken an interest in this matter, this alteration in the type of nervous activity does not take place in the thalamus, in the reticular formation, or in the sensory zones of the cerebral cortex to which the fluxes of afferent impulses are directed. However, he does not specify where the change occurs but leaves the question open. This cardinal problem, related to the etiology of both neurosis and corticovisceral pathology, can probably be resolved or clarified by long-term experiments, in which the classical, conditioned-reflex techniques and the method of electrode implantation in different areas of the cerebral cortex are used simultaneously. Nevertheless, the fact that direct stimulation of the premotor, limbic and orbital areas of the neocortex and of the hippocampus, amygdaloid nucleus and other archicortical and paleocortical formations produce corresponding autonomic effects, while stimulation of the receptors of internal organs or nerves produces changes of bioelectrical activity in just these areas and formations (see Chapter 1), suggests that these are the parts of the brain which are involved in corticovisceral disturbances. This is corroborated by the following experiments performed in our laboratory by Suplyakov (1971). Two cats had electrodes implanted in the anterior limbic cortex, the sensorimotor and optical areas of the cortex, the hippocampus and the amygdaloid nuclei, as well as infracortically, in the posteromedial and lateral parts of the ventral thalamic nuclei, the reticular formation of the brain stem and the posterior hypothalamus. "Psychogenic" stress was induced in the cats by a technique for disrupting higher nervous activity developed in our laboratory. This technique, like that adopted by Erofeeva's Pavlovian school, brings into conflict two biologically opposed inborn reflexes: the alimentary and the defense reflexes. In our modification, however, the animals were not confined to a stand in a conditioned-reflex chamber, but the experiment was conducted in a room in which they could move about freely. The procedure was as follows. After hunting and alimentary reflexes to a live mouse had been stimulated for a number of days, cat and mouse were connected to a 4-volt battery. When the cat caught and grabbed the mouse, the circuit closed, producing such a shock that the cat dropped the mouse and did not again attempt to take it into its mouth. The cat retained this negative reaction to a live mouse for a number of days. This change in its behavior was accompanied by significant disturbances of autonomic activity, manifested by changes in the ECG, in bromine metabolism, in the blood count and in

gastrointestinal secretion.   The somatic autonomic activity returned to
normal some weeks after the experiment.

In Suplyakov's experiments, changes in the bioelectrical activity of the
brain occurred immediately after the electrically stimulated conflict;
first in the mesencephalic reticular formation and the ventral thalamic
nuclei and then, though almost simultaneously, in the posterior hypothalamus,
the hippocampus and the visual cortex.   The changes were of a phasic,
rapidly fluctuating nature.   In the 3rd minute there was marked inhibition
in the anterior limbic region and visual cortex, posterior hypothalamus and
amygdaloid nucleus.   From the 5th minute excitation predominated.   The
changes in cortical and subcortical bioelectrical activity assumed a pathological nature on the third day after the conflict and in the course of the
neurosis: the amplitude of the biopotentials rose to $100 \mu V$ or more and
numerous slow waves were observed with occasional rapid spikes.

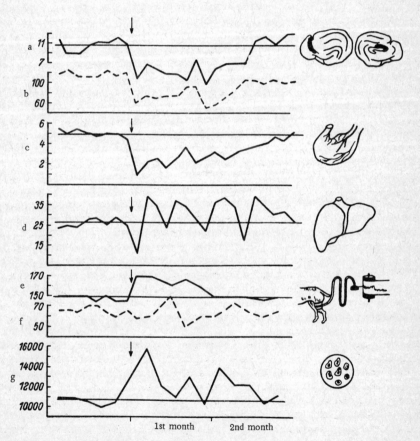

FIGURE 12. Changes in higher nervous activity and autonomic function after bilateral excision
(arrows) of parts of the limbic region of the cerebral cortex in dogs (after Kurtsin, 1960a):

y-axis: a) conditioned reflexes (drops of saliva); b) unconditioned-reflex salivation (drops);
c) gastric secretion (ml); d) bile secretion (ml); e) systolic pressure (mm Hg); f) diastolic pressure (mm Hg); g) leucocyte count in peripheral blood (thousands per mm³). Straight horizontal
lines indicate the mean levels of the findings.

Severe neurotic states with damage mainly of the conditioned-reflex mechanism have been found to arise in dogs and monkeys after "emotional shock" (Kryazhev, 1952), similarly caused by the conflict between the alimentary reaction and the electrodefense reflex. These states are distinguished by the disappearance of all conditioned reflexes and the paradoxical enhancement of the autonomic components: by respiratory, cardiac, and digestive disturbances, a rise in blood pressure, hyperglycemia and hyperadrenalinemia and trophic disturbances, such as eczema, loss of hair and loss of weight.

The suggestion that the above-mentioned cerebral structures play a part in the development of corticovisceral disturbances is additionally supported by the fact that such disorders occur in animals under certain specific conditions. They appear when the premotor, limbic or orbital areas of the cerebral cortex are alone involved in the conflict situation (Kurtsin, 1964; Suvorov, 1967, 1971), or alternatively, after bilateral excision or coagulation of these neocortical areas, as of the hippocampus, amygdaloid nuclei and other archicortical and paleocortical formations. The disturbances involve digestive, cardiovascular, respiratory, urinary and many other functions (Figure 12). They affect the protein, nucleic acid, carbohydrate, water-salt and other types of metabolism, as well as gas exchange, enzyme reactions and hormone synthesis. In other words, they resemble in many respects the autonomic changes which were found to occur in neurotic animals.

The nuclei of the visceral analyzer are also concentrated in the above-mentioned regions of the neocortex, archicortex and paleocortex. Their excision weakens or even severs the connection between the brain centers and the sources of information of the internal organs for a period of several months; if the excision is extensive all the previously established interoceptive conditioned reflexes are weakened or even lost and new ones cannot be established (see Chapters 1 and 2). No effect is produced by control excision of the same extent in the parietal area of the cerebral cortex. However, the fact that bilateral connections exist between the cerebral cortex and the infracortical formations, means that it is theoretically possible that neurosis and corticovisceral disturbances may arise when the strength and mobility of excitatory and inhibitory processes are overtaxed not only in the cortical cells, as believed by Pavlov and his colleages, but also in the cells of the subcortical nerve centers connected with the central mechanisms regulating autonomic-visceral activity, vascular tone, hormonal activity and cell metabolism.

This possibility has been experimentally demonstrated on decorticate animals in our laboratory. In experiments on cats Chechulin (1963) showed that electroconflict elicited disturbances of the "mechanical" secretion of gastric juice, often accompanied by multiple erosions and even by ulceration of the mucosa, which were more severe in decorticate than in intact cats. Simonov (1962) found similar differences between decorticate and intact rabbits with regard to leucocyte reactions. These findings seem to indicate that neurotic disturbances of autonomic activity following disruption of higher nervous activity may also occur in the absence of the cerebral cortex. However, since these experiments were performed on decerebrate animals, the autonomic disorders should be regarded as the result of hysteriosis [sic] in Vvedenskii's sense of the term, rather than of neurosis as understood by Pavlov. After all, a conflict of nervous mechanisms with overtaxing of their strength, leading to a pathologically dominant state of hysteriosis [sic] and parabiosis, can be created at any level of the CNS down to and including the lumbosacral region of the spinal cord. Thus it should be quite possible to reproduce a prototype of the neurotic disturbances of certain autonomic functions in the corresponding autonomic centers. As regards the intact animal, however, it is not known how long such disturbances would last, how they would be manifested, or even whether they would develop at all, in view of the structural features of the nervous system and the extensive adaptive and defense mechanisms which exist in the cerebral cortex (Pavlov, 1951; Asratyan, 1970; Lagutina et al., 1970; Startsev, 1971). Unfortunately, comparative experiments of this kind on one and the same animal were not carried out by either Chechulin or Simonov; nor has anyone else made such a study.

However, experiments of another kind carried out in our laboratory seem to shed some light on this basic problem. Working with dogs who had had electrodes implanted in the caudate nucleus and hypothalamus and in whom a stereotype of salivary conditioned reflexes had been established, Suvorov (1967) subjected the nerve cells of these subcortical formations to overexcitation for three successive days. The result was the appearance of classical neurosis with a whole series of autonomic disturbances, including inversion of the vascular reflexes and the salivary reaction, hypertension and angioneurotic phenomena. Thus, overtaxing of the excitatory mechanism in the subcortical nuclei had produced neurotic disturbances of higher nervous activity in addition to serious autonomic changes. It is not known how the visceral-autonomic disturbances would have developed and how long they would have persisted in these dogs, had damage to the activity of the subcortical centers been preceded by extirpation of the cerebral cortex, but in the above experiments on intact dogs, the neurosis and cortical-visceral disturbances persisted for 18 months. After the dogs had completely recovered, an attempt was made to reproduce the same phenomenon by pharmacological decortication, using chloralose and 10% alcohol. This failed, neither neurosis nor autonomic disorders being produced. In other experiments we clearly showed that the conditioned-reflex mechanism regulating autonomic activity is the first to suffer in the case of "psychogenic" trauma and corticovisceral disturbances, probably because it is not a genetically determined process. On the other hand, corticovisceral disturbances are often characterized by a pathological conditioned reflex reaction which is difficult to extinguish. All these findings suggest that a relationship exists between corticovisceral disturbances and a primary lesion of the cerebral cortex.

At this point two comments would be in place. The first concerns the general mechanism of production of neurosis and corticovisceral disturbances. The very fact that a single conditioned signal which had previously played a part in the situation which damaged the cerebral cortex can produce a neurotic state and corticovisceral disturbances in a relatively healthy animal, or in man (Apter's situational neurosis or Kupalov's conditioned neurotic reflex), suggests that besides "functional" exhaustion of nerve cells there exist other mechanisms of inducing pathological corticovisceral states and in particular the conditioned reflex mechanism. The same is indicated by American observations (Masserman and Pechtel,

1953) on monkeys which developed an acute disturbance of the conditioned alimentary reflexes as soon as they perceived a toy snake in their feeding box. However, unlike the situational neurosis, the pathological process apparently developed here along the lines of an innate, unconditioned reflex, although in both cases it was triggered via the cerebral cortex. The other remark concerns the part played by the subcortical cerebral structures in the mechanisms of this kind of disorder. The extensive material available from recent experiments in neurophysiology and neuropathology shows that neither neurosis nor corticovisceral disturbances arise or develop without the active participation of infracortical cerebral structures. Even in psychogenic stress, when the word serves as the decisive pathogenic factor and the entire action is played out in the sphere of the second signal system on the material substrate of the neocortex, the subcortical cerebral centers play a very active part. Moreover, there are indications that the depth and duration of corticovisceral disturbances depend on the degree of "breakdown" of the defensive-compensatory cortical mechanisms and of cortical-subcortical integration, as well as on the extent to which various subcortical autonomic centers, particularly the limbic and striopallidal systems, the reticular formation of the brain stem, the thalamus and hypothalamus and the cerebellum, are involved in the neurotic process.

These comments are inspired by the following considerations: in the first place, all these subcortical formations possess numerous structural connections between themselves and with the cerebral cortex and maintain certain functional interrelationships, all of which ensure that autonomic visceral activity is centrally controlled at a high level. Secondly, the electrical or chemical stimulation of these formations clearly affects the autonomic activity of the viscera. Moreover, in the case of certain infracortical formations, an organic lesion immediately affects the cerebral regulation of the internal environment of the organism. For example, significant autonomic changes, particularly in gastrointestinal secretion and motility and in vascular tone, occur in animals after extirpation of the cerebellum or destruction of the corpus striatum, globus pallidus and certain subcortical limbic formations.

Even more profound and prolonged autonomic changes, as well as disturbances of the internal milieu, including metabolic processes (Shvalev, 1971; Anichkov et al., 1971) and hemopoiesis (Kan, 1971), occur after destruction of the hypothalamic nuclei. Long-term stimulation of the latter in rabbits may give rise to ulceration of the gastric and intestinal mucosae. However, the gastric ulceration which usually develops in immobilized rats is suppressed by destruction of the medial surface of the orbital cortex and of the anterior hypothalamus.

The contribution of the reticular formation to the development of neurosis and pathological corticovisceral states can be judged from the fact that its stimulation or destruction affects the internal milieu. Further evidence is provided by the finding that the administration of chlorpromazine to animals 30—45 min before the nervous conflict in the cerebral cortex prevents any disturbance of higher nervous activity or of autonomic activity, including gastric secretion (Gulyaeva, 1965), hepatic secretion (Gaza, 1965b; Figure 13), intestinal motility, respiration and heat production (Bolondinskii, 1965), vascular tone (Bolondinskii, 1965; Gaza, 1965b; Gulyaeva, 1965; Suvorov, 1967, 1971), osmotic regulation by the liver and kidneys

(Balakshina et al., 1967), and intestinal absorption (Rybnikova, 1966). Chlorpromazine eliminates or significantly reduces pathological impulses from the receptors of diseased organs, such as the stomach, liver, or intestine (Raitses, 1966; Rybnikova, 1966; Kurtsin, 1971b). The actual mechanism of this latter phenomenon is still not understood, particularly the seat of action of the substance. It may act directly on the reticular cells in the cortex, suppressing their excitability, or it may block the impulses flowing to the cortex, at the level of the brain stem, thus protecting the cortical cells from particularly powerful stimulation, or it may block the adrenergic structures of the reticular formation, markedly reducing their activatory influence on the cortex and thereby diminishing the excitability of the cortical cells and rendering them refractory toward nonspecific and even specific impulse fluxes. In any case, chlorpromazine eliminates the influence of the subcortical centers which are the source of power and energy for the activity of the cortical cells (Anokhin, 1968). It is possible that it also exerts a parallel effect on the cortical structures (Uspenskii et al., 1964; Bolodinskii, 1965).

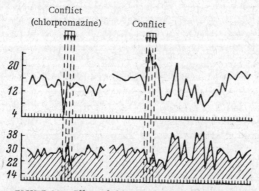

FIGURE 13.   Effect of chlorpromazine on higher nervous activity and autonomic activity in dogs after psychic conflict; left — after chlorpromazine (0.5 mg/kg); right — without chlorpromazine (controls).(after Gaza,1965):

Upper curve — sum of positive conditioned reflexes for the experiment (drops of saliva); lower curve — quantity of bile produced during the experiment (ml). Arrows — day of conflict; x-axis — day of experiment.

Hence, it can be seen that not only is the presence of the cortex and of the infracortical cerebral structures essential for the appearance of neurosis and corticovisceral disturbances, but that their cells must reach a certain degree of excitability. A pathological process does not develop at a low level of excitability, but once it appears it assumes a great variety of forms and manifestations. The state of adaptivity and sensitivity of the cortex at the moment that it is damaged is of major importance (Kurtsin, 1965b; Dolin and Dolina, 1972).

The experimental findings are paralleled by clinical observations in man, in whom pathological conditions of the diencephalic region of the brain, particularly the hypothalamus, give rise to complex and varied disturbances of the entire nervous system (Grashchenkov and Kassil', 1965).

Neuro-endocrine regulation is often affected, leading to disorders of fat, carbohydrate, salt and water, and catecholamine metabolism, and endocrine dysfunction. It is assumed that in such a case complex pathological cortico visceral mechanisms are involved. These may be direct, such as disturbances of the diencephalic regulation of visceral activity, or indirect (diencephalon → cerebral cortex → internal organs). It is of interest to note that the macrostructural changes in the blood serum proteins found in patients with hypothalamic lesions can be experimentally simulated by stimulating the reticular formation with adrenalin and the cortex with caffeine. A direct relationship has been noted between the degree of change in these proteins and the intensity of the excitatory disturbance in the cerebral cortex (Makarchenko and Dinaburg, 1971). Patients with a primar lesion of the mesodiencephalic region of the brain develop persistent changes in higher nervous activity, together with disorders of the cranial and peripheral blood vessels (Yaroslavtseva, 1966).

These findings provide direct and indirect evidence of the involvement of different nervous structures in the mechanism of corticovisceral disturbances.

An extensive system of projection fibers connects the cerebral cortex with the subcortical nervous structures which are directly involved in the control of visceral activity and autonomic reactions. This explains why, as is often observed in both clinical practice and experimental physiology, certain particularly powerful stimuli, or conflicting excitatory and inhibitory cortical processes, exert such wide-ranging visceral effects. Thus the activity of entire organs may be affected ("organ pathology") or an entire system may even be involved, such as the respiratory, digestive or cardiovascular system ("system pathology"). The crucial point is that the distribution of autonomic disturbances is largely governed by the specific involvement of the different cortical-subcortical structures in the pathological process. This, in turn, depends on the particular conditions under which the animal was subjected to trauma (Lagutina et al., 1970; Startsev, 1971). Among these conditions an important part is played by the state of the conditioned reflex mechanisms before the cerebral cortex was exposed to the trauma (Yakovleva, 1967). Disturbances in the activity of an entire system may be due to the fact that mechanisms for its organization and control have become involved in the pathological reaction (Murav'eva, 1970)

Intersystemic involvement in corticovisceral pathology is also possible. This has been demonstrated in the case of water-salt metabolism, which is known to be regulated by a most complex neurohormonal process. In Esipenko's laboratory (1965) it has been shown that in both hydration and dehydration of the organism, the appreciable changes in renal activity and gastrointestinal secretion are due to the involvement of a complex reflex mechanism which includes not only ismoreceptors and volumoreceptors, afferent renal and gastrointestinal innervation, hypothalamic structures and hormones, but also the sigmoid gyri of the cerebral cortex.

According to Tashenov (1969), the cerebral cortex regulates the relationships between the digestive and mammary glands in lactating animals. In dogs, Tagirova and Tursunov (1966) observed that changes in cerebrocortical activity induced by the administration of chloralose (25—27 mg/kg) or by extirpation, were accompanied by disturbances in the relationship between salt and water regulation by the kidneys and the salivary glands. In our laboratory, Britikova (1966) noted that in dogs a marked and prolonged impairment of the normally coordinated osmoregulatory activity of the kidneys and liver accompanied diminished activity of the cerebral cortex.

Consequently, a central pathological process may disturb the cortical regulation of autonomic activity not only at the cellular, organ and systemic levels, but also at the intersystemic level. Such disturbances may reflect a general or a local neurosis, which can be reproduced in the conditioned-reflex chamber or in unrestrained animals (Kupalov, 1961; Apter, 1970; Murav'eva, 1970; Startsev, 1971). We have already noted that even the normal structure of the central apparatus control is so complex and variable that the ensuing autonomic effect is the result of a highly complex process of cortical-subcortical nervous integration. These kaleidoscopic relationships and interactions form an even more complex pattern under abnormal conditions. For this reason the study of central disturbances has not yet provided an answer to the question why apparently identical trauma to the cerebral cortex and identical signs of general neurosis are accompanied by such widely-varying visceral manifestations, with the digestive, cardiovascular, urinary, or other organs being predominantly affected at different times.

This subject will be treated separately below (see Chapter 9). At this point it is sufficient to note that the peculiar nature of the central mechanism governing autonomic visceral activity naturally leaves its mark on many aspects of corticovisceral pathology which still require to be studied. For example, the orbital cortex exerts an influence on the cardiovascular system through the extrapyramidal pathways and the hypothalamus, while the promotor cortex influences it via both these pathways and directly through the bulbar centers. These particular connections, together with the heterogeneity of the cerebral structures participating in autonomic reactions, may partially explain the fact that in dogs, neurosis and vascular disorders were found to persist for 5 to 6 months following a conflict of processes in the premotor of the cortex, as compared with only 1.5 to 2 months after a conflict in the orbital cortex. According to experiments performed in our laboratory, this also depends on which of the subcortical centers is predominantly involved in the pathological process. For example, if the posterior hypothalamic nuclei are involved, the duration of the neurosis and vascular disturbances may be as long as 15 or more years. Here the degree of inertia of the particular subcortical formation may play a role in the persistence of the dominant pathological process (Levshunova, 1969; Biryukov and Bachurikhina, 1970; Budylin, 1970; Startsev, 1971); one of the features of such dominance being the capacity of the nerve cells to pass into a state of parabiosis on excessively powerful excitation. Such a condition is largely responsible for the occurrence in neurosis and pathological corticovisceral states of autonomic effects of different degrees in the form of equalizing, paradoxical, and inhibitory secretory and motor responses. Examples from laboratory experiments and clinical observations have been provided by many authors (Chernogorov, 1956; Bykov and Kurtsin, 1960; Havlíček, 1962; Rusinov, 1969; Borodkin, 1961; Startsev, 1971).

Cells of the higher divisions of the CNS are more likely to retain traces of stimulation over a long period than are the lower divisions. Thus, excitation produced in the nerve centers of the spinal cord by weak stimulation of the skin, lasts up to a few minutes, whereas excitation generated in the cortical centers by a reflex or direct stimulus persists for more than 24 hours (Kupalov, 1956). In pathological states these periods may be considerably prolonged and the nature of the reaction may be modified. In Asratyan's laboratory (1970), a sluggish increase in the excitability of the nerve centers in spinal dogs, produced by repeatedly stimulating the receptors of the skin of the tail and the hind paw in combination, was maintained for several weeks, displaying all the features of a pathological dominant. In Anokhin's laboratory (1958) a similar model was produced for the autonomic innervation at the level of the medulla oblongata, which serves the vasoconstrictor center. The state of the center was such that afferent impulses from the receptors in the aortic arch and carotid sinus were unable to produce a vascular depressor reaction. In Rusinov's laboratory (1969), weakened conditioned reflexes and a raised blood pressure persisted as aftereffects for many days following polarization of the hypothalamus. In Airapet'yants' laboratory (1962) conflict between a pathologically altered interoceptive locus on the cortex and a healthy exteroceptive locus, transformed the former into the dominant focus which gradually drew more and more cortical elements into the pathological reaction. Interoceptive signals evidently play an important part in the formation of stagnant dominant foci in the cortex and subcortex.

Findings of this kind have also been obtained in our laboratory (see Chapter 8). For example, in rabbits in whom a state of experimental neurosis had been induced, bilateral decortication produced the same abnormal leucocyte reactions as the neurosis. Again, in cats with an intact cortex the suppression of cortical activity under anesthesia did not prevent the onset of pathological reflex reactions from the intestine to the blood pressure and respiration, induced by the electroconflict. One obtains the impression that the subcortical formations become involved in the neurotic process later than the cerebral cortex. On the other hand, under certain conditions, trace reactions of traumatic effects may be retained longer by these formations. This may to some extent reflect the considerable compensatory capacity of cortical structures (Lagutina et al., 1970) and explain the fact that marked autonomic and trophic disturbances accompany neuroses in lower but not in higher mammals (Biryukov and Bachurikhina, 1970). Evidently, it is this property of the subcortex which holds the secret of the prolonged persistence of pathological manifestations of autonomic activity after higher nervous activity has returned to normal. This would explain the very common and readily reproducible exacerbation of cortico-visceral disorders. Furthermore, the emotional reaction associated with psychogenic stress causes the pathological trace reaction to persist for a longer period, just as in the normal state the emotions help to consolidate (fix) the traces of a memory.

However, a certain part in the development of the pathological condition of the brain centers may be played by endocrine disturbances and also by afferent impulses arriving from pathological changes in the internal organs (see Chapter 8). In such a case blocking of impulses is of great significanc

This may be brought about by many factors: by extremely powerful impulses which produce a breakdown of the synaptic transmission mechanism, or by the development of a parabiotic state of cells and nervous conductors under the influence of hormones, mediators and other biologically active substances, or by damage to the interoceptor structure of an organ by a local pathological process, such as gastric inflammation or ulcer (Raitses, 1966; Kurtsin, 1967a, 1967b, 1971b), myocardial infarction (Frol'kis et al., 1962), or enteritis [sic] (Budylin, 1970). The experimental blocking of impulses in the brain centers has been achieved by the arrival of conflicting fluxes of impulses via different afferent conductors and systems, as well as by means of chlorpromazine or other neuroplegic substances (Anokhin, 1958). The level of the nervous system at which this occurs depends to a great extent on the functional motility of the structure which is affected. The sympathetic ganglia with their limited lability are inhibited earlier than the labile hypothalamus and long before the cerebral cortex. At the biochemical level the blocking of synoptic connections is due to changes in the reactions of the sulfhydryl protein groups which play an important part in metabolic processes.

The structural changes must obviously be due to increased metabolic activity in the cytoplasm itself and in the synapses, as can be observed when the latter are stimulated over a long period. Thus, in Merkulova's laboratory (1970) it has been found that long-term stimulation of afferent somatic nerves produces an excitatory process in the CNS, which is followed by prolonged inhibition; these processes being accompanied by various changes at the cellular and subcellular levels. The following relationships may be postulated: a fall in the glycogen content of the synaptic end plates and neurons and changes in carbohydrate metabolism; a decrease in the number of synaptic vesicles and disturbances of mediator activity; alterations in the shape of the end-plate mitochondria from ellipsoidal to irregular with enzyme disturbances; an increase in the number of SH groups in the cytoplasm and nucleus of the neuron with disturbances of protein metabolism, as well as a change in the actual structure of the protein molecules; tigrolysis of Nissl bodies with a decrease in the RNA content and changes in nucleic acid and nucleoprotein metabolism; a significant increase of mitochondria in the nerve-cell cytoplasm and increased synthesis of ATP; an increase in the lysosomes, vesicles and vacuoles in the Golgi apparatus with increased neuronal discharge (Merkulova, 1970).

In addition to the type of higher nervous activity, the duration and strength of the stress and the form, severity and duration of the neurosis and of the corticovisceral disturbance, the mechanism of causation of the neurosis itself is obviously of importance. It may be predominantly cortical or subcortical, depending on the degree to which different cortical and subcortical nervous formations and structures are involved in the pathological process.

At this point it is necessary to reemphasize a concept that is important for an understanding of the trigger mechanisms of corticovisceral disturbances: the tone and activity of the neocortex are governed by a powerful stream of stimuli reaching it by specific and nonspecific pathways from the thalamus and the reticular formation. The breakdown of cortical mechanisms may to some degree be determined by the nature and extent of the injury to these infracortical formations and systems. In turn, the activity of the reticular formation and thalamus and their activating systems may vary with the intensity gradient of the impulse and the effects of mediatory hormonal and metabolic substances, in particular acetyl-choline, adrenalin, noradrenalin, hydrocortisone and carbon dioxide.

Among the central mechanisms involved in corticovisceral disturbances a significant part is probably played by disorders of the cerebral circulation associated with the psychogenic trauma and the development of the neurosis (see Chapter 11).

THE TRIGGER MECHANISMS OF STATES OF EMOTIONAL STRESS

The emotional factor, which is an essential component of the trigger mechanism of mental stress and of most or all of the alimentary, sexual, defense reactions, and above all, of the reaction to pain, plays an important part in the generation and development of psychosomatic and cortico-visceral disturbances. Its influence on psychosomatic processes has been the subject of numerous publications, including the well-known monographs by Cannon (1923), Cobb (1950), and Gellhorn and Loofbourrow (1963), in which the many findings are reviewed and original theories are advanced.

Pavlov (1951) attributed great significance to the emotions in the shaping of higher nervous activity and repeatedly emphasized that they constituted the source of power of the cortical cells. This concept is now attracting close attention in the Soviet Union and elsewhere, and emotional stress is being singled out from the enormous number of different stress situations which may affect the animal, and is being treated as an independent phenomenon.

Although emotional stress can be considered from various points of view all of them can be ultimately reduced to the study of the trigger mechanism responsible for the nature of this stress. As a result of the considerable amount of research which has been carried out on this subject in recent years, two suggestions have been put forward regarding the origin of the emotions. They may be the result of cerebral activity, that is, of inter-cortical impulses, or they may be caused by hypothalamic activity stimulated by afferent impulses from receptors, and there is still no consensus on this subject.

Olds (1958) and Delgado (1964, 1966, 1969), making extensive use of the technique of electrode implantation in the hypothalamus in a variety of animals, rats, monkeys, and bulls, described emotional-alimentary and behavioral reactions to direct electrical stimulation of strictly defined points in the lateral and medial hypothalamic regions. As a result it was thought by many investigators that the seat of the emotions and emotional states in the animal had been discovered. This idea, in a somewhat modified form, has also been developed by a number of Soviet workers (see Chapter 2). There exists, however, another opinion on the matter. It has been asserted that archicortical and paleocortical structures constitute the seat of the emotions at the higher level (Beritov, 1969), particularly the amygdaloid nuclei, septum and hippocampus which, together with the hypothalamus, form the so-called Papez circuit. From this point of view, Ordzhonikidze and Pkhakadze (1971) recently experimented on cats in whom the neocortex had been isolated by a procedure described by Khananashvili. They found that the emotional manifestations engendered by conditioned and unconditioned stimuli were scarcely altered, except for a slight difficulty in establishing new conditioned reflexes. They therefore concluded that the higher integrating mechanisms of emotional reactions are located not in the neocortex but in the archicortex and paleocortex. This conclusion was fortified by the fact that a large number of stellate neurons were found in the archicortex and in layer IV of the neocortex for, according to Beritov, these neurons are involved in the realization of subjective, emotional experiences. The above-mentioned authors suggest that the mechanism of the emotions possesses the following structure. Emotional behavior is integrated by the paleocortical pyramidal neurons. These latter are connected by axons to clusters of stellate cells in the archicortex where subjective sensations and emotional experiences are formed, as well as to the hypothalamus and thalamus which govern the autonomic component of the emotions. This view is supported to some extent by the fact that tranquilizers of the benzodiazepam series, including nitrazopam, act primarily on the structures of the limbic system (Vikhlyaev and Klygul', 1971) and that in animals the emotional or motivational state can be modified by the electrical stimulation of certain "points" in the limbic brain.

However, objections may be found to this view concerning the seat of the higher emotions, since the partial or total elimination of neocortical activity by cryogenic means was in some cases accompanied by a partial or total disappearance of emotional manifestations (Belenkov, 1971). Consequently, in the "integrated brain," made up of subcortical and cortical structures, responsibility for the emotional discharge must be attributed not to the archicortex and paleocortex but to the neocortex. Moreover, further experiments showed that, of the many neocortical areas involved, the temporal and frontal areas play the major part in the production of the emotions, as well as of certain higher activities of the brain. In experiments performed in Belenkov's laboratory (1971), decortication of the temporal areas completely suppressed brain activity and led to the disappearance of all the conditioned reflexes and many unconditioned reflexes and emotional manifestations. During the actual process of decortication, which consisted of cooling the temporal region, the animals showed reactions of fear: an urge to get out of the cage, cries, dilatation of the pupils, urination, defecation and other autonomic effects, while all the time maintaining the activity of the limbic system and the hypothalamus, both of which are said to take part in the mechanism of emotional reactions (Anokhin, 1964). Hence, the emotional activity of these nervous formations is wholly determined by the neocortex and mainly by the temporal area.

The weak spot of this, as of many other theories, is the impossibility of reproducing a true emotional state in the laboratory. Indeed, neither electrical stimulation of the lower and higher so-called emotional structures (Vainshtein, 1971; Vedyaev, 1971; Kozlovskaya, 1971), nor the microinjection of acetycholine, carbocholine or physostigmine into these structures (Allikmets, 1971) produces the same emotional effect as occur in animals under natural conditions. This difficulty has often been pointed out. Similarly, attempts at reproducing aggression or fear by the direct administration of catecholamines or adrenomimetic substances into the "emotional" structures: the anterior and posterior hypothalamus, the central gray matter of the midbrain and the amygdaloid nuclei, have repeatedly failed (Allikmets, 1971). Indeed, how could a complete emotional reaction be evoked by introducing substances into any single formation, since a behavioral reaction is implemented by nervous structures situated at various levels of the brain? Moreover, an animal experiment does not answer the fundamental question whether manipulation of these structures produces any sensation or experience that is absolutely characteristic of the emotional reaction. Nor can this problem be solved by the electrical stimulation of deep cerebral structures or individual cortical zones. In human subjects, during surgical operations, there is no certainty that even the highly-localized application of the stimulus by the electrodes will guarantee that the effect is related only to the actual point stimulated, and not to other structures (Belenkov, 1971). Most emotional reactions are complex and are formed with the help of intrabrain relationships based on the collaboration of numerous cortical and subcortical structures. One proof of this is the fact that the electrical or chemical stimulation of any single "emotiogenic" cerebral structure can be almost immediately recorded electroencephalographically in other "emotiogenic" structures (Borodkin, 1971).

Furthermore, emotional-behavioral and autonomic reactions in the integrated organism are triggered by cortical mechanisms after the cortex has sufficiently analyzed the ambient environmental phenomena, and particularly the nature of the stress stimulus. That is why a decorticate hare hardly reacts to an approaching predator, thus endangering its own life, and why a decorticate dog will die of starvation when surrounded by food. That is why a human being born without a cerebral cortex is a complete invalid, unable to exist without total assistance from others. Such a creature is incapable of thought, for the brain is incapable of mental activity and the surrounding world does not evoke emotions that are characteristic of the normal individual.

It is now clear why, in dogs with implanted electrodes, long-term stimulation of the amygdaloid nucleus, piriform lobe, medial preoptic region, hippocampus and caudate body, separately and in various combinations only elicits fragmentary elements of emotional manifestations but never produces an integrated behavioral reaction of an emotional nature (Khananashvili and Lapina, 1971). Here, however, one must again stress the basic principle that higher cerebral activity of a psychoemotional nature is implemented by the neocortex not on its own, but in cooperation with the archicortical, paleocortical, and subcortical formations and structures. For this reason, severance of the neocortical projection pathways in male dogs does not eliminate their emotional excitement on sighting a female in heat, even though the actual ability to copulate has been lost, whereas, on severance of both the neocortical and hippocampal conducting pathways, all sexual activity ceases (Khananashvili and Lapina, 1971).

It is clear that emotions are made up of complexes of inborn and acquired reactions, which reflect not only motor and autonomic phenomena

ut also the mental state, so that, depending on the subjective evalua-
ion of the stress factor, they may assume a great variety of forms ranging
rom fear, fright, or indignation to joy and delight. It should be obvious
hat each of these different forms and kinds of negative and positive emo-
ion can hardly possess its own "seat," yet the search for such "seats" is
till continuing. Moreover, since the emotions are made up of mental,
notor and autonomic components which form different combinations in dif-
erent persons and even in the same person, a search is also being made
or the hypothetical seats of the centers integrating emotional-behavioral
eactions at different levels. Its lower and higher divisions are being
ought in numerous structures, such as the anterior and posterior hypo-
halamus, the reticular formation of the brain stem, the thalamus, strio-
allidal system, archicortex and paleocortex, up to various neocortical areas
nd zones. This is a tremendous task and it is still very far from comple-
ion. In fact, the reports at the symposium on the subject of "The structural,
unctional and neurochemical organization of the emotions" (Leningrad,
971) showed that it is still in its very beginnings, continually encountering
bstacles and difficulties, especially with regard to the higher levels, that
s the seats of the mental component of the emotions. Dissatisfied
vith the search for a nervous basis of individual emotional states and dis-
nchanted with the theory of the fragmentary structure of the emotions,
ome investigators are now pinning their hopes on the discovery of a
'topography of the integrative centers (zones) of emotionally-expressed
nanifestations" (Val'dman, 1971), or of a "unified cerebral system"
Belenkov, 1971), or a "complex systemic organization" (Khananashvili and
Lapina, 1971), or finally, a "functional system of emotional behavior"
Vedyaev, 1971). It is easy to understand the dissatisfaction and disap-
ointment with the experimental study of these problems that is now be-
oming noticeable in the writings of certain investigators who have long
devoted themselves to the question of the nature and mechanisms of the
motions.

In fact, despite all the attempts of modern neurophysiologists to find a
oncrete, delimited basis for specific emotional states, nothing of this kind
as been discovered and the findings reported in the literature are of a
ighly conflicting nature. We possess no clear idea of the relationships
etween the lateral and ventromedial hypothalamic nuclei, on the one hand,
nd the cerebral cortex on the other (Marits et al., 1971); hence, the pre-
ent sharp controversy concerning the significance of various cortical and
ubcortical formations and structures in emotional states and emotions.
Though recognizing the dominant role of the lateral and ventromedial
ypothalamic nuclei (Sudakov, 1970; Marits et al., 1971), the emphasis is
ow being laid on the strategic importance of the pontomedullar reticular
structures (Shuleikina, 1971).

Thus even after the discussion at the symposium, a number of fundamen-
al problems remain unresolved. To what degree is the reaction evoked
y stimulating the pacemaker of the hypothalamus or of the reticulo-
imbic formations identical with natural emotions and emotional states?
What is the role of various cortical and subcortical neural structures and
f their central interactions in the regulation of the emotions? What are
he "trigger" mechanisms of the emotions? Where are the centers of

negative emotional states, such as rage, aggression and fear, and of positive
states, such as satiety, pleasure and enjoyment, or of the "social" behavior
of animals, individually and in the herd? Moreover, which structures, including those of the Papez circuit, constitute the seat of actual sensation
(emotional experience) which invests the different emotions with their
specific characteristics, coloring and nuances? The part played by the
emotions in many behavioral acts, including such reactions as self-stimulation, avoidance, encouragement and punishment, has been an open question
for many years and still remains so (Olds, 1958). Little is known of the
changes in emotional reactions in pathological conditions of the brain
centers, although these merit the closest study on theoretical and practical
grounds. Still obscure is the difference between the concepts of "emotion"
and "motivation" and whether any difference exists between an "emotion,"
an "emotional state" and an "emotional reaction." If these are different
concepts, what is the "emotiogenic" basis in each case? And as a final
question which has not yet received a satisfactory answer, I would like to
ask whether the reaction described as "hissing and growling," often
mentioned in laboratory reports, can be seriously considered as indicating
the presence of the emotions of rage and aggression, and the same applies to
the reaction of "flight," as an indication of fear or terror.

I fully share Smirnov's (1971) preference for using socio-psychological
rather than medico-biological methods to investigate human emotions
and their cerebral mechanisms. However, difficulties are still encountered
even if these methods are used, as can be seen for example from the report
of the International Congress on Emotional Stress (Sweden, 1967). There
was much detailed discussion of the clinical and physiological aspects, including the effects of various stressors on cardiovascular, respiratory and
endocrine activity. Procedures were described for determining and measuring these effects, as well as the stress reaction itself and for evaluating
the clinical significance of stress and the physiological reaction of different
subjects to different stress factors in the laboratory and in everyday life.
However, most interest was shown in the socio-psychological aspect, including methods of measuring subjective and objective variables of this
kind. There was much discussion of the methods of investigating and
modifying the psychological defense mechanisms, as well as of the significance of the psychological dependence which may arise during the period of
stress.

In reviewing the proceedings of the congress, Myasishchev (1970) summed
up its conclusions along the following lines. Emotional stress constitutes
an enormous problem with many aspects. It requires to be studied by the
joint efforts of psychologists, physiologists and clinicians. The significance
of the congress lay in the fact that the problems involved in studying emotional stress in man were considered not only from the medical, biological,
anatomical and physiological points of view, but also from the purely
psychological aspect; since a study on man cannot be complete without the
inclusion of specifically human psychological values. This line of thought
was pursued by many of the participants who noted the confusion which
surrounds the actual concept of stress. However, although a daunting
amount of literature has appeared on the subject, little real progress has
been made in our knowledge of the subject in recent years.

In order to study the physiological reactions to stress, one has to use stimuli which may affect the organism under normal conditions.   Moreover, not only physiological and biological effects but also the psychological aspects, which are affected by the intellectual processes, must be taken into account.   In certain occupations the combination of emotional and mental stress is incomparably greater than any physical (muscular) stress. For example, in a pilot who carries out acts of varying degrees of complexity at high altitudes, the preponderant stress is of a neuroemotional nature, resulting in a marked increase in the heart rate, up to 180 beats per minute, considerable water loss (up to 4—5% of the body weight), marked hyperventilation (respiratory rate of up to 50 per minute), as well as a number of other autonomic changes (Kosmolinskii, 1964).   In persons who operate heavy agricultural machinery the effect of overwork for several days is especially marked with respect to the activity of the CNS, that is, the activity of the auditory, visual and motor analyzers.   There is a diminution in the capacity for accurate perception and for the processing of information, in the ability to control the machine and in the precision of movement required for the work.   The mental component is evidently the most vulnerable in this kind of psychophysical stress (Golovacheva et al., 1966). A movie showing ritual operations being performed on the genitals of young Australian aborigines at the time of puberty evokes marked autonomic and mental reactions in the audience.   However, when the same movie is accompanied by a reassuring commentary, the psychological attitude and thus the autonomic reaction of the viewers assume quite a different character: there are no negative reactions or autonomic crises (Figure 14). Screening of the patriotic film "Zoya Kosmodemyanskaya"* has been found to produce feelings of distress and a sharp rise of blood pressure in young people suffering from hypertension (Volynskii, 1971).

It is obvious that the significance of the emotional factor must be studied primarily in its relation to psychogenic stress and to the trigger mechanisms of corticovisceral disturbances.   This is one of the most important problems of psychosomatic medicine today.

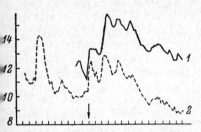

FIGURE 14.   Electrical conductivity of the skin during the screening of a film featuring a painful ritual among Australian aborigines, in a silent version (1) and when accompanied by a "protective" commentary (2) after Lazarus, 1970):

y-axis — electrical conductivity of the skin, microohms; x-axis — time marker, 15 sec. The arrow indicates the start of the film.

* [A film about a Soviet girl guerilla who was captured, tortured and executed by the Germans during World War II.]

Chapter 5

THE TRIGGER MECHANISMS OF PSYCHOGENIC STRESS

The trigger mechanisms of the pathological process and of the initial
phase of its development are two problems of corticovisceral pathology
which are of foremost concern to clinicians and physiologists alike. How
does an extremely powerful stimulus acting on the auditory or visual
analyzer produce a pathological reaction? How does this reaction develop
initially, when signs of disease have not yet appeared and the patient has not
yet sought medical attention? Why does the same pathogenic stress give
rise to a corticovisceral disease in some individuals and not in others?
Is a corticovisceral disease preceded by a premorbid period and if so, what
are its characteristic features and why does the latent period of the disease
sometimes last for days, weeks, or even many months?

These are only some of the problems which require to be given first
priority.

PSYCHOSOCIAL ENVIRONMENT AND CORTICOVISCERAL
DISTURBANCES. THE SIGNIFICANCE OF DIFFERENT
TYPES OF HIGHER NERVOUS ACTIVITY

In man, mental trauma, caused by negative emotions resulting from
a deed or from the spoken or written word, is the most common type of
powerful stress stimulus to produce corticovisceral disturbances. The
effect of mental trauma may be even greater than that of physical trauma
such as concussion, poisoning, avitaminosis, or endocrine disorders, all
of which are also able to produce corticovisceral disturbances.

In 1922 the well-known Soviet cardiologist Lang (1950) reviewing the
achievements of medical practice over the centuries and comparing them with
his own clinical observations, became convinced that the etiological basis
of hypertension was strain and trauma in the emotional sphere of higher
nervous activity, due to stimuli and emotions of a negative character. The
eminent Soviet pathologist Bogomolets (1929) later concurred with him,
adding that hypertension was liable to develop as a result of repeated minor
mental trauma occurring in everyday life. The same opinion has been
voiced more recently by the well-known Soviet clinician Chernorutskii
(1952) who stated that "the course and specific clinical features of conditions
such as peptic ulcer and hypertension are best understood if their etiology
is considered in the light of the corticovisceral theory. At present however

lthough we know something of the beginning and end of the chain of causes
nd effects responsible for the development of these and other cortico-
isceral conditions, the intermediate links and the mechanism of the patho-
ogical process are still something of a mystery"(p.17). Similar statements
ave been made by many other laboratory workers and clinicians in the
oviet Union and elsewhere, who have supported their conclusions with
xamples taken from everyday life and from clinical practice. Only a few
xamples from the scientific literature can be given here. Strazhesko
1949) described a patient who had never previously suffered from peptic
lcer but developed a perforated gastric ulcer after the city in which he
ived was bombed. A rise in the incidence of perforated ulcers during the
ir raids on London has also been reported (Figure 15). Similar findings
ith regard to hypertension have been described by Lang (1950). Again,
mother whose two sons died on the same night showed typical signs of
xophthalmic goiter in the morning (Harvát, 1955). A careful revision of
he histories of patients attending a cardiology clinic showed that 97% of
hose diagnosed as suffering from hypertension had a history of mental
rauma and nervous strain, brought on by negative emotions (Lang, 1950).
very day life presents such a plethora of conflict situations that the physician
ometimes finds it difficult to detect them all and to determine the significance
f the mental factors in the etiology and pathogenesis of the condition
see Chapter 12). In many cases, however, this is quite obvious (Luriya,
944; Lang, 1950; Kosenko and Paramonova, 1967; Nichkov and Krivitskaya,
960; Teleshevskaya, 1969).

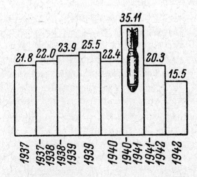

FIGURE 15. Annual average monthly incidence
of cases of perforated gastric ulcer in London
before, during and after World War II air raids
(after Bykov and Kurtsin, 1968).

Istamanova (1958) has observed that 92% of cases of neurasthenia
with manifestations of some disorder of visceral activity had a history of
severe psychogenic trauma and prolonged nervous strain. Mental
factors were detected in approximately the same percentage of peptic
ulcer cases (Chernorutskii, 1952). The significance of psychogenic
factors is more readily perceived when they affect large population
groups, as in the case of the unusual "outbreaks" of peptic ulcer and

hypertension in wartime and the very marked changes in the nature and course of psycho-autonomic disorders during floods or earthquakes. Draw on the experience of World War II and especially the 900-day siege of Leningrad, Chernorutskii (1952) has noted that: "A thorough investigation and careful examination of the causes, course and clinical picture of case of peptic ulcer and hypertension during the war leave no doubt that the common denominator of all the pathological changes was acute nervous ar mental trauma with excessive psycho-emotional stress."

An increased incidence of peptic ulcer in wartime with an atypical cou has also been reported from other countries. There are numerous repor of a 20 to 30% increase in new cases and a 70 to 80% increase in relapses Some authors have reported a rise of over 50% in new cases. However, whatever the exact number of new cases of a psychosomatic condition, it is clear that mental trauma is often the causative agent of corticoviscera disturbances in man, the "diseases of psychostasis," as they have been termed by Delgado (1969, 1971).

An interesting finding has been reported by Volynskii (1971). Medical examination of 109,000 persons showed that the prevalence of hypertensio was twice as high in soldiers at the front and three times as high in those who survived the siege of Leningrad and similar situations as in those wh had spent the war period in the rear. This is an important and in our opinion, a basic finding. At the same time we have only scant knowledge c the physiological mechanisms underlying such psychosomatic disorders. Some light on the problem has been shed by experimental physiology, by means of which extensive information has been acquired on the subjects of experimental neuroses and corticovisceral pathology. Yet, such findings quite unable to explain the actual cause of the trauma, the severity of its mani-festations and its psychogenic nature, because in man the disturbance occurs chiefly in the sphere of the second signal system which is absent in ani-mals. This aspect of mental trauma belongs to materialistic psycholo and to clinical neurology and psychiatry. Nevertheless, whatever the forn of the mental trauma, it affects the organism by physiological mecha-nisms which are common to man and the higher mammals.

This fundamental thesis was repeatedly emphasized by Pavlov (1951, Vol. 3, book 2, pp. 303 and 402; Vol. 4, p. 415) and it has been confirmed in medical practice by comparing clinical observations with the results of animal experiments. Interesting findings in this field were reported by Petrova (1946) during World War II, after a bomb fell on the building of the Institute of Physiology of the Academy of Sciences of the USSR in Leningrad. Out of 9 dogs in whom a Pavlovian stereotype of salivary conditioned reflexes had been established, eight developed an acute patho-logical condition of the cortical cells, which subsequently became chronic, accompanied by various autonomic disorders, despite the fact that the bom did not give rise to any bodily injury. This constitutes a spontaneous mod of the production of corticovisceral conditions by the instantaneous action an extremely powerful acoustic stress factor on the brain cells.

An equally vivid illustration is provided by the relationship between the typological features of the nervous system and the appearance of neuroses and corticovisceral disturbances. Of the four basic types of higher nervo activity (strong, unbalanced; strong, balanced, inert; strong, balanced, mobile; weak), as distinguished by Pavlov's school in animal experiments (and which in many ways resemble the four Hippocratic temperaments: choleric, phlegmatic, sanguine and melancholic), the incidence of neuroses and corticovisceral disturbances is highest in the two extreme types, that is strong, unbalanced (choleric) and weak (melancholic). Pavlov (1951) has written: "We have always been convinced that changes in higher nervous activity can be readily induced among our animals by traumatic agents; particularly among the uncontrolled and weak types, in which they took the form of neuroses."(Vol. 3, book 2, p. 346). In his paper "Basic Types of Higher Nervous Activity in Animals and Man" Pavlov pointed out that, notwithstanding great diversity in the ways of life of higher animals, such as dogs, which are close to man, their behavior is governed by the nervous system, just as in man, so that its main features and characteristics could well be similar. Furthermore, in the chapter entitled "A Physiological Study of the Types of Nervous System," that is, of temperaments, he writes: "I do not think it will be an insult to man if it is shown that his nervous system has the same general characteristics as that of the dog. Our education has already proceeded so far that no one will seriously oppose this view. We are perfectly justified in applying to man the results of experiments on the nervous system of the dog, for the resemblance is close."

In studies conducted in our laboratory for many years on over 400 dogs with an established stereotype of the conditioned salivary reflex it has also been shown that corticovisceral disturbances occurred mainly in animals with the weak and with the strong, unbalanced (uncontrolled) types of higher nervous activity. We were unable to produce either neurosis or cortico-visceral pathology in dogs of the strong, balanced type (whose numbers were very small, only 1% of the total), even though we used a variety of techniques for deranging higher nervous activity. We did not succeed even when the animal and its nervous system in particular had been previously weakened by such procedures as venesection or starvation. Similarly in Pavlov's laboratories various techniques for disrupting higher nervous activity were unsuccessfully used on this same type of dog. On one of his "physio-logical Wednesdays" Pavlov described dogs with these types of nervous system, such as the sanguine "Boi" and the phlegmatic "Zolotistyi," as outstanding, ideal types, combining the highest manifestations of the three characteristics: strength, equilibrium, and mobility. He noted that only a few dogs of these ideal types had been encountered among the thousands used in his work over 33 years.

However, it would be wrong to say that all animals with these types of higher nervous activity are immune to neurosis and corticovisceral dis-turbances. The literature provides evidence of neurosis produced in dogs of the strong balanced type (Yakovleva, 1967) and of chronic tension of cortical origin persisting for over 10 years (Danilova, 1965). In the last years of Pavlov's life it was shown in his laboratories that experimental neurosis could also be induced in dogs of the strong balanced type. This prompted Pavlov to modify his original view that neurosis is confined exclusively to the weak and uncontrolled types and to concede that nervous disorders might also be induced in strong, balanced animals, that is, in those with normal nervous mobility. However, in such cases considerable time and effort would need to be expended in trying out different techniques

(1951, Vol. 3, book 2, p. 300). Thus disturbances of higher nervous activi can be repeatedly and easily produced in dogs of the weak type, resulting ir persistent neurosis, whereas they are harder to produce in dogs of the strc type because of the strength and mobility which their nervous processes have achieved by training (Apter, 1969, 1970). Yakovleva (1967) attributes even greater importance to the degree of training of nervous processes as a factor affecting the production of experimental neuroses than to the typological characteristics of the nervous system.

A number of conclusions may be drawn from the experimental findings described in the extensive world literature on the subject. In the first pla the type of nervous system of the animal largely determines whether neu- rosis and corticovisceral disturbances will be induced and if so, what form they will assume. These conditions can be produced in practically 100% of animals of the weak and the strong unbalanced types. This conclusion accords with the numerous clinical reports that a definite correlation exists in man between certain forms of neuroses and psychoses, peptic ulcer, hypertension, and other corticovisceral conditions, on the one hand, and the constitutional and individual characteristics of the subject on the other. According to a study by Lang (1950), 80% of hypertensive patients possessed the weak type of higher nervous activity. Wartime residents of Leningrad suffering from hypertension were classified by Kupalov's associates, Yakovleva and Stozharov (1946), according to their type of highe nervous activity and it was found that 54% belonged to the weak type. It m be stressed that this kind of classification is based only on general physio- logical mechanisms, without taking into consideration the personality or an other specific features of human nervous activity, which are rendered still more complex and diverse by the social environment.

Because man alone possesses a second signal system, the mutual rela- tionship of the two signal systems is another characteristic feature of hum subjects. From this point of view three types of human nervous system ca be distinguished: 1) intellectual, in which the second signal system pre- dominates over the first; 2) artistic, in which the relationship is reversed; 3) intermediate, in which the two systems are more or less balanced. Thi additional characteristic by which the human nervous system can be clas- sified is a useful aid in studying the pathogenesis of psychoses and neurose (Ivanov-Smolenskii, 1971).

As regards corticovisceral pathology, experiments on animals show that the activity of the defense-adaptation mechanisms of the cortical-sub- cortical structures is more limited in the case of the weak and strong un- balanced types of nervous system, than with the strong balanced type. As a result, the depth and intensity of propagation of a pathological process, as well as its course and outcome, are more pronounced in the case of the weak and the unbalanced types, with a higher incidence of complications anc relapses.

The possible applications of this classification of the nervous system to various aspects of corticovisceral pathology have not yet been exhausted. For the purposes of this book some of these applications have been ignored including the relationship of the type of nervous system to the compensator processes called forth by general and local corticovisceral disturbances; as well as to the reaction of the corticovisceral structures and control mechanisms to various neurotropic and particularly psychotropic substanc in different stages of neurosis and corticovisceral pathology. In general, the treatment and the closely-linked question of prevention of cortico-visceral disorders have never before presented such a challenge. Cardio-vascular diseases have now become the outstanding problem in medical research and practice throughout the world, while the incidence of conditions such as peptic ulcer and metabolic diseases is rising annually and is coming to assume epidemic proportions. It is now widely recognized that the ner-vous factor, specifically, the nervous mental strain of the higher divisions of the CNS, resulting in corticovisceral disturbances, is the decisive factor in the etiology of these human ailments (Petrakov, 1972).

Apart from the type of nervous system, the nature of the trauma and the circumstances under which the neurosis was induced also exert an important influence on the nature, course, severity and outcome of the disease. Ob-servations on monkeys at the Sukhumi monkey farm have demonstrated that exposure to a new complex of ecologically inadequate stimuli exerts a powerful traumatic effect on animals which formerly lived in the wild (Lagu-tina et al., 1970). Conflicting defense and alimentary, or herd and sexual, natural conditioned reflexes have been found to produce serious autonomic disorders in sacred baboons, affecting in particular the cardiovascular system (hypertension, hypotension, coronary insufficiency, myocardial in-farction), the digestive system (gastric achylia, adenomatosis, polyposis and gastric ulcer) and the endocrine glands (hyperglycemia, amenorrhea) (Lagutina et al., 1970; Stratsev, 1971).

The general physiological mechanisms of the appearance and develop-ment of neurosis in a comparative series of vertebrates are basically the same as in the dog, which constitutes the classical Pavlovian subject for studies of experimental neuroses. At the same time, the lower mammals display a number of peculiarities in the development of the neurotic process as compared with the highly organized mammals (Biryukov and Bochurikhina, 1970). These are due to ecological factors and can be characterized as fol-lows: a) rapid appearance of the neurotic state; b) lability: frequent shifts between the pathological and the normal state; acute autonomic and trophic disorders; c) difficulty of returning to normal. In general, comparative physiological and phylogenetic studies of corticovisceral disturbances are of particular scientific interest. For example, it is important to know why the ce-rebral cortex (neocortex) of man and the higher animals is less resistant to psychogenic (cortical, emotional) stress factors, despite the presence of exten-sive compensatory adaptive mechanisms and the defensive ability to improvise, than the nervous structures of the paleocortex and archicortex, not to mention the subcortical formations.

PHYSIOLOGICAL, BIOCHEMICAL AND ULTRA-
STRUCTURAL BASIS OF THE INITIAL PHASE
OF CORTICAL (PSYCHOGENIC) STRESS

In man the trigger mechanism of psychogenic stress is characterized by an extremely curious feature that is of great importance for the de-velopment of the pathological process; the mental trauma is not

always followed immediately by obvious signs of neurosis and corticovisceral disease. Psychiatrists, neuropathologists, endocrinologists, car-
diologists, gastroenterologists and other clinicians have all reported that
the latent (premorbid) period is sometimes remarkably long.

Davydenkov (1963), an eminent Soviet specialist in neuroses, has described a patient who had suffered very severe mental trauma on the battle-
field, but only developed a neurosis six months later, after he had left the
fighting unit and had been transferred to the rear, where he lived and work
under quiet and relatively favorable conditions. Such "delayed reactions"
to extraordinary stimuli of vital importance are attributed by neuropathologists to the emergency mobilization of the human defense-adaptation
mechanisms. The duration of the latent period is thought to be related to
the strength and functional capacity of these mechanisms which may be differently developed in different persons, depending on numerous circumstances,
particularly the type of nervous system, its degree of training, and the physical
and mental state of the subject at the moment of trauma. Incidentally, the "flar
up" of corticovisceral conditions in civilian populations during World War II
did not die down immediately after the end of the war, but lingered on into the ea
postwar years, when there was no longer any apparent reason for it to be
sustained.

A latent period has also been observed by physiologists in cases of
experimental neurosis. On this subject, Pavlov has explicitly stated that
in dogs the profound disturbance of nervous activity does not take place
directly after the conflict or the extremely powerful stimulus, but a day or
more later. In our experiments on dogs subjected to a conflict of nervous
processes in the cerebral cortex, or to a brief exposure (for a few seconds
to an extremely powerful acoustic stimulus on one or on four successive day
the first signs of neurosis and corticovisceral disturbances did not always
appear on the day when the stress stimulus was actually applied. In some
of the animals they appeared more or less immediately after the
traumatic stimulus to the cortex, but in most cases they only appeared
one, two, or more days later and sometimes only after several weeks. The
well-known American physiologist Gantt (1953), a pupil of Pavlov, who has
carried out extensive research into experimental neuroses, has written that
in animals the severest forms of this condition do not become apparent
soon after the trauma to the nervous system but months or even years late
The cerebral cortex often "pays later" for a traumatic experience (Dolin
and Dolina, 1972). The writings of Pavlov and of his colleagues on the subject of experimental neuroses do not specify the nature of the physiopatholo
gical mechanism which gives rise to this latent period in neuroses and
corticovisceral pathology. Pavlov only made a general statement to the
effect that neuroses are caused by overtaxing the strength or mobility of th
basic nervous mechanisms of excitation and inhibition. However, just what
is meant by "tax" in physiological, biochemical and morphological terms is
not clear to this day, although it is known that Pavlov (1951) regarded the
processes of nervous excitation and inhibition as different phases of a
physicochemical process. Another well-known Pavlovian concept concerns
the high reactivity, easy vulnerability, limited working capacity and
excessive (protective) inhibition of the cortical cells. These characteristic

serve to protect the cell from exhaustion when its reaction to a stimulus reaches a certain limit.

All this is logical and sounds convincing as long as one is satisfied not to go beyond the limits of conditioned reflex salivation; or to use the terminology of cybernetics, if one does not go beyond the confines of the "black box."

The same may be said about the duration of the latent period of neuroses. We do not know the specific mechanisms by which it is determined. Maiorov has suggested the following explanation (Maiorov, 1954): functional trauma to the cerebral cortex brought about by conflicts or by exceedingly powerful stimuli causes only a diminution of activity of the cortical cells, whereas a true pathological state, with clear manifestations of exhaustion, sets in many days later as the result of the daily addition of ordinary, everyday stimuli to the psychogenic trauma. In the case of laboratory dogs, such stimuli are the daily conditioned reflex experiments which require intense cerebral activity. These ordinary stimuli, impinging on the already weakened background of the higher nervous activity of the organism, eventually cause this activity to break down and enter a pathological state. According to other authors (Yakovleva, 1967; Murav'eva, 1970), the duration of the latent period in a situational neurosis is determined by the rate of closure of the intracortical reflex arcs. An important role is ascribed by Kupalov (1961) to disturbances of the cortical-subcortical relationships, especially the disparity between the strength of cortical and subcortical excitation. This author, however, again reduces the problem to overstrain of the nervous processes, mainly the inhibitory mechanism. According to Anokhin (1958), at the basis of the neurosis lies a conflict not, as Pavlov thought, of excitation and inhibition, but of two independent excitatory systems. The conflict ends suddenly and at a high pitch of nervous intensity with the "victory" of one over the other which is inhibited for good.

These features of the interaction of the nervous processes probably determine the duration of the latent period. The victory of one system over the other and the consequent onset of neurosis and corticovisceral pathology are preceded by a period, presumably corresponding to the latent period of the neurosis, during which the two competing activities increase the strength of their excitations and mutually stabilize one another. This is why the conflict tends to persist for a prolonged period and at a high level of excitability.

However, Anokhin's purely physiological concept also lacks any indication of the relationship between the actual background of this conflict, against which the systems compete for a "strategic breakthrough" and the conflict taking place between the basic nervous processes of excitation and inhibition, which eventually serves to overtax their strength and mobility. The latent period of neuroses and corticovisceral disturbances following mental trauma must in the last resort be due to biochemical and morphological changes in the background structure itself, primarily in the cerebral cortex and possibly in the subcortical nervous formations. This approach is similar to Bykov's (1952) notion of a structural and functional relationship between the cortical neuron and its blood vessels. Together they constitute a functional unit which takes care of specific neuronal activity, the blood supply to the neurons, the rate of neuron metabolism and the prompt elimination of metabolites — in short, of everything implied by the terms "trophism" and "trophic" processes.

Bykov thus provides a more concrete interpretation of the nature of the latent period: the appearance and development of neurosis and of corti- covisceral pathology being attributed to trophic disturbances in the cerebr cortex, brought on by overtaxing the strength and mobility of the nervous processes, with simultaneous disturbances in the blood supply to the brain (Bykov and Kurtsin, 1960, 1968). Studies of axosomatic and axodendritic synaptic structures in the spinal and cortical neurons of cats, rats, and man have shown that many such formations which serve as the terminals of various efferent and afferent cerebral systems, are situated not only on the neurons themselves but also on the capillaries surrounding the neuron (Dolgo-Saburov, 1956). These findings suggest that excitation is transmitt not only from neuron to neuron but also to the blood vessels serving these neurons. This confirms Bykov's hypothesis (1952) that a cortical reflex change may take place simultaneously in the neurons and in their circulati so that the metabolic processes which accompany any changes in the nerves can be regulated as rapidly as possible. A histological connection of this kind between nerve cells and their blood vessels has also been de- tected in the digestive organs (Lavrent'ev, 1948; Kolosov, 1962, 1972; Lukashin, 1970) and it is therefore reasonable to assume that a similar principle of reflex regulation is found throughout the animal organism.

Thus, neurophysiological thinking has gradually merged with the ideas concerning the biochemistry of the brain and it has become recognized that it is necessary to study the metabolic changes occurring in the structure which serves as the arena for the conflict of nervous processes or as the actual place where they overtax their strength. An important contribution to the solution of this problem has been made by studies of the biochemistr of the animal brain, carried out in the laboratories of G. E. Vladimirov, A. V. Palladin, V. A. Engel'gard and E. M. Kreps. These have shed new light on the biochemistry of the nervous process of excitation and inhibition in the higher divisions of the CNS. They used a technique of instant freezi of brain tissue, which fixed the biochemical changes in a state as close as possible to the natural course of events and hence furnished highly reliable and valuable results. In rats it was found that changes in activity were accompanied by definite changes in the metabolic processes of the brain, involving redox potentials and the content of such substances as ammonia, phospholipids, carbohydrates, ATP and ADP. For example, increasing excitation was accompanied by a marked decrease in the tissue content of ATP and creatine phosphate with a simultaneous rise in the level of in- organic phosphate, whereas increased inhibition led to the accumulation of energy substances and a decrease in the metabolism of labile phosphorus compounds. Changes in the state of the brain were accompanied by signi- ficant changes in the carbohydrate-phosphorus compounds which are the principal, if not the only, source of energy for the specific activity of the CN

These studies paved the way for the study of the biochemical changes in the brain when it is acted upon by extra-powerful stimuli that experimental simulate the effect of psychogenic stress. The chief traumatic agent used was an acoustic stimulus. The reason for this is that the auditory analyzer together with the visual analyzer, plays a major part in bringing the orga- nism in contact with environmental factors. It was not by chance that Pavl made use of the acoustic stimulus as a stress factor to produce neurosis in dogs. This was employed in the laboratory both as an extremely powerful stimulus (a rattle) and as a conditioned signal of positive and inhibitory reactions in the form of a metronome beating 60 to 120 times per minute, or a tone. In our laboratory disturbances of higher nervous activity in dogs were often produced by means of an acoustic stimulus which served to overtax the strength or mobility of the nervous processes. The pathogenic effects of noise and other sound stimuli on human beings are also being widely studied and the findings then compared with the data obtained in animal experiments.

The effect of acoustic stimuli on higher nervous (mental) activity and autonomic activity in man and animals has been the subject of numerous investigations. Reviews on the subject have recently been published by Orlova (1965), Nichkov and Krivitskaya (1969) and Andreeva-Galanina and colleagues (1972). The main conclusion to be drawn from these investigations is that an acoustic stimulus which is strong enough and presented frequently enough can produce marked changes not only in higher nervous activity, but also in the activity of the cardiovascular, digestive, respiratory, urinary, endocrine and other systems, in both man and animals. Marked changes also occur in carbohydrate, protein, water-salt, lipid and other metabolic processes. Metabolic changes can already be detected after an acoustic stimulus of only 50 db (Orlova, 1965).

In our experiments on rats (Korobkina and Kurtsin, 1960) a weak acoustic stimulus, producing general motor excitement, increased the rate of oxidation in the cells and tissues of the brain by 21.2% on the average, while a strong acoustic stimulus of the order of 125 db and 2000 cps, such as an electric bell or automobile horn, produced a state of motor hyperexcitation and immobilization of the animal to the point of catalepsy and inhibited the oxidative processes in the brain by 6% on the average, as compared with intact [sic] rats. Studies were made (Dmitrieva and Kurtsin, 1960) of the content of macroergic phosphorus compounds in the brain tissues of rats that had been subjected for 10 minutes to an extra-powerful acoustic stimulus (125 db, 2000 cps). Immediately after the stimulus ceased and 2, 4 and 7 hours later the animals were killed in turn by instantaneous freezing in liquid air, as in the preceding series of experiments. The samples were taken and processed in the cold. The general behavioral reaction of the animals was found to differ according to their resistance to the sound. One group of rats, judging from their behavior, did not react to the stress stimulus and the brain indices studied differed little from those of the controls. A second group showed increased motor activity but without convulsions. These rats showed minor changes in brain phosphorus metabolism, expressed in a fall in ATP and creatine phosphate and a simultaneous rise in inorganic phosphate as compared with the control group. The third group showed the most severe reaction to the stress stimulus in the form of marked initial excitement, followed by convulsions and then by inhibition and a cataleptic state. In these animals the content of macroergic compounds in the brain showed significant changes, the ATP decreasing from 14.6 to 6.2 mg %, or by 55.0%, the creatine phosphate falling by 88.0%, from 6.0 to 0.8 mg %, while the inorganic phosphate content increased by 150%, from 18.2 to 46.2 mg % (all findings for wet tissue). The changes were detected immediately after the convulsion ceased but in most cases they were at their height two hours later.   The phosphorus metabolism in the brain rose after 7 hours, but did not reach the control level.

The significance of these findings is increased by the fact that the level of macroergic phosphates remained totally unaffected by slight conditioned reflex excitement.   Consequently, the marked drop in the content of macro-ergic phosphates in the brain must be attributed to the exhausting effect of the extremely powerful stress factor.   Another noteworthy finding in these and other experiments (Korobkina and Kurtsin, 1960) is that the acoustic stress stimulus induces metabolic changes not only in the brain but also in organs governed by the autonomic nervous system.   These reverberations are evidently caused by the spread of the excitement generated in the cortical-subcortical divisions of the auditory analyzer to the autonomic cen-ters of the cerebrum and medulla oblongata via associative neurons, the reticular formation of the brain stem and the limbic system.   The fact that autonomic changes in man are not confined to cases in which the acoustic stimulus penetrates to consciousness but also occur when the stimulus is not subjectively perceived and even during sleep, suggests that this excite-ment is propagated in the nervous structures of the brain by an inborn, un-conditioned-reflex mechanism.

Furthermore, the initial latent period of the disorder may to some exten be due to the time lag between the application of the extra-powerful stimul and a marked depletion of the energy resources of the nerve cell. Valuable findings in this respect have been provided by histochemical investigations. For example, in rats subjected to overstrain of cerebral cortical activity, changes in behavioral reactions were accompanied by changes in the rate o protein anabolism and in the content of nucleic acids in the cytoplasm and nuclei of the cortical nerve cells (Zhemkova et al., 1956).

We have found that on overtaxing the nervous processes in the cerebral cortex of dogs, changes were produced in the RNA content of the tissues of the cerebral cortex, particularly as regards ribonuclease activity (Gaza and Nechaeva, 1970).   An increase in their activity was already detected on the second day after the conflict, and from the fifth day on it became very obvious, persisting thus for the next six weeks.   The increase after the on-set of neurosis varied between 11% and 82% for alkaline ribonuclease and between 10% and 55% for acid ribonuclease.   The regularity of this increas suggests that the trigger mechanism of neuroses and corticovisceral patho logy is not confined to depletion of the cells of the cerebral cortex as a result of overstimulation of the mechanisms of excitation and inhibition.

Voronin and Danilova (1966) have shown that the injection of ribonucleas into the hippocampus of a rabbit inhibits conditioned reflexes.   Consequent. the changes occurring in the ribonuclease content of the brain following ex-posure to stress may affect the course of metabolic processes and the ac-tivity of the cerebral structures responsible for higher nervous activity an for the control of autonomic activity, by involving in the pathological re-action the hippocampal complex which is one of the inhibitory systems of the brain. A contributory factor, as shown in our laboratory (Mikhailov et al., 1962), is that experimental neurosis causes profound changes in the metabolism of bromine which, according to the Pavlovian school, acts as a most potent stimulator of inhibition in the cerebral cortex.   These dis-turbances were detected between the 4th and 7th days after the conflict.

However, the changes in the chemical activity of the brain are not confined to the ribonucleases. Kuzokov (1971b), working in our laboratory,
studied the cholinesterase activity in the cerebral hemispheres of rats,
at rest and in a state of acoustic stress (automobile horn of 120 db and
2000 cps). While the initial cholinesterase activity in the brain was
0.468 ± 0.48 mg, or $66.8 \pm 9.0\%$ decomposed acetylcholine, there was a
sharp drop to 0.281 ± 0.024 mg, or $40.1 \pm 4.0\%$, after a 20-minute exposure
to the extra-powerful acoustic stimulus. The low level of enzyme activity
persisted for 3 to 4 days after the exposure. Using the UV microabsorption
method, Hamberger and Hyden (1945) found that an acoustic stimulus of 80 db
at 6000 cps immediately led to a virtual disappearance of RNA from the
cytoplasm of cells in the cochlear ganglion and to a five-fold decrease in
their protein content. The RNA and protein content only regained their
initial levels in the third week after the single exposure. When an extra-
powerful acoustic stimulus was used (12 revolver shots in the course of
6 days), full restoration of the RNA and protein levels was not achieved even
8 weeks later. Exposing rats to an extra-powerful acoustic stimulus,
Zhemkova et al. (1956) found the rate of uptake of ^{35}S by the cerebral cortex
to be higher in animals of the excitable type than in those of the inhibited type
or in the controls. It was found, moreover, that the cells of the pyramidal
tracts of the excitable rats often contained irregularly shaped nuclei and
their chromophilic substance had a somewhat increased RNA content.

Histological studies of the brain of albino rats subjected to acoustic
stress (Nichkov and Krivitskaya, 1969) showed that oxygen deficiency
developed in the neurons, glia and blood vessels. These findings are in
agreement with the results of an experiment in which acoustic stress
produced cerebral hypoxia with the inhibition of certain enzymes,
including histaminase which is particularly sensitive to oxygen deficiency.
In this case a whole complex of biochemical chain reactions, with the
participation of many enzyme systems, is probably involved. For example the
diminished activity of histaminase will give rise to the accumulation of
histamine in the tissues and since histamine inhibits oxidizing enzymes
such as the dehydrases, the oxygen deficiency of the brain tissues is
exacerbated. As a result of such chain reactions a local vicious circle
is produced, which consolidates the pathological condition of the brain
centers. It seems to us that such findings regarding the changes occurring
in the metabolic processes and in the activity of the enzyme systems
provide the key to an explanation of the latent period which precedes the
manifestations of neurosis and corticovisceral disturbances. This is the
more so since certain biochemical processes taking place in cells and
tissues consist not only of chain reactions but also of protracted processes
which will require a much longer time for the performance if their enzyme
mechanism is impaired.

Equally important is the effect of an acoustic stimulus on the absorptive
properties of cell membranes. In his early studies Nasonov (1959) already
showed that the protoplasm and nucleus of cells in the spinal ganglia, which
do not normally stain in vivo, actively absorb the dye after exposure to noise,
while strong acoustic stimuli paralyze the activity of the cell and produce
structural changes of a paranecrotic [sic] nature which are, however,
reversible. Exposure of a cell to the stimulus primarily affects the protein

component of the protoplasm, resulting in the subsequent biochemical and structural changes.   The degree of injury to the cell has also been found to be related to the strength and duration of the stimulus.   According to Romanov (1956), the brief action of an extra-powerful acoustic stimulus alters the absorptive capacity of the sympathetic ganglion nerve cells in the rabbit by over 20%, and the initial level is not restored until 20 —24 hou: later, while painful stimulation of the sciatic nerve for 5 minutes produces a change in the absorptive capacity of the brain cells that persists for as long as 5 hours.   Romanov observed that an acoustic conditioned-reflex stimulus can produce changes in the absorptive capacity of cortical cells which persist for several days.

A new page has been added to the theories of neurosis production as a result of electron-microscope studies.   Manina (1971) found that the major of cortical neurons retain their ultrastructure in neurosis.   Although the organelles show some local degenerative changes, their regenerative capacity is increased.   However, these changes persist for many days and even weeks after the trauma and give rise to abnormal activity of the neuron. Using an optical microscope, Nichkov and Krivitskaya (1969) showed that the neurons of the cerebral cortex are the most vulnerable to acoustic stres: followed by those of the subcortical formations.   Of the latter the neurons which are most susceptible to injury are firstly those in the structures of the auditory analyzer and then the neurons of the limbic system, reticular formation of the brain stem, hypothalamus and cerebellum, that is, nervous formations which are closely related to the mechanism governing the autonomic activity of the organism.   The pathological changes noted included marked chromatolysis of the Nissl bodies in some neurons and hyperchromatosis in others; the presence of binucleolate cells; varicose swellings of the dendrites; deformation, fragmentation and vacuolization of myelinated fibers; swelling and disintegration of synapses; thickening and coarsening of presynaptic connections; deformation of the dendrites and hyperplasia, hypertrophy, and disintegration of the glia.   Structural changes were also observed in the blood vessels: the nuclei of the endothelial cells were swollen, and the lumen was sometimes markedly constricted, with perivascular edema and sometimes showed extreme paralytic dilatation, with hyperemia, erythrocyte stasis, extravasation of plasma and angionecrosis: a condition which, in rats, was often found at the cortical end of the auditory and dermomotor analyzers.

It cannot be asserted that structural changes form the basis of all the above biochemical disturbances which play such an important part in the processes of excitation and inhibition, since the reverse can also occur. In other words, biochemical disturbances within the nerve tissue may give rise to structural changes.   It must be stressed, moreover, that certain structural changes are reversible, disappearing after prolonged rest. Others are manifestations of reactive, proliferative processes and are essentially compensatory and adaptive.   Finally, some changes are irreversible, ending in disintegration and degeneration of the nervous structure.

These physiological, biochemical and histological changes all help to she light on the extraordinarily complex structural and functional pattern resulting from overstimulation of the processes of excitation and inhibition, which was formerly so puzzling a phenomenon.

It may thus be assumed that the length of the latent period of a neurosis, the nature of the neurotic condition of the cerebral cortex and the duration of corticovisceral disturbances are all determined by the degree of bio-chemical and structural damage to the cortical cells. It is still impossible to demarcate the boundary beyond which the first signs of neurosis can be detected. This seems to vary with the organism and to depend on the typological characteristics of the nervous system, as well as on the state of activity of the cells and of the entire cerebral cortex at the moment of ex-posure to the psychogenic trauma. The contributory factors are not limited to disturbances of enzyme activity and of cellular synthesis and break-down, mainly of protein and nucleic acids. An important part in the genesis of neuroses and corticovisceral disorders seems to be played by structural changes in the cell, in such components as the membranes (plasmatic, nuclear, endoplasmatic and mitochondrial), canaliculi, nucleus, endoplasmatic reticulum and mitochondria. These structures are associated with the acti-vity of the sodium, potassium, calcium and other ionic pumps, with the synthesis of nucleic acids and protein molecules, and with many other func-tional and genetic properties of the cells. The significance of a "breakdown" of the cellular structures as a whole and of individual cell components requires to be determined by further studies of the central effects of neu-rosis on the cerebral cortex in warm-blooded animals, at the subcellular, molecular, and possibly even submolecular levels.

Another important aspect is the cyclical nature of the involvement of the enzyme systems or metabolic reactions. Thus damage to one enzyme system affects another and so on along the chain. It would, however, be naive to imagine that the trigger mechanism of the initial phase of stress is capable of sustaining the development of the pathological reaction over a period of many days. What probably happens in this period is that the initial trigger effect is taken over by other local and general mechanisms which maintain the force of the explosive wave and extend the initial changes in all directions. Prominent among these numerous mechanisms is the action of hormones and mediators on the cerebral structures. The hormones of the adaptatory system, that is, of the pituitary and adrenals, may play the leading part in the initial phase of stress. They may become involved in the initial pathological process in the brain in the very first minutes or hours after exposure to the psychic trauma. This has been endorsed by studies at the Institute of Physiology of the Academy of Sciences of the Ukrainian SSR on the effect of ACTH and hydrocortisone on the content of carbohydrate-phosphorus compounds in the brain of guinea pigs. It was found that with a single intramuscular injection of ACTH the content of ATP, creatine phos-phate, or inorganic phosphate in the brain was not affected, although the glycogen content rose. However, repeated administration of the hormone resulted in a fall in the content of ATP and creatine phosphate and a rise in inorganic phosphate and glycogen. Since ACTH usually acts indirectly, by activating the secretion of corticosteroids by the adrenal cortex, it is not surprising that the administration of extra hydrocortisone accelerated the onset of cerebral effects. Only one hour after single intramuscular injection of 12.5 mg hydrocortisone to the guinea pigs, the content of ATP and creatine phosphate in the brain dropped from 15.0 to 12.6 mg % and from 12.7 to 11.6 mg %, respectively, while the content of inorganic phosphate and glycogen rose from 4.8 to 5.6 mg % and from 85.8 to 99.0 mg %, respectively; the effect reached its peak in 2 to 4 hours.

Thus, the speed at which the hormonal mechanism is brought into play ar the action of the hormones on the brain (reflex as well as direct) should no doubt also be taken into account in explaining the varying duration of the latent period. However, this is merely an assumption and requires direct experimental confirmation. Also to be clarified is the role of mediator systems, such as noradrenalin and adrenalin, which exert a significant influence on various metabolic processes, particularly glycolysis. It is known from the literature that certain stress agents, such as abrupt changes in the ambient temperature, pain, narcosis and surgical trauma, cause a drop in the noradrenalin level in the brain within $1-2$ minutes of the onset of exposure to the stimulus. It is also known that the administration of large doses of insulin or hydrocortisone to guinea pigs subjected to stress by immobilization for $4-5$ hours raises the adrenalin content of the adrenals and noradrenalin content of the brain (Table 3).

TABLE 3. Content of noradrenalin in the brain and of adrenalin in the adrenals of a guinea pig under different kinds of stress (after Maevskaya, 1968), $M \pm m$

Experimental conditions	Content, mg/g	
	noradrenalin	adrenalin
Normal state	0.38 ± 0.26	308.0 ± 32.0
Stress:		
Immobilization for $4-5$ hr	0.52 ± 0.03	458.0 ± 31.0
Administration of hydrocortisone, $5-10$ units/kg	0.41 ± 0.024	437.0 ± 20.0
Administration of insulin, 10 units/kg	0.55 ± 0.03	608.0 ± 78.0

Note: 0.01.

The involvement of the hormonal link is probably just as rapid in the presence of a mental stress factor, since this is certainly no weaker, and may even be stronger, than all the above-mentioned stress stimuli. This is an important consideration, because the rate of neurosecretion in the neurons of the hypothalamus through which the "main lines" pass from the cerebral cortex to the internal organs is directly dependent on the content of adrenalin and especially of noradrenalin in the hypothalamus. All this suggests that adrenergic mediators may play an important part in the trigger mechanism of neurosis and visceral-autonomic disturbances of cortical (psychogenic) origin. The role of the cholinergic mediator acetylcholine merits separate discussion, since the major events occurring in psychogenic stress take place in the cerebral cortex where the cholinergic structures are now believed to be mainly located.

CHEMICAL NATURE OF THE TRIGGER MECHANISM OF NEUROSIS AND OF CORTICOVISCERAL PATHOLOGY

It has been seen that overtaxing the strength or mobility of the excitatory and inhibitory processes by stimulating the cerebral cortex

in various ways will produce, after a shorter or longer latent period, a
neurotic condition of the cortical cells, which disturbs the functional relationships between the cortical and subcortical brain centers and leads to
corticovisceral pathology. In the last few years it has been learned that
this kind of overstrain is accompanied not only by weakening and inversion
of the activity of the cortical neurons, as manifested by the conditioned
salivary reaction, but also by other neurotic changes in the brain, including
disturbances in the metabolism of carbohydrates, phosphorus, proteins,
and the nuclei, and in gas exchange, as well as changes in the
absorptive properties of the cells. Moreover, certain changes in the bioelectrical activity of the brain have also been observed in neurosis. Yet
all these physiological, biochemical, electron-microscope and electrophysiological findings, while broadening our understanding of the nature of neurosis,
of the central mechanisms of corticovisceral disturbances and of the latent
period in psychosomatic disorders, have not yet solved the riddle regarding
the initial mechanism which actually triggers off the pathological process.
Nor have they revealed how the mental excitation sets in motion all
the successive biochemical, physical, physiological, and morphological chain
reactions and ultrastructural changes in the cells and tissues of the brain.
    On general physiological considerations, it may be assumed that psycho-
genic trauma, like any other stimulus to nervous tissue, produces a state of
excitation in the substrate by means of acetylcholine which mediates the
nervous excitation in the cortical synapses and in the postganglionic endings
of the cholinergic fibers. This substance is released into the synaptic gap
by the evacuation of a large number of submicroscopic granules or vesicles
ranging from 200 to 1000 $\overset{\circ}{A}$ in diameter. Most of it is found in a bound form
which is rapidly decomposed by the enzyme cholinesterase (MacIntosh and
Oborin, 1953; Robertis, 1964). The question arises whether strong stimuli
do not cause large concentrations of acetylcholine to be released into the
synaptic gap, while the cholinesterase activity is depressed. We have assumed
that acetylcholine is the chemical agent in the cerebral cortex, which triggers first the neurotic process and then the corticovisceral disturbances,
following exposure to an extremely powerful stimulus, or when the mobility
of the nervous processes in the cerebral cortex is otherwise overstrained
(Gaza, 1969). There were also grounds for associating this chemical assault
on the cells with the limbic cortex. In our early studies on dogs we had
shown that excision or coagulation of this cortical area alone, and no other,
gives rise to chronic disturbances of both higher nervous activity and autonomic activity: that is, of vascular tone and bile secretion (Gaza, 1962),
blood pressure, diuresis [sic] and the secretion of gastric juice (Gulyaeva,
1962). There were also other considerations, taken solely from the literature, based on the important part played by the limbic area of the cortex
and by the limbic system as a whole, in the mechanism controlling autonomic
activity (see Chapters 1 and 2). This hypothesis was tested in our laboratory by experiments on dogs with an established stereotype of conditioned
salivary reflexes, in whom the normal pattern of autonomic reactions (bile
and gastric secretion, blood pressure) had previously been determined.
A single dose of either 200 or 2000 gamma acetylcholine was injected into
the limbic cortex (areas L_2 and L_1) through a previously prepared window
in the skull. Between 1 and 3 days later the animals developed changes in

both higher nervous and visceral activity, which persisted for many weeks. In the controls the injection of physiological solution into the same cortical areas had no such effect, nor did the injection of large doses of noradrenalin or serotonin which also mediate nervous excitation, nor even the administration of smaller doses (20 gamma) of acetylcholine. On the other hand, the injection of large doses of acetylcholine into the occipito-parietal region of the cortex produced neither neurosis nor corticovisceral disturbances (Gaza, 1971).

Hence, acetylcholine and no other mediator is the chemical agent which triggers the development of neurosis and corticovisceral pathology, while it is in the limbic cortex that psychic or some other cortical stress (emotional or interoceptive) overtaxes the nervous processes (Kurtsin and Gaza, 1970). The power of the "blow" in producing not only severe disturbances of cerebral and visceral activity but also a prolonged aftereffect lasting weeks or even months apparently contributes to the fact that the strong stimulus entering the brain "smashes" the complex yet fragile structures made up of the neurons and their circulatory system and at the same time "disorganizes" the equally complex and fragile enzyme system. Thus, for example, the cholinesterase activity is markedly reduced (Kuzovkov, 1971b), while the ribonuclease activity is increased (Gaza and Nechaeva, 1970).

Some of the other paleocortical regions, such as the hippocampus and amydaloid nuclei, as well as certain neocortical areas, including the orbital cortex and the premotor area (areas 4 and 6), may also be capable of producing such cortical and corticovisceral effects on the administration of high concentrations of acetylcholine. However, nothing definite can be said in this regard until such experiments have been carried out. Also to be studied is the part played by the adrenergic structures and adrenergic mediators in the development of a pathological reaction when acetylcholine is injected into the limbic cortex. It is probably of some importance, since in the same dogs the injection of acetylcholine into the limbic cortex produce neither neurosis nor corticovisceral disturbances, if chlorpromazine in a dose of 0.5 mg/kg was administered 45 min before the chemical "blow" (Kurtsin and Gaza, 1970, 1971) (Figure 16). The mechanism of this phenomenon is complicated, the possibilities being as follows: 1) a direct effect of chlorpromazine on the cholinergic systems of the reticular formation of the brain stem and on the cerebral cortex itself, leading to reduced susceptibility of the cortical neurons to acetylcholine; 2) a central cholinolytic effect of chlorpromazine, resulting in the partial or total destruction of the acetylcholine injected into the limbic cortex; 3) a paralytic effect of chlorpromazine on the adrenergic structures of the reticular formation and the thalamus, thus shutting off the activating effect of the subcortex on the cortical cells of the limbic region and reducing the excitability of the latter. All three hypotheses can be supported by a good number of experimental findings reported in the extensive literature dealing with the mechanism of the effect of chlorpromazine on the brain. On the basis of our observations on the effect of different doses of chlorpromazine on higher nervous activity and on corticovisceral relationships (Bolondinskii, 1965; Gaza, 1965b; Gulyaeva, 1965; Rybnikova, 1966; Balakshina et al., 1967; Suvorov, 1967), we support the third suggestion and assume that the thwarting of the acetylcholine effect is due to a marked diminution in the reactivity of the cells of the limbic cortex following the lytic action of chlorpromazine on the adrenergic structures of the reticular formation, subcortex and cortex.

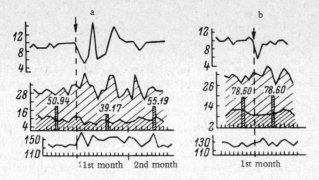

FIGURE 16. Changes in higher nervous activity, bile secretion and blood pressure
in a dog following injection of 200 µg acetylcholine into the limbic cortex (a)
and without chlorpromazine (b) after the administration (after Kurtsin and Gaza,
1970).

Curves (from above downwards) — sum of positive conditioned reflexes for each
experiment (drops of saliva); alimentary bile secretion; spontaneous bile secretion
(ml); bars: bilirubin content (mg%); blood pressure (mm Hg). Arrow — time of
acetylcholine administration.

Thus, the experimental findings tend to show that the "overtaxing of the
nervous processes," which is generated in the cortical cells by the action
of an extra-powerful stress stimulus and which leads to their functional
exhaustion, the development of neurosis and then to corticovisceral pathology, is probably rooted in profound changes in metabolic processes and
enzyme reactions as well as in the properties of the cell membranes and
of the ultrastructure of the cells. This "breakdown" of the structural and
functional organization of cells is initiated by the chemical "blow" dealt by
a high concentration of acetylcholine, the mediator of nervous excitation.

However, research into the biochemical basis of the trigger mechanism
of corticovisceral disturbances is only in its early stages. Much experimental work still requires to be carried out regarding the part played in the
production and development of the neurotic state by a) the adrenergic and
serotoninergic cortical and subcortical structures, in addition to the cholinergic structures and b) the choline-histamine-serotonin-mimetic and adrenomimetic mediators. These biologically active substances are all produced
as a result of the psychogenic trauma and impaired blood supply to the
cerebral cortex and to the subcortical neural structures.

Damage to enzyme systems and in particular the suppression of cholinesterase activity and the increase in nuclease activity are of vital importance in all stages of the initiation and development of neurosis and corticovisceral disturbances. It would be most desirable to learn something
about the changes in these and many other important enzymes during the
period of stress itself and in the course of development of the neurosis,
up till the time when the corticovisceral relationships are completely
restored to normal. Disturbances in monoaminoxidase activity have also
been reported.

However, the significance of many biologically active substances is not limited to their share in injuring the nervous mechanisms; they are also instrumental in causing disturbances of visceral activity, particularly secretion and motility; as well as of hormone production and enzyme activity, of urine formation, of the metabolism of proteins, nucleic acids, carbohydrates, lipids, phosphorus and trace elements, and of oxidation and other processes of growth, repair and energy production. If this problem can be solved at the molecular, subcellular, and cellular levels in the intact animal, by the use of Pavlovian techniques, it will be possible to understand (Kurtsin, 1963) and evaluate the role and significance in corticovisceral pathology of such substances as adrenalin, noradrenalin, dopa and other catecholamines, acetylcholine, serotonin, histamine and other mediators, gamma-aminobutyric, lysergic and citric acids and many other biologically active substances which play a part in the metabolic processes, including growth, energy production and repair. A comprehensive study of the biochemical changes which take place in corticovisceral disturbances and which themselves give rise to these disturbances to a significant extent, constitutes one of the important tasks of corticovisceral biochemistry.

A neurochemical approach to the study of the initial stages of corticovisceral disturbances is prompted not only by the above biochemical and electron-physiological investigations, but also by the wealth of discoveries made in the field of psychopharmacology over the last 15 — 20 years and particularly the part played by certain chemical substances, such as acetylcholine, serotonin and its product lysergic acid, in the development of psychoses (see the review by Gaito, 1966; Il'yuchenok, 1972; Megrabyan, 1972).

One of the many intimate mechanisms which may play a part in the development of the pathological state, is the process whereby the ionic equilibrium is maintained between the neuron and the ambient fluid medium. According to present views (Tobias, 1964), the mechanism by which an axon passes from a state of rest to a state of excitation consists in the migration of potassium ions from the cytoplasm of the axon into its membrane, with the result that the latter takes up water and its structure becomes looser and less connected. It is thought that this process, which is reversible, is essential for the acceleration of ionic fluxes through the canals (pores) of the membrane and for the formation of the nerve impulse. However, this ionic mechanism is liable to break down under excessive strain; hence its significance in the development of the primary stress effect (Manina, 1971).

Neurotic manifestations of the internal organs are usually only functional and gradually disappear once higher nervous activity returns to normal. However, the fact that the changes which occur are not limited to the ultrastructure of the cells and tissues of the cerebral cortex but also extend to the internal organs, suggests that the preconditions for a transition to the stage of organic lesions is already to be found in the organs during the stage of disturbed activity. It is evident that prolonged disturbances of this kind, particularly in metabolic processes, can also give rise to serious dystrophic phenomena, so that the condition acquires a markedly organic character. The investigations described above have succeeded in showing that certain disorders of visceral activity or structure may be due to a primary disturbance in the cortical mechanism governing autonomic activity, thereby

validating the corticovisceral theory of the pathogenesis of certain psychosomatic diseases.   They also objectively demonstrate the initial stage of
the pathological process (the premorbid period of the disease), which lies
outside the sphere of activity of the clinician who is usually confronted with
what might be termed the "finished product," since by the time the patient
seeks medical aid, the symptomatology is generally quite evident.

Chapter 6

NEUROENDOCRINE MECHANISM OF CORTICO-
VISCERAL DISTURBANCES

The problem of neuroendocrine relationships in the processes of adaptation of the animal organism to the external environment is one of the main aspects of the theory of corticovisceral disturbances now being studied by many physiologists and clinicians. However, prolonged investigations in this field have not yet produced a consensus of opinion on the subject. On the contrary, there exist at present at least two sharply diverging views, which might be termed the reflex theory and the hormonal theory. The first is based on Pavlov's view that the reflex is the most common reaction in the life of a complex organism, ensuring that a correct and precise relationship is continuously maintained between the different parts of the organism and between the organism as a whole and the environment. Adaptation is the biological aim of all reflexes, innate and acquired, but the highest degree of adaptation of the organism and of its parts is achieved by means of conditioned reflexes.

THE GENERAL ADAPTATION SYNDROME AND
THE REFLEX THEORY OF ADAPTATION

The hormone theory of adaptation is embodied in Selye's work on stress and its relationship to what is now known as the general adaptation syndrome (Selye, 1950, 1952, 1959, 1971, 1972). Briefly, this can be summed up as follows. A highly complex series of defense and adaptation reactions is produced in the animal organism in response to the action of any stimulus (stress factor). This is implemented by two mechanisms, one specific and one nonspecific. The specific mechanism is conditioned by the character and specific nature of the stimulus, its form and quality. Thus, a particular antigen stimulates the organism to produce specific antibodies; ionizing radiation gives rise to the syndrome known as radiation sickness, brought about by ionization of the water molecules in the tissues, damage to the protein, carbohydrate, lipid and other cell and subcellular components, toxicosis [sic] and reflex changes in cellular and tissue activity. In the same way a psychogenic factor which is usually accompanied by an emotional reaction, produces cardiovascular and respiratory effects and digestive and sexual disorders. The nervous system often plays a part in the initiation of specific effects.

The other mechanism bears no relation to the quantitative and qualitative characteristics of the stress factor. Through the pituitary-adrenal cortex axis, it produces a complex of functional and structural changes, which are always of the same nature but vary in severity. Thus, the same response is elicited to antigens, ionizing radiation, psychogenic trauma and a great variety of other stimuli differing both qualitatively and quantitatively. This second mechanism for the development of the adaptation and defense reactions was considered by Selye (1972) to be the more important. It generates a special kind of stress in the different physiological systems and in the body as a whole, to which he gave the name of the stress syndrome, or the general adaptation syndrome. Stress gives rise to a) marked enlargement of the adrenal cortex with a simultaneous decrease in its lipid and cholesterol content; b) involution of the lymphatic system: the lymph nodes, spleen and especially the thymus, manifested by lymphopenia and eosinopenia; c) gastrointestinal hemorrhage and ulceration. These phenomena develop in stages: the first stage represents the state of anxiety or shock, the second, resistance, or countershock, and the third, exhaustion. The stage of anxiety is dominated by breakdown processes and lesions caused by the pathogenic stimulus, manifested by muscular hypotonia, low blood pressure and body temperature, an increased permeability of the blood vessels and cell membranes, hemoconcentration, tissue acidosis, hypoglycemia, eosinopenia, lymphopenia, hypochloremia, hyperkalemia, a high rate of cell katabolism, and certain gastrointestinal lesions. This stage gives rise to degenerative changes in the lymphatic system while, on the other hand, as Selye noted, the adrenal cortex "flourishes." He thus regarded this stage as an alarm reaction, a very useful defense phenomenon in the nonspecific adaptation reaction. These changes take place suddenly but persist for some time, unless the stressor is sufficiently powerful to exhaust the adrenal cortex at once. Thus, the acute phase of resistance subsequently becomes transformed into a chronic state.

The stage of exhaustion is marked by the same autonomic changes as the initial stage. It results from the prolonged action of the pathogenic factor and may have a lethal outcome if the adaptation reaction is not successful.

Thus, the stress reaction involves changes resulting both from the pathogenic stimulus and the defense processes, and it is not always easy to differentiate between them; just as it is difficult to decide whether stress is useful or harmful to the organism (Söderberg, 1967). The reaction is generated by a great variety of agents, such as trauma, infection, poisoning, narcosis, high and low temperatures, ionizing radiation, emotional factors, and even physical and mental strain. Yet the reaction should always be regarded as an attempt by the organism to restore the state of equilibrium and to establish homeostasis. In response to stress, the anterior lobe of the pituitary vigorously produces two hormonal substances which exert opposing effects on the cells and tissues: the adrenocorticotropic hormone (ACTH) and to a lesser extent, the somatotropic hormone (STH). The degree of stimulation of ACTH or STH production and of their release into the blood determines the trend and the actual nature of the adaptation reaction. However, the process is mediated by the adrenal cortex which is stimulated by these hormones to vigorously produce the corticosteroid hormones which actually influence the effectors. The stimulation of corticosteroid production is based on the increased synthesis of enzyme proteins, which itself depends on increased RNA metabolism (Voitkevich and Tkacheva, 1969). The corticosteroid level in the blood during stress may be high or low, depending upon the stage of the reaction and the characteristics of the individual organism (Lazarus, 1967). In the resistance stage which follows the stage of damage ("shock"), the production of corticosteroids is intensively stimulated by ACTH, so that their content in the blood and tissues is high. For example, in rats the synthesis of corticosterone in the adrenal tissues during the stress reaction rises to 100 mg/hr. In dogs, the secretion of hydrocortisone into the blood increases from negligible amounts to 18 and 23 μg/min, respectively, 10 and 15 min after exposure to stress. In man the content of adrenal hormones in the blood increases tenfold in the hours following surgical trauma. The corticosterone content also rises when the adrenal cortex is stimulated by ACTH.

At present there are about 40 corticosteroids known, some of which have been isolated in the crystalline state. The most important are cortisone (17-hydroxy-11-dehydrocorticosterone), hydrocortisone (17-hydroxycorticosterone), prednisone, prednisolone, aldosterone and corticosterone (11-21-dehydroxyprogesterone).

The production of corticosteroids and their entry into the blood are regulated and controlled by ACTH. This hormone is secreted by the basophil cells of the anterior lobe of the pituitary. It stimulates the production of the glucocorticoid hormones, such as cortisone, hydrocortisone and cortisol which produce atrophy of the thymus and lymph nodes and changes in the blood (neutrophilic leucocytosis, lymphopenia, eosinopenia) and in the metabolism of carbohydrates, fats and proteins, and inhibition of inflammatory and katabolic processes. Glucocorticoids enhance the activity of succinic dehydrase, peptidase, nucleotidase, acid phosphatase and certain other enzymes; they also accelerate the absorption of glucose and lipids by the small intestine and increase glycogenoplastic and inhibit glycogenolytic processes in the tissues.

STH stimulates the production of the mineral corticoids, DOCA, and aldosterone which promote inflammation and give rise to nephrosclerosis [sic], hypertension and inflammatory processes in the cardiovascular system and joints. They also regulate the metabolism of sodium, calcium, chlorine, potassium, phosphorus and iron.

It is still not clear why different hormones are predominantly released in different cases of stress, although a relationship has been noted to various physiological states of the organism, for example to excessive muscular fatigue, cooling, oxygen lack or changes due to age. The adaptation syndrom may help or harm the organism. Under certain conditions, the vigorous production of adaptive hormones, unrelated to the strength of the stressor, leads to exaggerated reactions of adaptation. Reactions of this kind can then no longer be considered as an adaptation-defense response. They have been transformed into obviously pathological manifestations, to which Selye (1972) has given the name of "diseases of adaptation." For example, a rise in the blood content of mineral corticoids may produce a syndrome known as aldosteronism which is characterized by edema, hypertension, nephrosclerosis and myocarditis. However, a disease of adaptation may equally be caused by a fall in the content of adaptive hormones in the blood and particularly by a change in the concentrations of different hormones in relation to one another (Gorizontov and Protasova, 1968; Selye, 1972).

Diseases of this kind are liable to give rise to serious complications. ACTH, hydrocortisone and other steroid hormones exert an adverse effect on the course of such a corticovisceral condition as peptic ulcer, resulting in exacerbation, relapse, perforation and the production of new ulcers. Hence, the hormonal link, the pituitary-adrenal system, is believed to play a definite role in the corticovisceral genesis of peptic ulceration. The appearance and development of chronic gastric ulcers under the influence of corticosteroid hormones, particularly hydrocortisone, have also been demonstrated experimentally. Large doses of DOCA produce nephrosclerosis, hypertension, an increase in tendency to inflammation, hemorrhage and hyalinization of the kidneys (Selye, 1952). Prolonged administration of ACTH or glucocorticoids may result in "steroid diabetes" and in the presence of factors predisposing to atherosclerosis. When ACTH and cortisone are given simultaneously, their effects on the tissues are usually summated, as is also the case with the simultaneous adminstration of STH and DOCA.

An important part in the appearance and development of adaptation diseases is played by concomitant factors which create a suitable background for the action of the hormones. These may be of external origin, such as diet, heat or cold, or of internal origin, such as heredity, constitution and previous trauma (Clegg and Clegg, 1969).

Such, essentially, is the stress theory. Its validity is confirmed by the fundamental finding that the appearance of stress is prevented by removal of the pituitary or the adrenals. In Selye's experiments on hypophysectomized rats (Selye, 1952), factors such as cold, trauma, and toxic substances did not produce a state of stress. It was this that prompted Selye's categorical and uncompromising assertion that all stressors influence the adrenal cortex solely through the pituitary and that any other explanation is quite superfluous. However, the more one knows about the adaptation reaction to different stressors, particularly the psychogenic agents, the more one encounters aspects of the reaction that cannot be accommodated within the classical theory of stress. In particular these include the part played by the nervous system in the development of stress, as has been pointed out by a number of authors (Bykov and Kurtsin, 1960, 1966b; Kurtsin, 1966c, 1969g, 1971a, 1971d; Gorizontov and Protasova, 1968; Kositskii and Smirnov, 1970) who have critically analyzed Selye's theory. They have quite correctly noted that the failure of the theory to make due provision for the nervous mechanisms detracts from its scientific value (Durmish'yan, 1960; Myasishchev, 1970). This basic shortcoming was also perceived by the initiator of the theory himself. It is significant that in recent years he has begun to speak much more of the hypothalamic-pituitary-adrenal system; admitting that the stress reaction is not mediated directly through the pituitary and adrenal cortex but indirectly via the hypothalamus (Selye, 1971, 1972) and this view is shared by others (Vunder, 1972).

This is a significant amendment to the original explanation of the genera adaptation syndrome. Most important, it reflects the actual situation, since the production of the hormones of the pituitary-adrenal system and their release into the blood are indeed regulated by the hypothalamus (Harris, 1962; Schreiber, 1963). The regulation is affected by the medial hypothala mic, tuberal nuclei and the zone lying between these nuclei and the para ventricular nuclei. This region of the hypothalamus contains the supra optic nucleus which is the starting point for two pathways leading to the pituitary: the supraoptic-hypophyseal tract, connecting the supraoptic nucleus with the posterior lobe of the pituitary and the humoral pituitary tuberal system which provides a connection between the hypothalamic nuclei and the adenohyphysis via the blood. The control is carried out by chemomediator substances (neurosecretions) in the blood, secreted by the neurons of the hypothalamic nuclei. Outstanding among the neurosecretion is the corticotropin-realizing factor (CRF) which can regulate the secretio of all the pituitary tropic hormones. For the stimulation of ACTH produc tion two forms have been distinguished, α-CRF and β-CRF: the latter bein the more active. In an animal the administration of this factor increases the 17-hydroxycorticosterone content; as little as one millionth of a milli gram of the neurosecretion causes the pituitary gland to release ACTH. However, regulation of the pituitary is the task not only of the anterior and postoptic regions of the hypothalamus, as was formerly assumed, but also of its posterior region where a sympathetic structure secretes a substance which inhibits the production of ACTH by the pituitary. According to Alesh (1971), the neurosecretory nuclei of the anterior hypothalamus and the functions of the pituitary gland are intricately related. The supraoptic nucleus evidently acts on the hypothalamic-adenohypophyseal system, increasing the secretion of the corticotropin-realizing and gonadotropin activating factors, while simultaneously inhibiting the synthesis and ex cretion of the thyrotropin-activating and prolactin-inhibiting factors.

This recognition of the important influence of the hypothalamus, and particularly of the hypothalamic neurosecretions, on the activity of the pituitary-adrenal hormone system appears to favor a merger of the hormonal and reflex theories. Yet two fundamental aspects remain unclea 1) the mechanism of the initial phase of the stress reaction; 2) the part played by the higher cerebral divisions in the adaptative activity of the hypothalamus-pituitary-adrenal system and as the leading element in neuroendocrine relationships.

According to Selye, the nature of the initial mechanism which transmits the stimulus from the "target," the area of the body affected by the stressor to the anterior lobe of the pituitary is still practically unknown. On this point Durmish'yan (1960) has reasonably suggested that Selye is still stubbornly searching for something that was discovered long ago. Support ers of the reflex theory are able to supply an unequivocal answer to this question, in the light of Pavlov's teachings. The inaugural phase of the stress reaction is based on a reflex initiated by stimulation of the peri pheral endings of the centripetal nerves, that is, of the numerous receptors which are the first to receive the stimulus. The nervous excitation then proceeds along the afferent conducting paths to the brain centers, where it is analyzed, integrated and synthesized. From here it passes, in the forr of "command" impulses, along the nerves to the organs and tissues which are responsible for adaptation of the organism to environmental changes, unless the stressor belongs to the category of highly traumatic stimuli. However, stressors of this type are strange for the organism concerned, so that they act as "specific stimuli for those defense mechanisms of the organism which are designed to combat the particular factors involved" (Pavlov, 1951, Vol. 2, book 2, p. 265). This passage is in fact referring to the "overall mechanism for the general adaptation of the organism to an encounter with pathogenic conditions" (ibid).

Thus, the stress reaction is initiated at the moment that the stress factor acts on the receptor devices of the external or internal analyzers and the stimulus proceeds along afferent conductors, via the complex of cerebral structures, to the hypothalamus-pituitary system (Figure 17). Consequently, the first mediator of the stress is a reflex mechanism. This mechanism has been precisely determined and studied in the case of stressors which act preferentially on the acoustic, optic, proprioceptive and interoceptive analyzers. In the hypothalamus the stress excitation is switched over from the neural to the humoral pathway, along which the neurosecretory substances convey the excitation to cells of the anterior lobe of the pituitary. The stress stimulus travels from the analyzer receptors to the pituitary along very complex pathways. Most, if not all, of the exteroceptive and interoceptive stimuli reach the higher divisions of the analyzers. Many of the cortical and subcortical mechanisms exert their regulatory influence on autonomic and somatic activity mainly through the hypothalamus with which they are connected both directly and indirectly (see Chapters 1 and 2).

Supporters of the reflex theory have also provided a clear and well-documented explanation in reply to the second question (Bykov and Kurtsin, 1960, 1966a, 1968) which Selye himself did not even raise, let along answer (1972). It was succinctly formulated in the following manner by Speranskaya (1961): the nervous and endocrine systems are very closely linked, both functionally and structurally, constituting a single regulatory system in the organism, in which the leading part is played by the highest division of the nervous system: the cerebral hemispheres (pp. 49-50).

The most important aspect now being studied is the role of the hormonal factor in corticovisceral pathology, namely 1) the pathogenic action of the adaptive group of hormones and 2) the part played by hormones in the development of corticovisceral disturbances.

THE PATHOGENIC ROLE OF HORMONES

When ACTH and the glucocorticoids were first used in clinical practice attention was already drawn to the mental disturbances which often accompanied such a course of treatment. Large doses of ACTH, cortisone, hydrocortisone and other corticosteroids were found to induce euphoria, insomnia and delirium, or sometimes depression, and in many cases even gave rise to Cushing's syndrome, or to the so-called cortico-suprarenal psychosis. The convulsive effect of these hormones, even in relatively small doses, has been reported by many authors. In some dogs between

2 and 6 mg/kg hydrocortisone hemisuccinate or 1.5 mg/kg prednisone are sufficient to produce severe convulsions. In rats and cats the administration of $300-400$ mg/kg of 17 α-hydroxy-11-desoxycorticosterone gives rise to tonic and clonic convulsions within 15 to 35 minutes, usually followed by decerebrate rigidity and then by death.

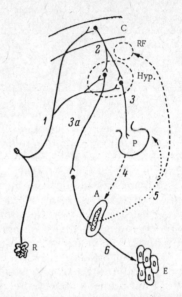

FIGURE 17. Diagram showing the role of reflex and hormonal mediators in a stress reaction:

R: receptor; C: cerebral cortex; P: pituitary; A: adrenal gland; E: effector; Hyp.: hypothalamus; RF: reticular formation; 1) afferent pathways from receptor to cerebral cortex; 2) efferent pathways from cerebral cortex to hypothalamus and then by 3) to pituitary and by 3a) to adrenal medulla (stippled area); 4) humoral pathway for transmission of nervous excitation from hypothalamo-pituitary region (ACTH) to adrenal cortex (unshaded area); 5) humoral (adrenalin) stimulation of pituitary and brain stem reticular formation; 6) humoral pathway for transmission of excitation from adrenal cortex (corticosteroids) to effector.

Electroencephalographic studies on animals and human subjects have shown that the adaptive hormones may either stimulate or inhibit the electrical activity of the CNS, depending on the dosage and on whether the hormones are glucocorticoids or mineral corticoids. Malyshenko (1971), working with rats and rabbits with electrodes implanted in the brain, studied the effect of DOCA by topical application or intramuscular injection (10 mg/kg). Desynchronization of bioelectrical activity was observed, first in the neocortex and hippocampus and then in the various subcortical formations: the anterior and posterior hypothalamus, the supraoptic and ventrolateral hypothalamic nuclei and the reticular formation of the brain stem. According to Nikolov (1964, 1969) and to Mityushe et al. (1970), ACTH, cortisone and hydrocortisone affect the bioelectrical activity of both the cortex and the subcortex, so that the affected animals react much more strongly to pain and light stimuli than do the controls. In experiments on rabbits the prolonged administration of 10 mg/kg hydrocortisone daily for 15 days inhibited the bioelectrical activity of cortico-subcortical structures (Table 4).

TABLE 4. Biopotential frequency (sec^{-1}) in specific regions of the rabbit brain on prolonged daily administration of 10 mg/kg hydrocortisone (after Efimova, 1967)

Location of electrodes	Before administration	Day of administration		
		2nd	5th	15th
Motor cortex	9.7 ± 0.5	9.0 ± 0.66	7.9 ± 0.35	5.8 ± 0.74
Visual cortex	9.0 ± 0.6	8.0 ± 0.62	8.0 ± 0.57	6.9 ± 0.42
Brain stem reticular formation	10.1 ± 0.68	9.0 ± 0.67	7.3 ± 0.49	7.8 ± 0.31
Mediodorsal thalamic nucleus	7.0 ± 0.27	8.2 ± 0.64	6.0 ± 0.44	7.9 ± 0.49
Posterior hypothalamus	8.1 ± 0.49	8.1 ± 0.36	5.2 ± 0.31	6.4 ± 0.66

The initial level of activity is not restored sooner than 10 days after the cessation of administration of the hormone.

In other experiments on rabbits with implanted electrodes, Nikolov (1964) observed that hydrocortisone regulates the electrical rhythm in the cortical and subcortical nervous structures and produces the typical spike of electrical activity, first in the reticular formation and then in the sensorimotor, temporal and occipital areas of the cerebral cortex and in the posterior hypothalamus. Sometimes, however, the changes in bioelectrical activity begin in the medial part of the thalamus and subthalamus and then pass to other subcortical and cortical formations. In general hydrocortisone intensifies spinal bioelectrical activity when the initial impulse is weak but diminishes it if the latter is strong (Nikolov, 1964, 1969).

The administration of ACTH produces a two-stage effect. There is a stage of intensification in the first 30−35 minutes after intramuscular injection of the hormone and a phase of attenuation of the spinal bioelectrical activity in the following 30−35 minutes (Figure 18). The effect of very large and very small doses of cortisone, and of ACTH, on the production of skin ulcers has been described by Azhipa (1964). As a general principle, it must be borne in mind that variations in the blood content of the individual adaptive hormones and particularly in their ratios (Selye's "diseases of adaptation", 1952), together with the associated changes in the interaction of these hormones with mediators, metabolites, enzymes and the other biologically active substances which help to maintain homeostasis ("diseases of homeostasis" according to Kassil', 1969), will all necessarily affect the physiological state of the nervous system.

ACTH and corticosteroids also influence higher nervous activity in animals and man, conditioned reflexes being more affected than unconditioned reflexes (Nikolov, 1964; Lissak and Endröczi, 1965, and others.) It has been shown in our laboratory that in dogs even a single dose of ACTH or cortisone causes changes in higher nervous activity, which manifest themselves in a decrease or increase of positive conditioned reflexes, increased successive inhibition or deeper differential inhibition, depending on the typological characteristics of the nervous system. The duration of the effect was found to bear a relationship to the dose of hormone administered. In healthy animals the conditioned reflexes were not significantly affected by 1 — 2.5 units ACTH or 1 — 2.5 mg cortisone. Five units of ACTH produced changes in higher nervous activity which lasted for 3 — 5 days; 20 — 40 units of the hormone elicited more prolonged changes (Table

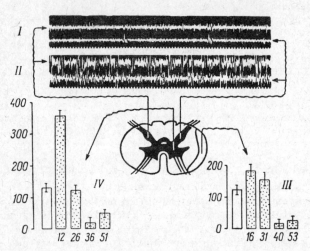

FIGURE 18. Effect of ACTH on the spinal cord (after Kurtsin and Nikolov, 1966):

I) electromyelogram before administration of ACTH; II) 21st min after suboccipital administration of ACTH (1 mg/kg); III) changes in excitability of the pyramidal tract; IV) changes in excitability of right anterior horn. Vertical: number of integrator impulses per 10 sec (300 impulses = 20 μV); horizontal: time (min) following intramuscular injection of 2 mg/kg ACTH. White columns: controls.

Cortisone in doses of 25 — 30 mg disrupted conditioned-reflex activity for 12 — 16 days, with a parallel change of the same duration in the unconditioned reflexes (salivation and secretion of gastric juice).

TABLE 5. Changes in conditioned reflexes in a dog after a single dose of 40 units ACTH (after Kurtsin and Yaroslavtseva, 1960)

Conditioned stimulus	Magnitude of conditioned reflex (drops of saliva per 20 sec)			
	before administration	days after administration		
		1st	2nd	9th
Bell (+)	16	5	8	10
Light (+)	10	6	7	11
M_{120} (+)	14	5	7	10
M_{60} (−)	0	0	0	0
Bell (+)	14	6	3	0
Light (+)	9	6	7	10
M_{120} (+)	12	8	6	10

In dogs, according to Nikolov (1964), the effect of a single dose of ACTH or cortisone on the conditioned reflexes varies with the dose. Small doses (0.25 mg/kg) of cortisone stimulate the excitatory process in the cerebral cortex; medium doses (1 mg/kg) do so in some dogs, but in other dogs they appear to inhibit it; large doses (2 mg/kg) exert an inhibitory effect.

With the repeated administration of 0.5 unit/kg ACTH for 8 to 15 days, the changes in higher nervous activity usually began with the first injection, continued throughout the period of administration, and often persisted after it. The changes were characterized by a predominance of either excitation or inhibition or by a disturbance in their relationship. Small and medium doses of ACTH and cortisone produced a two-stage effect: the stage of excitation being followed by a stage of inhibition. Large doses apparently overstepped the limit and inhibition prevailed. There was a significant disturbance of differential inhibition. These results have been confirmed by others (Mityushov et al., 1970). A dose of 3 units of ACTH per kg is apparently so excessive that it causes inhibition not only of alimentary but also of defense conditioned reflexes.

Marked disturbances of higher nervous activity in dogs, particularly of motor-defense conditioned reflexes, also followed bilateral adrenalectomy, especially during a period of crisis, caused by suspension of the daily injections of cortisone, DOCA and saline which are essential for the maintenance of life after such an operation (Filippov and Valueva, 1964). Attenuation of the conditioned reflexes rapidly ceased once substitution therapy was recommenced and even the lost reflexes soon reappeared, but they again became weakened in these animals 1.5 − 2 years later and the establishment of new reflexes became extremely difficult. Similar findings have been reported in adrenalectomized rats, in whom a system of conditioned motor-defense reflexes had been established (Mityushov et al., 1970).

In all these cases changes in higher nervous activity were accompanied by changes in visceral activity and these too were prolonged and far-reaching (Kurtsin and Yaroslavtseva, 1960). Similar corticovisceral disturbances occurred after the intravenous injection of DOCA and sodium chloride daily for two months or more. The changes were superficial or profound, depending on the dose of hormone administered (Vartapetov et al., 1969). In dogs a dose of 0.5 mg/kg DOCA with 5 g sodium chloride produced neurosis, with cyclic increases and decreases of conditioned reflex activity and with a corresponding lability of vascular tone. A dose of 2 − 3 mg/kg produced marked inhibition of higher nervous activity and persistent hypertension. Further evidence of the participation of the cerebral cortex in DOCA-induced corticovisceral disturbances was the finding that sodium bromide retarded the development of persistent hypertension, while chlorpromazine restored the blood pressure almost to normal levels (Vartapetov et al., 1969).

In physiological doses the hormones of the pituitary-adrenal system thus stimulate the activity of the higher divisions of the CNS. Under their influence, the optimum tone of the cerebral cortex becomes more than optimal, the conditioned reflexes are enhanced, the latent period of the reflexes is shortened and differentiation is stable. In short, the cerebral cortex functions at a higher physiological level. The prolonged administration of high doses is liable to cause typical neurotic changes in higher nervous activity, as well as in the general behavior of the animals. In such a case the hormones act as a factor producing neurosis, particularly if they are injected suboccipitally, when the neurosis is accompanied by severe inhibition of conditioned reflexes, ataxia and paralysis. Nikolov (1964) compares this condition with that occurring in different stages of the development of the stress reaction. Since higher nervous activity suffers heavily in these cases, he concludes that the general adaptation syndrome is dependent on the physiological state of the higher brain centers.

The fact that the activity of the CNS is disrupted under the influence of these hormones is a further indication that, besides their adaptive function they may, under certain conditions, upset the mechanisms regulating the activity of the organism and produce a corticovisceral vicious circle or intensify one that already exists. The relevant conditions are not only larg doses of the adaptive hormones but, even more important, the type of nervous system involved. Stress produced by the subcutaneous injection of turpentine, by the administration of ACTH or caffeine, develops different in dogs with different types of higher nervous activity, the reaction being most pronounced in the weak type and less clearly expressed in the strong balanced type. In the weak type the reaction to the hormones consists of the prolonged inhibition of cerebral cortical activity and inductive excitatic of the hypothalamic-pituitary-adrenal system (Nikolov, 1964). The typologi characteristics also appear to be largely responsible for the individuality of the organism which, as emphasized by non-Soviet scientists, is expresse by the varying autonomic reactions to hormone administration and in man by the development of emotional stress (Lazarus, 1967; Levi, 1967b). Studi on the effect of hormones do not reveal any specific changes in higher nervous activity. Such changes are apparently nonspecific type of reaction with certain standard features and relationships. Thus the strength and duration of the effect is a function of hormone dosage, of the type of nervou system involved and of the initial state of activity of the organism. Anothe characteristic feature is the stimulatory effect of small doses of hormones on the excitatory process in the cerebral cortex, together with a concentrat ing effect on the process of inhibition. Large doses, on the other hand, having exceeded the limits, act as an extra-powerful stimulus on the cortical cells, resulting in their exhaustion and inhibition.

The complex effects of hydrocortisone and ACTH on the brain and spinal cord could be mediated in the following ways: 1) a direct action of the hormones on cells and nervous conductors of the brain and spinal cord; 2) an increase of cerebral activity due to stimuli from the activating reticular formation which is directly affected by the hormones; 3) reflex changes in cerebral activity due to the action of the hormones on vascular and tissue receptors; 4) changes in the physiological state of the brain centers and th conducting nervous pathways due to changes in the composition of the blood and the cerebrospinal fluid and in the enzyme processes in the cells and tissues, brought about by the adaptive hormones.

The following fundamental aspects require to be stressed.

1. In his discussion on the effect of hormones on the animal organism, Ukhtomskii particularly noted the absence of a precise destination. On entering the bloodstream they are addressed "to whom it may concern." However, it has now been established that a hormone in the blood can cause changes in corticovisceral and cerebroendocrine relationships not only by direct action on an organ or a system of organs, but also by means

of a reflex originating in the chemoceptors of the blood-vessels and tissues. This is the most widespread mechanism of hormonal influence on the effectors (Kurtsin and Nikolov, 1966). It also plays an important part in the actual production of hormones and in their release into the bloodstream as well as in disturbances of hormone interactions which Vunder (1972) has named "diseases of feedback."

2. In speaking of the direct action of hormones on nervous structures, one is primarily referring to their effect on the activity of enzymes, or of their inhibitors and histones which depress the activity of nerve cells. They particularly affect the cell and mitochondrial membranes which contain multienzyme systems (Surikov, 1969) but they also influence various metabolic processes, including carbohydrate-phosphorus metabolism, aerobic and anaerobic respiration, the synthesis of proteins and nucleic acids and elements of the Krebs cycle. It is also possible that the hormones act directly on the mitochondrial membrane, since when they are added to brain or liver tissue, vacuolization is distinctly observed in the cell mitochondria (Clegg and Clegg, 1969).

It must be borne in mind that the hormones in the tissues interact with other chemical substances such as mediators, metabolites, ions and enzymes. This may take place locally or at distance, depending on the concentration of the hormones, their rate of circulation, neutralization and excretion from the body and many other factors (Kassil', 1969). Action takes place at a distance not only by carriage of the hormones in the bloodstream but also by their effect on reflexes at various levels of the nervous system. Damage to the blood-brain barrier may significantly alter the direct effects of these hormones on the CNS. On the whole, the metabolic changes of the corticosteroids have been adequately discussed in the literature. Yet no data are available regarding the effect of disturbances of higher nervous activity on hormonal action on the cells, although, judging from reviews of the literature (Mityushov et al., 1970), the influence of hormones on metabolism in stress has been the subject of numerous investigations.

The crux of the matter is that stress can produce severe disturbances of enzyme and metabolic reactions (Nikolov, 1964). Theoretically, the hormones may directly participate as coenzymes in redox reactions, or they may affect the coenzymes and cofactors by interacting with them, or they may simply affect enzyme activity. Here, however, the following circumstance must be taken into consideration. At one time it was thought that the tissue requirements of corticosteroids increased under stress, so that the blood level of these hormones fell. This led to a rise in the secretion of ACTH which stimulated the production of corticosteroid hormones by the adrenal cortex and their release into the blood. Such a chain reaction satisfactorily conformed with the general concept of the state of stress. However, the assumption that the hormone requirements of the tissues are increased under stress was not confirmed, nor was it found in human subjects that hormonal activity was increased during an operation, although surgery must be classified among the extremely powerful stress agents. Whatever the mechanism of hormonal action may be, it is clear that the nervous system which transmits the stress stimuli to the pituitary-adrenal system is itself affected by these hormones, including ACTH, during the period of stress and that the corticosteroids modify the activity of the nervous centers and conducting pathways either directly, or indirectly through reflex and humoral mechanisms.   In this manner, by the reciprocal influence of nervous and humoral factors, under the leadership and guidance of the higher divisions of the CNS, a pattern of activity is established in the organism which is known as the general adaptation syndrome.

Our knowledge of the interactions between the pituitary adrenal hormones and the nervous system is still far from complete.   Nevertheless, i may be asserted that a stress factor from the external environment can trigger the pituitary adrenal adaptation system by acting on the cerebral cortex.   In other words, the higher cerebral divisions of the brain are able to activize the hormonal mechanism of adaptation reactions, while the hypophysis-adrenal system acts as an intermediate link or mediator for the complex reflex reaction.   This neuroendocrine cycle incorporates a feedback mechanism which regulates the operation of the cerebral control centers in accordance with the particular state of the cells and tissues and thereby renders it more efficient and apparently also more reliable.   This mechanism also improves the functioning of the endocrine system itself, the hormones of which play a significant part in the development of the general adaptation syndrome and in the maintenance of homeostasis.   It would therefore seem that the entire body of clinical and experimental data concerning the effect of adaptive hormones on the CNS, up to and including the cerebral cortex can be regarded from two points of view: on the one ha as manifestations of the self-regulation principle which underlies the integrating, coordinating, and regulating activity of the higher brain centers and on the other hand as a confirmation of the pathogenetic role of the adaptive hormones.

In discussing this subject, one must not neglect the well-known fact that the sex hormones exert a powerful influence on the nervous system.   Thus in man and mammals castration gives rise to severe functional and structural changes throughout the body.   Members of Pavlov's school used castration as a technique for producing experimental neurosis; Pavlov's close associate Petrova often used it on dogs.   Recent detailed studies by Vartapetov and his colleagues (1969) have shown that postcastration disturbances are not confined to higher nervous activity but affect the entire organism, including digestive, circulatory, respiratory, metabolic and other autonomic activities, and producing highly complex syndromes which these authors have named "postcastration disease."

The reaction of organs and of the organism as a whole to stress factor has been found to be significantly modified by changes in the relationships between organs and systems, particularly between the different endocrine glands and between them and the nervous system, as occurs after removal of the sex glands.   It is no accident that myocardial infarction is more commonly observed and more severe in persons in whom the climacteric has been accompanied by pathological manifestations.   Castration following an existing neurosis aggravates the corticovisceral disturbances (Mirzoev, 1958).   This further confirms the idea that though the endocrine glands normally function as the intermediate hormonal link in the implementation of the complex reflex reaction and of the special feedback connection betwe the brain centers and the internal milieu of the organism, under pathologica conditions they may act as a factor which maintains and aggravates the morbid condition of the brain centers and of the internal organs (Kurtsin, 1962b, 1962c, 1965d, 1968e, 1969c, 1969g).

The initiatory mechanism of neuroses of endocrine origin consists of a disturbance in the correlation of endocrine activity, which leads to changes in the hormone content of the blood. The trigger in these cases is constituted by the rise or fall of these hormone levels in the blood, which should be regarded as extraordinary stimuli from interoceptive systems (Berko and Trofimov, 1971).

THE HORMONAL LINK IN PSYCHOGENIC STRESS

The assumption that hormones play a part in the development of psychogenic stress rests on the following evidence: 1) the proved possibility of altering the hormonal activity of glands by direct stimulation of the cerebral cortex and by the formation of a conditioned reflex; 2) the fact that hormonal changes have been found to accompany changes in the activity of the cerebral cortex, particularly in psychogenic or emotional stress. Studies in experimental physiology and pathology have now provided sufficient evidence on both these points (Vunder, 1972).

It is now known, for example, that the influence of the cerebral cortex is mediated through both conditioned and unconditioned reflexes: ACTH secretion depending on the conditioned excitation and excitability of the cerebral cortex (Eskin et al., 1959), while corticosteroids are produced by direct stimulation of the cerebral cortex. While in dogs the normal hydrocortisone level averages 355.3 mg % within the adrenals and 4.6 mg % in the blood issuing from the adrenals, these values decline to 207.7 and 4.2 mg %, respectively, on long-term stimulation of cells in area 6 of the cerebral cortex (Nikolaichuk, 1954).

The cerebral control exerted by the limbic system extends to the synthesis and secretion of many hypophyseal hormones (Söderberg, 1967) and the development of the stress reaction is largely dependent on the degree of tonic influence exerted by the orbital area of the frontal cortex on the hypothalamus (Kaada, 1951). A prolonged increase in the hormonal activity of the adrenal cortex is observed in animals during the establishment of conditioned reflexes. A similar phenomenon has been noted in man in states of mental strain, depression, anger, or euphoria (Gellhorn and Loofbourrow, 1963). Regular changes in the hydrocortisone content of the blood and adrenals also occur on long-term stimulation of the brain (Nikolaichuk, 1963) which sometimes results in excitation of adrenal activity, rather than inhibition. The hippocampus exerts a constant inhibitory influence on the activity of the pituitary-adrenal system (Lissak and Endröczi, 1965), which is stimulated by the amygdaloid nucleus: destruction of the latter diminishing the secretion of ACTH. Changes in the activity of the cerebral cortex due to bromine or caffeine affect the hydrocortisone content of the blood. Stimulation of the orbital cortex activates the secretion of ACTH. There is an increase in the activity of the pituitary adrenal system in narcotic-induced sleep. Bilateral decortication causes a rise in the 17-OCS level in the blood plasma.

There are also findings with regard to the effect of cerebrocortical activity on the pituitary-adrenal system (Eskin et al., 1959; Lissak and Endröczi, 1965). In his studies of emotional stress in relation to fatigue and work capacity, the eminent Polish physiologist Missiuro (1960) came to the conclusion that the excessive strain imposed by modern industrial technology, and particularly by strenuous but monotonous work, results in nervous disorders, hypertension, coronary disease, metabolic disturbances and premature atherosclerosis. He considers that the underlying mechanism is constituted by the effect of adverse, psychogenic factors on the hypothalamic-pituitary-adrenal complex and on the ascending activating system of the reticular formation of the brain stem. Under conditions of mental stress, as during athletic competitions, while waiting for a medical diagnosis and particularly, during surgical operations, in mental trauma of various kinds and in emotional stress in general, the content of adrenal cortical hormones in the plasma and of 17-hydroxycorticosteroids in the urine is raised (Levi, 1967a). The relationship of this hormonal activity to the activity of the cerebral cortex has recently been demonstrated in experimental neurosis. In emotional stress, however, the release of ACTH is also due to the involvement of the sympathetic-adrenal system (adrenalin and noradrenalin) under the influence of discharges from the limbic neocortex and posterior hypothalamus, although extirpation of the adrenal medulla does not entirely block the secretion of ACTH.

Working in our laboratory on dogs with Pavlov pouches, Gulyaeva and Seregin (1969) have made simultaneous studies of higher nervous activity, gastric secretion, blood pressure and blood 11-hydroxycorticosterone (fluorimetric method), under normal conditions and when neurosis was induced by Pavlov's method of conflicting nervous processes. They found that the neurosis gave rise to changes, not only in higher nervous activity, gastric secretion and blood pressure, but also in the content of 11-hydroxycorticosterone. Disturbances of higher nervous activity were elicited immediately the conflict occurred and this was followed by a rise in the blood pressure. Disorders of gastric secretion appeared from the 5th or 14th day in different dogs, while changes in the blood corticosteroid content were detected on the preceding day. Thus, the hormonal effect depended on the changes in higher nervous activity during "psychogenic" stress. This is a very important finding from the point of view of cause and effect, as regards the part played by neural and hormonal factors in the pathogenesis of corticovisceral conditions, such as peptic ulcer and hypertension. Another noteworthy phenomenon was the wavelike fluctuation in the blood corticosteroid content, the rise and fall corresponding with the similar changes in the conditioned reflexes. However, once higher nervous activity had returned to normal, the blood corticosteroids returned to their initial levels a few months after the breakdown of higher nervous activity, the actual period varying with the different dogs. Finally, it is to be noted that the preliminary changes in the blood corticosteroid content were not the same in all cases but depended on the initial level. When this was high, the conflict was followed by a fall in the blood level of these hormones and vice versa. For example, in one dog with a high initial blood hormone content, the level dropped from 11.2 to 5.7 mg % after the conflict, and fluctuated around that level for a month. In another dog, with an initial low blood corticosteroid content, the level rose from 2 to 10 mg % after the conflict, although only for a short while; after which it dropped to 3.8 mg % and remained at that low level for about four weeks.

Havlíček (1962) found an increase in 17-ketosteroid secretion and in the weight of the adrenals in animals with experimental neurosis, as compared with healthy animals.   The literature includes reports of many other cases in which functional or structural lesions of the cerebral cortex or changes in its activity due to neurotropic drugs produced marked and prolonged changes in the activity of the hormones of the pituitary-adrenal system. From many years of observations on dogs, Vartapetov et al. (1969) established that the changes in activity of the adrenal cortical hormones which followed a disturbance of higher nervous activity and the development of a neurotic state with systemic hypertension, in fact took place in two stages: a stage of intensification, followed by a stage of attenuation.   With the second stage the initial corticovisceral changes, particularly the neurosis, became more firmly established, while supraliminal inhibition develops in the cortical cells and the hypertension becomes persistent.   The influence of disturbed activity of the higher divisions of the CNS on hormonal action in rats has also been reported by Voznesenskii (1963).   Groza (1964) attributes the inhibition of gastric secretion accompanying disorders of activity of the higher divisions of the CNS to abnormal adrenal cortical activity, namely to the adverse effects of DOCA.

Numerous cortical and subcortical nervous formations play a part in the mechanism of hormonal changes, particularly the limbic areas.   Electrical stimulation of these areas has been shown to increase the 11-hydroxycorticosterone content of the blood by 70%, if the intitial level was low, and to lower it by 66%, if it was initially high.   There are grounds for believing that the considerable secretion of ACTH and corticosteroids into the blood, which occurs in psychogenic stress, is due to stimulation of the hypothalamic-pituitary-adrenal system by the limbic nuclei.   However, at present it would be very wrong to limit a review of the mechanisms of corticovisceral disturbances to the hormones of the pituitary-adrenal cortex system. During many years of experimental study of autonomic visceral effects in psychogenic stress, we repeatedly noted that different hormones were involved in the psychogenic stress reaction under different experimental conditions (Figure 19).   Sufficient evidence has now been produced in the field of experimental physiology for it to be stated with confidence that, however significant the role of the pituitary-adrenal cortical hormones in the mechanism of corticovisceral disturbances, an important part is also played by other endocrine organs.

Since all the endocrine glands are interrelated, changes in the hormonal activity of one gland inevitably react on the others.   For example, increased production of thyrotropic hormone causes increased synthesis of thyroxin and its release into the blood; loss of sexual function (hypofunction, castration, climacteric)stimulates thyroid activity; thyrotoxicosis diminishes the activity of the sex glands; thyroxin suppresses the activity of the islets of the pancreas and causes hyperplasia of the thymus.   There are similar relationships between the adaptive hormones and the internal secretions of other glands: for example, ADH affects ACTH and is affected by cortisone. The interrelationships between the pituitary and the thyroid, sex and adrenal glands are controlled, on the one hand, by the stimulatory effect of the pituitary tropic hormones (thyrotropic, gonadotropic, somatotropic, adrenocorticotropic) on the activity of the secretory cells of those glands (an influence which disappears on removal of the anterior lobe of the pituitary, while, on the other hand, a change in the blood content of corticosteroids, sex hormones and thyroxin affects the hormonal activity of the adenohypophysis. Such antagonistic and synergic effects manifest themselves in many different combinations and aspects, so that findings with regard to the influence of the endocrine glands may vary widely (Clegg and Clegg, 1969).

The functions of this "nonadaptive" group of hormones from the point of view of corticovisceral interrelationships under normal physiological conditions have been previously reviewed by us (Bykov and Kurtsin, 1960, 1966; 1968; Kurtsin, 1968b). In the context of physiopathological stress in man they have been discussed in the proceedings of the International Symposium on Emotional Stress (Lazarus, 1967; Levi, 1967a, b; Söderberg, 1967; Myasishchev, 1970, and others). Here we shall therefore only consider the experimental findings which shed light on the part played by these hormonal substances in psychogenic stress; above all, their role as the hormonal link in corticovisceral disturbances. Among this group of hormones it is fully justified that adrenalin has attracted close attention. Following Cannon's well-known researches (1953), it became clear that the autonomic phenomena demonstrated in "emotional" stress in animals, such as tachycardia, high blood pressure, dilatation of the pupils, weakened intestinal peristalsis, increased sweating, a rise in the blood sugar and in the red cell count, contraction of the spleen and an increase in the circulatory volume, result not only from the marked sympathetic excitation of the nervous system, but also from overfunctioning of the adrenal medulla (Lissak and Endröczi, 1965). This sympathetic-medullary effect is greatly diminished and may even be lost if exposure to the emotional stress factor is preceded by removal of the adrenals or severance of the nerves passing to them. The same effect can be obtained by chemically blocking transmission of the impulses to the adrenal medulla along the sympathetic nerves.

The emotions also give rise to considerable autonomic changes in man. As in animals, the blood contains increased concentrations of adrenalin and noradrenalin. This phenomenon was recently reproduced by showing different kinds of films to a group of subjects (Levi, 1967b). It was found that films evoking feelings of aggresion and animosity, or anxiety and horror, as well as comedies which elicited positive though excessive emotions, gave rise to increased synthesis of adrenalin and noradrenalin, whereas restful movies, particularly nature films, which evoked a feeling of calm and balance, had relatively little effect on the sympathetic-adrenal system (Table 6).

TABLE 6. Average secretion of adrenalin and noradrenalin, mg/min, in healthy women during the showing of films evoking different types of emotional stress (after Levi, 1967b)

Emotion evoked	Adrenalin	Noradrenalin
Calm and balance (nature film)	3.0	12.0
Aggression and animosity	7.0	16.0
Strong positive emotions (comedy)	7.0	18.0
Anxiety and horror	10.0	20.0

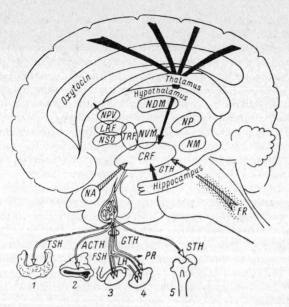

FIGURE 19. Effect of the nervous system on the endocrine glands in psychogenic
stress (after Kurtsin and Nikolov, 1966):

Hypothalamic nuclei : NDM: dorsomedial; NP: posterior; NVM: ventromedial;
NPV: posteroventral; NSO: supraoptic (related to ADH secretion), NM: mammillary;
GTH: area of gonadotropic hormone secretion; TRF: area of secretion of thyroid-
releasing factor regulating secretion of thyroid-stimulating hormone (TSH); LRF:
factor regulating luteinizing hormone secretion (LH); CRF: corticotropin-releasing
factor, stimulated by amygdaloid nucleus (NA) and mesencephalic reticular formation
(FR) and inhibited by cerebral cortex and hippocampus; FSH: follicle-stimulating
hormone; PR: prolactin; STH: growth hormone; 1) thyroid; 2) adrenal; 3) testis;
4) ovary; 5) bone-marrow. Black arrows — inhibitory influences; light arrows — stimulatory influences.

Another important finding was that the secretion of noradrenalin was
greater than that of adrenalin in those who were in an aggressive or angry
mood without anxiety, while adrenalin secretion predominated in a state of
anxiety. This pattern has not yet been satisfactorily explained but it has
been observed by others in healthy persons under stress, as well as in
neurotics and psychotics (Gellhorn and Loofbourrow, 1963).

Working in our laboratory, Sergeeva (1969) studied the chemical changes
in the blood of dogs with a Pavlovian experimental neurosis, over a period
of several months. A tendency to the predominance of adrenalin-like substances accompanied the disturbances of higher nervous and autonomic activity, as manifested by changes in the blood pressure, diuresis and
gastric secretion. The level of these substances returned to normal
together with the restoration of normal higher nervous activity and corticovisceral relationships.

The extensive literature on the influence of the higher brain centers on insulin secretion by the pancreas (Mityushov, 1964) tends to show that psychogenic factors may play a part in the development of diabetes mellitu (Teleshevskaya, 1969). The activity of the islets of Langerhans increases in emotional stress. The excitation travels from the cortex via the parasympathetic hypothalamic nuclei and the vagus nerves. A high blood insulir level has been found in mental patients during a state of excitement. Increased activity of the vago-insulin system has also been observed in certain forms of neurosis. This is supported by findings in dogs with experimental diabetes from partial removal of the pancreas as reported by Mityushov (1964). When neurosis was induced by means of a Pavlovian nervous conflict, the diabetic state became exacerbated during the next few days, although it subsequently improved.

Apparently, the general adaptation syndrome (stress) also involves the hormones of the pars intermedia and pars posterior of the pituitary, which itself maintains the closest relationships with the adrenocortical-pituitary hormones. Suffice it to say that the secretion of all the pituitary hormones is regulated through the hypothalamus (Sager, 1960; Aleshin, 1971) and that emotional stress in man is accompanied by a) increased activity of both the pituitary-adrenocortical system (Levi, 1967a) and the sympathetic-adreno-medullary system (Patkai, 1967; Söderberg, 1967), and b) increased synthesis of pituitary thyrotropic and gonadotropic hormones, as well as of the thyroid and sex hormones (Levi, 1967a).

Psychogenic stress in dogs affects not only the blood corticosteroid content (Vartapetov et al., 1969; Gulyaeva and Seregin, 1969) but also the hypothalamic neurosecretory (ADH) regulation of water-salt metabolism (Balakshina, 1954; Britikova, 1966; Balakshina and Britikov, 1968; Kurtsin and Sergeeva, 1971), as well as respiratory exchange in the body, which is governed by the secretion of thyrotoxin by the thyroid (Alexander et al., 1961; Nikolaeva, 1966, 1971) and of thyrotropic hormone by the posterior lobe of the pituitary (Kakhana, 1959). Other stress effects are also accompanied by a rise in the blood content of both ACTH and thyrotropic hormone. Finally, bilateral extirpation of the cerebral hemispheres causes severe dystrophic changes not only in the pituitary and adrenals but also in other endocrine glands (Bayandurov, 1949), while thermal injury to the hypothalamus produces functional and structural changes in the pituitary, thyroid, and sex glands (Kakhana, 1960). All these experimental findings confirm clinical observations regarding the profound effect of mental factors on endocrine function. Cases have been described in which acute mental trauma was followed by such a severe disturbance of water metabolism that the patient was obliged to drink as much as 20 liters water daily to quench his thirst; the diurnal diuresis being of course of approximately the same volume. An experimental model of this kin of human disorder has been produced in our laboratory by derangement of high nervous activity in dogs. Over a period of many months we were able to observ the appearance and prolonged persistence of such an increased desire to drink (Sergeeva, 1958), with marked polyuria (Balakshina, 1954) under more or le normal environmental conditions, in the presence of stereotyped stimuli an on a normal diet and water and salt intake. The phenomenon was elicited in dogs many times, although in some cases the development of psychogenic stress was accompanied by oliguria instead of polyuria (Balakshina and Britikova, 1968).

In rats the secretion of antidiuretic hormone is increased under the influence of pain or emotional excitement and even by placing the animals in unfamiliar surroundings.   Diuresis in dogs is abruptly halted by rage.

Within the hypothalamus itself a leading part is played by the supraoptic nuclei which receive all the information from the volume receptors and from the osmoceptors of the blood vessels, organs and tissues.   It is here that the regulation of water and salt metabolism by integrated unconditioned reflexes takes place.   Here too is formed the neurosecretion that is the precursor of the neurohypophyseal hormone (ADH or vasopressin) which regulates the reabsorption of water (and possibly also of sodium) in the renal tubules. Some of the conditioned reflex pathways which participate in homeostasis and in the regulation of diuresis probably also pass through these hypothalamic nuclei, enabling the cerebral cortex to exert a regulatory effect on renal activity via the hypothalamic neurohumoral mechanisms.   The renal cortico-visceral disturbances which occur in psychogenic stress are also imple-mented via these pathways.

In our laboratory (Kurtsin and Sergeeva, 1971) experiments have been carried out on dogs with a permanent vesico-gastric fistula in which electrodes had been implanted on the right and left sides of the hypothalamus. Following the establishment of neurosis which lasted for about three months, the hypothalamic mechanisms for regulating the urinary functions of the kidneys were found to show the following disturbances: a) diminished spon-taneous diuresis and urine volume in response to a water-milk load; b) di-minished rather than increased diuresis and a reduced chloride content in the urine, in response to right or left hypothalamic stimuli; c) diminished diuresis on the day of hypothalamic stimulation and even on the next two or three days, when the water-milk load was used alone, without electrical stimulus.   During the neurosis the diuretic effect became asymmetrical, the effects of hypothalamic stimulation being stronger on the right than on the left.   Diuresis gradually returned to normal in line with the state of higher nervous activity.   These findings tend to confirm the assumption that the kidney disturbances of water and salt metabolism and urinary function occurring in psychogenic stress are due to dysfunction of the cortical mechanisms controlling the integrative and regulatory activity of the hypothalamic-pituitary system.   There are indications that ADH plays a part in the release of ACTH and is itself affected by corticosteroids. It is true that conflicting findings appear in the literature regarding the influence of cortisone on water and salt metabolism; yet, the inhibitory effect of cortisone on the production of ADH has been emphasized by most authors.   This property seems to be shared by all the glucocorticoids, since they promote diuresis and the excretion of sodium in the urine following sodium retention (Pronina, 1969, 1971).   According to observations in our laboratory (Balakshina, 1954; Kurtsin, 1960; Britikova and Balak-shina, 1969), polyuria and disturbances of sodium excretion are specifically found in psychogenic stress.   Hence it is possible that the disorders of water and salt metabolism which occur during disturbances of higher ner-vous activity and in the neurotic state are related to primary changes in the activity of the cerebral cortex, limbic system, reticular formation and hypothalamus and only secondarily to disturbances in the hypothalamic mechanisms of ADH neurosecretion.

There are a number of indications that the thyroid also plays an importa
part in the stress reaction. In the first place, its internal secretion, thyro:
possesses an extremely broad range of action, affecting every cell in the
animal body. This is seen by the influence of thyroxin or thyroidin on cell
ular respiration in the CNS, the internal organs and striated muscle. In th
thyrotoxic state in man a complex of corticovisceral disorders accompanie
the raised blood content of thyroid hormone. Finally, participation of the
thyroid in the stress reaction is also indicated by the fact that its hormona.
activity is controlled by the hypothalamus via nervous formations (supraoptic nuclei) as well as humorally, through the thyrotropic hormone (Lissal
and Endröczi, 1965; Grashchenkov, 1965; Tonkikh, 1968).

In this connection one might also refer to studies which have demonstra
ted the conditioned-reflex regulation of the respiratory exchange (Bykov,
1942; Ol'nyanskaya, 1964). Similarly, cases have been described in the
literature of increased respiratory exchange in workers before starting
work, or even when visiting their place of work on a day off and the same
holds for athletes before the start of a race. The reader is reminded
of the original study carried out by Alexander and colleagues (1961) who
used radioisotopes to demonstrate increased thyroid activity in subjects
watching a dramatic film. Such references are, however, unnecessary, sin
phenomena of this kind have been repeatedly observed in different laboratories and can hardly be doubted. However, the situation is different with
regard to the mechanism of cortical influences on respiratory exchange in
human and animal tissues and cells. In animals, the gas exchange level
is influenced not only by general factors, such as the ambient temperature,
muscular activity, the ingestion of various foods and their quantity and
quality, the intensity of the illumination, spatial perception and the time
period, but also by such phylogenetically specialized stimuli as being together with a group of similar animals. In the case of man, the general,
natural factors fade into the background, being overshadowed by social factor
the most important of which are the stimuli of the second signal system.
The cortical influences on tissue respiration take two pathways: 1) along
the nerve fibers; the nervous stimulus passing through the cortico-subcortical formations to the thalamic-hypothalamic region, where it mainly
switches over to sympathetic nerves, through which it reaches the cells,
tissues and organs and 2) the neurohumoral pathway, in which the
excitation first passes along the common nervous pathway until it is
switched to the humoral pathway in the hypothalamic-pituitary system,
where it is transmitted by the thyrotropic hormone, and in the thyroid
gland, where thyroxin takes over. In dogs thyroidectomy destroys an established and consolidated gas exchange conditioned reflex and makes it
impossible for new conditioned reflexes of this kind to be formed
(Ol'nyanskaya, 1964). In the intact animal the hormonal component of the
corticovisceral reflex may be, and probably is, binary and ternary; a whole
complex of neurohormonal chain reactions being associated with the main
reaction (Bykov and Kurtsin, 1960; Durmish'yan, 1960; Lissak and Endröcz:
1965; Tonkikh, 1968; Bulygin, 1970, 1971).

It should also be noted that the production of thyrotropic hormone by the
pituitary may be modified by a conditioned-reflex mechanism, thereby diminishing thyroid activity (Eskin et al., 1959) and that a conditioned reflex

may be formed to the effects produced by the administration of a thyrotropic preparation. It has been shown that the compensatory increase or decrease of pituitary thyrotropic activity which results from the chemical blockade of the thyroid gland by methylthiouracil, or from the prolonged administration of thyroxin, can be reproduced purely by conditioned reflexes (Eskin et al., 1959). Thyroid secretion in dogs can be stimulated and suppressed under the influence of positive and inhibitory conditioned defense signals (Amiragova, 1971). Thyroid activity is weakened by repeated superficial stimulation of the cerebral hemispheres with a gauze swab. In rabbits the application of silver plates to the surface of the cerebral cortex in the region of the retrosplenial area produces the same sluggish state of thyroid activity as is observed in typical colloid goiter. Thyroid function in puppies is markedly disturbed by extirpation of the cerebral hemispheres. The fact that cortical mechanisms play a part in the regulation of the hormonal activity of the thyroid has also been demonstrated from other points of view (Voitkevich and Gordina, 1954; Kakhana, 1960, 1970), particularly as regards the interaction between thyroid and pituitary hormonal activity (Arkhipenko, 1956; Eskin et al., 1959; Amiragova, 1968, 1971; Vunder, 1972).

However, the thyroid, like other endocrine glands and all the viscera, is also connected with the brain centers by feedback mechanisms which continually supply information regarding the state of nutrition and blood supply of the secretory cells and of the rate of hormone production and of its release into the bloodstream. Such information reaches the brain along nervous and humoral pathways, as can be seen from the following data: a) in dogs the administration of thyroidin (0.5 g/kg) in the food for 10 to 15 days produced pathological disturbances of higher nervous activity, vascular tone, gastric secretion and gas exchange; all typical of psychogenic stress (Kurtsin and Nikolaeva, 1966) and a similar state has been produced in rabbits by the same method (Vartapetov et al., 1969); b) cardiovascular and respiratory disturbances and changes in metabolic reactions resulting from a nervous conflict in the cerebral cortex were more severe and persistent if the animal was in a hyperthyroid state; c) stimulation of the thyroid receptors resulted in changes in the bioelectrical activity of the innervation of the thyroid, hypothalamus, and cerebral cortex (Kakhana, 1959); d) strengthening of both conditioned and unconditioned reflexes by the injection of thyroxin in a dosage of 0.1 mg/kg (Amiragova, 1971).

To this should be added the direct action of thyroid hormones on the brain centers. Thus, injection of threshold doses of thyroxin and triiodothyronin into the anterior or posterior hypothalamic nucleus, or the mammillary complex, affects the electrical activity of the hypothalamus itself and of other subcortical and cortical formations in the following sequence: hypothalamus → hippocampus → amygdalar complex → cerebral cortex (frontal and sensorimotor areas) (Amiragova, 1971).

This review of findings regarding the influence of the cerebral cortex and subcortical formations on the activity of the thyroid gland in the normal physiological state is far from complete. It does suggest, however, that the thyroid may also be involved in stress reactions provoked by psychogenic factors. This has, in fact, been so frequently demonstrated, both clinically and experimentally, that it may be confidently asserted rather than surmised.

In his time, the famous French neurologist Charcot regarded exophthalm goiter as a neurosis, while the equally famous Russian physician Botkin remarked that anger, loss of various kinds and fear may produce the most severe and characteristic manifestations of that disease, sometimes very rapidly, within a few hours. Moreover, he asserted that the influence of mental factors on both the course and development of this form of the disease was beyond any doubt. The clinical literature abounds in statements of this kind and particularly from the period of World War II, when the incidence of cases of neurosis caused by severe mental shock greatly increased. According to some authors, mental trauma is the cause of 80—85% of such cases. It became obvious that the main pathogenetic factor in hyperthyroidism was a disturbance in the activity of the cerebral cortical and subcortical centers. Recently, the importance of mental trauma in the etiology of thyrotoxicosis has again been repeatedly noted (Zhukova, 1969; Teleshevskaya, 1969).

These clinical observations conform with the laboratory findings. Experimental models of psychogenic stress in animals have produced similar chronic changes in the basal metabolism and in the hormonal activity of the thyroid, along with chronic changes in higher nervous activity and in visceral function. The following is typical of the many findings of this kind obtained in our laboratory. Five dogs were exposed to a series of successive stimuli: a particularly loud sound (95db) was accompanied by switching off the light in the conditioned-reflex chamber, which produced a conflict, the animal was finally exposed to a single "electroconflict" on each of 4 successive days. This resulted in a disturbance of higher nervous activity (weakening of positive conditioned reflexes, disinhibition of differentiation, phasic activity of the nerve cells), changes in general behavior and increased thyroid activity which was manifested by a 10 to 36% rise in the basal metabolic rate (Table 7) and a 25% increase in the uptake of radioactive iodine by the thyroid. The gastric secretion in response to alimentary stimulation was increased by 46 to 134.9% (Table 8).

TABLE 7. Oxygen uptake (ml/min) by dogs in experimental neurosis (after Kurtsin and Nikolaeva, 1966)

Name of dog	Initial state	Neurosis		
		Disturbance of higher nervous activity	aftereffect	
			1—2 weeks later	3—4 weeks later
Jack	84	89	94	93
Shaloon	61	—	71	78
Okrat	91	94*	103	104
Tomik	85	94	94	—
Zhuk	78	86	88	75*

Note: P < 0.1 for data marked with an asterisk and P < 0.001 for other data.

TABLE 8. Gastric secretion in dogs (ml) in response to sham feeding with 600 ml milk during neurosis (after Kurtsin and Nikolaeva, 1966)

Name of dog	Initial state	Neurosis	
		disturbance of higher nervous activity	aftereffect 1—2 weeks later
Okrat	151.1 ± 8.1	—	266.7 ± 17.2
Tomik	63.0 ± 6.7	148.0 ± 48.3	112.0 ± 12.2
Zhuk	40.5 ± 4.4	—	59.2 ± 6.8

In these and many other experiments carried out by Nikolaeva (1966, 1971) the level of the oxidative processes was always found to be related to the degree of activity of the cerebral cortex: a deterioration in the higher nervous activity indices being accompanied by an increase in cellular oxidation while, when they returned to normal, there was a fall in the gas exchange level. A number of important findings have also come from other laboratories. Thus, dogs with an experimental neurosis produced by an "electroconflict" showed increased activity of the thyroid and thyrotropic hormone of the pituitary, associated with a decrease in the radioactive iodine uptake by the thyroid, in some cases by as much as half of the initial value (Arkhipenko, 1956). In stress, the absolute and relative weight of the thyroid increases, while the follicular diameter diminishes. Disturbance of higher nervous activity with forced immobilization, produced typical exophthalmic goiter in dogs, manifested by tachycardia, an increased respiratory rate, marked exophthalmos, a significant rise in the uptake of radioactive iodine by the thyroid and the release of more protein-bound (hormonal) iodine into the blood (Zubkov and Furdui, 1965).

Changes in thyroid activity in animals undergoing psychogenic stress have also been described by Kakhana (1960) and by Amiragova (1968, 1971). Disturbances of normal activity of the cerebral cortex and subcortex were transmitted to the thyroid gland via the hypothalamus and adrenals (Amiragova, 1968). In dogs some part in this process seems to be played by the adrenergic structures of the reticular formation, since chlorpromazine (1—1.5 mg/kg) represses the specific reactions of the thyroid to this kind of stress factor (Amiragova, 1971). In such types of stress, a change occurs in the secretory cycle of the thyroid, with inhibition of the phase of hormone production and stimulation of the phase of release of the hormone into the blood. In such a case the cortical influences are exerted indirectly, through stimulation of the release of adrenalin into the blood. The thyroid is influenced by adrenalin indirectly, via the pituitary, apparently through the stimulation of ACTH synthesis, since the development of stress is prevented by hypophysectomy and denervation of the adrenals (Amiragova, 1968). Kakhana (1960) reported emotional stress in dogs teased by a cat, manifested by an increase of thyroid activity and of blood adrenalin. Similar findings have been reported in rabbits and cats subjected to this kind of stress. According to other workers, such cases are not confined to changes in activity, but also involve structural changes in the thyroid, such as vasodilatation, follicular petechiae and enlargement of the epithelial cells. Kakhana noted the increased weight of the gland and histological examination showed the extensive development of interfollicular tissue and a prevalence of small follicles. However, in rabbits such changes were only observed after repeated exposure to stress for weeks or months, when the animals had developed hyperthyrosis [sic] with an increase of up to 39% in the gas exchange, as compared with the controls, a rise in the blood sugar of 10 to 25 mg %, a 53% increase in the pulse rate, sinus tachycardia, a 13% rise in the respiratory rate and a 20% decrease in the body weight. The EEG showed increased bioelectrical activity in the motor zone of the cortex and in the posterior hypothalamus. Together with hyperactivity of the gland there was an increase in the thyrotropic activity of the anterior pituitary. Afferent pathways from the thyroid lead via the vagus and sympathetic nerves through the medulla oblongata and the reticular formation of the brain stem to the cerebral cortex, where the area of representation of the thyroid gland forms a feedback by means of the closure mechanism with structures which play a part in the control of thyroid activity.

Thus the experimental findings suggest the following mechanism of action in corticothyroid disturbances. In psychogenic stress, excitation involving the cortical representation of the thyroid (the anterior part of the cerebral hemispheres) and the projection zone of the vagus nerves acts through a series of subcortical nervous structures, such as the caudate nucleus and the thalamus and reaches the anterior and posterior hypothalamus. Thence it proceeds to the thyroid gland along a neuro-conductor pathway, consisting of the vagus and sympathetic nerves and a neurohumoral pathway made up of the pituitary, thyrotropic hormone, ACTH and corticosteroids . It may be added that histological studies of the thyroid gland of dogs in a chronic state of experimental neurosis lasting 4 to 8 years, with a raised BMR, showed that the gland can maintain its hormonal activity for several years without showing pathological structural changes (Nikolaeva and Loskutova, 1969).

Thus, experimental physiology has now provided weighty evidence of the participation of the thyroid in psychogenic stress, in a dual capacity. It serves both as an intermediate hormonal link in the complex reflex to the reaction stress factor and as one of the factors maintaining and exacerbating the pathological condition of the brain centers and internal organs.

Another possibility to be considered is that the sex hormones are involved in the stress reaction, as Selye mentioned in passing in one of his early papers. This has also been suggested by Richter (1958). The estrous or menstrual cycle depends on the secretory cycle of the anterior pituitary and ovarian hormones, while these secretions are in turn influenced by the higher divisions of the CNS. Clinicians are clearly aware of the influence emotional disorders on menstrual-ovarian disturbances and on the complex processes which determine libido. The cerebral influences are mediated by the hypothalamus which plays some part in the production of the gonadotropic hormones: the follicle-stimulating hormone which excites growth of the follicles and the formation of estrogens in the ovary and spermatogenesis in the testes; the luteinizing hormone which controls ovulation and the formation of the corpus luteum and stimulates the production of the male sex hormone in the testes, and the luteotropic hormone or prolactin which stimulates hormone production in the corpus luteum and lactation. Severance of the connection between the hypothalamus and the pituitary, or damage to the hypothalamic nuclei markedly disturbs or

even interrupts the estrous cycle.   Clinical observations have shown that
tumors of the posterior hypothalamus may lead to precocious sexual matu-
rity, while tumors of the anterior hypothalamus often produce hypo-
gonadism.   Human sexual disturbances may also be related to damage
to the activity of the limbic system.   Cases have been reported in which a
tumor of the gyrus cinguli, uncus, or temporal lobe was accompanied by
sexual disorders and spermatogenesis is commonly impaired following
severe mental trauma (Stieve, 1952).

According to experimental findings, electrical stimulation of the septum,
or the preoptic region of the brain and particularly of the limbic system,
affects the synthesis of gonadotropic hormones, their release into the blood
and the process of ovulation.   Stimulation of the tuber cinereum increases
the production of luteinizing hormone and causes ovulation; if this structure
is damaged, the estrous cycle and ovulation cease.   A lesion of the region
anterior to the tuber cinereum increases the follicle-stimulating activity
of the pituitary and at the same time the synthesis of luteinizing hormone
ceases.   The production of androgens is markedly affected by electrical
stimulation of the caudate nucleus, septum and hypothalamus (Selye, 1952;
Gellhorn and Loofbourrow, 1963).   In cats, rats and rabbits a relationship
has been established between the electrical activity of the base of the
forebrain and sexual function.   The coupling sequence of the neurohormonal
mechanisms which regulate the sexual cycle has been demonstrated.   Thus,
a rise in the level of estrogens in the blood during the period of follicular
maturation inhibits the secretion of follicle-stimulating hormone, while the
hypothalamic trigger mechanism stimulates the release of luteinizing
hormone.   The estrogens are now known to accumulate selectively not only
in the uterus and vagina, but also in the hypothalamus, preoptic region and
in the nuclei of the septum pellucidum.   Consequently, regulation by the
brain centers of the secretion of sex hormones proceeds according to their
knowledge concerning the state of activity of the glands.

This information is relayed to the brain centers via a feedback system
from the sex organs themselves.   Thus, in cats stimulation of the vaginal
receptors was found to modify the electrical activity of the anterolateral
region of the hypothalamus.   Stimulation of the uterus in cats (Gorchakova,
1972) or of the vagina in rabbits affected the electrical activity of the
neocortex, limbic cortex, hippocampus, septum, reticular formation and
hypothalamus (Gellhorn and Loofbourrow, 1963).

Partial denervation of the ovaries arrests the maturation of follicles and
corpora lutea and induces atrophy of the ovarian tissues.   The implementation and development of the embryo is markedly disturbed by denervation
of the region of the uterine horn.   In some cases bilateral denervation of
the uterine horns in sheep did not abolish the rutting instinct and the
animals mated, but the cells of the embryos failed to divide and even if fission
took place, growth was retarded and the embryos often died.   Histological
examination of such cases showed that the walls of the denervated uterine
horns and of the uterus itself had become very thin and atrophied; at the
site of implantation of the embryos the connection of the placenta and
embryo with the wall of the uterine horn was destroyed.   In a sow
denervation of one uterine horn resulted in slower development in this
horn, so that the embryos were smaller than in the other horn.

In female rabbits the induction of acoustic and other forms of psychogenic stress during the first third of pregnancy was found to inhibit embryonic development and often result in abortion, while the newborn showed
signs of marked physiological immaturity (Pronin, 1954). In red Belorussian
bulls Kolesnikov and Borisov (1967) established a definite correlation between the type of higher nervous activity and the spermatogenic activity of
the sex organs. Their findings prove beyond doubt that the spermatogenic
function of the sex glands is regulated by the higher divisions of the central
nervous system.

For normal fertilization to occur a number of organs and systems must
work in harmony, particularly the ovary, where the ovarian follicle matures
and the uterus, the endometrium of which undergoes estrous changes.
Fertilization also requires a reaction on the part of the brain and pituitary
hormones, as can be inferred from the marked decline in the reactivity of
cerebral structures in rutting animals. A detailed study of the changes
taking place in higher nervous activity and in certain autonomic functions
in rutting dogs, under normal and pathological conditions, has been carried
out in our laboratory (Balakshina et al., 1960). This has shown that
rutting itself gives rise to marked changes in conditioned-reflex activity.
This had early been discovered in Pavlov's laboratories, but it was now found
in addition that these conditioned-reflex changes are not confined to exteroceptive stimuli but also extend to interoceptive stimuli. Moreover, different changes were found in dogs with different types of nervous system.
In dogs of the strong type, with suitably mobile nervous processes, the
changes in conditioned reflexes occurred mainly during the actual rutting
phase, when a sharp decline was noted, mainly in the positive conditioned
interoceptive reflexes. In the strong variant of the weak type changes in
higher nervous activity were found to occur even in the prerutting phase
and were marked by an intensification of exteroceptive and interoceptive
conditioned reflexes, followed by disturbance of internal inhibition at the
peak of rut. In these dogs changes in higher nervous activity were accompanied by changes in autonomic activity, including a diminution of drink
excitability and of carbohydrate metabolism in the gastric glands, inhibition
of biliary activity, increased absorption of glucose by the intestine and
of sodium chloride by the gallbladder, increased gastric secretion and
heightened excitability of the mechanoreceptors of the urinary bladder and
esophagus. These are probably not the only autonomic changes which
occur. Our investigations on dogs with corticovisceral pathology also revealed a reciprocal relationship between the rhythm of the estrous cycle
and the duration of rut. The relationship was retained after excision of
the premotor and limbic fields of the cerebral cortex.

The effects of experimental neurosis on ovarian function in rats has been
studied by Maisuradze (1971). Korzhova (1967) has reported that in preg-
nant rats experimental neurosis affects the development of the fetuses and the
newborn. The neurosis was induced by means of an extra-powerful acoustic
stimulus (95 db) applied for 1.6 minutes, which gave rise to epileptiform
attacks or motor excitement. All the rats were very sensitive to the
acoustic agent. In addition to the above changes in their general condition,
the following manifestations were noted: a rise in blood pressure; a fall
in the blood hemoglobin, especially toward the end of pregnancy and its slow
recovery after delivery; marked hypoproteinemia and significant changes in

the serum protein ratios with a sharp fall in the gamma globulin; albuminuria and retarded weight gain. All such findings indicate the presence of serious corticovisceral disorders induced by the pathogenic agent. Furthermore, reabsorption of the embryos occurred in 28.5% of the experimental rats, as compared to only 8.5% in the controls; the traumatized rats produced only 5 or 6 embryos in the uterus, as compared to the normal 8 or 9, while in 7.4% of these rats delivery was premature and in 60.7% it was delayed. The incidence of stillbirths and of postnatal mortality was high. The fetuses and newborn of traumatized rats were smaller and lighter and their physical development lagged behind that of normal offspring.

These researches have thus established a fact of the greatest theoretical and practical importance: functional trauma of the higher divisions of the CNS during pregnancy produces corticovisceral disturbances in the mother and exerts a detrimental effect on the condition and fate of the fetuses and newborn.

Significant observations have been made by Prosvirina (1966) on male patients with disorders of sexual function. Marked disturbance of higher nervous activity was diagnosed on the basis of the conditioned vascular and respiratory responses. An inert focus of pathological excitation was discovered in the second signal system (concentration on the ailment), together with marked inhibition of the orientating unconditioned and conditioned reflexes of the first signal system and of the conditioned reflexes of the second signal system in 56 to 78% of cases. After appropriate treatment these pathological phenomena disappeared, higher nervous activity returned to normal and normal sexual function was restored.

Through the hypothalamus the higher cerebral divisions also affect lactation which is stimulated by oxytocin, the hormone of the paraventricular nucleus and posterior pituitary, and by the lactogenic hormone of the anterior pituitary.

A change in the physiological state of the cerebral cortex affects the permeability of mammary gland tissue, the regulation of milk production and the utilization of substances by the cells of the mammary gland (Berkovich et al., 1967b). For example, the marked state of excitation produced by caffeine, or by amphetamine sulfate, was accompanied by a greater uptake of ^{35}S-methionine by the albumin, α-lactalbumin, immune globulins (euglobulin and pseudoglobulin), α-2-β-casein fractions and β-lactoglobulin in the milk. There was also a statistically significant rise in mammary gland activity and specifically in the production of γ-casein and milk fat. Intensification of the inhibitory processes by means of chloralose, chloral hydrate, nembutal or sodium bromide, resulted in inhibition of the uptake of ^{35}S-methionine by the α-2-casein, albumin and the γ-casein fractions of the milk. Mammary-gland activity rose as the inhibition weakened. Tashenov (1969) showed that the cerebral cortex takes part in the coupling mechanism of the mammary and digestive (salivary and gastric) glands in lactating sheep and goats. A conditioned reflex to a bell was established in all the experimental animals, based on the secretion of saliva and gastric juice in response to stimulation of the udder and papillary receptors (milking and udder massage). The reflex which has a rather complicated structure became established in goats after 20 to 25 combinations of the bell with milking and with udder massage and in sheep after 25—30 such combinations. The cerebral cortex also plays an important part in the lactation reflex in mares which develop a conditioned lactation reflex after only 11 to 18 combinations. It follows that the higher divisions of the central nervous system govern the hormonal activity of the glands involved in the synthesis of the gonadotropic hormones and estrogens, as well as the estrous cycle, ovulation, spermatogenesis, reproduction, pregnancy and embryonic development. As a result the hormonal activity of these glands is seriously impaired in psychogenic stress.

Of the hormones of local importance those of the digestive system will be considered here since their physiological significance has been thoroughl studied and determined, while their activity in pathological conditions is attracting increased attention (Kurtsin, 1962c, 1969c; Harper, 1972). There is already a fair amount of evidence showing that the higher divisions of the CNS influence these hormones: 1) blocking of the effect of the adrenergic structures of the reticular formation of the brain by chlorpromazine alters the nature of hepatic secretion evoked not only by reflexes but also by hormones (Gaza, 1965a); 2) experimental neuroses and structural lesions of the premotor and limbic areas of the cerebral cortex give rise to disturbances of bile formation lasting many months (Gaza, 1962, 1965a, 1966) and also of the discharge of bile (Gorshkova and Kurtsin, 1967a, 1967b; Klimov, 1969), both of which are partly under hormonal control; 3) the destruction or stimulation of certain subcortical nervous formations, such as the amygdaloid nuclei, the septum and the hippocampus, lead to changes in the secretion of bile and in its discharge into the duodenum in both the complex reflex phase and the hormonal phase (Bakuradze and Nikolaeva, 1965; Danilova and Klimov, 1967; Klimov, 1969). All these influences are exerted through the autonomic nervous system.

Thus, the production and effects of the hormones regulating bile formation and discharge, such as cholecystokinin, secretin, urocholecystokinin and antiurocholecystokinin, are under the controlling influence of the nervous system, up to and including the level of the cerebral cortex. This also applies to the hormonal regulation of exocrine pancreatic activity. In the first place the combination of an acoustic stimulus with the injection of secretin into the blood produces secretion of gastric juice in response to isolated applications of the stimulus. Secondly the production of experimental neurosis in dogs gives rise to changes in the reactivity of the secretory cells of the pancreas to endogenic and exogenic secretin, which persist for many months (Shostakovskaya, 1960; Kurtsin and Suplyakov, 1964; Kuznetsova, 1971). The powerful light stimulus produced by a 300-watt electric bulb placed at a distance of 30 cm from the head or to the auditory stimulus produced by exposure to noise for 5 minutes, gave rise to a state of inhibition in most of the dogs, followed by an increase in pancreatic secretion on the introduction of 0.25% hydrochloric acid solution into the duodenum. Occasionally, the secretory process was increased immediately on exposure to the light or sound (Murav'eva, 1967), with a resultant increase in the enzyme content of the juice. This means that the stimuli affected the production of the hormones secretin and pancreozymin. Cortical influences on the pancreas and duodenum, where these hormones are produced, are also mediated by autonomic innervation.

This has been demonstrated by blocking the adrenergic nerves with ergo-toxin (Solov'ev, 1959, 1971) and the cholinergic nerves with atropine, which considerably diminished or even abolished the hormonal effect, while pre-liminary irrigation of the duodenal mucosa with tetracaine diminished the pancreatic reaction to the introduction of hydrochloric acid solution into the duodenum. Hence, the synthesis of secretin and pancreozymin and their stimulatory effect on the pancreatic secretory cells are similarly controlled by the cerebral cortex.

Finally, a third group of digestive hormones is also subject to the control of cerebrocortical influences. Thus, the sight of food or sham feeding, in dogs in whom the pyloric antrum had been removed, scarcely provoked any secretion of gastric juice, in contrast to intact dogs. Consequently, during the complex reflex phase gastric secretion is triggered through the hormone gastrogastrin which acts as the intermediate link in this pro-cess. Dogs subjected to experimental neurosis suffer for months and sometimes years, from disturbances of gastric secretion to various kinds of food, not only in the complex reflex phase, but also in the neurohormonal phase (Kurtsin, 1952, 1962c; Gulyaeva, 1956; Golovskii et al., 1960; Baladzhaeva, 1971). Gastrogastrin synthesis is also modified in neurosis. Thus, when the mucosa of a denervated gastric pouch formed from the region of the pyloric antrum is irrigated with a 5% peptone solution, the secretion from a denervated pouch in the fundus may be greater or less than usual until the neurosis disappears and higher nervous activity returns to normal (Gulyaeva, 1969; Kurtsin, 1969c; Kurtsin and Gulyaeva, 1969; Gulyaeva et al., 1971a). If these isolated gastric pouches preserve their nervous connections with the CNS, hormone production increases and correspondingly, the hor-monal effect of the glands of the fundus will be maximal for the same stimulus (Kurtsin and Gulyaeva, 1969). It is also possible that conditioned reflexes stimulate or inhibit gastrogastrin production. Thus, the group of digestive hormones which plays a part in the regulation of gastric secretion, such as gastrogastrin, pylorin, pyloric antrum gastrin, gastric-juice depressor, enterogastrin, enterogastrone, secretin and cholecystokinin-pancreozymin, like the two groups discussed above which regulate the activity of the pan-creas, liver, and biliary tract, is also under the controlling influence of the cerebral cortex. This is why psychogenic stress is accompanied by profound disturbances in the synthesis of these hormones and leads to protracted changes in the hormonal mechanism stimulating the secretory and muscle cells of the digestive system.

The hormone system thus participates in psychogenic stress as one of the links in the chain of corticovisceral disturbances. The first and main link in the process is the disturbance of the cortical mechanisms for regulation, integration and correlation. The next link consists of distur-bances of cortical-subcortical interactions. The result is a serious dis-turbance of hypothalamic function, leading to a derangement of the inte-gration and regulation of autonomic activity, metabolic processes, blood supply to the cells and the activity of the homeostatic mechanisms, and of the hormonal activity of the endocrine glands, particularly the pituitary adrenals, thyroid, sex glands and the islets of the pancreas and the digestive system. From the hypothalamus, the stress stimulus reaches the viscera and the peripheral endocrine glands along two pathways: the humoral, or transpituitary pathway is made up of the neurosecretions and the pituitary hormones while the nervous parahypophyseal pathway originates in the anterior and posterior sympathetic nuclei of the hypothalamus.   This disorganization of activity of the internal organs and systems and of the endocrine glands, in its turn plays an independent part in the further spread of the pathological process.   A pathologically changed organ sends increased fluxes of afferent impulses to the central nervous formations, aggravating the pathological state of the cerebral cortex and subcortical autonomic centers.   The hormonal system also plays an important part at this stage in the development of the condition.   The increased or attenuated secretion of hormones affects the organs both directly and through the vascular and tissue receptors which are strongly influenced by the hormones particularly those of the adaptative group.   Normally, the endocrine glands serve as information centers, playing a very important part in integrating, coordinating and regulating the activity of the higher brain centers (the principle of self-regulation).

In psychogenic stress, however, this derangement of the neurohumoral mechanisms for the secretion of hormones and for their discharge into the blood, transforms the endocrine glands into a pathogenic factor: maintaining and aggravating the pathological condition of the cerebral control centers, as well as of all the cells and tissues of the internal organs. Because of the close functional relationship between the different endocrine glands, a disorder of one gland alone is rarely if ever encountered.   Clinical and experimental observations have demonstrated that endocrine involvement in psychogenic stress is most commonly multiglandular.   However, this does not preclude the possibility that the predominant lesion may occur in one particular gland, particularly if this happened to possess a "weak spot" before the exposure to stress.

Besides the adaptive hormones of the pituitary and adrenals other hormones also play an important part in the reaction to stress.   These include the pituitary hormones, ADH, the thyrotropic and gonadotropic hormones, oxytocin and the lactogenic and follicle-stimulating hormones; the adrenalin and noradrenalin produced by the adrenals; the thyroid secretion, thyroxin and the sex hormones.   In addition, locally-acting hormones, such as gastrin secretin and cholecystokinin, are also involved.   The physiological effects of the hormones in psychogenic stress form a rich mosaic.   Within the cells and tissues of the organs, changes occur in the rate and even in the direction of the metabolic processes, and of their activity and blood supply.   There are ultra-structural changes in the cells, especially in the mitochondria which are the principal cell-laboratories where the processes of oxidation take place and various forms of chemical energy are transformed into the energy of the phosphate bonds of macroergic compounds.   Thus, the hormones too become actively involved in the maintenance of the "vicious circle" between the brain centers and the periphery, which results from the corticovisceral disturbances.   In this way they further complicate the disease pattern, adding a new complex of neurohumoral chain reactions.   At a certain stage in the development of the pathological process stagnant (dominant foci of excitation and inhibition showing all the features of parabiosis may arise in the central nervous structure, particularly in the limbic system thalamo-hypothalamic region, hippocampal complex, striopallidal system, reticular formation and the overlapping or projection zones of somatic and autonomic activity.   These foci may strengthen or weaken the prevailing reflex reaction, or they may on the other hand distort it, thus evoking inadequate responses.   Under certain conditions these stagnant foci can partly or wholly block the passage of impulses from the visceral organs and endocrine glands to the neocortex and from the neocortex to the periphery.   In either case they set the stage for the pathological process to run a chronic course. Some part in this process may be played by the blocking of afferent and efferent impulses in various elements of the central and peripheral nervous systems, as a result of functional and possibly even structural damage to the synaptic formations and nerve tracts.   Again, an important part in these central and peripheral blocking mechanisms may be played by certain hormones, such as the tropic hormones of the pituitary, the adrenal corticosteroids and the thyroid and sex hormones.

Chapter 7

CENTRAL AND PERIPHERAL MEDIATORS
OF PSYCHOGENIC STRESS

The problem of the conducting pathways which mediate the psychogenic stress merits the closest attention, for any major advancement in our knowledge of the theory of corticovisceral relationships and of the treatmen and prevention of corticovisceral disturbances (diseases) will depend on its solution. We have still to learn more about the ways in which psychogenic trauma is mediated in man. Our theories are mainly based on findings obtai ed from experiments in the field of corticovisceral physiology and to some extent on corticovisceral pathology. However, the findings obtained in expei iments on animals, particularly in short-term ("acute") experiments under anesthesia, cannot be automatically extrapolated to the human organism. It is, however, beyond doubt that the point of onset of the psychogenic stress lies wholly within the nervous structures of the auditory or visual analyzer. It is also clear that the initial target of psychogenic stress is the peripheral component of these analyzers, through which the sound or light stimuli, after being suitably transformed into nerve impulses by the recep- tors, reach the cortical divisions of the auditory and visual analyzers. Thi probably constitutes the site of origin of the stress wave which is propagate along the nervous pathways of the brain, medulla oblongata and spinal cord via the autonomic nervous system to the viscera, giving rise to changes anc disorders of visceral activity.

The mechanism of the corticovisceral reflex in an organism exposed to an acoustic stress can be outlined as follows: the impulses proceed along th conductors of the auditory analyzer: the receptors and processes of the bi- polar cells of the spiral ganglion, auditory nerves and other nuclei, olives, nuclei of the lateral lemniscus, inferior colliculi and the medial genicu- late bodies. Reaching its cortical end in the temporal cortex, the stimulus travels along associative neurons to the limbic, premotor and orbital areas It then proceeds along efferent conductors to the hypothalamus which trigger the hormonal system of the pituitary and adrenal cortex, and finally reaches the adrenal medulla via sympathetic pathways. The intensified discharge of adrenalin into the blood and its passage to the brain increases the activity o the reticular formation, both directly and by a reflex from the aortic recep tor area and the carotid sinus. The acoustic excitation generated in the cor tical end of the auditory analyzer is mediated by the limbic cortex which possesses numerous connections with the reticular formation, the hypotha- lamic region and the cerebello-olivary system (see Chapter 1) which, in the turn, play a part in the regulation of autonomic activity. This gives rise to complex of heterogeneous visceral-autonomic disturbances in the initial phas

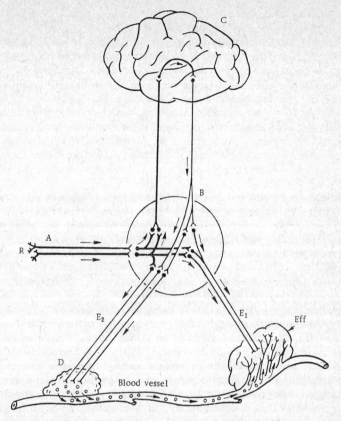

FIGURE 20. The two pathways of the corticovisceral reflex in psychogenic stress (after Kurtsin, 1968):

A) afferent nerve fibers; B) lower CNS divisions; C) cerebral cortex; D) endocrine gland; R) receptor; E_1) nervous pathway; E_2) neurohumoral pathway; Eff) effector.

of development of corticovisceral disorders. As the pathological process unfolds, this initial and fundamental trend in the development of pathological processes is abetted by other factors, central and peripheral, nervous and hormonal, ionic and mediator, metabolic and structural. All of these take over the task of "triggering" the disturbances in a kind of relay and render the pathological process chronic by maintaining it and spreading it through-out the body or through individual organs and systems. Thus the stress wave is propagated by two mechanisms, neuroconductor (E_1) and neurohumoral (E_2) (Figure 20). Initially both use a common pathway, consisting entirely of ner-vous structures. Much of our knowledge concerning the propagation of stress waves is based on studies of corticovisceral integration (see Chapters 1 and 2). Reverberations of the mental trauma apparently reach the viscera, blood vessels, and endocrine glands via the extrapyramidal (phylogenetically old) and pyramidal (phylogenetically new) tracts. The former passes through numerous subcortical centers, while the latter connects the neocortex directly with the nuclei of the cranial nerves (the corticopontine tract) and the anterior horn of the spinal cord (the corticospinal tract). According to French (1962), the fibers from the cerebral cortex form a thick bundle in the region of the septum lucidum and then become distributed over the whol of the cephalic part of the brain stem; another pathway possibly leads through the hippocampus and the entorhinal area along the striae medullare

A stress wave of excitation can be transmitted from the premotor, front and orbital areas of the cortex to the cardiovascular system along a number of neuroconductor pathways (pyramidal, frontopontine, extrapyramidal, sub callosal tracts) via the pallidum, the paraventricular and ventromedial hypo thalamic nuclei, the nuclei of the striopallidal system and the bulbar center (Figure 21).

The efferent pathway from the limbic cortex probably continues to the posterior hypothalamus and supraoptic and paraventricular nuclei (Figure 22), since their destruction diminishes the visceral effect produced by stimulation of the limbic cortex (Chernigovskii, 1967). Cardiac inhibitory influence from the cerebral cortex also pass through the posterior hypothalamus, since after coagulation of the nervous structures of this part of the gland, cardiac activity is no longer affected by the development of differential or extinguish ing inhibition in the cortex. Another pathway from the hypothalamus to the effector proceeds via the vagus and sympathetic nerves. These pathways have been described in detail in monographs by Suvorov (1967), Kositskii an Chervova (1968), and Makarchenko and Dinaburg (1971), with regard to the cardiovascular system and by Kurtsin (1952), Chernigovskii (1967) and Gorshkova and Kurtsin (1967b), with regard to the digestive system.

The stimulatory and inhibitory cortical influences are thought to pass through the mesencephalic reticular formation and the nonspecific thalamic regions, respectively. Consequently, an excitatory or inhibitory autonomic visceral effect may be induced not only by the basal ganglia and reticular formation, but also by the neocortex.

A significant part in the development of corticovisceral pathology is play ed by functional and structural damage to the hypothalamus which forms a two-way link between the cerebral cortex and the internal organs (see Chapters 1 and 2). In rabbits it was found that overstimulation of the posterior hypothalamus with an electrical current gave rise to dystrophic processes in the stomach, heart, lungs, uterus and other viscera (Anichkov et al., 1971; Shvalev, 1971).

Moreover, at the level of the hypothalamus the stress wave divides into two impulse fluxes, one of which proceeds along nervous pathways via the medulla oblongata and spinal cord to the effectors, while the other travels partly to the posterior and medial lobes of the pituitary and partly to the hypothalamic nuclei, where it stimulates the production of neurohormones which act on the pituitary. Here, in the hypothalamus is the origin of the powerful neurohumoral pathway which transmits the psychic stress reaction to the viscera through the endocrine system (Figure 20).

Selye (1952), his colleagues and numerous others consider that this neurohumoral pathway which has to pass through the pituitary, exerts the decisive and controlling influence on any stress reaction, including psychogenic stress. However, in view of new experimental findings regarding the

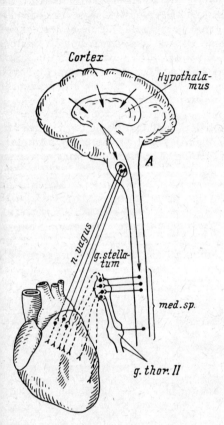

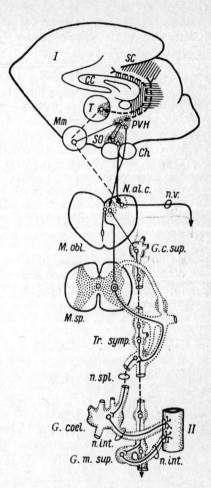

FIGURE 21. The nervous pathway for cortical influences on the heart:

A—vagal nucleus in medulla oblongata; med.sp. — cord segments sending sympathetic fibers to the heart; g.thor. and g. stellatum — thoracic sympathetic ganglia. Solid lines — preganglionic fibers (vagus, sympathetic nerves); lines of dashes — postganglionic vagal fibers in the heart; interrupted lines — postganglionic fibers (sympathetic) to the heart. Arrows show cortical influences transmitted to the heart via the hypothalamus, vagus and sympathetic nerves.

FIGURE 22. Conduction of efferent influence on intestinal motility from the limbic cortex (after Chernigovskii, 1967):

I) medial surface of cerebral hemisphere (hatched area, limbic cortex); II) segment of small intestine; SC: cruciform sulcus; CC: corpus callosum; T: thalamus; Mm: mammillary bodies; PVH: paraventricular hypothalamic nucleus; SO: supraoptic nucleus; Ch: chiasma; N.al.c.: nucleus alae cinereae; n.v.: vagus nerve; G.c.sup.: superior cervical ganglion; M.obl.: medulla oblongata; M.sp.: spinal cord; Tr.symp.: sympathetic trunk; n.spl.: splanchnic nerve; G.coel.: coeliac plexus; G.m.sup.: superior mesenteric ganglion; n.int.: intestinal nerve.

paths along which stress reactions develop, including psychogenic stress, this idea now requires to be modified.

In our laboratory neurosis was produced by Pavlovian conflict in hypophysectomized dogs with an established stereotype of conditioned salivary reflexes. It was found that the development of the neurosis was accompanie by the same autonomic disturbances of gastric secretion and blood pressur as those observed after conflict in dogs with an intact pituitary (Figure 23). This would mean that a state of psychogenic stress may arise without the participation of the hypophysis. This type of stress reaction has been simi larly established by our colleague, Balakshina (1964), who has studied diure sis in dogs with a severed hypophyseal stalk, and by Sever'yanova (1965) whose studies on hypophysectomized dogs in Nekrasov's laboratory were designed to determine the part played by the pituitary in the development of neurogenic hypertension. In Nikolaichuk's experiments (1963) on hypophysectomized dogs, stimulation of the motor or occipital region of the cerebr cortex over a period of several weeks resulted in the doubling or tripling the corticosteroid content of the adrenal cortex and blood plasma.

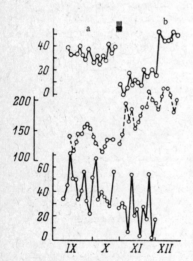

FIGURE 23. Quantitative changes in conditioned reflexes, blood pressure and gastric secretion in a hypophysectomized dog suffering from "psychogenic" stress (after Kurtsin and Chubarova, 1968):

a) initial values (8 months after hypophysectomy); b) neurosis. Top to bottom: sum of positive conditioned salivary reflexes for the experiment (scale divisions); arterial pressure, mm Hg; gastric secretion over 4 hr of the experiment, ml. X-axis — months preceding and following the nervous conflict in the cerebral cortex (arrows).

There are also indications that hypophysectomy does not prevent the hepatic dystrophy usually produced by powerful stimulation of the duodenal receptors. Hence, there also exists another pathway for the realization of the stress effect via the nervous system (the parahypophyseal pathway), in addition to that via the hypophysis (the transhypophyseal pathway). The development of the general adaptation syndrome can therefore be represented in the following manner. Impulse fluxes generated in the exteroceptors and interoceptors by various stimuli (stressors) reach the effector organs via reflex arcs of varying degrees of complexity. Some arcs are limited to ner vous structures, whereas others use both nervous and endocrine pathways. The basic mechanism underlying the production of psychogenic (emotional) stress may be represented thus: stressor → receptor → afferent fibers (neurons I and II) → subcortical nervous formations (thalamus; reticular formation) → afferent fibers (neuron III) → cerebral cortex (nuclei and fibers of analyzers, premotor, orbital, limbic and other areas) → efferent fibers of cells of the layer V of the cerebral cortex → subcortical centers for so-mato-autonomic correlation (reticular formation, limbic and striopallidal nuclei, thalamo-hypothalamic region, particularly the supraoptic and para-ventricular nuclei) → medulla oblongata (or cerebellum), spinal cord → efferent fibers of the autonomic nervous system (cholinergic and adrenergic fibers), sympathetic ganglia → nervous mechanisms in the walls of the viscera → effectors.

In other cases, the stress reaction may proceed along the following path: stressor → receptor → afferent nerves (neurons I and II) → medulla oblongata, thalamus, reticular formation of the brain stem, limbic and striopallidal systems → cerebral cortex (analyzer nuclei and peripheral elements, limbic, orbital, premotor, and other forebrain areas, hippocampus, amygdaloid complex) → central efferent nerves → subcortical autonomic ganglia (reticular formation, limbic and striopallidal systems, hypothalamus, especially the neurosecretory nuclei) → portal circulation (neurosecretions) → pituitary → systemic circulation → adrenal cortex (corticosteroids) → systemic circulation → end effector (organ, cells, tissues). In this scheme the nervous pathway is interrupted at the level of the hypothalamus—pituitary system but this may occur at the level of the adrenal medulla. From here the stress excitation is relayed by adrenalin and noradrenalin via the bloodstream, often directly to the anterior lobe of the pituitary. It may also take place through the reticular formation and hypothalamus, provided that the permeability of the blood-brain barrier is sufficiently high for these chemical mediators, or possibly by a reflex from the receptors of the aortic arch and carotid sinus. The sympathetic innervation is considered to be of great importance by Graham (1953) and certain other researchers (Maevskaya, 1968). When stimulated, the production of adrenalin is increased and through the blood this, in its turn, stimulates the nervous system itself, as well as cell and tissue metabolism and ACTH production. Thus, Graham bridges the gap between Selye's concept that only the anterior pituitary and adrenal cortical hormones play a part in adaptation reactions and Cannon's theory (1953) that the leading role in many stress reactions, especially those in which emotional factors are involved, must be ascribed to the sympathetic nerves and to the adrenalin produced by their stimulation. Involvement of the sympathetic nervous system in the stress reaction has also been reported by other authors (Gorizontov and Protasova, 1968). In such a case the stress reaction would be mediated by the autonomic nervous system, the stimulus being transmitted by chemical mediators.

In this context the role of catecholamines in the "first stress mediator" also becomes clear. The pathway might then run as follows: stressor → receptor → thalamus → reticular formation → cerebral cortex → efferent fibers → structures reacting to adrenalin, acetylcholine, histamine or serotonin in the limbic system, mesencephalon, thalamus and reticular formation → hypothalamus → reticular formation → spinal cord (sympathetic trunk) → sympathetic fibers → adrenal medulla (adrenalin and noradrenalin) → bloodstream → peripheral structures reacting to adrenalin → hypothalamus → anterior

pituitary (ACTH) → bloodstream → adrenal cortex (corticosteroids) → blood
stream → effector. Within the adrenals and pituitary, the nerve impulse
(stress stimulus) may be transmitted with the aid of acetylcholine, since the
adrenals possess nicotine-sensitive choline receptors, while the pituitary
contains an amount of acetylcholine equaled only by the sympathetic ganglia

Graham has made the interesting suggestion (1953) that insulin plays a
part in stress. He shares our opinion that the stress reaction also involves
the parasympathetic nerves which, when stimulated, increase the secretion
of insulin and its discharge into the blood. The insulin then activates the
secretion of corticosteroids by the adrenals.

Others have suggested that there may be reflex transmission of stress
stimuli to the posterior pituitary which secretes or already possesses the
hormone vasopressin. This hormone exerts a strong tonic effect on the vas
cular system and also directly stimulates pituitary hormonal activity (Pole
nov, 1968; Voitkevich, 1970; Aleshin, 1971).

According to Bugaenko (1963), the second stage in the development of
stress consists of interrelated nervous phenomena arising from the involve
ment of the reticular formation of the brain stem which excites the pituitary
adrenal system by means of cyclic feedbacks. The cerebral cortex also
becomes drawn into the process, stimulating the anterior pituitary (ACTH)
as well as the hypothalamus and the parasympathetic nervous system. These
stimuli eventually lead to hypersecretion by the adrenal cortex, resulting in
an excessive corticosteroid content in the blood. This is regarded by Buga
enko as the third and last stage in the development of the stress reaction.
Actually, this is not quite correct; the decisive point being the level at which
the stress wave of excitation passes through the central nervous system and
gives rise to the general adaptation syndrome. It may take place at the level
of the spinal cord or medulla oblongata, or of the thalamus and hypothalamus
or at the level of the mesencephalon and cerebral cortex.

The mechanism by which the general adaptation syndrome develops will
thus depend to some extent on the above level. If the wave of excitation is
confined to the spinal cord and medulla, the stress reaction may be mainly
brought about by efferent sympathetic stimulation of the adrenal medulla.
The output of adrenalin and noradrenalin then brings into play the hormonal
pituitary-adrenal adaptation system. If the wave passes at the level of the
thalamic-hypothalamic region, the range of nervous structures involved is
increased, as has been shown above, and the pituitary-adrenal adaptive
system can be brought into play not only by catecholamines, but also directly, by stimulation of the pituitary, probably mainly by hypothalamic neurosecretions. Finally, when the stress excitation involves the cortical mecha
nisms as, for example, in emotional stress, such as pain, fright, fear or
rage, not only is the adaptation reaction at its most extensive but all the
mechanisms of development of the general adaptation syndrome are finally
set in motion. The stress wave of excitation now travels along the nervous
and neurohumoral pathways to every part of the body which becomes involve
in the stress reaction. At certain levels the excitation wave is overlapped b
a new impulse flux generated as the receptor formations are stimulated by
the adaptive hormones and by new reflexes. Onto this complex set of neurohormonal phenomena are superimposed, in their turn, new situations created
by changes in cortical-subcortical relationships. These changes are due to
activation of the cerebral cortex by impulses arriving via specific nervous
structures and by the powerful activating influence of the reticular formation

However, participation of the nervous system is not limited to the period of functioning of the "first stress mediator." On entering the blood, the pituitary and adrenal hormones stimulate numerous cardiovascular receptors even before they reach the cells and tissues, thereby creating a number of new reflex reactions, and the resulting chain reaction involves ever more structures. Some of these constitute ultimate substrates; others, which are intermediate, comprise not only a great variety of organs but also the hormonal system itself. As a result, once the pituitary and adrenals have become involved in the complex reflex reaction, they are repeatedly subject to reflex stimulation.

The development of the general adaptation syndrome is thus an extremely complex matter. In its different stages and to varying degrees, it involves both nervous and endocrine factors; its reflex components, which constitute the initial stage in the development of the stress reaction, are overlain by hormonal reactions which, in turn, come to involve a new complex of reflex reactions. All this creates a tangle of interwoven, neural and hormonal phenomena. Nevertheless, from the biological point of view the first, nervous pathway consisting of highly sensitive tissue, evidently bears the main responsibility for the action of the organism as an integrated whole in its relation with environmental factors, as well as for protecting the cells and tissues against harmful agents. However, our ideas in this respect are inevitably arbitrary and schematic, because we are trying to delineate the pathways of development of the stress reaction on the basis of insufficient knowledge.

Both the pathways described, together with certain variants, are of course utilized almost simultaneously by the organism. The adaptive organs and systems go into operation within fractions of a second of receiving the signals arriving via the nervous pathway and very soon after, within a few tenths of a second, the final effector is reached by signals traveling along the other pathway. The important part played by various biological substances in the interaction between the nervous system and the pituitary—adrenal hormone system, must also be borne in mind, particularly such mediators of nervous excitation as noradrenalin, acetylcholine, histamine, serotonin, dopa, polypeptides, unsaturated hydroxylipid acid, glutamate (which mediates the excitation in noncholinergic cerebral synapses) and gamma-aminobutyric acid (which inhibits synaptic transmission). It must be assumed that they take part in producing the psychogenic stress reaction in the central nervous system, since on microinjection into various parts of the brain acetylcholine and dicarboxylic amino acids (mainly glutamic acid) were found to produce excitement, while the monocarboxylic acids (gamma-aminobutyric, beta-alanine, and delta-aminovaleric acids) gave rise to inhibition.

It is now known that the monoamines and acetylcholine are to be found in the synapses of the cerebral neurons, that the brain possesses special mechanisms for synthesizing and breaking down these substances and that specific chemical structures exist which react selectively to noradrenalin, acetylcholine and serotonin. It has also been established that the biological activity of individual mediators varies during stress (Mityushov et al., 1970). A special role in intracerebral relationships in pathological states is played by histamine which not only mediates the nervous excitation but also increases the sensitivity of the cholinoceptors in nervous tissue and blood vessels to acetylcholine and diminishes the sensitivity of their adrenoceptors to catecholamines (Putintseva, 1970). There are grounds for relating the paralyzed condition of the cerebral vascular system in severe stress to these effects of histamine. Naumenko (1971) has shown that local stimulation of sero- tonin-sensitive structures of the medial part of the anterior, middle, and posterior divisions of the hypothalamus and limbic system (ventral hippo- campus, septum, preoptic region) excites the activity of the hypothalamus pituitary-adrenal system, whereas the stimulation of nervous structures in the dorsal part of the hypothalamus and in the region of the amygdaloid nu- cleus inhibits such activity.

The brain centers can therefore affect the pituitary-adrenal hormone system in two ways: by excitation and by inhibition produced by the effect of serotonin on those nervous structures which are sensitive to it. The adrenal cortex is not stimulated by serotonin in hypophysectomized animals.

The pituitary-adrenal system is also excited by the stimulation of cere- bral structures which are sensitive to adrenalin. In guinea pigs, for example local stimulation of the posterior hypothalamic nucleus, mammillary nuclei and the nuclei of the ventral mesencephalic tectum by $1\mu g$ noradrenalin lead to a statistically significant rise of corticosteroids in the blood ($P < 0.01$). No such effect occurs after the mesencephalon is sectioned in a caudal di- rection, away from the site of stimulation (Naumenko, 1971). The effect is due to primary excitation of peripheral structures sensitive to adrenalin. The same applies to M- and N-parasympathomimetics. For example, in Naumenko's experiments on guinea pigs, the subcutaneous administration of $5-10 \, mg/kg$ of the anticholinesterase substance galanthamine which readily crosses the blood-brain barrier, significantly raised the blood corticosterone content ($P < 0.001$), but the same dose proved ineffective after mesencephal section. In guinea pigs the activity of the adrenal cortex was also stimulat by the local application of $5\mu g$ doryl to the posterior hypothalamus and ros- tral regions of the mesencephalon (Naumenko, 1971), but the effect did not occur when the mesencephalic part of the brain stem was sectioned before the substance was applied.

Mediators are essential for transmission of the stress reaction along nerves and across synapses (Eccles, 1964; Il'yuchenok, 1972). Electron microscopy has revealed numerous mediator-containing vesicles, both in the axons which make contact with the cell membrane and actually inside the cells, directly beneath the membrane (Robertis, 1964; Gaito, 1966). Hence, even the nervous pathway of the stress reaction is not purely neural but is neurohumoral; the only difference between it and the second pathway being that psychogenic stress is transmitted not by hormones but by nervous me- diators of excitation. Thus the production of psychogenic stress should be viewed as a series of complex reflex reactions which are dominated and controlled by the nerves, while the pituitary-adrenal system acts as a spe- cific intermediate or terminal transmitter of nervous excitation (Speran- skaya, 1961; Kurtsin, 1965e; Nichkov and Krivitskaya, 1969; Mityushov et al. 1970). This latter system thus serves to extend the range and duration of the nervous influences on the cells and tissues. In psychogenic stress, as in pathological corticovisceral conditions in general, disturbances occur in the nervous regulation of the synthesis and inactivation of hormones and me diators. A high concentration of these substances in the blood and cerebro- spinal fluid exacerbates the pathological condition of the brain centers, there by reinforcing the "vicious circle" produced by the central nervous mechanism and the internal secretions. The hormones of the pituitary-adrenal system and the mediators of the brain centers evidently play a very important part in the establishment of this vicious circle which plays an essential part in the production of corticovisceral disorders (Kurtsin, 1965d, 1965f, 1965g, 1969c, 1969g, 1971c).

Chapter 8

THE STRUCTURE OF THE VISCERAL ANALYZER AND THE INTEROCEPTIVE MECHANISMS OF CORTICOVISCERAL DISTURBANCES

The progress achieved in neurohistology and neurophysiology over the past few decades has increased our knowledge of the sensitivity of internal organs (interoception) to the extent that it is now essential to determine the structure of the visceral (interoceptive, internal) analyzer (Sherrington, 1906; Bykov, 1942; Chernigovskii, 1943, 1960, 1962, 1967; Airapet'yants, 1952, 1962, 1971; Kurtsin, 1952, 1966, 1967b, 1971c; Bykov and Kurtsin, 196 1966a; Karaev and Loginov, 1960; Rikkl', 1961; Durinyan, 1965; Kurtsin ar Nikolaeva, 1966; Airapet'yants and Sotnichenko, 1967; Varbanova, 1967; Ermolaeva, 1969; Nozdrachev, 1969; Bulygin, 1970, 1971; Gasanov, 1970; Kullanda, 1970; Sitdikova, 1970; Raitses, 1971; Sotnichenko, 1971).

THE STRUCTURE OF THE VISCERAL ANALYZER

Like the external analyzers (visual, auditory, olfactory, gustatory, or cutaneous), the visceral analyzer is made up of three parts: a peripheral division containing the sensitive nerve endings; an intermediate division comprising the conducting pathways for the impulses and switching mechanisms ("relays") in the peripheral ganglia, subcortical nervous structures and synapses; and a central division made up of the cortical nuclei and the other nervous elements scattered throughout the cortex.

The analyzer is peripherally represented by interoceptors which are present in all the viscera, endocrine glands and blood vessels of vertebrate including man (Lavrent'ev, 1948; Grigor'eva, 1954; Dolgo-Saburov, 1956; Granit, 1956; Stöhr, 1957; Gilinskii, 1958; Heymans and Neil, 1958; Kolosc 1962, 1970, 1972; Kadanoff, Gurowski, 1963; Abraham, 1964; Shvalev, 1965; Milokhin, 1967; Kolosov and Milokhin, 1970; Mel'man, 1970; Volkova, 1972 and others).

Structurally, all the interoceptors fall into two large groups, free, or uncapsulated and enclosed, or encapsulated. The former lie free within the tissues and cells. In form they may be reticular, glomerular, tree-like, bushy, or of other shapes. Those of the second group are encased in a thic laminated capsule. They often lie in direct contact with the cell cytoplasm and take a number of forms, such as the corpuscles of Pacini, Meissner or Golgi, or the end bulbs of Krause. In man the interoceptors are highly differentiated and of a complex nature. They are highly specialized structure capable of reacting to specific mechanical, thermal, osmotic or other stimul and of transforming them into nerve impulses. The mechanoreceptors are divided according to the rate at which they adapt to stimuli. The rapidly adapting types do so within a few milliseconds, but the slowly-adapting take several hours (Mendelson and Loewenstein, 1964; Il'inskii, 1967).

It is still unclear whether the varied shapes and structures of the sensitive nerve endings reflect their different functions, or whether any receptor, irrespective of shape and structure, is capable of reacting to mechanical, chemical, thermal and other stimuli. There are observations suggesting some specialization of receptors; for example, the Pacinian corpuscles are only sensitive to deep pressure, and the glomerular and tree-like interoceptors are confined to chemoreception. However, exposure of the mechanoreceptors, for example, to various chemical substances, such as solutions of potassium, sodium, chloride or calcium ions, adrenalin, acetylcholine or gamma-aminobutyric acid, may increase or weaken their activity. Temperature also exerts some influence. Nevertheless, this question is still open. Thus, it is assumed that the chemical substances do not act directly on the mechanoreceptor mechanism but indirectly through its blood supply. Again the glomus has been reported to contain only chemoceptors and the carotid body only mechanoreceptors.

Another controversial matter is the existence of nociceptors. It is possible that sensations of pain are produced by excessive stimulation of the same interoceptors that are normally receptive to mechanical, chemical, thermal or other stimuli. Nevertheless, it is not excluded that the peripheral division of the visceral analyzer possesses sensitive nerve endings and conducting afferent paths resembling the pain, touch and temperature receptor mechanism of the skin analyzer.

It is widely admitted that the chemoceptors fall into at least two sharply delimited groups, one of which is distinguished by its complex structure and selective sensitivity to certain chemical substances, while the other comprises receptors of comparatively simple structure, which react to general changes in the chemical composition of interstitial fluid. Thus, a fall in the oxygen tension of arterial blood excites the carotid receptors but has no effect on those of other blood vessels. On the other hand, substances such as sodium, chloride, hydrochloric acid and histamine stimulate all the vascular system receptors, apart from those of the carotid sinus. Thus, at least two different chemoceptor mechanisms appear to exist (Chernigovskii, 1960; Lebedeva, 1965). One of them is selectively sensitive to carbon dioxide and certain other acids and particularly sensitive to thiolic inhibitors. The other mechanism, responsible for the spontaneous activity of chemoceptors and their reaction to potassium chloride, nicotine and alkaline solutions, is more resistant to sulfhydryl-blocking agents. The end organ of chemical sensitivity is constituted by special ganglion-like cells, of two types: one being sensitive to acetylcholine and to ganglial poisons, such as nicotine, while the other is sensitive to oxygen deficiency, cyanides, sulfonamides and azides.

Receptors of electrical stimuli have recently been discovered in strongly and weakly electric fishes, as well as in a number of nonelectric fishes (Il'inskii et al., 1970), mainly among the sensor elements of the lateral line. However, there are grounds for assuming that they also exist in warm-blooded animals and particularly in the muscles and nerves where biocurrents are continuously gener-

ated. The electroreceptors are highly sensitive to electrical stimuli, of the or
der of 10^{-11} or of $10^{-2} \mu V/cm$, according to different authors. The chemocepto
are also fairly sensitive, responding to certain chemical substances, such a
adrenalin, in dilutions of $2 \cdot 10^{-10}$ or even $1 \cdot 10^{-18}$ (Bykov and Kurtsin, 1960
In addition to this sensitivity, they are also extremely stable, both structu
ally and functionally (Karaev and Loginov, 1960; Chernigovskii, 1960). The
sensitivity of the thermoreceptors is somewhat low, their threshold of dis
crimination being $> 0.25°$. The mechanoreceptors (baroreceptors, presso-
receptors, distension receptors) are fairly sensitive: thus, those which ar
stimulated by microdistension react to a difference of hundredths or even
thousandths of a micron (Il'inskii, 1967; Volkova, 1972). The latent period c
a receptor potential is 0.06 msec, or less than the synaptic delay, which is
0.2 msec.

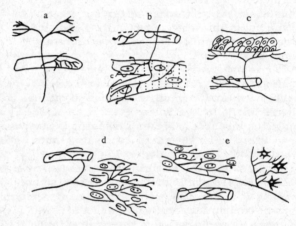

FIGURE 24. Diagrammatic representation of polyvalent interoceptors
in various organs (after Lavrent'ev, 1948).

Sensitive nerve endings on blood vessel and in tissues in: a) pia mater;
b) myocardium; c) urinary bladder; d) stomach; e) intestine.

The molecular basis is assumed to be similar for all types of receptor
(Vinnikov, 1971), just as is their mode of operation (Granit, 1956). So too,
are the energy aspects of the transformation of a stimulus into a nerve
impulse, which involves the participation of various substances, including
cholinesterase, adenosinetriphosphatase, alkaline and acid phosphatases,
succinic dehydrogenase, and cytochromoxidase. Acetylcholine, released
from the nerve endings, plays an important part in the excitation process.
The sensitive nerve endings of one and the same receptor may be connecte
to more than one structure; as, for example, to smooth muscle and to a
blood vessel, in the walls of the gastrointestinal tract (Lukashin, 1970); or
to a ganglion nerve cell or the surrounding glia and to a nearby capillary,
as is found in Auerbach's plexus in the small intestine; or to a neuron of th
cerebral cortex and a nearby blood vessel (Lavrent'ev, 1948; Dolgo-Saburo
1956; Kolosov, 1972) (Figure 24). This polyvalent structure of the receptor

obviously serves to provide the cerebral regulatory centers with simultaneous and parallel information on the state of activity of the cell and on the condition of its blood supply. Possessing this information the circulatory system can immediately respond to the stimulus, ensuring an adequate supply of blood, or rather nutrients, to the active cells.

Neurohistological studies carried out in Kolosov's laboratory have recently furnished incontrovertible proof of the existence of a special form of interoceptor (Milokhin, 1967). These are closed annular formations, usually rather large, which may be found along the length of the terminal branches of the nerves, from the receptor to the main afferent fibers. Their physiological significance is still obscure. It is assumed that they do not participate in the reception of nervous stimuli, but modify the conduction of the nerve impulse by, for example, markedly diminishing interference and noise during the transmission of sensory information along the afferent conductor. In other words, they act as noise- or shock-absorbers when the nervous impulse is powerful or of high intensity. They may also act as special collectors for subliminal stimuli, accumulating the impulse energy until an impulse of the optimal magnitude can be despatched to the cerebral centers. Such a device may serve to mitigate the damaging effects of extra-powerful stimuli on the fragile synaptic devices (defense function).

These receptors possess yet another noteworthy feature. They may be found on the actual nerve cells of autonomic and spinal ganglia (Milokhin, 1967; Kolosov and Milokhin, 1970), or even in the cerebrum (Dolgo-Saburov, 1956; Kolosov, 1972). In all probability, they have but one function: to keep the cerebral centers controlling autonomic activity informed about the condition of the nervous system itself; its conducting mechanism, the rate of conduction of impulses along the nerves, the excitability of the nervous structures, the performance, state and activity of the synapses and finally, the quality of the excitation in the neuron itself. As yet, it is difficult to pinpoint the actual nerve centers which perform such a controlling function. Possibly they are the same as those which control and regulate all the vegetative and somatic processes according to the principle of self-regulation. At any rate, there is no doubt that this information service would alone ensure the reliability and prompt operation of the nervous system. Furthermore, in interpreting the phenomena arising in the organism, whether it is in a normal or pathological state, one must constantly bear in mind the fact that the nervous system is itself a powerful receptive structure, capable of "responding" to many environmental influences.

The discovery of receptors in all the viscera, blood vessels, endocrine glands, bone marrow, musculo-skeletal system and now, finally, in various peripheral and central nervous structures, has demonstrated that vital substances such as oxygen, carbon dioxide and water are not perceived only by central nervous structures but also by numerous somatic and visceral receptor devices. The regulation of an important function such as respiration, in relation to tissue (cell) oxidation, is not only carried out by so-called "automatic" stimulation of the cerebral centers (that is, humorally) and by vascular reflexes from the carotid sinus and aortic arch, but also by interoceptive reflexes from every part of the body. Similarly, regulation of the water content of the body and of water and salt metabolism in general, including the sense of thirst, are due to signals not only from pharyngeal

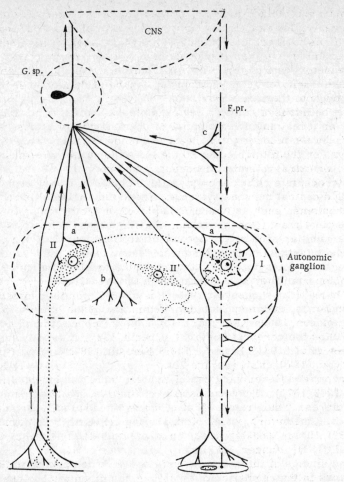

FIGURE 25. Diagram of interneuronal relationships of an autonomic ganglion
(after Milokhin, 1967).

G.sp.: spinal ganglion (or ganglion of the vagus nerve); F.pr.: preganglionic
nerve fiber; I) efferent autonomic neuron (Dogel's type I cells); II and II')
sensitive neurons (Dogel's type II cells). Dotted lines: afferent nerve fibers
of central (spinal or vagal) origin and their receptor endings; a) receptors of
autonomic neurons; b) receptors in the capsule and stroma of an autonomic
ganglion; c) receptors in nerve bundles and in trunks of autonomic plexuses.

receptors but also from osmoceptors and volume receptors in tissues and
organs throughout the body.

Although man possesses a very large number of receptor devices, these
are not uniformly distributed throughout the body. The large reflex-produc-
ing areas of the gastrointestinal tract: the pyloric antrum of the stomach,
the duodenum, the ileocecal region and the rectum, possess numerous inter-
ceptors; similarly, those of the cardiovascular system are to be found in th

carotid sinus and the aortic arch. Stimulation of the interoceptors gives rise
to a series of reflex reactions which, if they take place in the organ where
the receptor is located, are known as intraorgan interoceptive reflexes.
Such, for example, are the reflexes from the gastric mechanoreceptors to
gastric secretory and motor cells, or from the myocardial receptors to the
myocardium itself, or from the depressor zone of the aortic arch to arterioles throughout the vascular system. In other cases, the interoceptive
reflex may be intrasystemic as, for example, the reflex from the stomach to
the liver; or it may involve a number of physiological systems, such as the
reflexes from the bladder to the heart and blood vessels, from the lungs to
the kidneys, or from the bladder to the intestine, which are thus known as
conjugate, or extrasystemic interoceptive reflexes.

The interoceptive reflex arc may pass through different levels of the peripheral and central nervous systems. These may be local intramural nervous mechanisms, such as Auerbach's plexus or Meissner's plexus in the
gastrointestinal tract (Gorshkova and Kurtsin, 1967b; Kurtsin, 1968c); or
vegetative ganglia, such as the coeliac plexus, the cervical sympathetic
ganglia, the inferior and superior mesenteric ganglia (Bulygin, 1970, 1971),
or the ganglia of the sympathetic trunk. At the level of the spinal cord and
medulla oblongata, they may pass through the spinal autonomic centers and
the vagal nuclei (Grashchenkov, 1965; Rosin, 1965); or they may pass through
the hypothalamus, thalamus, reticular formation of the brain stem (Durinyan,
1965; Ermolaeva, 1969; Kullanda, 1970), hippocampus, limbic system (Kullanda, 1970) or the cerebral cortex (Gal'perin, 1937; Airapet'yants, 1952,
1962; Delov et al., 1961; Petrova, 1966; Kurtsin, 1967a, 1971b; Chernigovskii,
1967; Bulygin, 1970, 1971) (Figure 25).

Interoceptive reflexes vary widely in their form and extent (Rikkl', 1961;
Poltyrev, 1962, 1971). They are usually chain-like, involving numerous nervous structures. Their range of influence is extended still further by the
hormones and mediators, which often play a part in their formation (Kurtsin,
1967a, 1969f, 1971c; Tonkikh, 1968; Pronina, 1969, 1971; Bulygin, 1970, 1971;
Larin et al., 1971; Vunder, 1972).

Detailed studies of interoceptive reflexes have demonstrated the role of
interoceptors in the regulation of digestion, the circulation of the blood,
respiration, urine formation and other autonomic processes (Bykov, 1942;
Heymans and Neil, 1958; Solov'ev, 1959, 1971; Chernigovskii, 1960, 1967;
Rikkl', 1961; Poltyrev, 1962, 1971; Frol'kis et al., 1962; Gorshkova and Kurtsin, 1967c; Suvorov, 1967; Kassil', 1968), as well as of musculo-skeletal
activity (Merkulova, 1959; Bulygin, 1971; Mogendovich and Temkin, 1971).
Moreover, experimental studies of visceral-visceral reflexes have provided an
explanation of the numerous clinical observations of so-called concomitant
or secondary disorders in organs not necessarily belonging to the same
physiological system as the primary lesion. Such combinations of diseases
occur, for example in the liver and the stomach, in the form of hepatitis and
gastric ulcer; in the gallbladder and heart, as cholecystitis, cholelithiasis
and stenocardia [sic] [angina pectoris]; and in the stomach and heart,
as the gastralgic [sic] form of myocardial infarction (Samson, 1962; Teregulov, Mayanskaya, 1962; Gubergrits, 1963; Zaitseva, 1969, 1971; Stepanov, 1970;
Volynskii, 1971).

The course taken by the visceral-visceral reflex depends on the chemical
composition of the interstitial fluid surrounding the receptors, nerves, synapses

and nerve centers. For example, the excitability and conductivity may be modified by the products of digestion of proteins, fats and carbohydrates; b mediators, metabolites or vitamins, or by hormones such as the adrenocor cotropic hormone, thyroxin, follicle-stimulating hormone and hydrocortiso or by catecholamines such as adrenalin and noradrenalin which themselve serve as stimuli for chemoceptors. However, a special role in the implementation of these reflexes belongs to the higher divisions of the CNS and the cerebral cortex in particular, for the rate of production of the reflex a a whole depends on the functional state of the cortex (Bykov and Kurtsin, 1960; Chernigovskii, 1960; Rikkl', 1961; Gorshkova and Kurtsin, 1967; Gas nov, 1970; Balakshina, 1971), as has now been sufficiently demonstrated by experimental physiology. Thus, it has been found that excitation or inhibit of cerebral cortical cells can respectively increase or decrease the magni tude of interoceptive reflexes. Extirpation of the entire cerebral cortex (Asratyan, 1970) or excision of particular areas, such as the premotor and limbic (Gulyaeva, 1962; Gaza, 1965a; Gasanov, 1970), frontal and orbital (Bogach, 1971) areas, as well as temporary dissociation of the cortex by means of neuroplegic (neuroleptic) substances (Suvorov, 1967) or by the exper mental induction of a neurotic state (Kurtsin, 1965e, 1966a, 1967a, 1967b, 1969a, 1971d, and others), significantly modifies the activity of the entire reflex arc including, of course, the peripheral portion of the visceral analyze

The intermediate division of the visceral analyzer consists of conductin pathways along which the impulses from the peripheral part of the analyze reach its central, cortical division. It would appear that spinal (somatic), sympathetic and parasympathetic nerves all serve as afferent conductors c impulses from the visceral interoceptors, but this is not universally ackno ledged. On this question three points of view are expressed in the literatu the conductors being exclusively spinal nerves, or exclusively autonomic nerves, or both. The third view is shared by most authors and it is suppo ed by a good number of experimental findings. Recent histological studies Kolosov's school have incontrovertibly shown that on ganglionic cells of the autonomic nervous system are to be found receptors consisting, in the first place, of sensitive neurons of the spinal ganglia (sensitive somatic cells), a well as of cells of Dogel's type II. Hence, it seems justified to postulate th existence of special sympathosomatic and sympathosympathetic pathways (Kolosov and Milokhin, 1970). Bulygin (1971) and his staff have made most pair taking studies of the interoceptive pathways from the bladder, rectum, stomach and ileocecal region and have concluded that afferent impulses fro these organs travel along autonomic, especially sympathetic nerves, as we as along somatic (spinal) nerves. Recordings of biocurrents from afferent visceral nerves show two types of impulses: rapid, high-voltage and slow, low-voltage. Severance of the preganglionic fibers of the nerves causes im pulses of the first type to disappear, while those of the second type persist It can thus be concluded that the first type of impulse is related to spinal, somatic nerves, and the second type to sympathetic nerves.

The pathways from the receptors in the heart, lungs, stomach, ileocecal region, rectum and bladder have been fairly well studied. These are multi afferent pathways, consisting of both trunk and supplementary routes. The former are direct; the latter indirect, acting mainly in reserve. The dire pathways lead from the viscera to strictly defined segments of the spinal cord; as from the bladder and rectum to the sacrólumbar region or from t stomach to the region of the 2nd—5th thoracic vertebrae. For long stretches the indirect afferent pathways are constituted by the sympathetic nerves and periarterial plexuses and they enter the spinal cord mainly through the posterior roots but partially also through the anterior roots, without keeping to specific segments. Afferent spinal fibers usually pass through autonomic nervous ganglia of the pelvic region, abdominal and thoracic cavities. Within these ganglia the interoceptive excitation is transmitted by special adrenalin-like and choline-like mediators (Bulygin, 1970). The pathways are most complex within the CNS, including the spinal cord, medulla oblongata and subcortical regions and especially in the mesencephalic reticular formation, thalamus, hypothalamus and cerebral cortex (see Chapters 1 and 2). Our knowledge of these pathways is still incomplete. There is no doubt that the visceral impulses arrive in the cortical division of the analyzers, that is, in the limbic, premotor, orbital and other areas, and in the hippocampus, having passed through specific and nonspecific structures of the thalamus and of the reticular formation of the brain stem (Raitses, 1971, and others). In addition to the known supplementary pathways, it has been reported that other, indirect pathways pass through nonspecific structures, intralaminar nuclei and midline nuclei, to the hippocampal-limbic formations and lateral neocortical areas (Sotnichenko, 1971).

Unlike the external analyzers, the central representation of the viscera in the cerebral cortex is not concentrated in any single place but is scattered over the cerebral hemispheres, particularly the premotor, orbital and limbic areas (Figure 26). According to electrophysiological data reported by Chernigovskii (1960, 1967) and by his colleagues, the cortical representation of such autonomic nerves as the vagus, splanchnic, glossopharyngeal, pelvic, pudendal, chordae tympani and superior laryngeal, is narrowly localized, with foci of maximum electrical activity mainly around the sylvian and cingulate gyri. The representations of the splanchnic, mesenteric and pelvic nerves are characterized by the somatotropic location of their cortical projections within the somatosensory areas I and II. The representation of the vagus is distinguished by three projection zones, one of them on the medial surface of the cerebral hemispheres, another within somatosensory area II and the third in the region of the coronary gyrus (Kullanda, 1970). On the other hand, studies of higher nervous activity seem to indicate that the cortical end of the visceral analyzer is diffusely located. These two views regarding the location of the central part of the visceral analyzer have recently shown a tendency to become reconciled, as can be seen from a study of the representation of the vagus (Chernigovskii, 1967). This nerve which serves almost all the organs in the thoracic and abdominal viscera, has a multiple representation in the cortex, including the somatosensory region adjoining the projection zones of the splanchnic nerves. All 18 areas of viscerosensory representation (Chernigovskii, 1967) are located in the anterior part of the cortex; none are to be found in the parietal, occipital or temporal lobes. The cortical nuclei of the visceral analyzer are responsible for the final and most accurate analysis of the stimuli. However, the activity of the cortical end of this analyzer is closely related to that of other nervous formations, particularly the hippocampal and amygdaloid nucleus, caudate nucleus, globus pallidus, septum, thalamus, mesencephalic reticular formation and, of course, the hypothalamus. They exchange a great variety of ascending and descending, horizontal and vertical, diagonal and annular impulse flux (see Chapter 1).

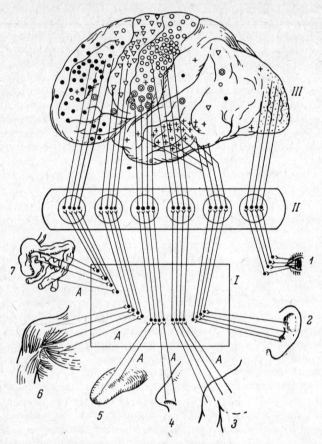

FIGURE 26. Structure of analyzers (after Kurtsin, 1968b):

1—7) receptors (visual, auditory, cutaneous, olfactory, gustatory, motor, visceral); I) region of spinal cord or medulla entered by afferent fibers (A), the impulses then being transmitted to the local neurons whose axons end in the region of the optic thalamus (II); the axons of the optic thalamus nerve cells end in the cerebral cortex (III) which contains the nuclei of the analyzers: visual (stippled), auditory (crosses), cutaneous (circles), smell and taste (double circles), motor (triangles) and visceral (large dots) and their peripheral elements.

The structure of the visceral analyzer has thus become increasingly cle in recent years and it is now known to include not only cortical, but also su cortical representation of visceral activity; its cytoarchitectonics reflectir the analyzer's stereoscopic mode of activity.

It must be agreed that only a part of the interoceptive stimulus required for supplying information to the higher cerebral centers controlling the viscera and for accurate analysis, reaches the cerebral cortex. This part then interacts in a complex manner with the cortical excitatory and inhibitory processes which modify the conditioned reflexes (Gal'perin, 1937; Bykov, 1942; Airapet'yants, 1952, 1971, and others). Apparently the rest of the afferent interoceptive impulses are blocked by afferent stimuli transmitted to the cerebral cortex by somatic structures (Durinyan, 1965; Kullanda, 1970).

However, under certain physiological conditions, such as overdistension of the stomach, rectum, or bladder, the afferent interoceptive impulsation arriving at the cerebral cortex is so abundant that it evokes the sensation that these organs are full. Similarly, in visceral lesions marked by severe pain, such as acute appendicitis, ileus, peptic ulcer, cholecystitis, nephritis, or pleurisy, the afferent interoceptive impulsation entering the cerebral cortex is certainly far greater than is usually the case. At the same time, there is probably continuous supervision on the part of the cerebral cortex over the subcortical analysis of the interoceptive stimuli. The connections between the limbic area of the cerebral cortex and the hypothalamus, on the one hand, and with the phylogenetically younger formations of the anterior part of the cerebral hemispheres, on the other, enable the higher autonomic centers in the anterior part of the cortex to correct the integrative activity of the hypothalamus and other subcortical formations. The overlapping of somatovisceral functions in the limbic system also permits the efferent somatic structures to participate in these responses. Corticofugal discharges of the giant pyramidal cells of layer V of the cerebral cortex may constitute the initial efferent link in such combined responses (Kullanda, 1970).

Projection areas of visceral nerves are also found in the cerebellar cortex (Bratus', 1969; Kullanda, 1970). At first thought, the presence of interoceptive connections in the cerebellum may seem surprising, nevertheless there also exists an autonomic representation in the motor areas of the cerebral cortex. The autonomic activities represented in the cortical motor analyzer and cerebellum are mainly those concerned with muscular activity and with the closely-related regulation of tissue metabolism. All this lends credence to Chernigovskii's (1960) concept of the cerebellum as a component of the interoceptive analyzer. That cerebellar perception of interoceptive impulses does not duplicate the activity of the cerebral cortex, is attested to by the following findings: a) different pathways are used to conduct the signals to these two parts of the brain; the main pathways to the cerebellum being located in the anterior quadrant and anterolateral spinal tracts, but in the posterior part of the spinal cord on the way to the cerebral cortex; b) different types of fibers conduct the interoceptive impulses in each case: fine fibers of the A-Δ type pass to the cerebellum, while fibers of the A-β type go to the cerebral cortex; c) different periods of subnormal excitability (relative refractoriness) are elicited in response to testing stimuli, the period being more prolonged in the case of the cerebellar cortex. Moreover, the limiting frequency of reproducible stimuli is always lower for the cerebellum, at 4 to 5 per second, than for the cerebral cortex, for which it is 7 to 8 per second.

The differences between the cerebellar and the cerebral cortex with respect to interoceptive impulses can be explained by the fact that the activizing influence of the reticular formation differs at different levels of the central nervous system (Narikashvili, 1965). Nevertheless, both types of cortex function concurrently in the reception and processing of interoceptive information. This is confirmed by the finding that changes of evoked potentials occur in both when the activity of one alone is intensified by strychnine (Bratus', 1969).

The view that the visceral analyzer is connected with efferent mechanism of the cerebral cortex also requires to be revised. In studies of cerebral function over almost a century, experimental physiology has accumulated a body of findings which unequivocally demonstrates that stimulation of well-defined zones of the cerebral cortex produces corresponding autonomic effects. Modern microelectrode techniques have now succeeded in pinpointing the loci in the visceral analyzer area which produces the strongest autonomic effects when stimulated (Chernigovskii, 1967).

Hence, the visceral analyzer may be assumed to constitute one of the major components of a highly complex, neurodynamic afferent-efferent cerebral system.

Yet another aspect requires to be mentioned in discussing the role and significance of the visceral analyzer in the integrative activity of the central nervous system. This is the theory of reverse afferentation which was advanced by Pavlov and was already confirmed by Anokhin in 1935. It has been widely employed in cybernetics as applied to higher nervous activity and corticovisceral relationships. The receptors of any effector involved in the response to stimulation of a receptor field do not remain indifferent. As the organ begins to function, changes occur in the nature and rate of cellular metabolism: the content of oxygen and carbon dioxide, ions and hormones, metabolites and trace elements in the tissues at rest become altered, the tissue temperature usually rises and there are changes in osmotic pressure and certain other physicochemical and biological parameters. All these changes stimulate the baroreceptors, chemoreceptors, thermoreceptors and osmoreceptors of the activated organ itself.

Thus, the active organ itself becomes a source of intense interoceptive stimuli which inform the centers governing visceral activity of changes in the physiological state of the organ and of the mode and degree of its activity. Ordinary information from the internal organs is mainly transmitted along slow-conducting systems consisting of fibers of the $A(\gamma, \Delta)$ and C types with a conduction rate of 30 to 15 m/sec and partly along a rapid-conducting system. It reaches the reticular formation and limbic system, arriving, in other words, at the divisions whose task is the continuous regulation of visceral activity. Urgent information apparently proceeds along fibers of the $A\beta$ type with a rapid rate of conduction of 70 m/sec (Kullanda, 1970). Reaching the cortical projection zones, these signals stimulate the formation of trigger, regulatory and corrective influences on the viscera. As a result of this feedback, the activity of the organ is correlated as far as possible with the activities and condition of all the other organs and systems of the body.

Last, but not least, stimulation of the receptors of a viscus, such as the esophagus, stomach, intestine, gallbladder, or urinary bladder, simultaneously with a stimulus evoking an innate reaction, such as salivation, is liable to result in the establishment of an interoceptive conditioned reflex, according to the principle of temporary connection and this may remain consolidated for a prolonged period. The discovery of interoceptive conditioned reflexes (Bykov et al., 1928) was of fundamental importance. Since then numerous studies have been carried out not only on the unconditioned interoceptive reflexes but even more on the conditioned reflexes of this kind; the characteristics and properties, their interaction with exteroceptive reflexes and the significance of interoceptive stimuli in the formation of such physiological manifestations as the sensations of thirst and satiety, hunger and appetite and recovery from illness.

With this discovery the relationship of interoception to the corticalization of autonomic activity came to be viewed in quite a new light and in a broader and deeper context. The two problems indeed became inseparably linked and assumed a central position in the theory of corticovisceral relationships. It was quite evident that the cerebral cortex is also greatly influenced by the nervous impulses arising in the receptors of the viscera, vessels and endocrine glands. These impulses reach the cerebral cortex via the nerves and provide the nerve centers governing autonomic activity with information regarding the state and performance of the internal structures. This information is then compared with that which the cerebral centers receive from the external environment. Only after a most complicated and detailed analysis of both these sources of information is that cortical response produced which determines not only the subsequent performance of the internal organ from which the information was received, but also the general behavior of the body as a whole.

The discovery of interoceptive conditioned reflexes has led to a reappraisal of the relationships between the cerebral cortex and all the internal organs and systems of the body (Bykov, 1942; Bykov and Kurtsin, 1960, 1966a). An understanding of the part played by interoceptive information, not only in higher nervous activity (Gal'perin, 1937; Bykov, 1942; Airapet'yants, 1952, 1971) but also in the production of emotional manifestations (Gellhorn and Loofbourrow, 1963; Anokhin, 1964; Sudakov, 1970; Badikov, 1971), has helped to resolve a number of fundamental problems of corticovisceral pathology.

THE INTEROCEPTIVE MECHANISMS OF CORTICOVISCERAL DISTURBANCES

Clinical observations suggest that certain disorders of the viscera and blood vessels may be caused by exteroceptive damage to the cortical mechanisms governing autonomic activity. Corticovisceral pathology of this kind may manifest itself in the form of disorders of function, such as cardiac and gastric neuroses, biliary and gastrointestinal dyskinesia, bronchial asthma and stenocardia [sic] [angina pectoris], or secretory disorders of the digestive glands, but it may even give rise to structural lesions, such as gastric or duodenal ulcer, myocardial infarction, endarteritis or ulcerative colitis. Studies in experimental physiology have endorsed these clinical observations. Moreover, they are daily providing fresh findings which convincingly show that overtaxing the strength and mobility of the nervous processes in the cerebral cortex and subcortical formations, by means of extra powerful stimuli or conflicting excitatory and inhibitory stimuli, produces a derangement of higher nervous activity (neurosis), with the development of a chronic disturbance of visceral activity. On the other hand, clinical medicine has long shown that in man disorders of higher nervous activity may occur on the basis of a primary pathological process in the internal organs, particularly inflammation of the stomach or rectum, or the development of a neoplastic condition in these organs.

Of recent years, the significance of the somatic factor in the etiology of neurosis and psychosis has repeatedly been emphasized by neuropathologist and psychiatrists. Moreover, such secondary disorders of higher cerebral activity are the source of further pathological manifestations, this time in the viscera. Consequently, clinical observations of this kind require separate consideration and discussion from the point of view of the corticovisceral theory. In the first place, the question arises as to whether it is possible t create an experimental model of a corticovisceral disease. Recent laboratory experiments show that this, in fact, can be done. It has been firmly established that local pathological processes in internal organs are often accompanied by neurotic changes in higher nervous activity as, for example, in experimental cholecystitis (Gaza, 1957; Budylin and Zinchenko, 1969), proctit: (Andreeva and Kurtsin, 1958), gastritis (Kurtsin et al., 1965; Raitses, 1966) enteritis and pneumonia (Budylin, 1969). The phenomenon can also be observed when dogs with an established stereotype of conditioned salivary reflexes are subjected to various surgical procedures on the intestine (appendectomy), stomach (resection from one- to two-thirds), or on the heart (experimental aortic insufficiency), or to long-term stimulation of a nerve or of a spinal root (Budylin, 1969, 1970).

However, neither experimental physiology, nor clinical practice has revealed the actual mechanism of development of cortical disorders by this approach. Indeed, it has been claimed that the disturbances of higher nervous activity in cholecystitis, gastritis, proctitis and other so-called local pathological processes are due to hormonal changes and toxic effects mediated by the blood, in other words, to humoral factors (Horvath et al., 1966 Poltyrev, 1971). Only through intensive studies of interoception has sufficient factual evidence been produced to unequivocally demonstrate that disturbances of higher nervous activity can be caused by interoceptive, that is by purely nervous factors. In our laboratory an experimental model of neu rosis was created in dogs by producing a conflict in the cerebral cortex between positive and inhibitory conditioned interoceptive impulses; for exampl from the stomach (Gulyaeva, 1956), gallbladder (Gaza, 1965a), or urinary bladder (Balakshina, 1954). The resultant disturbances of higher nervous activity, followed by disturbances of autonomic activity, differed but little from those occurring in experimental corticovisceral disorders produced b external environmental factors (Figure 27). In both cases, the nature and duration of the corticovisceral disturbances are determined by the type of nervous system concerned and by the degree of participation of the differen cortical and subcortical structures, rather than by the actual nature of the stimulus (Kurtsin, 1960; Gorshkova and Kurtsin, 1967b; Suvorov, 1967, 1971)

It would thus appear that a significant part in the production of disturbanc of higher nervous activity occurring in the presence of a local pathological process in an internal organ may be played by the fact that the interoceptiv stimulus shifts from the organ to the cerebral centers. The changes in hig er nervous activity may result from either unconditioned-reflex or conditioned-reflex stimulation. In some cases, however, interoceptive impulsati does not initiate the corticovisceral disturbances, but acts as a factor sustaining the development of the pathological process. This was the case in Rybnikova's experiments on dogs. Long-term electrical stimulation of area

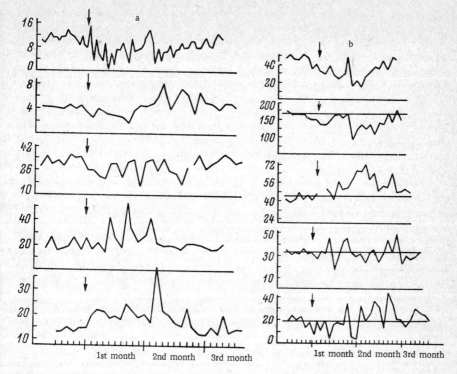

FIGURE 27. Changes in higher nervous activity and secretion of digestive juices in dogs in experimental neuroses produced by exteroceptive (a) and interoceptive (b) factors (after Kurtsin, 1960).

From above down: a) conditioned reflexes (drops of saliva); secretion of gastric juice, bile, pancreatic and intestinal juices (ml); b) conditioned reflexes, unconditioned reflexes (scale divisions), secretion of gastric juice, bile and pancreatic juice (ml). Arrows indicate conflict.

of the premotor area of the cerebral cortex resulted in inhibition of glucose and water absorption in an isolated loop of small intestine. This constituted the first stage of a disturbance of absorption initiated by the cerebral cortex. The electrical stimulation of the cerebral cortex, which had continued for many months, was then stopped and the electrodes were removed from the brain by a further operation. The dogs showed no change in their behavior or in autonomic activity, except for intestinal absorption which remained abnormal. The absorption of both glucose and water diminished markedly, although the absorption of glucose showed the greatest change, in contrast to the normal state in which the reverse relationship obtains. This represented the second stage of the pathological process, and now the factor maintaining the pathological state, both at the center and at the periphery, was the interoceptive impulsation from the internal organ caused by the presence of a rubber tube in the intestinal loop during the period of the experiment.

This condition of the intestinal villi persisted for years, rather than months, and did not respond to treatment with drugs. Yet, atropinization of the intestinal loop before the experiment was sufficient to guarantee that the absorption of glucose and water remained normal. The same result was obtained after preliminary irrigation of the intestinal mucosa with a solution of novocaine. Apparently, a bilateral connection became established and consolidated between premotor area 6 of the cerebral cortex and the intestine, which maintained the pathological condition of both the cerebral centers and the intestinal villi. Some part in the development of this condition might be due to increased reactivity of the receptor apparatus of the intestine and cerebral centers, of the type which Vvedenskii has called hysteriosis and which arises when an organ is subjected to long-term stimulation (Safarov, 1965). The return to normal took place when the vicious circle was broken at the organ level, by blocking the efferent and afferent impulses, respectively, in each case (Kurtsin, 1964). Normal absorption by the intestine also took place when the interoceptive impulses were centrally blocked, at the subcortical level, by the dissociative effect of chlorpromazine on the adrenergic structures of the reticular formation (Rybnikova, 1966).

However, the significance of pathological interoceptive impulsation is not limited to its ability, alone or together with hormones, to alter higher cerebral activity and to consolidate pathological corticovisceral connections. The appearance of a pathological process in an internal organ is usually associated with disorders of other organs (Volynskii, 1971). Thus, for example, gastric ulcer is associated with disorders of function in the liver, pancreas, intestine, heart, blood vessels and many other organs. Such findings have been obtained in the laboratories of Poltyrev (1962, 1971) and of Raitses (1966) and also in our own. Dogs with experimentally produced gastric ulcers developed disorders of secretion not only of the stomach but also of the pancreas (Chumburidze, 1970) and biliary secretion by the liver was also affected. Dogs with experimental proctitis developed a prolonged disturbance of the external secretion of the pancreas and of gastric juice (Andreeva and Kurtsin, 1958). In both cases the "associated" disorders of the organs were accompanied by profound changes in higher nervous activity.

Thus, the etiology of such conditions is not necessarily limited to a reflex effect from the pathologically affected organ (visceral-visceral reflex), or to a toxic, hormonal effect transmitted humorally from blood to lymph, but may also include the influence of the higher divisions of the central nervous system, that is of cortical-subcortical mechanisms. Such a corticovisceral origin has been proposed for dyskinesia of the biliary system of the liver (Gorshkova and Kurtsin, 1967b). According to this theory, the dyskinesia is not due to the psychogenic injury alone. It is also thought to result from a conflict between processes of excitation and inhibition in the cerebral cortex associated with interoceptive signals, such as arise, for example, from the different parts of the gastrointestinal tract.

This has been corroborated by studies made in our laboratory. The receptors of an organ which is the site of a pathological process undergo a series of morphological changes depending on the degree of development of the process. These changes range from the stage of irritation demonstrated by thickening of the nerve fibers with increased argentophil properties, to the stage of irreversible structural alteration, in the form of fragmentation and lysis of the nervous elements, as is found, for example, in gastric ulcer (Shvalev et al., 1963). Thus, all or part of the internal organ comes to show structural changes (Kurtsin, 1960). The development of a pathological process in an organ markedly and for a prolonged period alters the nature of the afferent impulsation in the nervous pathways which connect the organ with the cerebral centers. Thus, in experimental gastritis the biopotentials in the gastric nerves are diminished, or even disappear and later their magnitude and frequency increase, as is the case in acute gastritis (Figure 28). Alternatively, their magnitude and frequency may increase at the beginning and then decrease or even disappear, as in experimental gastric ulcer (Yuldasheva, 1966).

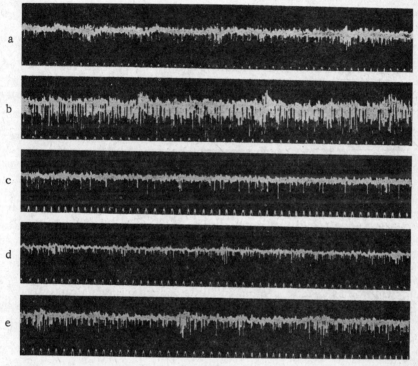

FIGURE 28. Afferent impulsation in gastric branches of the vagus nerve in a tomcat. In the normal state (a), in different stages of acute gastritis (b—d) and in convalescence (e) (after Zakharzhevskii and Ermolaeva, 1965).

Time mark, 0.2 sec

The bioelectric activity is also modified in subcortical nervous structures, such as the thalamus, hypothalamus, reticular formation and amygdaloid nucleus, as well as in the limbic, sensorimotor and other areas of the cerebral cortex, by the experimental induction of local ulceration in the stomach (Milenov, 1966). The same phenomenon had previously been observed by Raitses (1966) in dogs with experimental gastritis, proctitis and gastric ulcer induced by atophan [cinchopen]. He found that the bioelectrical activity of the cerebral cortex, spinal centers and thalamic and hypothalamic nuclei in these animals showed either an increase or a decrease. This change in the bioelectrical activity of the cerebral cortex became the dominant type, to which the reactions of other cerebral centers to interoceptive stimuli were subordinated.

However, alterations in the frequency and magnitude of the afferent impulsation from the diseased organ do not constitute the only factor of importance. A significant part seems to be played by the dissociation of activity of various receptors in the pathologically altered organ. Most important of all seems to be the reactivity of the cortex itself and of the subcortical neural structures to the chronic flow of pathological information (Budylin, 1969, 1970). Such a state of excitation in an organ may result in a great variety of reflex responses; they may be markedly intensified, or markedly attenuated or even absent. It is also possible to envisage a state in which one part of an organ is pathologically altered, while the rest remains normal. Such a model has been produced in cats by our colleague, Dzhagiika. An inflamed part of the spleen was isolated from the rest and both parts were then perfused with an irritant fluid. Stimulation of the chemoreceptors of the healthy part evoked normal blood pressure and respiratory reflex responses, whereas identical stimulation of the chemoreceptors in the inflamed area gave rise to a response which was initially increased but then either disappeared or became markedly attenuated. Oscillography performed by Suplyakov, another colleague of ours, showed that the impulsation in the nerve fibers serving the inflamed lobe increased in magnitude and frequency in the initial phase of the condition, in contrast to the normal impulsation in the fibers leading to the intact lobe. A similar phenomenon was observed by Zakharzhevskii and Ermolaeva in cats with experimentally induced inflammation of a loop of the small intestine. The spontaneous impulsation from the loop, as recorded from the greater splanchnic nerve, showed a rise in frequency from between 60 and 100 to between 120 and 220 per second and an increase in amplitude from between 40 to 80 to between 70 and 130 μV. The leads of action potentials from the intestinal branches of a noninflamed loop of intestine did not show any appreciable changes in spontaneous impulsation.

A change in afferent impulsation, particularly an increase in intensity, is liable to give rise to dominant foci of excitation and inhibition (Ukhtomskii, 1966), which may lead to prolonged disturbances of normal activity in the cerebral cortex and internal systems. A successful model of such pathological dominance has been created by Levshunova (1969). A local inflammation was produced in the sciatic nerve, which gave rise to its prolonged stimulation, resulting in chronic inhibition of higher nervous activity and dystrophic somatic changes. Nikolaeva and Denisova (1969) produced a pathological dominant by interoceptive means. Equally important are long-term experiments on dogs with a Pavlov pouch, in which a stereotype of conditioned interoceptive and exteroceptive reflexes had been established. In some of these dogs it was found that when interoceptive conditioned reflexes from the lesser curvature were involved in the conflict situation, very severe disturbances ensued in the secretory activity of the glands of this part of the stomach. However, when the same type of reflexes from the greater curvature was involved, the secretory disturbances were most severe, not in the lesser but in the greater curvature (Gulyaeva, 1956; Kurtsin, 1967a, 1971b). A cortical conflict involving simultaneous interoceptive impulsation from the lesser and greater curvatures produced a neurotic state with pronounced secretory disturbances in both curvatures.

Such circumstances apparently set up a vicious circle, not only in the cortical-subcortical integrating system, but even between cerebral centers and internal organs or between cerebral centers and endocrine glands, particularly the pituitary and adrenals which are directly involved in the general adaptation syndrome. In our opinion, the formation of a vicious circle of this kind is not due solely to the fact that the increase in efferent impulsation whips the cells of the organ into excessive activity and forces the blood vessels into providing an abnormally great blood supply. It must also be attributed to the afferent impulsation which proceeds from the pathologically altered organ to the cerebral centers and exacerbates their abnormal state. Sometimes there is attenuation or even total suspension of the feedback from the cerebral centers to the internal organs and the blood vessels.

Thus, a local pathological process in an internal organ may either be limited to a local association with a particular group of cerebral centers, maintained by the conditioned-reflex mechanism or it may involve many centers connected with many internal organs, producing a diffuse disease picture. If the impulsation from the organ is stronger or weaker than normal, or is absent, the state of activity of the cerebral centers will be correspondingly altered and, as a result, the efferent impulsation proceeding from the centers to the pathologically altered organ also becomes abnormal. Thus, an experimentally produced gastric ulcer modifies both the afferent and efferent impulsation, as recorded oscillographically, the vagus innervation to the stomach showing a significant increase in both magnitude and frequency (Yuldasheva, 1966). Participation of the cerebral cortex is also demonstrated by the fact that suitable doses of chloral hydrate or alcohol prevent induction of the neurosis, despite the fact that pathological impulses from the abdominal organs are arriving in the brain (Suvorov, 1967, 1971).

The results of our experiments on dogs with injury to part of the limbic and premotor areas of the cerebral cortex (Gaza, 1962, 1965a; Gulyaeva, 1962, 1965; Bakhtadze, 1967) tend to show that these areas participate in the mechanism of viscerocortical disorders. However, they are not the only part of the brain involved, since some weeks or months after their excision or destruction the interoceptive conditioned reflexes are restored and new reflexes can be established. The disturbances of higher nervous activity and of visceral activity also disappear. Moreover, the corticovisceral disturbances produced in these dogs when the interoceptive conditioned reflexes become involved in the conflict of cortical processes are of the same nature and duration as when the limbic and premotor areas of the cerebral cortex are intact (Gaza, 1965a; Gulyaeva, 1966).

Some information has also been obtained regarding the part played by the reticular formation. In dogs chlorpromazine was found to prevent neurosis and corticovisceral disturbances after a conflict situation involving interoceptive conditioned reflexes from the gallbladder (Gaza, 1965a), Pavlov pouch (Gulyaeva, 1965), or intact stomach (Suvorov, 1967). This drug also prevents the occurrence of pathological dominance in the cerebral cortex on long-term stimulation of a nerve and soon abolishes any dominance which has already arisen (Levshunova, 1969). Besides the reticular formation, the hypothalamus also plays a significant part in the production of viscerocortical pathology (Budylin, 1970; Chereshnev, 1971; Shvalev, 1971).

Thus, viscerocortical pathology is determined by a neurohormonal mechanism, in which the decisive part is played by changes in the interoceptive impulsation. Viscerocortical pathology must, however, be regarded as a particular aspect of corticovisceral pathology.

Chapter 9

AUTONOMIC RESONANCE IN PSYCHOGENIC STRESS:
POSSIBLE MECHANISMS OF ITS ORIGIN AND THE
PROBLEM OF SELECTIVE DAMAGE TO AN
INTERNAL ORGAN

In the experimental study of corticovisceral pathology, the question conti
nually recurs as to why neurotic disturbances of the cortical regulatory
mechanism should sometimes give rise to hyperactivity in an internal organ
and sometimes to hypoactivity. Clinically this has long been recognized, a
number of internal conditions being classified according to the predominance of
one form or the other. Thus, a differentiation is made between hypersecretion and hyposecretion in such conditions as hyperacidic and hypoacidic gastritis; between gastrointestinal and biliary hyperkinesia and hypokinesia;
between spastic and atonic enteritis and colitis; vegetative cardiac neurosis
sometimes with tachycardia and sometimes with bradycardia; vascular
hypertension and hypotension; hyperglycemia and hypoglycemia; and hyperthyroidism and hypothyroidism. Unsuccessful attempts have been made to
explain the origin of such functional deviations on the basis of differences in
the physiology or pathology of the affected organs, or of changes in the excitability of the parasympathetic and sympathetic nervous systems leading t
vagotonia or sympathicotonia, dystonia or vegetosis and such views have
even found their way into modern textbooks of internal medicine. From our
own experimental studies on the subject, it would seem rather that the hyper
functional and hypofunctional forms of vegetative disorders brought about by
corticovisceral disorders primarily reflect the functional state of the higher
divisions of the central nervous system. In brief, it is suggested that
they are brought about by two pathophysiological mechanisms: parabiotic
and subordinative.

THE ROLE OF THE PARABIOTIC AND SUBORDINATIVE
MECHANISMS IN PRODUCING PATHOLOGICAL
CHANGES IN AN ORGAN IN NEUROSIS

The parabiotic mechanism is a postulate of the theory of parabiosis,
devised by Vvedenskii (1901) on the basis of experiments on nerve-muscle
preparations, with regard to the lower cortical centers and later applied by
the Pavlov school to the cells of the cerebral cortex. This theory has repeatedly been utilized by physiologists and clinicians in the diagnosis and
treatment of neurological and internal diseases (Chernogorov, 1956). Seriou
attempts have been made to explain the nature of different forms of secretor

disorders of the stomach, liver and pancreas (Razenkov, 1948; Linar, 1968) by a parabiotic state of the actual glandular apparatus. Razenkov (1948) who considered that the functional state of the substrate, that is, of the viscus itself plays an important part in its response to stimuli, has stated that in the case of the digestive glands the response to stimuli is markedly altered by metabolites such as urea, histamine, insulin or adrenalin, by the products of digestion: extracts, peptone, or amino acids, or by the administration of foreign substances, including sodium salicylate, chloral hydrate, sodium bromide, thyroidin and pituitrin. Reactivity may, for example, be high with small doses or low with large doses of these substances, thus giving rise to the hyperfunctional or hypofunctional form of a disorder.

On the basis of electrophysiological investigations, it has recently been asserted that "the cells of very different tissues (muscular, connective and epithelial) may react to a variety of external agents with gradual changes in the cell potentials, which develop relatively slowly. The features of this cell reaction resemble the successive stages of development of the parabiotic process as established by Vvedenskii's galvanometric experiments" (Latmanizova, 1965, p. 79). At the same time, Razenkov has admitted that the functional state of the glands may also be modified by the nervous system. According to him, general neurohumoral regulation is reciprocally related to the substrate controlled, whether organ, tissue or cell. His laboratory has produced numerous experimental findings to support this assumption, for example, the changes which occur in higher nervous activity in animals on a high protein or high carbohydrate diet, or with a "satiated" or "hungry" state of the blood.

The state of parabiosis may possibly occur in any excitable tissue and is not necessarily confined to nervous tissue. This seems to be demonstrated by the theory of paranecrosis (Nasonov, 1959). However, in man and in animals with a highly developed nervous system it is doubtful whether it is possible to produce a parabiotic state in secretory cells, for example, so long as the nervous system is functioning normally and controlling their condition and activity. Pavlov and his associates, who often encountered parabiotic phenomena in their experiments on conditioned salivary reflexes, never considered them as a parabiotic state of the salivary gland cells, but always as a parabiotic state of cerebral cortical neurons, manifested by the quantity of conditioned-reflex saliva. It would thus seem more correct to regard such alterations in the functional state and activity of a parenchymatous cell as being primarily due to changes in the central nervous influence on its activity and biochemical processes.

The subject has already been discussed in the literature from this point of view (Bykov and Kurtsin, 1948, 1960, 1966a; Busalov, 1958). Changes in gastric secretion have been used to indicate the development of various kinds of internal inhibition in the cerebral cortex (differential, conditioned, extinguishing and retarding), which the Pavlov school usually determined from the salivary reaction. According to Linar (1968), who has produced an excellent monograph on acid production in the normal and pathological stomach, "parabiosis can only develop when two kinds of stimuli are present, a parabiotic (humoral) stimulus which produces a non-wavelike impulse and which itself then forms the background for a stimulus producing a wave of excitation. Characteristic of the non-wavelike excitation is the fact that its effects depend on the rhythm of the waves of nervous impulses reaching the functional substrate along a centrifugal nerve, as well as on the rhythm of the wave of excitation which arises in the functional substrate itself in response to these nervous influences" (p. 318).

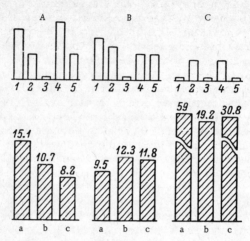

FIGURE 29. Changes in higher nervous activity and pancreatic secretion in a dog following a conflict (after Kurtsin, 1953b).

Top — magnitude of conditioned reflexes (in drops of saliva): 1, 4) bell (positive); 2, 5) M-120 (positive); 3) M-60 (inhibitory). Bottom — quantity of pancreatic secretion (ml) in 4 hr on eating bread (a), meat (b), milk (c). A) initial level; B) 10 days later; C) two months after conflict.

In our studies on dogs in whom various corticovisceral disorders had been experimentally induced, we consistently observed that the occurrence of hypnotic phases in cerebral cortical activity, as determined from the conditioned salivary reflexes, was accompanied by similar phases in pancreatic secretion. Sometimes the quantity of secretion in response to strong (meat) and weak (milk) stimuli was the same (equalization phase), sometimes it was large in response to a weak stimulus, but small in response to a strong stimulus (paradoxical phase) (Figure 29); while at other times the cells did not react to either the strong or the weak stimuli (inhibitory phase). This was particularly noticeable with regard to the activity of the gastric secretory cells (Kurtsin, 1952), for which five types of secretory activity could be distinguished, according to precise, quantitative and qualitative characteristics: normal, excitable, inert, asthenic and inhibited. This has been confirmed in human subjects from whom pure gastric juice was obtained by means of a double stomach tube made of rubber and designed by Kurtsin and Slupskii, using the method described by Bykov and Kurtsin (Kurtsin, 1953; Baladzhaeva, 1968; Zvorykin, 1968; Ibragimova, 1968). Our ideas concerning the corticovisceral origin of this condition (Bykov and Kurtsin, 1948, 1949, 1954, 1966a) are based largely on findings of this kind obtained in patients suffering from peptic ulcer. The occurrence of pathological types of secretory activity in other digestive disorders has been utilized clinically in differential diagnosis and in the evaluation of different therapeutic methods (Zhgenti,1956; Samson,1962; Shilov, 1962; Gurskaya, 1964; Vilyavin and Nazarenko, 1966; Baladzhaeva, 1968; Zvorykin, 1968; Ibragimova, 1958). By the same method five types of gastric motility have also been demonstrated (Kurtsin, 1952; Baladzhaeva, 1968), showing that the parabiotic state of the cerebral centers is also reflected in the condition of the smooth muscle of the viscera during the development of a corticovisceral disorder.

Such resonance of the parabiotic state of the brain cells has also been observed by our colleagues with regard to vascular tone. Thus, in the course of a neurosis in dogs, Suvorov (1967) observed that a positive conditioned stimulus produced marked vasoconstriction (the paradoxical phase) before the usual prolonged vasodilatory effect. In her studies, on neurotic dogs, of reflexes from the mechanoreceptors, chemoreceptors and thermoreceptors of the uterine-horn and ileocecal mucosa to the limb vessels, Bokeriya noted changes in the conditioned and even in the unconditioned vascular reflexes. For several days she witnessed the development of the inhibitory, paradoxical and other phases. The occurrence in dogs of various types of cardiovascular disorder in experimental neurosis has also been determined in our laboratory by Zakharzhevskii (1966a, 1966b), using special transducers implanted in the coronary vessels to record the changes in the circulation rate. He noted that at certain stages of development of the neurosis, reflex (feeding) and humoral (adrenalin, pituitrin) stimuli reduced the myocardial blood supply instead of increasing it, as is normally the case. Previously, Pshonik (1952), using a plethysmograph, had detected various disturbances of the vasomotor centers in animals with experimental angioneurosis, including the occurrence of the paradoxical state, when the conditioned-unconditioned stimulus produced dilatation of the vessels instead of constriction (Figure 30). Similar vascular manifestations have been observed by many authors in human subjects with hypertension or peptic ulcer, as well as in neurasthenia and other neuroses. It would thus appear that the functional state of the cells of the viscera and the blood vessels is dependent on that of the cells of the cerebral cortex and of the subcortical neural structures. Moreover, a parabiotic condition of these nerve cells may be reflected in the activity of the cells of the viscera and blood vessels. If this is so, it must be concluded that the parabiotic mechanism plays an important role in the production of various forms of autonomic disorder.

The concept of a subordinative mechanism underlying the development of hyper- and hypoactivity in the viscera and blood vessels is based on certain tenets of Pavlov's theory of higher nervous activity and in the first place on the principles of interaction of the processes of excitation and inhibition, which he discovered. The irradiation, concentration and reciprocal induction (positive and negative, parallel and consecutive) of these processes are now known to be responsible for the varied patterns of cortical activity. Moreover, highly complex relationships also exist between the cerebral cortex and those subcortical centers directly involved in the visceral innervation (see Chapter 2). Thus the subcortical formations undergo negative induction (their activity is inhibited) when the cortex is active and positive induction (their excitability and tone are increased) when the inhibitory processes in the cerebral cortex are strengthened, as when cortical activity is weakened, or when transmarginal inhibition develops. In neurosis and various forms of

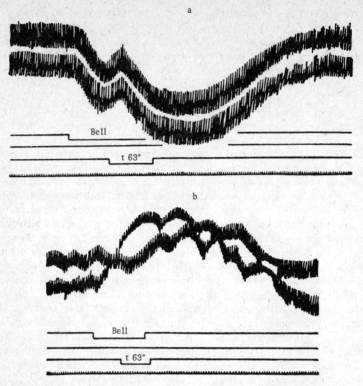

FIGURE 30. Inversion of the vascular reaction to conditioned and unconditioned stimuli in human neurosis (after Pshonik, 1952):

a) vasoconstrictor conditioned reflex to combination of bell + pain (water at 63°C);
b) paradoxical vascular reaction to the same stimuli. From above down: plethysmogram of left arm, plethysmogram of right arm, conditioned stimulus mark, base line, unconditioned stimulus mark, time mark in sec.

corticovisceral pathology, the integration of the processes of excitation and inhibition becomes inert and sluggish, so that the phenomena arising in the brain appear as in a slow-motion film.

My colleagues have made a number of studies on this subject. In experiments on dogs, Frolov, Golovskii and Gulyaeva have shown that the incidence and duration of gastric hyper- and hypoactivity are often clearly determined by the state of activity of the cerebral cortex and subcortex in promoting either irradiation of the excitation and inhibition, or else their reciprocal induction (Figure 31). The effect of cortical-subcortical relationships was also very marked in Sung Ling's studies of disturbances of intestinal secretion in experimental neurosis. The changes in the nature of the cortical-subcortical relationships were found to follow a definite sequence. During the period of derangement of higher nervous activity the cortex showed increased excitation while the subcortex showed increased inhibition, that is the phenomenon of negative induction. Then, the cortex also entered a state

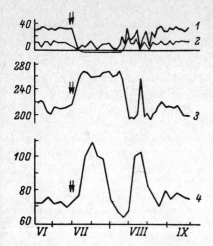

FIGURE 31. Correlation between higher nervous activity and gastric secretion in a dog with experimental neurosis (after Kurtsin, 1959):

1) conditioned alimentary reflex; 2) conditioned differentiation reflex; 3) unconditioned alimentary reflex (scale divisions); 4) gastric juice (ml). Arrows — days on which conflict took place; Roman numerals — months.

of increased inhibition which irradiated into the subcortex, followed by a positive subcortical induction in the latter. Two months after the psychogenic trauma, when higher nervous activity began to return to normal, the cortical inhibition was supplanted by excitation which irradiated into the subcortical centers. It was these developments which produced the wavelike pattern of higher nervous activity which determined whether the pathological manifestations took the form of intestinal hypo- or hyperactivity.

In a dog Rybnikova has studied the intestinal absorption of glucose and water during neurosis. It was found that as the magnitude of the positive conditioned reflexes diminished from 49 to 35 scale divisions, the unconditioned reflex salivation fell from 970 to 602 divisions and the intestinal absorption of glucose from 80% to 40%, showing that the inhibition was being irradiated from the cortex into the subcortex. When the magnitude of the conditioned reflexes increased from 35 to 64 scale divisions, while the unconditioned salivary reflexes remained at the previous low level of 602, the percentage of glucose absorbed by the intestine remained low (60%), that is, there was negative induction in the subcortex. In both cases the intestine displayed hypoactivity in its ability to absorb glucose. In another dog, the neurosis was marked by a predominance of excitation which again developed in two stages: first, the sum of positive conditioned reflexes increased from 74 to 123 scale divisions, together with an increase in unconditioned salivation from 374 to 400 scale divisions and the absorption of intestinal glucose increased from 50% to 80%, demonstrating that the inhibitory process was being irradiated from the cortex into the subcortex. The conditioned reflexes then fell to 63 divisions, the unconditioned reflexes rose above the initial value (427 divisions) and the intestinal absorption of glucose remained high at 60%, due to positive induction of the subcortex. In both cases the disorder took the form of hyperactivity of intestinal absorption.

Such a pattern was also noted in Skorik's studies of vascular tone in dogs with disturbances of higher nervous activity due to a conflict between interoceptive conditioned reflexes, or between interoceptive and exteroceptive conditioned reflexes. The normal sum of positive,-conditioned and unconditioned reflexes was 40 to 50 and 50 to 70 scale divisions for each experiment, while the blood pressure was 130 to 140 mm Hg, with a fluctuation of not more than 10 mm Hg. These indices fell to 30 and 45 scale divisions and 115 mm Hg, respectively, on the 9th day of the neurosis: a sign that the inhibition had irradiated from the cortex into the subcortex, thus lowering the blood pressure. By the 15th day after the conflict, the conditioned reflexes had risen to 65 divisions, the unconditioned to 60 divisions and the blood pressure to 165 mm Hg, showing that the excitation had now irradiated from the cortex into the subcortical centers, increasing the blood pressure.

In other cases, the activity was modified by the phenomena of positive and negative induction. Reciprocal induction in neurosis may also take place between the different parts of the subcortical centers which are involved in the regulation of digestive activity or of the blood circulation, for example. Consequently, the same complex pattern usually produced in the cerebral cortex by the interplay of excitation and inhibition may exist in the subcortical neural structures, thus accounting for the differences in the reactions of individual organs belonging to the same or different functional systems. Moreover, this dependence of the different forms of functional disorder of an internal organ on the functional state of the higher divisions of the central nervous system may manifest itself not only in reflex stimuli but also in humoral effects as, for example, in hormonal action (Emel'yanova and Trofimov, 1970).

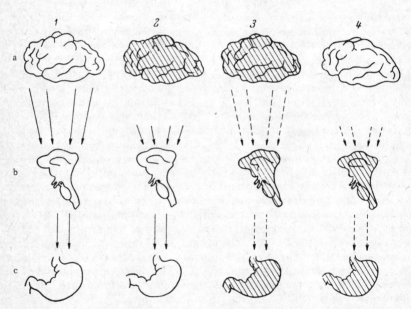

FIGURE 32. Types of functional relationship between the cerebral cortex and subcortex in the hyperactive and hypoactive forms of visceral disorders (after Kurtsin and Bolondinskii, 1967):

a) cerebral cortex; b) subcortical and vegetative centers; c) internal organ (stomach); clear — excitation, hatched — inhibition; 1) irradiation of excitation from cortex to subcortex, hyperactivity of organ; 2) cortex inhibited, subcortical centers highly excited (positive induction), hyperactivity of organ; 3) irradiation of inhibition from cortex to subcortex, hypoactivity of organ; 4) cortex in state of excitation, increased subcortical inhibition (negative induction), hypoactivity of organ.

Hence, hyper- and hypoactivity, the two basic forms of functional disturbance of the viscera and blood vessels which occur in corticovisceral disorders, may be produced by the four variants of cortical-subcortical interactions shown in Figure 32.

UNDULATORY PATTERN OF VEGETATIVE DISORDERS

Functional disorders of internal organs often take the form of a wave. Throughout the condition the deviations of activity of the organ from the norm take the form of a periodic alternation of hypo- and hyperactivity. In some cases, such periods of alternation may last for weeks or even months, in others only for days, so that the scale of the undulation may be large or small. In our investigations a phenomenon of this kind was observed in secretory disorders of the stomach, liver, pancreas and intestine, in disorders of gastrointestinal motility and in functional disturbances of the cardiovascular system and of the kidneys. Alternations of increased and diminished activity of the endocrine glands in neurosis and corticovisceral disturbances have also been reported by many authors. In our laboratory, they have been observed in an experimental neurosis of dogs involving the pituitary-adrenal system (Gulyaeva and Seregin, 1969). An undulatory effect has also been noted by us in studies of general processes, such as carbohydrate, protein, nuclear and water and salt metabolism, intestinal and gallbladder absorption, vascular permeability of glands, the blood-brain barrier and the cell-blood-skin barrier. The findings were especially striking in studies on dogs made by our colleague Nikolaeva (1965, 1966) over a number of years. Here the normal indices of higher nervous activity and respiratory exchange were compared with the findings obtained during the state of neurosis and in convalescence. Each period of increased activity and inhibition in the cerebral cortex was accompanied by an increase of activity of the oxidative processes of the organism. Conversely, the level of the respiratory exchange diminished during the period of increased cortical activity (see Figure 11). The pattern persisted throughout the neurosis, whether the latter had been induced by the classical Pavlovian technique or by overstrain of the higher cerebral centers caused by increased interoceptive stimuli; nor did it bear any relation to the type of nervous system of the animal (Nikolaeva and Denisova, 1969). In healthy dogs that have not been subjected to neurosis, increased excitation in the cerebral cortex is usually accompanied by the activation of redox processes in the cells of the body, as is indicated by an increase in the respiratory exchange and the pulmonary ventilation and by the high coefficient of oxygen utilization by the lungs (Ovcharova, 1966).

Hence, in the normal state there also exists a direct relationship between the intensity of oxidation in the organism and the functional state of the higher cerebral centers. In a pathological state (neurosis), an increase of excitation in the cerebral cortex produces a concomitant decline in the respiratory-exchange level. In our experiments on dogs (Kurtsin et al., 1965), the pattern established by Nikolaeva was confirmed by simultaneous gas analysis, using a Haldane apparatus, and measurement of the tissue respiration of an organ in the same animal, by biopsy of the gastric mucosa through a fistula.

Summarizing all our experimental findings on the subject, we must conclude that the undulatory nature of the autonomic disorders in neurosis reflects the pattern of development of the pathological process.

This leads us to the question of the nature of undulatory vegetative disorders. The answer may be sought in a number of directions, with regard to both the hyperfunctional and hypofunctional forms. The undulatory nature of the pathological process may be related to a disturbance of the synergism between the cholinergic and adrenergic innervation of an organ. Such disorders may be related to specific disturbances of the hormonal regulatory mechanism, particularly the effect of the pituitary-adrenal system on the gastrointestinal tract and the diverse hormonal requirements of the cells and tissues of the organism during the period of stress. Finally, the undulatory nature of functional disorders in organs may reflect specific disturbances in the local mechanisms regulating the organ.

All these suggestions may be justified to some extent. Yet, comprehensi studies of the cortex, subcortex and organs in experimental neurosis increasingly suggest that the form taken by the disorder must largely be attributed to the irradiation and reciprocal induction of excitation and inhibiti in the cerebral cortex and the infracortical nerve centers which directly govern the viscero-vegetative reactions. Indeed, cortical nervous process are not linear but undulatory, due to the interaction of the two opposed processes of excitation and inhibition. This is distinctly seen, for example, i differential and extinguishing inhibition. The undulatory nature of higher nervous activity was emphasized more than once by Pavlov and in our opinion it is this which also provides the clue to the undulatory form taken by autonomic disorders in neuroses. However, it must also be taken into consideration that while fluctuations of higher nervous activity and of visceral activity are normally insignificant, on account of the equilibrium maintaine between excitation and inhibition in the cerebral centers, in neurosis the balance is usually markedly upset in favor of one of these processes. Irradiation and reciprocal induction become inert, often stagnant. This tends t increase the duration and amplitude of the oscillations, that is, it modifies "the wave in time and in space" as Pavlov put it.

Experimentally, it has been established, in the first place, that the onse development and disappearance of autonomic disorders are directly related to the onset, development and disappearance of disturbances of higher nervous activity. Disturbances of visceral activity, or of general physiologica processes, usually follow deviations of higher nervous activity from the norma Furthermore, their severity and duration are similar to those of the cortic disturbances. Finally, when cerebral activity returns to normal, this is usually soon followed by a return to normal of visceral activity. Secondly, hypoactivity of an internal organ arises when the cerebral cortex is domina ed by inhibition which then radiates into the subcortical centers or, in the case of negative induction of these centers, by increased excitation in the cerebral cortex. The hyperactive form of autonomic disorders is due eithe to positive induction of the subcortex from the inhibited cortex, or to irradi ation of the excitation from the cortex into the subcortex. The alternation these forms of corticovisceral disorders has been clearly demonstrated in Melikova's (1971) experiments on interoceptive conditioned and unconditione metabolic (glycemic) reflexes in dogs with experimental neurosis. In the first stage of neurosis, when inhibition prevailed in the cerebral cortex, th interoceptive reflexes underwent synchronous inhibition; in the second stag with persistent cortical inhibition, the interoceptive metabolic reflexes wer initially at a high level, but during the period of increasing excitation in the cerebral cortex, the glycemic reflexes fell abruptly. Thirdly, the undulator form of vegetative resonance in neurosis does not arise immediately, but i formed gradually, beginning with a disturbance in the normal interaction ar balance of excitation and inhibition in the cerebral cortex.

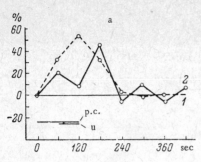
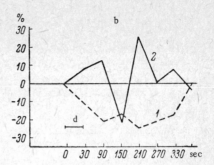

FIGURE 33.   Course taken by a positive (a) and by an inhibitory (b) conditioned reflex in a dog in a normal state (1) and in experimental neurosis (2) (after Kurtsin, 1959, 1965):

y-axis — deviation of pulmonary ventilation from the initial level (%); x-axis — time (sec); p.c.: effect of positive conditioned stimulus; u: unconditioned; d: differentiated.

This has been aptly demonstrated by our colleagues Golodov and Sapov from the Department of Physiology of the Military Academy of Medicine.   Golodov studied the changes in pulmonary ventilation and composition of the alveolar air in experimental neurosis, in a number of dogs in whom systems of conditioned antacid-defense and respiratory reflexes had been established. He used his own method whereby the automatically recorded variations in pulmonary ventilation served to indicate the course of development of the inhibitory process from the base line, first in the normal state and then in neurosis (Figure 33b).   He also studied the development of the excitatory process (Figure 33a).   In both cases, the neurosis was accompanied by distinct inversion of the different stages of development of the nervous processes, while the variations in both inhibition and excitation assumed an undulatory form.

Sapov obtained similar findings with regard to the blood pressure level. Even during the actual experimental conflict, at the moment of the "psychotrauma," a distinct increase in the rate of variation of the blood pressure level in response to the conditioned signal was noted, as well as the obviously undulatory nature of the variations themselves (Figure 34).   In neurosis, the positive conditioned stimulus first caused a drop in blood pressure, instead of the normal rise; the drop was followed by a rise 30 sec later, which was again followed by a drop and a rise.   The height of the [systolic] pressure was 50 to 55 mm Hg and its variations were clearly of an undulatory nature. The process of inhibition also underwent a drastic change and assumed an undulatory form.

Suvorov's (1971) experiments are also of interest; like the previous ones, they were concerned with the initial phase of formation of the neurotic process and its resonance in the vegetative sphere. He found that a few days after the derangement of higher nervous activity, vascular disorders in dogs, as determined plethysmographically, already show a change in the pulse volume without any stimulation whatsoever.   At first the undulation is barely visible on the plethysmogram and resembles the "play of the vessels," when vascular dilatation rapidly alternates with constriction. However, within the

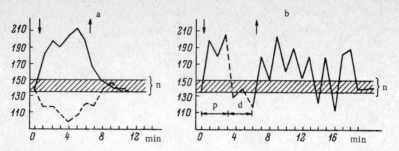

FIGURE 34. Course taken by a positive (solid line) and by an inhibitory (broken line) conditioned vasomotor reflex in a dog in the normal state (a) and during conflict (b) (after Sapov, 1958):

y-axis — systolic blood pressure (mm Hg); x-axis — time over which blood pressure measured (min); n — fluctuations in resting blood pressure. Arrows — start and finish of the conditioned signal; p: positive stimulus; d: differentiated stimulus.

first three days the undulation becomes distinct and permanent (Figure 35). From then on, even if neurosis lasts for some months, the undulation consti tutes a characteristic feature of the angioneurosis. A marked "play of ves- sels" takes place in human subjects, especially at the height of neurosis and in acute attacks of hypertension, peptic ulcer and other conditions (Pressman and Pressman, 1968), at a stage when the vascular reactions to stimuli are also particularly mobile and strong. At the same time, the reaction to stimuli is very sluggish and the vascular undulation appearing in response to a condi- tioned or unconditioned stimulus does not disappear for a long time. In our opinion, this feature of the reaction is an indication of the presence of the dominant pathological state in the vasomotor centers.

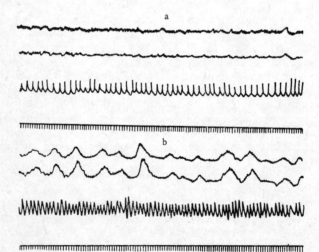

FIGURE 35. Vasomotor condition in a dog in the normal state (a) and on the 3rd day after an extero-interoceptive conflict — "play of vessels" (b) (after Suvorov, 1967).

From above down — left paw plethysmogram; right paw plethysmogram; time mark, 2 sec.

Hence, the pathological process in neuroses and corticovisceral disturbances does not develop in a linear fashion but undulates, since the types of
damage which give rise to hyperactivity or hypoactivity of the organ alternate
at short or long intervals of time over many days, weeks, months or even
years. The nature of these undulatory changes of autonomic-visceral activity
is far from clear. However, the experimental findings suggest that central
nervous mechanisms constitute the leading factor, particularly the irradiation and reciprocal induction which take place in the cortical and infracortical
structures related to the regulation of autonomic-visceral activity. This does
not mean that disturbances in the tonal balance of the cholinergic and
adrenergic autonomic nervous systems play no part at all in the production
of these different forms of the disorder, or of the phenomenon of undulation.
Nor can one neglect the possibility of disturbances in the local, neural and
humoral (hormonal) mechanisms regulating the affected viscera. Probably
all these factors play a part, but they do not trigger off the manifestations.
They only secondarily become involved in the development of the pathological
process, following the alteration in the functional state of the cerebral
cortex resulting from the psychotrauma, the changes in the cortical-
subcortical interactions in the cerebral centers and the onset of the neurosis.
However, in our opinion the autonomic resonance hypothesis in neurosis suffers from one important shortcoming. It does not indicate why some cases
of corticovisceral pathology give rise to inductive interactions between the
cortical and subcortical cerebral centers, while in other cases the vegetative
resonance is due to irradiation of the nervous process. Our knowledge of the
subject is still insufficient to understand why a particular form of pathological activity appears in an organ, so that we are still unable to determine the
likely development of the pathological process, let alone control it.

SELECTIVE DAMAGE TO INTERNAL ORGANS

Studies of the physiological mechanism underlying the functional relationships between the cerebral cortex and internal organs have provided a new
approach to the problem of selective or predominant damage to an internal
organ or a system of organs in neurosis. This question of specificity, as it
has been succinctly called by American workers in the field of psychosomatic
medicine, is one of the most important in corticovisceral pathology.

For some decades now, the clinicians have confronted physiologists, pathologists and other laboratory workers with the following question. Why does
trauma to the brain produce cardiovascular disease in some persons (stenocardia [angina pectoris], myocardial infarction, ischemic heart disease,
or hypertension), while in others it gives rise to digestive disorders (gastric or
duodenal ulcer, disorders of gastrointestinal or biliary motility, esophageal,
cardiac or pyloric spasm), respiratory conditions (bronchial asthma), or
endocrine disorders (diabetes, hyperthyroidism, dysmenorrhea, impotence)?

This question has assumed a particular interest in recent years, since
the establishment of the corticovisceral theory of origin of certain diseases,
particularly among the internists who encounter the different visceral guises
of neurosis more often than other practitioners (Kassirskii, 1970). It is not
so long since Myasnikov (1958) wrote: "Unfortunately, we still know little

about the mechanisms connecting cortical and autonomic reactions, includi
the actual manner in which the nervous system influences specific interna
organs (that is, the effectors) and thus creates the specific pattern of a pa
ticular disease. The doctrine of corticovisceral physiology and pathology
developed by Bykov and his colleagues suffers from a gap in this respect
which is acutely marked by the clinicians" (p. 32). As pointed out by Zaits
(1971), one aspect of the corticovisceral mechanism of production of pepti
ulcer, that is still not understood, is the reason why the pathological centr
influences concentrate on the stomach and duodenum in this condition. Kakhana (1959) has asked: "Why are severe emotional disturbances liable to
give rise to thyrotoxicosis in some patients and gastric ulcer in others, wh
still others suffer from conditions such as bronchial asthma, diabetes mel
litus or hypertension?" Apter (1969) has followed him in asking: "Why does
psychogenic damage to the cerebral cortex produce a cardiovascular condi
tion in some persons, but respiratory and digestive disorders in others?"
Why, indeed? And why has nobody succeeded in providing a satisfactory
answer to these questions, although they have attracted considerable atten
tion and have been the subject of extensive research for very many years?
Psychosomatic medicine, as developed outside the USSR, has offered num
ous hypotheses and speculations on the subject, but a paucity of facts. Thu
importance has been ascribed to constitutional, chiefly hereditary factors
(Alvarez, 1951) which are said to shape the functional systems of the organism and the specificity of the organs with respect to the perception of stir
li, so that certain organs possess less resistance than others. According t
the well-known American psychoanalyst Alexander (1953), everyone has a
vulnerable spot, an Achilles heel, laid down by the genetic code.

Clinical observations by Soviet neuropathologists and psychiatrists, who
are often confronted with cases of psychogenic trauma, have not yet confirme
the role of genetic and other constitutional factors in the pathogenesis of
psychosomatic disease (Apter, 1969). It is true that in certain families ove
several generations the incidence of psychosomatic conditions, such as ga
tric and duodenal ulcer and cardiac and vascular disorders, was found to b
2 to 3 times the average (Dubarry et al., 1959; Ryvkin, 1960; Rabinovich ar
Kublanov, 1963). At the same time, it is becoming increasingly evident tha
peptic ulceration occurs as a consequence of exposure to unfavorable facto
in the social environment, to which the human body is slow in adapting
biologically. According to the internists (Zaitseva, 1971), hereditary bio
logical traits play no determinant role in this matter. The condition is, by
its very nature, essentially determined by social factors. Clinical studies
have shown that under such conditions peptic ulcer may develop in persons
belonging to very different families, with different hereditary characteristics of the nervous system, particularly the type of reactivity. It must
be admitted, however, that both experimental physiology and genetics have
failed to provide convincing factual evidence one way or the other.

A significant finding in monkeys at the Sukhumi monkey farm is that
neurotic sacred baboons are very prone to circulatory disorders, while
neurotic rhesus monkeys are most likely to develop digestive disorders
(Lagutina et al., 1970). It is difficult to say how these findings should be
translated into human pathology, particularly as they have not yet been explained with regard to the two species of monkeys, for whom the ecologica

conditions were more or less identical. However, lack of knowledge does not warrant a total denial of the significance of heredity in the genesis of corticovisceral diseases. The possibility must be admitted that a from generation to generation there may be transmitted a predisposition to a pathological process in just that organ or that functional system which was severely damaged in an earlier generation. The final answer to this problem is most likely to come from genetic studies, both in the clinic and in the laboratory. Some workers ascribe significance to the emotional factor itself. They claim that a specific emotion, such as anger, fear, or grief, is capable of evoking a reaction from a particular organ or system of organs. However, the scientific value of most of these hypotheses is greatly diminished by the fact that they are based on Freudian concepts of the subconscious, of regression and conversion and of infantile libidinous fixations (see the reviews by Wells, 1956, 1966; Kurtsin, 1965b; Bassin, 1968).

A wider hypothesis has been presented by Alexander (Alexander, 1953; Alexander et al., 1961). According to this, every psychosomatic disease possesses a core of emotional conflict which is responsible for the damage to an internal organ or a physiological system. Thus, hypertension and tachycardia are expressions of rage, repressed anger, or fear; attacks of bronchial asthma are correlated with the subconsciously repressed impulse of a mother to shout, while peptic ulcer is related to a feeling of dependence. This concept further postulates the involvement of two antagonistic, affective-instinctive human urges, on the one hand for protection (infantile dependence) and on the other hand for aggression, power and possession. Repression of the second urge gives rise to hypertension, stenocardia [angina pectoris] or cardiac neuroses, while repression of the first results in peptic ulcer or ulcerative colitis. It is claimed that repressed anger chiefly affects the cardiovascular system, the need for closer relationships and the desire for help affects the digestive system, while specific conflicts between sexual desires and tendencies of dependence particularly affect the respiratory tract. Some of the effects are mediated mainly by the sympathetic innervation, others by the parasympathetic. The former leads to hypertension, arthritis, migraine, diabetes and thyrotoxicosis and the latter to gastric ulcer, bronchial asthma and ulcerative colitis.

Alexander's hypothesis is in many ways similar to certain Western theories in the field of psychosomatic medicine, including such concepts as the "receptivity" of an internal organ to a conflict situation, the symbolic language of the organs and the specific capacity of the viscera to reflect emotional experiences.

Not long ago, similar statements also appeared in the Soviet literature on the subject. It was claimed, for example, that cardiac disorders are related to the emotion of fear, hepatic disease to anger and gastric disease to apathy and depression.

However, Alexander's concept has not been fully accepted even outside the USSR. It has been criticized for resorting to Freudian psychoanalysis and for interpreting the findings from a Freudian point of view. The American Psychoanalytical Association has plainly admitted that no correlation has yet been proved to exist between a particular type of person and hypertension, or between specific changes in organs and specific subconscious conflicts and that all the findings require to be cautiously evaluated. Moreover, there is a

need for improving methods of investigation which make use of both psycho
logical and physiological measurements.

Weitbrecht (1955) altogether considers that Alexander's ideas are specu
lative, intangible and like algebraic equations with such a large number of
unknowns that they must be considered as assumptions, not scientific
conclusions. The well-known American psychoanalyst, Kubie (1954), has al
noted the great difficulties involved in applying the specificity theory to var
ious psychosomatic disorders.

Alexander's postulates have also been criticized by us (Kurtsin, 1965b).
Nevertheless, his ideas, like similar American theories in the field of psy
chosomatic medicine, do contain a rational nucleus, in our opinion. This
consists of the emphasis on factors that affected the organ or system of
organs in a certain manner at some earlier period in the life of the individual, thereby producing the conditions for psychogenic (emotional) trauma t
be selectively reflected on them at a later period. For example, psychosomatic diseases in adults have been said to result from exposure to stress
stimuli in early childhood (Stephens, 1962). Once the Freudian overlayers
have been discarded, the factual core of this concept is revealed and one ca
perceive its most important aspect: the importance of acquired factors in t.
development of selective damage to an internal organ during a general neurosis. It is evident that a certain part in such damage is played not only by
hereditary factors but also by traumatic influences on the organ throughout
the period of life preceding the psychogenic trauma, including early childhood. One would also agree that the specificity of the trauma itself is of the
greatest importance, although this should be considered in a somewhat different aspect from that chosen by Alexander and other representatives of
Western psychosomatic medicine.

Each individual possesses his own cycle of emotions, depending upon his
way of life, upbringing, education and skills, his experiences in life, his
work, living conditions, diet and social relationships. A certain word used a
a stimulus may not produce any noticeable corticovisceral changes in one
person, while it may give rise to a severe disorder in another, for whom it
is charged with intense meaning. That such a connection and relationship
exist, seem to us practically beyond dispute. At any rate, actual experienc
of life provides convincing evidence to this effect. In our opinion, the part
played by the emotional factor is confined to the production of a general neu
rosis which, being a nonspecific reaction, elicits the same manifestations
for all types of negative emotions, such as grief, fear, or aggression. More
over, ignoring the psychological aspect of the emotional state and consider-
ing only the physiological effects, a neurosis may also be produced by certain positive emotions, such as joy and rapture which, just like the negative
emotions, suddenly overtax the nervous processes, so that the cerebral
cortical cells rapidly reach the limits of their capacity and enter a state of
functional exhaustion. However, neuroses are certainly much more common
ly caused by negative emotions and they are probably elicited by positive
emotions only in persons with a weak type of nervous system.

Our own ideas on the subject may thus be summed up as follows: a) an
acknowledgement of the emotional factor as an etiological agent in psychosomatic disorders; b) a denial of any connection between particular emotions
such as anger, fear or grief, and specific internal organs, such as the heart

liver or kidneys, or functional systems, such as the digestive and cardiovascular systems. In all probability, the same emotion, such as anger, is able
ultim' tely to produce cardiovascular, digestive or respiratory disorders.
The particular system affected in a given person depends not on the specificity of the emotions but on their particular significance for the individual affected and on the presence of a weak spot in an organ or a system of organs.
This weak spot is probably produced by both general and local factors (Kurtsin, 1965a, 1965h, 1971b, 1971c).

The general factor consists mainly of conditioned-reflex mechanisms, and
is based on Pavlov's suggestion that isolated pathological foci may appear in
the cerebral cortex. Such foci have been repeatedly observed in experiments
with conditioned reflexes as well as in patients. For example, there have
been reports of asthmatic or stenocardial attacks [attacks of angina pectoris]
of conditioned-reflex origin and of human cases of hypertension, thyrotoxicosis, disorders of intestinal motility and certain other pathological
phenomena, due to seemingly insignificant stimuli, such as the sight of an
elevator stuck between floors, of a goldfish or of a rose, a word uttered that
is charged with some specific personal meaning, or the sound of a specific
melody. In dogs, if pituitrin injections are combined with the ring of a bell,
the latter will soon provoke the same changes in the circulation rate and in
the coronary vessels, resulting in myocardial ischemia, as those previously
produced by the injections (Teplov, 1962; Zakharzhevskii, 1966a). If a type
of food which is inacceptable to a dog, such as honey, is combined with stimulation of the visual and auditory analyzers, eventually these effects alone
will provoke the same marked inhibition of the gastric glands which was
originally caused by the honey (Bykov and Kurtsin, 1960). In a similar fashion, it is possible to reproduce a cataleptic state that was originally caused
by bulbocapnine, or a whole complex of somatic-autonomic effects that are
characteristically caused by morphine, apomorphine, aconitine, dinitrophenol,
or camphor (Dolin, 1962).

After introducing food together with sodium arsenite into the rumen of
sheep and goats through a fistula, Margolin (1967) found that when this had
been repeated several times, the animals refused the type of food that had
previously been combined with the administration of the poison. This negative
reaction persisted for over a month. In Speranskii's laboratory (1935) the
manipulations involved in the intravenous injection of horse serum produced
the same state of shock as the serum itself. In all these experiments, the
tenacity of the conditioned-reflex effect is striking. We recall an experiment
performed some 20 years ago by the epidemiologist A. P. Kazantsev in the
Department of Physiology of the Military Academy of Medicine. In dogs, the
taking of blood from a vein under the same laboratory conditions as those
used for the previous injection of dysentery toxin, now provoked all the signs
of dysentery infection. Two weeks later, after all the signs of illness had
disappeared, the experiment was repeated with sterile meat broth, the entire
procedure being identical with that used for administration of the toxin. On
the following day, the dogs showed the typical picture of dysentery: they were
unable to rise from the floor, they refused food and the pulse rate had
risen to 180 per minute and was scarcely perceptible. Somewhat later,
a liquid, mucous, bloody stool was produced and all the previously established
conditioned salivary reflexes disappeared. The conditioned reflexes reappeared within three days, the pulse returned to normal within 6 days and the

intestine also soon returned to its normal state. Such conditioned reflex reproduction of manifestations of the disease was then provoked twice again, at intervals of 3 to 4 weeks.

Thus, selective, or predominant, damage to an internal organ or a system of organs by a pathological process may be due to a previously established conditioned-reflex connection between the cerebral cortex and the organ or system. The conditioned-reflex mechanism also underlies the selective damage to internal organs and functional systems produced experimentally in monkeys at the Sukhumi monkey farm (Lagutina et al., 1970; Startsev, 1971). Here, the reaction of an organ or system was found to be related to the persistent pathological state of the cerebral centers, and the activity of the organ and all the stimuli triggering and correcting it then assumed the role of signals initiating the development of some pathological condition of the organ or system. The technical procedure was as follows. A pathological condition of the digestive organs was produced when feeding was followed by immobilization. After a number of repetitions, the monkey acquired a pathological dominant in the motor analyzer, so that the feeding now served as a conditioned signal which itself evoked the entire gamut of kinetic changes, accompanied by functional and morphological changes in the organ itself. For example, in the stomach it gave rise to gastric achylia, hypopepsia, adenomatous polyps and gastric ulcer. In sacred baboons similar experiments were carried out in which the genital system was associated with pathological dominance of the motor analyzer, giving rise to an experimental model of neurogenic amenorrhea in the females and psychogenic impotence in the males. In rhesus monkeys the combination of an interoceptive chemical stimulus and a pathological defense dominant produced a model of chronic neurogenic hyperglycemia. These model pathological conditions in the various organs were all very persistent.

Havlíček (1962) found that experimental neurosis in dogs, rabbits and monkeys takes an especially severe course if it assumes the form of a defense dominant. The importance of the latter in the mechanism of protracted corticovisceral disturbances has also been emphasized by Biryukov and Bachurikhina (1970). Damage predominantly to a particular organ or a system of organs can be reproduced experimentally, in a dog or monkey, by overtaxing the central regulatory mechanisms of the system. Thus, daily disturbance during feeding or even changes in the feeding schedule (the feedings being too frequent, or infrequent, or irregularly spaced) eventually produced severe functional disorders of the stomach, pancreas, liver and intestine, with the development of dystrophic processes which often resulted in an organic lesion, such as gastritis or gastric ulcer (Putilin, 1968). Incidentally, these experimental findings agree with clinical observations (Zaitseva, 1971) which have shown the importance of various dietary factors in the pathogenesis of peptic ulcer. According to Pavlov, both conditioned reflexes and innate reactions are involved in the procedure of feeding.

Hence, selective damage to an organ or organ system may be caused by overtaxing the central mechanism by which it is controlled. Psychogenic trauma is particularly likely to occur in an organ or system whose cerebral regulation centers have been overstrained. The cardiovascular disorders which have been experimentally reproduced in monkeys at the Sukhumi monkey farm include hypertension, hypotension, coronary insufficiency and myocardial infarction (Lagutina et al., 1970; Startsev, 1971). According to

Istamanova (1958, p. 94) the predominance of cardiovascular disorders in neurotic patients may also be caused by excessively severe and prolonged physical exertion, accompanied by an emotional stimulus.

The intracerebral mechanism which consists of the partial involvement in the pathological process of various divisions of the central nervous system, mainly the limbic and premotor regions of the cortex, the thalamohypothalamic region, the reticular formation and the striopallidal system, may also be included among the general factors which produce selective damage to the internal organs. The important factors here are firstly the interaction of excitation and inhibition between different areas of the cerebral cortex itself and between the cortex and the subcortical centers and, secondly, the degree of involvement of a given cortical or subcortical nervous structure in the cortical conflict of nervous processes. Thus, the derangement of conditioned respiratory reflexes in dogs produced a "respiratory neurosis," while the derangement of salivary reflexes caused persistent and severe disturbances of secretion and motility in the digestive organs (Saragea and Foni, 1962).

Working with dogs in whom the limbic areas of the cerebral cortex had been destroyed, our colleagues Gaza (1966) and Gulyaeva (1966) observed a prolonged pathological condition of the vascular system, on a background of marked changes in higher nervous activity, while the state of the digestive system remained normal. According to Startsev (1971), female sacred baboons suffering from a neurosis with the predominant disturbance in the region of the alimentary center, showed no significant changes in the cardiovascular system or the sexual cycle. The isolated, or partial disturbance of intracerebral interactions in neurosis may involve not only various areas of the neocortex, but also parts of the subcortical systems with which the cortex is anatomically and functionally connected. Moreover, a nervous conflict within the caudate nucleus gives rise to prolonged hypertension, whereas a conflict in the globus pallidus produces hypotension (Suvorov, 1967). Thus, the manifestations may differ even within a single physiological system.

The most significant findings are those reported by Suvorov (1971), which show that the effect evoked depends on the degree of involvement of a structure in the conflict situation. Thus, hypertension does not occur in dogs with a neurosis caused by a nervous conflict in the orbital area of the cerebral cortex; the effects being confined to manifestations of angioneurosis which persist for 6 weeks to 2 months. Yet, in neurosis due to a nervous conflict in the premotor area, the angioneurosis is accompanied by hypertension which persists for 5 to 6 months. In neurosis due to a nervous conflict in the striopallidal system, vascular disturbances accompanied by hypertension persist for 9 to 11 months. Finally, a stable hypertension persists for 18 months or longer in neurosis due to a nervous conflict in the hypothalamic region.

It should be noted that overstrain of the nervous activity of the nuclei of the striopallidal system and hypothalamus does not in itself lead to neurosis and autonomic disorders. These only occur when the cortical regulatory mechanism has been damaged. It must be assumed that the cerebral centers are closely knit in an integrated morphofunctional system which regulates autonomic activity. Within this system there is evidently a strict differentiation and localization of the cortical and subcortical mechanisms governing the activity of the autonomic nervous system as a whole, and specific sympathetic or parasympathetic activity. It is this which determines whet the ultimate effect will be hypertension or hypotension, hypersecretion or hyposecretion, or a disturbance in both parts of the autonomic nervous sys tem or only in one of them.

The main local factor responsible for damage predominantly to one org is the interoceptive mechanism. Even before the appearance of the neuros this serves to separate the afferent impulsation coming from the internal organ from the total flux of afferent impulses proceeding to the central ner vous system from all the receptor areas of the body. The separation is achieved by repeated stimulation of the organ in question. Separation of th kind by "blazing a trail" (Sherrington, 1906) may become consolidated in th form of an interoceptive conditioned reflex in the cerebral centers (Bykov, 1942), thus forming the connections by which a psychogenic or emotional blow, for example, will affect the organ or system into which it has been incorporated.

There are a number of experimental findings to support this hypothesis including the results of special studies on the subject which have been car- ried out in our laboratory over the past 10 years. It has been found, for example, that in dogs and cats, various pathological conditions affecting ar organ, such as gastritis, proctitis, cystitis, cholecystitis, and gastric or duodenal ulcer, tend to inhibit the conditioned-reflex activity of the cerebr cortex for many weeks or even months (Gaza, 1957; Kurtsin, 1967a, 1971c). The organs themselves showed structural alterations in the afferent and ef ferent nerves (Shvalev et al., 1963) and marked changes in the afferent im- pulsation in the nerves (Zakharzhevskii and Ermolaeva, 1965; Yuldasheva, 1966) as well as changes in the bioelectrical activity of the subcortical cen- ters, the thalamus, hypothalamus and reticular formation and of the orbita sensimotor and limbic areas of the cortex (Milenov, 1966). It has thus beer experimentally demonstrated that when an internal organ is in a pathologic state, the receptors generate pathological impulses which proceed to the higher divisions of the central nervous system and reach the subcortical an even the cortical level, drastically altering their functional state and higher nervous activity. In this way a trail is blazed from the organ to the higher cerebral centers and the connection is consolidated by a conditioned-reflex mechanism.

Budylin and his colleagues have also described changes in the conditioned reflex activity and bioelectrical activity of cortical and infracortical struc- tures in animals suffering from experimental cholecystitis (Budylin and Zin chenko, 1969), a focal inflammation of the sciatic nerve (Levshunova, 1969) and neurosis of interoceptive origin (Emel'yanova and Trofimov, 1970). Distur bances of higher nervous activity were distinguished by external inhibition, pathological cortical dominance, hyperasthenia, hyposthenia and mixed form of neurosis (Budylin, 1970). Chemical "neurotomy" by the intravenous ad- ministration of 0.25% novocaine solution blocked the impulse fluxes proceed ing from the pathological foci to the cerebral centers, so that higher nervo activity, the bioelectrical activity of the cerebral structures and the auto- nomic visceral activity all returned to normal (Berko, 1969; Budylin, 1970).

The Rumanian physiologists Saragea and Foni (1962), working in our labo- ratory, have studied the significance of pathological overstrain of the visce in the development of the autonomic disorders which follow a conflict of the alimentary and defense reflexes (electroconflict). They found that in dogs with a chronic fistula of the digestive tract, the most marked and prolonged autonomic disturbances occurred in organs which had been "traumatized" (by inflammation, for example) before the neurosis; while the regulatory systems affected were those which had been overstrained before the neurosis by such manipulations as repeated loading with sugar, or the administration of adrenalin.

In other experiments in our laboratory, an experimental neurosis was produced in dogs by a conflict of the interoceptive conditioned reflexes established to stimulation of the gastric receptor area from a Pavlov pouch. In this case, the resulting disorders of gastric secretion were more pronounced and prolonged than the changes in the other activities studied, such as the blood pressure and the blood count (Gulyaeva, 1956). A similar pattern was also observed when one gastric secretory area was involved in the cortical conflict, while the other remained intact, the secretory disorder being more severe in the affected part of the stomach. Such consolidation of a conditioned-reflex pathological reaction is liable to be very persistent. Rybnikova studied variations in the intestinal absorption of glucose and water in dogs with a Thiry fistula when stimulation was applied to the electrodes implanted in the premotor cortical area. It was found that the stimulation produced a general neurosis and general autonomic disorders, such as disturbances of intestinal absorption, changes in the blood count and a rise in the blood pressure. Higher nervous activity returned to normal within 2 years, as did the blood pressure and blood count, but intestinal absorption remained defective for 7 years. However, if the experiment was preceded by administration of atropine or by irrigation of the intestinal mucosa with a novocaine solution, thus disconnecting the efferent or the afferent impulses, respectively, intestinal absorption was not affected (Kurtsin, 1964). The same result can be achieved by blocking the afferent impulses at the level of the reticular formation of the brain stem with chlorpromazine (0.5 mg/kg).

Chubarova twice induced experimental gastritis in dogs and, following their recovery, produced a derangement in their higher nervous activity which resulted in a prolonged neurosis and corticovisceral disturbances. The disorders of gastric secretion were more severe and prolonged than the functional damage to the cardiovascular and urinary systems and to the blood. Gastric ulcer of corticovisceral origin was found to develop 2 to 3 times more rapidly in animals after gastritis than in animals with a normal stomach (Kurtsin et al., 1965). This has been confirmed in dogs by Sergeeva (1965) who overstrained the regulatory mechanism of the blood, producing a marked and prolonged anemia by the administration of phenylhydrazine or acetylcholine. After the blood count had returned to normal, a neurosis was induced. She found that the red cell changes occurring in psychogenic stress were the same as in phenylhydrazine or acetylcholine poisoning. Moreover, they persisted for 224 days, whereas the changes in higher nervous activity lasted for only 160 days, while the changes in the blood pressure and in gastric secretion lasted for 81 and 170 days, respectively.

It is of interest to note that when the nervous mechanisms regulating vascular tone were again subjected to the same kind of overstrain, long after the above experiments had ended, the blood pressure changes which followed the damage to the activity of the cerebral cortex and the development of the neurosis persisted for many months, whereas the changes in the blood coun gastric secretion and conditioned reflexes lasted for only a few weeks (Ser-geeva, 1966).

In the above experiments with psychogenic stress, the pathological reac-tion is of the type of Speranskii's (1935) "second blow", which possibly also involves the participation of the conditioned-reflex mechanism. Evidently, the development of the pathological process, predominantly in a single orga or system of organs, is due to the presence of traces of long-time memory the "trails" which had long ago been "blazed" through the central nervous system. Although the above findings are inadequate to finally solve the problem of specificity, in our opinion they suggest that characteristics acquired during the life of an individual person or animal play an important part in determining the location of the selective damage to an internal orga which may occur in general neurosis. Moreover, they provide an objective foundation for the further investigation of this complicated problem.

Hence, selective, or predominant, damage to an internal organ or syste of organs in general neurosis may be due not only to hereditary, constitu-tional traits, but also to a complex of other factors, including the roles of conditioned-reflex, intracerebral and interoceptive mechanisms.

Chapter 10

MATHEMATICAL ANALYSIS AND CYBERNETIC EVALUATION OF CORTICOVISCERAL DISTURBANCES

The existing techniques for the determination of corticovisceral disturbances make no provision for a detailed quantitative study of these conditions.
The necessity for detailed quantitative analysis of physiological phenomena
was already pointed out by Pavlov who said that "all life, from the protozoa
up to the most complex organisms including man, is made up of a long
series of progressively more complicated states of equilibrium with the
external environment. The time will come, remote though this may be, when
it will be possible to express all these states in the form of mathematical
equations" (1951, Vol. 3, book 1, pp. 124–215). The time predicted by this
great Russian physiologist is now at hand, since mathematical analysis and
the principles of cybernetics are beginning to be adopted by biology, physiology and medicine (Grodins, 1963; Milsum, 1966; Bailey, 1967). It seems to
us that this stage of development has also been reached as regards the
theory of corticovisceral relationships, although certain cybernetic principles, such as information theory, had become basic constituents of this
theory even before cybernetics became an independent science. Suffice it
to say that feedback from the internal organs to the higher cerebral centers,
including the cerebral cortex, was regarded as the source from which the
centers governing the functional state and activity of the internal organs
received a constant flow of information on the continuous processes of
adjustment of the animal organism to the conditions of the external environment (Bykov, 1942). The question is now being raised as to whether our
knowledge concerning the visceral information service cannot be extended
and whether quantitative indices and estimates cannot be obtained regarding the activity of the internal organs and of both normal and pathological viscerocortical and corticovisceral relationships. In fact, however,
the practical realization of this goal is more difficult than it would seem to
be at first sight. The point is not just to introduce cybernetic principles
and techniques of mathematical analysis into these branches of physiology
and pathology, but to establish thereby the fundamental, theoretical principles
of corticovisceral pathology and physiology, just as has been achieved, for
example, in theoretical physics or theoretical biology. This new branch of
knowledge calls for an equally new approach to the study of the phenomena,
a new understanding and, of course, new methods of analysis and investigation. Another difficulty lies in the fact that the phenomena of animal biology
do not perform harmonic oscillations as a rule; they are nonlinear, although
they are to some extent repetitive. Moreover, the large amount of information which is inevitably obtained when a physiological process is fractionally
investigated tends to confuse the investigator and lead him away from the

correct interpretation.   To put it otherwise, excessive information always contains not only useful data but also random findings which interfere with the analysis and may obscure the characteristic features of the pheno-menon.   For this reason, research into physiological phenomena calls for quantitative evaluation, with precise measurements being made of many similar processes, so that their common characteristics can be determined from which general laws can be established.   It is then possible to create a model of the particular phenomenon, or to otherwise predict its development in a specific direction under both normal and pathological conditions.   Once this has been achieved, it becomes possible to control the process in any desired direction.   This is the basis of theoretical corticovisceral physio-logy and pathology and as such possesses great practical significance for the future.

The following findings obtained in our laboratory (Kurtsin, 1952, 1953a, 1960; Dzidziguri, 1953; Kurtsin and Dzidziguri, 1965), which have been sub-jected to mathematical analysis by Dzidziguri (1968) together with a mathe-matician, Genkin, may be regarded as a first attempt to use this approach to investigate certain disorders of visceral activity in dogs subjected to ex-perimental neurosis, as well as in patients suffering from neurosis and pep-tic ulcer.   An attempt has been made to base theoretical conclusions on the quantitative evaluation of the visceral effect.   The findings were subjected to statistical analysis, including calculation of frequency distribution curves for the investigated parameters on both absolute and relative scales, cal-culation of the total variation, coefficient of variation, difference between the means, and ratio of variances.   The coefficient of correlation between the investigated parameters and various functions was calculated whenever necessary.

THEORETICAL SUBSTANTIATION OF THE QUANTITATIVE ASSESSMENT OF GASTRIC MOTILITY

When describing any activity of the animal organism, including gastric motility, the different levels of such activity must be taken into account.   In our opinion (Kurtsin and Dzidziguri, 1965; Dzidziguri, 1968), these levels can be classified into five discrete stages: 1) reserve, 2) functional, 3) mobility 4) activity, and 5) disordered activity.

When any excitable system (organ, tissue or cell) is in a state of reserve the amplitude of its rhythmic activity is minimal, it is not acted upon by stimuli and its metabolic processes function at a low level.   The amplitude increases somewhat in the stage of functional rest.   The cells now function mainly for their own needs and the sources of energy for future activity are accumulated.   When the system begins to assume functional activity, it enters the stage of mobility.   The amplitude now becomes much greater and the maximum shifts toward the midpoint of the cycle.   As the activity in-creases the living system becomes fully mobilized and as the action of the stimulus continues the cycle assumes a symmetrical form.   However, if the action of the stimulus grows still stronger, the system may pass from the stage of mobility into the stage of disordered activity, in which the function of the cell, tissue, organ, or system exceeds the critical value.   The amplitude of oscillation becomes still greater and its maximum shifts to the initial part of cycle.   When the living system is in the state of maximal energy strain, waves of second and higher orders usually appear signifying that the system is starting to switch over from the point of maximal energy strain to another, more frequent but more symmetrical, rhythm of activity. However, if the action of the stimulus ceases, the state of functional activity gradually comes to a halt and becomes superseded by the stages of functional rest and reserve, with the amplitude shifting toward the end of the cycle.

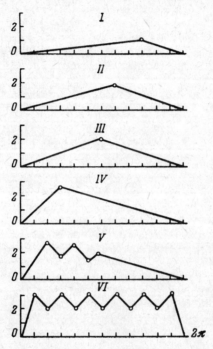

FIGURE 36. Energy curves for different states of an organ (after Dzidziguri, 1968):

I) state of functional rest; II) beginning of activity; III) state of mobility; IV) maximum activity; V) switch to a new rhythm; VI) switch to a more frequent rhythm; y-axis — amplitude (arbitrary units); x-axis — phases (in units of the complete cycle).

These stages are schematically represented by the graphs in Figure 36, in which the energy activity (intensity of the action of the stimulus) is plotted against time.   Since we are concerned here with gastric motility, they take into account the characteristics of the contractile process in smooth muscle.   Thus, the latent period of the latter is several seconds, as against 0.01—0.025 sec for striped muscle, while the entire contraction cycle in response to a single brief stimulation may be 20 sec or more, as compared with 0.01 sec for a single contraction of striped muscle.   Again, the threshold of stimulus is higher for smooth than for striped muscle. Further more, for objective analysis it is necessary to consider the general trend of the motor activity and not just the curve of a single cycle.

The curves of gastric motility obtained by the balloon technique are distinctly asymmetrical, due to the difference in the duration of the phase of increasing muscular contraction (the ascending part of the gastrogram) and that of muscular relaxation (the descending part). The curve of the contrac-tion cycle may be skewed to the right or left in different cases. The shape of the gastrogram shows that the usual analysis of the gastric motility findings, based exclusively on measurements of the amplitude, the frequency of contraction and the duration of the muscular contraction—relaxation cycle (Kurtsin, 1952, 1953), fails to utilize other important characteristics of the contractile act and leaves the nature and dynamics of the process itself scarcely investigated. One important shortcoming of the balloon-mano-metric technique for the investigation of gastrointestinal motility in man and animals is the arcuate path described by the arm of the recording sys-tem (the Marey capsule) in the presence of powerful muscular contractions. Thus, at slow scanning rates, for example, it is very difficult and often im-possible to determine the degree of asymmetry from graphs based on these curves. Moreover, the great majority of the recorders used for motility investigations of the stomach, intestine and other hollow organs, are not sufficiently sensitive, linear, free from inertia and stable to reveal the required information and they may even obscure the findings. Calibration of the recordings in absolute or even in relative values is often omitted and the scales along the x- and y-axes are not indicated when the gastrograms and enterograms are replotted as graphs, so that these graphs cannot be com-pared with others. Interpretation of the recordings and their mathematical analysis is particularly impeded by the low speed of kymograph rotation, between 0.2 and 1 mm/sec, which is often used for recording motility. How-ever, these and certain other shortcomings of the recording techniques can easily be overcome (Dzidziguri, 1968). Thus, for example, replacement of the Marey capsule by a float on the surface of the liquid in the open arm of the water manometer entirely eliminates these recording defects, so that the muscular contractions of the organ can be recorded as they really are, without distortion in the phase of maximum intensity and all the necessary data can then be made available for the analysis of any asymmetry of the oscillatory process.

This technique was first used by Gorshkova for recording gallbladder motility, then by Genkin and Dzidziguri for the intestine and then by Dzidzi-guri and myself for the stomach. In principle, it can also be used to deter-mine the motility of the esophagus, urinary bladder and other hollow organs. As a result the principles of mathematical analysis can be more widely and accurately applied, particularly to the phenomenon of asymmetry, as a definite relationship exists between the degree of asymmetry and the state of activity of the organ, such as the amplitude and frequency of contraction of the gastric and intestinal musculature. Moreover, it has been shown that changes in the asymmetry occur earlier than the onset of changes in the amplitude of the muscular contractions.

The asymmetric nature of the activity of organs has been noted and used by me for the classification of different types of gastric secretion and motility (Kurtsin, 1952, 1953a). The need for taking this asymmetry into account in any analysis of intestinal or gastric motility was demonstrated later (Kurtsin and Dzidziguri, 1965; Dzidziguri, 1968). Recently the importance of this phenomenon has also been shown in the case of corticovisceral urinary disturbances (Dzidziguri, 1968; Balakshina, 1971; Kurtsin and Sergeeva, 1971).

In all these investigations it was very important to find a quantitative expression of the muscular contraction asymmetry, which would reflect the ratio of the time interval between the beginning of each unit cycle and the moment of the maximum reaction of the cell or organ (ascending phase) to the time interval from the maximum to the end of the cycle (descending phase). The mathematical constant (λ) was adopted by us to express this quantitative evaluation of gastric motility. This quantity, which is the ratio of the durations of the phases of the cycle, is dimensionless and merely indicates the factor by which the recovery or descending phase (t_d) in the reaction of the cell, tissue, organ or system is longer or shorter than the developing or ascending phase (t_a). Thus, the phase-duration ratio for each oscillation was estimated from the formula:

$$\lambda_i = \frac{t_{d_i}}{t_{a_i}} \ (i = 1, 2, 3, \ldots, n).$$

The total duration of the cycle is $(T) = t_a + t_d$.

The above relationships for a given time interval were expressed by the mean asymmetry of all the successive contraction cycles.

Experience showed that when gastric motility takes a complex form, it is useful to consider the curve at a discrete moment in time. The curve is encoded in a manner which reveals the duration of the ascending and descending phases. The coding principle is that the series of discrete moments of time are associated with a sequence of ones and zeros according to the following rule: a "one" is used when the value of the curve is greater at the second than at the first point selected and a "zero" or dot is used in the converse situation. Again, a one is used if the value of the gastrogram at the third discrete moment of time is greater than at the second moment, a zero or dot if it is less; and so on. The number of ones in the quantization interval corresponds to the duration of the ascending phase of the curve, while the number of zeros or dots corresponds to the duration of the descending phase.

Special experimental studies (Kurtsin and Dzidziguri, 1965; Dzidziguri, 1968) have shown that the asymmetry parameter λ, passing through the above activity stages, can assume values ranging from 3 to $\frac{1}{3}$, the most common value being 1. While the amplitude is a quantitative measure of the strength of the excitatory or contractile process, λ provides a quantitative expression of its mobility.

The λ values are small, <1, when an excitable system is weakly stimulated, so that its energy activity is relatively low. As the stimulation becomes stronger and the energy activity of the excitable system increases, the λ values correspondingly increase to >1, although they do not rise beyond the maximum value $\lambda = 3$. Analysis of variations in the asymmetry of gastric motility showed that it reflects a definite pattern which can often be revealed by presenting the results of the analysis in generalized, relative coordinates instead of in particular, absolute values. The phase of the cycle of gastric motor or secretory activity was used by Dzidziguri (1968) as such a coordinate. The cycle phase may be indicated as fractions of the angle of the complete cycle, that is, as $\varphi = \frac{t_a}{t} \cdot 2\pi$, where t_a indicates the duration of the ascending part of the curve and t the duration of the complete cycle. This is a most convenient definition; it is widely used in mathematics and permits construction of reaction intensity curves. In practice, this is achieved by dividing the motility or secretion curves into 24 consecutive stretches, irrespective of the time and intensity scales, and the areas subtended by the curve are then summed (Figure 37). The result is an S-shaped curve with its point of inflection corresponding to the maximum amplitude. At the critical asymmetry values 3 and $\frac{1}{3}$, the generalized graph will assume the form in which the phase values are in the coordinates

$$\varphi_\lambda = \frac{1}{3} = \frac{3\pi}{2}, \quad \text{or} \quad 270°,$$

$$\varphi_\lambda = \frac{\pi}{2}, \quad \text{or} \quad 90°.$$

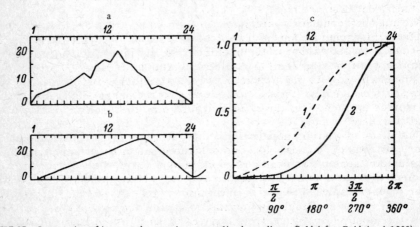

FIGURE 37. Construction of integrated curves in a generalized coordinate field (after Dzidziguri, 1968):

a) gastric juice secretion, ml; b) gastric motility, relative units; c) integrated curves in the coordinate field; gastric activity: 1 — secretion; 2 — motility. In graph c the y-axis denotes accumulated energy in fractions of unity. In graphs a and b the x-axis denotes phases in fractions of the complete cycle.

The general form of the S-shaped curve reflects the process of increasing work, while the energy characteristic of the cycle's asymmetry is provided by the inflection point. The state of energy activity of the system, organ, tissue or cell is reflected by the position of the S-curve in the coordinate field. The difference of phase at the inflection points of the integral curves for different processes in the generalized coordinate field represents a quantitative measure of dissociation as, for example, between gastric motility and secretion. Thus, it serves as an indicator of the onset, progress and termination of the pathological state.

Applying these mathematical parameters, that is, the relative cycle amplitude A (t) and its asymmetry characteristic, to the stages of energy activity of a living system as classified above, it is found that $\lambda \sim \frac{1}{3}$, $\varphi_m \sim \frac{3}{4}$ for the reserve stage, $\frac{1}{3} < \lambda < 1$, $\frac{1}{2} < \varphi_m < \frac{3}{4}$ for the functional resting stage, $\lambda \sim 1$, $\varphi_m \sim \frac{1}{2}$ for the mobility stage, $1 < \lambda < 3$, $\frac{1}{4} < \varphi_m < \frac{1}{2}$ for the activity stage, and $\lambda \sim 3$, $\varphi_m \sim \frac{1}{4}$ for the stage of disordered activity. Apparently, the transition of an excitable system from one stage to another does not proceed smoothly and gradually, but by jumps; this is evidently connected with the functional features of the governing and regulating mechanisms. The energy lost in overcoming internal resistance is inversely proportional to the degree of the phase asymmetry of the action cycle, while the efficiency is maximal $(\lambda = \frac{1}{3})$ in the stage of functional rest and minimal in the stage of mobility (down to the minimal permissible level for a living system in the stage of disordered activity). It is important to reemphasize the fundamental premise that the value of the amplitude of the activity of any excitable system subjected to stimulation does not increase more than three times; the degree of temporary asymmetry does not exceed $\lambda = 3$; and the energy lost by the living system in overcoming the resistance within the system itself amounts to $\sim \frac{1}{4}$ of the amplitude value of the action cycle of the system in the functional resting stage.

We must now consider what information the physiologist or clinician can obtain from this technique for the quantitative evaluation of physiological activity.

It has been shown that in the healthy organism there is a definite correlation between the degree of asymmetry and the amplitude of contraction of the smooth muscle of the stomach. A high amplitude value is always associated with a high asymmetry coefficient and vice versa. In a sick organism, the indices become dissociated, so that high amplitudes are associated with small values of and vice versa.

The study of gastric motility in healthy subjects and in cases of peptic ulcer, gastritis or neurosis has demonstrated pathological manifestations quite unlike those of the norm. The maximum value of the asymmetry coefficient is greater in healthy than in sick subjects. Patients with peptic ulcer exhibit disturbed motor synchronism — the curves being shifted to the right, that is, the maximum and minimum values are reduced to <1 (0.8). Thus, the most prevalent contractions are those in which the ordinate maximum is shifted toward the end of the cycle. Besides the dissociation and the reduced absolute asymmetry values, neurotic patients also display a distortion in the S-shape of the motility curve, which usually approaches a straight line. In cases of gastritis the curve loses its S-shape and tends toward the median.

The quantitative expression of gastric motility in healthy and sick persons can thus provide a basis for the quantitative classification of the typological traits. Based on the asymmetry coefficient range of 3.0—0.3, the previously established types of gastric motor function can now be given numerical expression as follows: excitable and asthenic types, 3.0—1.0; inert and inhibited types, 1.0—0.3. This constitutes a most convenient method of describing the degree of the pathological lesion in an organ, which may be not only of diagnostic value, but can also serve to evaluate the efficiency of treatment. Even if a patient shows qualitative signs of improvement of gastric motility, it does not necessarily mean that recovery is complete. This must be confirmed by quantitative investigation, by estimating the degree of asymmetry. Furthermore, this criterion is very sensitive, revealing the onset of normal gastric motility even when the signs of recovery are still difficult to detect by qualitative indices. This would be indicated, for example, in the inert type, by a change in the coefficient of asymmetry from 0.3—0.4 to 0.6—0.8, in the absence of changes in the amplitude and frequency of contraction.

Applied to human subjects, the technique of testing gastric function by means of a double stomach tube (Kurtsin, 1953a; Bykov and Kurtsin, 1960, 1966a, 1966b; Kurtsin et al., 1960; Shilov, 1962; Gurskaya, 1964; Rashap, 1966 Baladzhaeva, 1968; Zvorykin, 1968; Ibragimova, 1968) has provided information not only on gastric motility but also on secretory activity and has afforded an opportunity of comparing these two functions of the same organ by similar quantitative indices. For this purpose, the initial results were represented on the same scale, being reduced to the complete cycle on the x-axis and to fractions of the maximum amplitude on the y-axis. The general shape of such integral curves reflects the increase in activity, while the energy characteristic of the cycle is yielded by the inflection point of the integral curve. An analysis of this kind carried out by Dzidziguri (1968) showed that in healthy human subjects the degree of asymmetry of gastric motility and secretion attained equally high values, with complete coincidence of the generalized field coordinates as regards both the complete cycle phase and the form of the curves. The same was true of healthy dogs.

The relationship between the form of the integral curves of secretion and motility is quite different in sick and in healthy persons (Figure 38). In peptic ulcer the synchronism of the curves is disturbed: the motility curves are shifted toward the end of cycle, coinciding with the curves showing little asymmetry with regard to λ, whereas the secretion curves show a fairly large measure of asymmetry. As a result, the integral curves of secretion and motility cross in some patients, while in others they diverge in different directions from the coordinate field center. In gastritis, the integral curves of motility are similar to those in cases of peptic ulcer, whereas the secretion curves, unlike those for peptic ulcer, always lie either above or below the median line of the coordinate field. In neuroses the integral curves for both motility and secretion coincide and lie in the central part of the generalized coordinate field. Similar pathological changes in the degree of asymmetry of the gastric secretory and motility cycles, with dissociation of their curves, are displayed by dogs subjected to experimental neurosis.

The analysis demonstrated that low values of the asymmetry phase of the curves of gastric secretion and motility and their corresponding position in the generalized coordinate field were the normal findings, while dissociation of the curves occurred in pathological states. Dissociation may also take place with regard to the secretion of individual substances, such as water, salts, hydrochloric acid or pepsin. Consequently, the degree of dissociation may reflect the degree of pathological involvement.

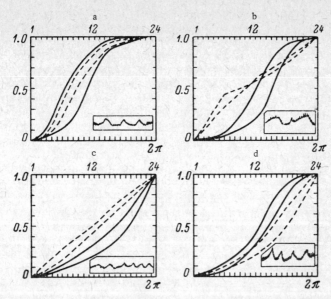

FIGURE 38. Integral curves of gastric secretion and motility in a healthy subject and in patients suffering from various forms of corticovisceral pathology; from the results of two measurements (after Dzidziguri, 1968):

a) healthy subject; b) case of peptic ulcer; c) case of neurosis; d) case of gastritis. In the right bottom corner of each diagram a portion of the gastrogram is shown. Remaining notation as in Figure 37.

Such, in brief, are the results of the first attempt to apply mathematical analysis to the quantitative evaluation of the visceral effect in disturbances of the cortical mechanisms governing autonomic activity of the organism.

APPLICATION OF CYBERNETIC METHODS TO THE COMPREHENSIVE EVALUATION OF CORTICOVISCERAL DISTURBANCES

In the same way as Dzidziguri (1968) applied mathematical analysis to the visceral effects due to a particular disturbance of higher nervous activity (experimental neurosis), Genes and Rashap (1963) used cynernetic methods for the comprehensive evaluation of corticovisceral disturbances in cases of peptic ulcer. Their idea was to obtain a numerical statement of the principal qualitative features of the disease, involving higher nervous activity, on the one hand, and the autonomic reactions, on the other. These numerical indices would then be used for the compilation of a coding table representing the numerical statement of the results of the clinical analysis of a particular case. Each major sign of disease is represented by one digit of a multidigit number which thus expresses the entire disease syndrome. These signs are always encoded in a particular order. The multidigit numbers are included in special tables, or are fed directly to the computer, which sorts them by groups according to a set program.

From among the main signs of peptic ulcer which reflect the changes in higher nervous activity and in autonomic visceral activity, the authors concentrated on the following indices: type of higher nervous activity (1), mean latent period of speech reaction in verbal test (2), overall evaluation of the results of the speech-motor test (3), functional evaluation of the state of autonomic reactivity by the cerebral, cardiac, dermoautonomic and vascular tests (4), stability of the blood capillaries (5), blood acetylcholine level (6), blood cholinesterase level (7), quantity of gastric juice (8), acidity of gastric juice (9), test-breakfast residue (10), and gastric motility (11). These findings were grouped according to similar and common features. Thus, there were "2—3" and "1—2—3" combinations with regard to higher nervous activity, "4—5" and "6—7" combinations with regard to autonomic reactions, and a "8—9—10—11" combination for gastric activity.

When studying corticovisceral disturbances in this way, important information is provided by correlating signs or combinations which indicate the state of higher nervous activity with those which refer to the autonomic visceral reactions. Thus, tests were often made for such sign combinations as "2—3—4", "1—2—3—4", "2—3—4—5", "1—2—3—6—7", "2—3—4—5"and "2—3—8—9—10—11". These combinations immediately provided generalized data on the state of higher nervous activity, or of the autonomic nervous system of the patient, as well as on the level and dynamics of chemical mediation and the state of gastric motility and secretory activity, which lies at the heart of peptic ulceration.

All patients were also classified according to the severity of the disease (mild, medium, severe) and the presence or absence of complications, for example, following resection of the stomach), and these were then correlated with the above sign complexes. In this somewhat crude manner a certain concentration of the material was achieved, thus obviating that wide scatter of cases which is such a frequent cause of error in the analysis of quantitative data.

The results obtained by this cynernetic approach to an analysis of the pathological process were as follows. Comparison of the clinical groupings with the "1—2—3" and "2—3" test combinations showed some abnormal changes in higher nervous activity in all severe cases of peptic ulceration in 97—98% of cases of medium severity and in 56—59% of mild cases. Similar correlation with objective indices of higher nervous and autonomic activity (complexes "2—3—4" and "1—2—3—4") revealed some degree of disturbance of these reactions in 100% of severe and medium cases and in 70—85% of mild cases. Again, in all cases in which ulceration was associated with some other disease, the "2—3—4" and "1—2—3—4" combinations showed some disturbance. In particular, in most cases (97—100% of severe and medium cases and 90% of mild cases) both higher nervous activity and gastric secretion and motility showed specific deviations from the norm when compared with the "2—3—8—9—10—11" combination.

Genes and Rashap concluded that these indices of corticovisceral relationships offer a reliable assessment of the clinical severity of peptic

ulcer and that such cybernetic methods for the comparison of sign combinations offer new prospects in the field of study of the pathogenesis and
diagnosis of the disease (Rashap, 1966). However, the patient's condition
should be evaluated by signs which reflect the essential pathogenesis of
the disease, since redundant, minor signs only interfere with the analysis
and should be discarded. The comprehensive evaluation of higher nervous
and autonomic activity by cybernetic methods has confirmed the principle, important for the interpretation of the mechanisms of corticovisceral
disturbances, that the lower divisions of the CNS possess a lesser degree
of mobility and thus tend to remain in a pathological condition longer than
do the higher divisions and the cerebral cortex in particular (Rashap, 1966).
The correlation of different constitutional types of higher nervous activity
with cases of peptic ulcer and hypertension has confirmed the assumption
that the type of nervous system is of significance in various corticovisceral
pathological states (Rashap, 1966).

It should be mentioned that a number of pediatricians (Abolenskaya, 1967;
Darovskaya, 1967; and Ul'yanycheva-Yudintseva, 1967, and others) have
carried out parallel corticovisceral investigations of this kind in older
children, making extensive use of the quantitative indices of higher nervous
and autonomic activity, as well as correlating the indices of activity of the
cerebral cortex and internal organs in normal and pathological states. The
state of cerebral cortical activity was determined by Ivanov-Smolenskii's
conditioned-reflex method (1971), using a motor technique with speech reinforcement. The changes in cerebral cortical activity were quantitatively
evaluated, using a scale based on a successive series of phase states of
the cortical cells. The level of the balance of excitation and inhibition was
expressed by a phase index graded in arbitrary scale units. Vegetative
activity was tested by the usual clinical, laboratory and instrumental methods.

The authors claim that this comparison of the state of higher nervous
activity and of autonomic function shows the degree of correlation for the
argument value of the phase index of higher nervous activity, on the one hand,
and of the activity of the internal organ, on the other. To put it differently,
the calculated probabilities of the corticovisceral connections were compared by means of the correlation ratios of the investigated indices. We
shall not deal here with details of the techniques used or with the mathematical analysis of the data. Those interested in these aspects are referred
to the original papers. We will only note that the stereotype of conditioned
reflexes consisted of acoustic stimuli alone: a tone of 300 cps (strong) and
another of 300 cps damped by 30 db (weak), being offered repeatedly. The
development of the pathological process and of recovery were accompanied
by changes in the excitability of cortical cells and by the occurrence of
different phases of their parabiotic state (simple, equalization, paradoxical,
and narcotic) which could be fairly readily determined from the effects of
the strong and weak conditioned stimuli. The order of the phases was reversed in the transition from the pathological to normal state, that is, in
the course of recovery. Each of the four basic phases manifests itself in
three variants. An increase or decrease of the cerebral cortical tonus
passes successively through the 12 variants of the four basic phases, proceeding cyclically along nine successively rising or falling levels of cerebral

excitability. Statistical processing of these 12 variants of the phases of the excitability levels of the cortical cells yielded a mathematical description of 108 phase varieties, a scale being made of the consecutive series of phases.

Technically, the determination of a phase index, or of the position of the phase in the series, is based on the results of conditioned-reflex experiments and on the formula $N=m+12\,(n-1)$, where N is an index indicating where the phase appears in the series (the phase index), m indexes the phase within the particular level of cortical excitability and n indexes the level of cortical excitability to which the phase belongs. Each phase variety has its own index on this scale, that is, the phase index which reflects the parallel process of improvement or deterioration of the conditioned-reflex activity of the cerebral cortex. It is based on the interplay of excitation and inhibition, that is, on the fairly rapid variations in the lability of the cerebral cortical cells, and it therefore assumes a wave form.

The application of the method of calculating correlation coefficients and plotting correlation curves to corticocardiac pathology has produced a number of valuable findings which are of importance for the study of the pathogenesis of cardiac disorders. Abolenskaya (1967) found, in a large group of children, that the degree of correlation between the investigated indices was least in healthy children and greatest in children with heart failure (Table 9). On account of the high degree of corticocardiac correlation, it is possible to use this method for the detection of incipient cardial disorders. For example, the corticocardiac correlations revealed cardiac deviations from the norm in a group of children in whom no lesions of this kind had been detected on clinical or laboratory examination (Darovskaya, 1967).

TABLE 9. Increase in the degree of correlation between the phase index of higher nervous activity and the heart rate in the transition from a normal to a pathological cardiac condition in children (after Abolenskaya, 1967)

State of the heart	Corticocardiac indices	
	phase index of higher nervous activity	heart rate
Healthy heart	0.62	0.43
Mild systolic murmur	0.78	0.55
Severe systolic murmur	0.78	0.80
Mitral insufficiency	0.93	0.95

Another example is the application to gastric pathology (Ul'yanycheva-Yudintseva, 1967). The transformation of gastric lesion from functional to organic is an old, but still topical problem of gastroenterology, especially as regards the disorders of gastric secretion manifested in both the early and the chronic forms of gastritis. During the period of development of functional gastritis, the indices of higher nervous activity and of acid production vary directly.   In children low excitability of the cortical cells was found to be associated with low gastric acidity and vice versa.   This parallelism is lost, however, as soon as the gastritis enters the transitional stage and then finally becomes an organic lesion.   Apparently this is to some extent due to a disturbance of the direct and indirect relationships between the stomach and cerebral centers, associated with an organic lesion in the gastric exteroceptive and interoceptive mechanisms, such as the receptors, the afferent and efferent fibers and the intramural ganglia. Indeed, an absence of parallelism in the corticogastric indices was observed in children suffering from a prolonged inflammatory process in the stomach. It is important to note that the importance of the correlation method was revealed by its application to gastric pathology, since in this way it was possible to detect transitional and organic stages of gastritis, for which clear and convincing data could not be obtained with the standard clinical and labora- tory techniques.   This method may for the first time enable the clinician to obtain valuable information on the preclinical stage of the condition, which so often escapes the physician's notice.

Further studies of correlations of this kind with regard to other organs and systems promise to produce even more information, from which it will be possible to draw general conclusions of importance for the diagnosis, treatment and prevention of internal diseases of corticovisceral etiology, as well as for the theory of corticovisceral relationships itself.

Summarizing the material presented in this chapter, it can be said that the first attempts to introduce mathematical and cybernetic methods and principles into the field of corticovisceral interrelationships in normal and pathological states appear to have been justified.   Research in this field should be encouraged and still more use should be made of the methods discussed in this chapter and also of other mathematical methods for the identification of pathological processes (Gubler, 1970; Linar, 1971; Papa- sova, 1971).

Chapter 11

THE ROLE OF THE VASCULAR FACTOR
IN CORTICOVISCERAL DISTURBANCES

Circulatory disorders, both in the cerebral centers themselves and in the internal organs, appear to play an essential role among the many factors which influence the development of corticovisceral disturbances. Indeed, whatever the cause of disturbances of cellular activity and whatever their nature, form, duration and outcome, the corticovisceral disorders must be largely governed by the changes in the cardiovascular system which follow damage to its neurohumoral regulatory mechanisms. This stems from the basic fact that corticovisceral pathology involves serious lesions not only in the functional and trophic innervation of an organ, but also in its vascular innervation. It is difficult to estimate the relative part played by these circulatory disorders in an organ. No comparative physiological investigations of this kind have ever been carried out and they would be somewhat difficult to devise. A most ingenious experiment would be required to differentiate between the damage and other effects on the organ caused by three (usually paired) nerves which have close functional relationships. Nevertheless, over recent years both experimental physiology and clinical practice have provided a fair amount of information suggesting the importance of vascular pathology in two particular areas: a) in the development of the pathological process in the cardiovascular system itself and b) in the development of disorders of visceral activity. These aspects will be briefly described in this chapter, although such brevity is not in accordance with the increasing flow of literature on these matters, including a number of monographs (Rogov, 1951; Pshonik, 1952; Bykov and Kurtsin, 1960, 1966a; Chernigovskii, 1960; Teplov, 1962; Suvorov, 1967; Kositskii and Chervova, 1968; Pressman and Pressman, 1968; Orlov, 1971a; Startsev, 1971), and it accords even less with their theoretical and practical significance and importance.

MECHANISM OF CHANGES IN VASCULAR TONE
IN CORTICOVISCERAL DISTURBANCES

As is well known from the clinical literature, the disturbances of higher nervous activity which follow mental trauma and nervous shock in human subjects may be accompanied by various cardiovascular disorders which are often protracted and chronic, with frequent relapses and complications. These have been observed in persons suffering from certain forms of psychosis and neurosis, as well as from peptic ulcer and hypertension of corticovisceral etiology (Lang, 1950; Chernorutskii, 1952; Vilyavin and Nazarenko, 1968). Such disorders always accompany experimental neuroses in animals (Pshonik, 1952; Prikhod'kova and Omel'chuk, 1955; Bykov and Kurtsin, 1960; Suvorov, 1967, 1971; Kurtsin, 1968b, 1971b; Lagutina et al., 1970; Startsev, 1971). They are mainly of purely cortical origin, developing through unconditioned-reflex, conditioned-reflex, or subordinate mechanisms.

The unconditioned-reflex mechanism. The vascular pathology is engendered by long-term stimulation or extirpation of the cortical vasomotor centers. It can be experimentally reproduced by electrical, chemical or mechanical stimulation of certain areas of the cerebral cortex, such as the limbic, premotor and orbital areas (Suvorov, 1967, 1971; Gaza, 1969, 1971), or by coagulation or extirpation of the cortical premotor and limbic areas (Gaza, 1962; Gulyaeva, 1962; Bakhtadze, 1967). Both hypertensive and hypotensive states can be reproduced in this way.

The conditioned-reflex mechanism. The vascular lesions result from the establishment and consolidation of a pathological conditioned vasomotor reflex (Rogov, 1951; Pshonik, 1952; Teplov, 1962; Pressman and Pressman, 1968; Pastukhov, 1970). The resulting vascular reflexes may be strictly localized and may be sustained by the same signals which participated in the establishment of the conditioned vasomotor reflex. They are often masked by other conditioned reflexes associated with the vascular reactions as, for example, in the case of defense, orienting or alimentary stimulation (Orlov, 1971a). Experimental models can be created of hypertension, hypotension, angioneurosis and of various types of angiopathy. The degree and duration of the vascular pathology are in this case governed by the degree to which the vasomotor points in the cortex and the closely associated subcortical, bulbar and cerebrospinal vasomotor centers are involved in the pathological process.

The subordinate mechanism. Here the vascular pathology is due to a general neurosis. It is based on changes in the normal interactions between the cortical and subcortical vasomotor centers. The vascular changes themselves are governed by the movement (irradiation) and interaction (positive and negative induction) of excitation and inhibition in these cerebral divisions. They are often also accompanied by pathological changes in other systems, such as the digestive and urinary tracts and the endocrine glands.

The vascular pathology is characterized mainly by changes in smooth muscle tone and in vascular permeability. It is a product of the cerebral cortical effects of exteroceptive and interoceptive signals, whether isolated or in complexes. Thus, Suvorov (1967, 1971), working in our laboratory, produced an experimental vascular neurosis in dogs by Pavlov's method of conflict of nervous mechanisms as applied to interoceptive conditioned reflexes. The dogs developed a chronic disturbance of higher nervous activity, as manifested by the conditioned and unconditioned salivary reflexes, as well as a severe, chronic disturbance of vascular tone, as indicated by the blood pressure level and by the plethysmographic reactions of the hind-limb vessels of the animals. The disorders were manifested in the following ways: marked undulation of the plethysmogram; inversion or absence of vascular reactions to positive conditioned stimuli; attenuation or inversion of unconditioned vascular reflexes; presence in the vasomotor center of equalization, paradoxical and even ultraparadoxical phases, resulting in inadequate response to stimuli of the cells of the cerebral center.

Experimental neurosis in monkeys is distinguished by a profound disturbance of higher nervous activity and is often accompanied by hypertension and myocardial ischemia (Lagutina et al., 1970; Startsev, 1971).

The detection of vascular pathology in experimental neurosis is an important aid in the understanding of certain human vascular disorders. Moreover, a knowledge of the subject is essential for an understanding of the mechanism of chronic disturbances of specific functions of organs because disorders of vascular tone, often lasting a number of months, nearly always accompany changes in the activity of the stomach, kidneys, intestine, pancreas, heart and other internal organs (Bykov and Kurtsin, 1951, 1952, 1960; Kurtsin, 1962a; Zakharzhevskii, 1966b; Pastukhov, 1970; Bugaev, 1971; Kuznetsova, 1971; Khaleeva and Petrenko, 1971). It is now known that 1) the vascular reaction of the digestive organs to stimulus (food) takes place before or simultaneously with the specific reaction of the internal organs, 2) those cells of an organ which do most work are provided with the best blood supply and 3) organs possess a complex circulatory system with an equally complex neurohumoral governing mechanism.

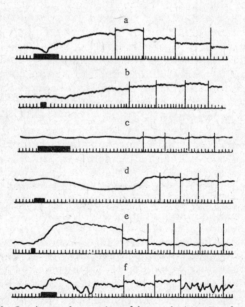

FIGURE 39. Gastric vascular reactions of dogs to the ingestion of meat (a) in the normal state and (b–f) in experimental neurosis (after Golovskii et al., 1960):

from above down: circulation rate in the gastric vessels; black horizontal bars indicate the ingestion of meat; hatching, circulation rate 1, 2, 3 and 4 hr after meal. Time mark, 10 sec.

The vascular reaction of an organ to the same alimentary stimulus becomes altered in the course of a neurosis (Figure 39). In some cases, the circulation rate rises rapidly, but then equally rapidly decreases, often down

to the starting level (the asthenic type); in other cases, the vascular reaction is either totally absent (the inhibitory type) or else it only starts after a delay of up to 3—4 hours following the ingestion of food (the inert type).   In still other cases, the circulation rate rises and falls alternately over short time intervals, thus describing a wave-form (the undulatory type).
In severe neurotic states the ingestion of food may sometimes cause a marked reduction of the circulation rate in the vessels of the organ, instead of an increase, on account of vascular spasm (the inverted, or spastic type).
This phenomenon may persist for a few minutes or for as long as 1—2 hours after the meal.

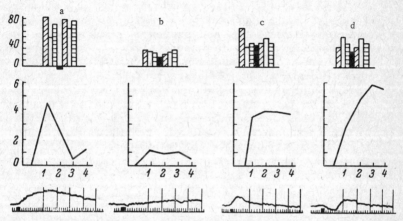

FIGURE 40.   Relationships of higher nervous activity, gastric secretion and blood supply of the stomach in dogs (a) before onset of experimental neurosis and (b—d) in various forms of experimental neurosis (after Golovskii et al. 1960):

from above down: bars — salivary conditioned reflexes (scale divisions) to bell, light, M-120, M-60 (differentiation), bell, light, M-120; curves — secretion of gastric juice (ml); 1—4: hour of the experiment; circulation rate in the gastric vessels. The remaining notation is the same as in Figure 39.

Vascular disorders follow derangements of higher nervous activity and then persist throughout the neurosis which, in dogs, lasts several months (Figure 40).   According to Pastukhov (1970), changes in higher nervous activity occur on the very first day after the conflict and overstrain of the nervous processes in the cerebral cortex: disturbances in the vascular reactions of the organ (intestine) appear after 2—3 days, disturbances of the specific activity of the organ (intestinal secretion) appear 6—10 days after the conflict; all these being dependent on the degree of excitability of the organ.   In our observations (Golovskii et al., 1960), disorders of gastric secretion occur less than 1—2 days after the derangement of higher nervous activity, and are even then preceded by changes in the vascular reaction.   These changes, and particularly the disturbances of the specific activity of the organ, are preceded by a change in tissue metabolism (Putilin, 1968; Rikkl', 1971).   In most cases, the latent period of vascular reaction to feeding lengthens in neurosis, especially in the inert and inhibitory types of the disorder, from 27 to 74 sec in the case of meat, from 36 to 56 sec for bread and from 11 to 270 sec for milk.

Vascular disturbances are not confined to feeding, but are provoked by humoral and particularly by hormonal stimulation. Pastukhov irrigated the intestinal mucosa with a solution of hydrochloric acid (the hormone enterokinin). In the normal state this evoked a moderate flow of intestinal juice and a slight increase in the circulation in the vessels supplying blood to the intestine, but in neurosis it produced an abnormal secretory reaction and various pathological vascular reactions in the intestine, such as the undulatory, inert, inverted and inhibitory reactions. Changes also occurred in intestinal motility, such as a lengthening of the latent period, a weakening of the muscular contractions and a decrease in peristalsis. Comparison of the vascular disturbances with those of gastric and intestinal secretion showed frequent dissociation of the two reactions, that is, an increase of the vascular reaction and a decrease in secretion, or vice versa, while other cases showed parallel secretory and circulatory disturbances, both reactions being either increased or diminished.

It already has been pointed out by us (Kurtsin, 1952) and subsequently also by others (Gurskaya, 1964; Baladzhaeva, 1968; Ibragimova, 1968; Chumburidze, 1970) that it is possible that in certain functional disturbances of organs not all the cells may be involved in the pathological process. For example, in some cases of neurosis and gastric ulceration, the secretory activity of the stomach may be impaired, while its motility remains intact, or vice versa. Again, there may be a severe quantitative disturbance of secretion (hyper- or hyposecretion), while its qualitative aspect (pepsin or hydrochloric acid) remains unaffected, or vice versa. Furthermore, dissociation may occur between specific functions of the same organ, in this case between the secretory and motor activities of the stomach or intestine and its vascular reactions. Such dyscoordination, as in the secretory-vascular mechanism of an organ regulated by a complex of cerebral centers, results from the functional and possibly also from the organic breakdown of these centers, or of the paths connecting them with the internal organs.

The mechanism of such a functional dyscoordination between an organ and its blood supply is evidently very complex; it is not confined to a derangement of the normal cholinergic and adrenergic synergism of the autonomic nervous system. A certain significance should also be ascribed to the fact that weakening of cerebral cortical activity is accompanied by marked changes in the functional relationships between the alimentary, respiratory and vasomotor nervous centers, both between their cortical and subcortical divisions and within the centers themselves which are responsible for the delicate regulation of autonomic activity. It is not by chance that the circulation rate in the gastric vessels is increased on stimulation of the anterior hypothalamic nuclei but diminished on stimulation of the posterior hypothalamic nuclei; these hypothalamic divisions are extensively utilized by the cerebral cortex for the control of autonomic reactions.

Neurosis also gives rise to serious functional changes in the finest vessels of the organs, as is particularly well demonstrated by changes in the resistance of the afferent and efferent arterioles of the renal glomeruli (Khaleeva and Petrenko, 1971). In dogs the glomerular filtration was determined by the creatinine clearance coefficient, the renal circulation by the diodrast clearance and the total resistance of the renal vessels, afferent and efferent arterioles and venules was calculated. These determinations were carried out first with the dog in the normal state and then again after derangement of higher nervous activity in the course of the subsequent neurosis. Against the background of the hypertension which was thus induced, it was then readily seen that the glomerular filtration was increased in some dogs and diminished in others, but that the total resistance of the renal vessels was increased in all the animals. In the five dogs used in the experiment the total resistance increased by 75.1, 87.5, 87.3, 150.4 and 209.6%, respectively, owing to the increased resistance in the afferent and efferent arterioles and venules.

Thus, the kidneys in neurosis develop a strong resistance to the circulation, impairing urine formation and also the blood supply to the renal tissue itself, renin thus being a major factor in the etiology of hypertensive disease. This has been clearly demonstrated by Gulyaeva et al. (1965) in dogs suffering from experimental neurosis. Parallel observations were made of the changes in higher nervous activity (using the conditioned salivary reflex method), in gastric secretion (by means of a Pavlov pouch and gastric fistula) and in the histology of the gastric mucosa (by biopsy through a chronic fistula and light microscopy of Bilszowsky-Gross preparations). Edema of the gastric mucosa, dilatation of the capillary bed and contraction of the mouths of the gastric glands were already observed on the second day after the infliction of trauma. On the following days, in the course of the development of neurosis and of gastric hypersecretion, preparations of the mucosa revealed marked venous stasis and erythrocyte diapedesis as well as edema of the secretory cells. Parallel with these findings there occurred changes in the nervous system of the organ: the nervous elements, particularly the receptors, were entirely impregnated, the fibers were somewhat convoluted and the argentophil properties were intensified. As the corticovisceral disturbances progressed, the sensory nerve endings of the gastric mucosa showed marked hyperreactivity; in places, the nerve fibers developed small varicose swellings which persisted through the period of the neurosis. As higher nervous activity and gastric secretion gradually returned to normal, so did the histological picture of the gastric mucosa (Figure 41).

Consequently, in mild corticovisceral disorders the structural changes in the gastric vessels and nerves may be limited to the stage of irritation and be reversible. If, in the course of such a neurotic state, the organ is subjected to additional stimuli, such as irrigation of the gastric mucosa with a solution of gastric juice through a fistula for 2 hours daily, the afferent and efferent nerves of the stomach develop degenerative and dystrophic changes in addition to the hyperreactivity (Shvalev et al., 1963; Kurtsin et al., 1965). The nervous changes are accompanied by marked changes in the gastric vessels. The mild hyperemia without any lesion of the vessel walls or infiltration of the tissues which arises in the early days of such combined stimulation of the stomach, is superseded by a marked hyperemia, venous stasis, multiple lesions of the vessel walls and lymphoid infiltration of areas of the mucosa with marked swelling. In the third week the mucosa may develop a structural lesion, such as erosion or ulceration,

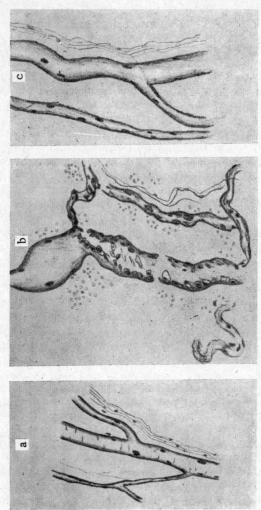

FIGURE 41. Changes in the neurovascular system of a dog's stomach in experimental neurosis (after Kurtsin et al., 1966): a) normal; b) neurosis; c) period of recovery.

the vessels may show a state of paralysis, with damage to their walls in places and there may be marked argentophilia of the receptor endings and twigs of the efferent nerves, with varicosity, fragmentation, vacuolization and disintegration of the nerve tissue in places.   In gastric ulceration the degenerative and atrophic changes in the nerves are accompanied by reactive changes which also spread to nerves remote from the ulcerative lesion in the stomach wall.   In this way, a "functional" condition becomes "organic" and gives rise to irreversible structural changes of the substratum.   Somewhat similar developments take place in ulceration of human gastric mucosa.   Consecutive biopsy of the stomach wall in human patients suggests that the appearance of the ulcerative lesion in the mucosa is preceded by severe trophic alterations in the mucosal cells, tissues and vessels (Kurtsin, 1969b).

The vascular factor is thus one of the main pathological agents in the preulcerative period.   The disorders of the neurohumoral regulation of the gastric vessels associated with neurosis play an important part not only in producing disturbances in the specific activity of the organ, but also in transforming the functional condition into an organic lesion: in this case, peptic ulceration.   Immobilized animals often develop such ulceration, starting as a dilatation of the superficial vessels of the mucosa within 30 min of the immobilization (Jacobson, 1967).   It is accompanied by changes in the fat cells and the production of vasoreactive substances which give rise to circulatory disturbances.   This is our view of the role of the vascular factor in the etiology of gastric ulcer which is one of the most impressive syndromes resulting from corticovisceral disorders.

This too is our idea of the part played by the vascular factor in the development of functional and above all of organic lesions of other digestive organs, particularly the pancreas and intestine, about which a certain amount of information is already available (Pastukhov, 1970; Kuznetsova, 1971).

The course of the vascular lesions described above and its correlation with disturbances in the specific function of the organ are also found to occur in association with corticovisceral pathology of the heart.   For many years Zakharzhevskii (1966a), a staff member of our laboratory, has studied the changes in higher nervous activity, blood supply and cardiac contraction (ECG) in the course of experimental neurosis.   For this he has carried out long-term experiments with dogs in whom transducers had been implanted in a coronary vessel and in the heart muscle, using an established system of conditioned reflexes.   In the course of his complex and laborious investigations, he determined the effect of an extremely strong acoustic stimulus on the cerebral cortex and the coronary circulation by means of the famous rattle which was so often used in Pavlov's laboratories for the derangement of higher nervous activity in dogs.   In some of our dogs it evoked an extraordinarily marked behavioral reaction when used in a dark conditioned-reflex chamber before the beginning of experiments on conditioned reflexes. As shown in Kupalov's laboratory, the darkness enhances the effect of the hyperstrong acoustic stimulus on the cortical cells of the auditory analyzer, which soon show functional overexcitation, exhaustion and chronic deviations from the norm in their activity.   Indeed, the sound of the rattle for a period of only 30 sec was sufficient to cause all but one of our dogs to become highly excited.   They tore at their harness and threw themselves about, whimpered and tried to jump out.   They developed marked dyspnea, muscular tremor, periodic yawning and signs of "fear" and axiety.   These external emotional manifestations were accompanied by sudden changes in cardiac action and in the blood supply of the heart.   The changes in the coronary circulation, which started after either 0.5—2 sec or 6—10 sec, displayed a brief initial phase lasting 20—60 sec, during which the circulation was increased, followed by a prolonged phase of up to 30 min, during which the circulation was slowed.   The maximal increase and decrease in the circulation were 35 and 70 mm, respectively,* and the heart rate increased by 80—200%.   A conditioned association was rapidly formed.   On the day following the application of the hyperstrong acoustic stimulus to the dogs, the approach of the experimenter to the stimulation switchboard (Figure 42) alone was enough to produce the entire external emotional response to the rattle and within 10—25 sec a marked drop of 35—50 mm was noted in the coronary circulation which persisted for 3—10 min, although the hyperstrong stimulus was not actually applied.   The changes in the coronary circulation in dogs exposed to an extreme stimulus and to a conditioned signal associated with it, have recently also been reported by Bugaev (1971).

Noteworthy in all these experiments is a) the rapid establishment of the conditioned pathological reflex to the circulation in the heart muscle and b) the ready reproduction of the pathological coronary effect under the influence of only one component of the conditioned stimulus complex.   It may be added that, in Zakharzhevskii's experiments, only one dog escaped neurosis among the six who were subjected daily, for four days, to the exceptionally strong acoustic stimulus.   The other five dogs developed a neurosis which persisted for several months, with marked changes in the myocardial blood supply (Figure 43).   The animals exhibited inert, undulatory, inverted (paradoxical) and other types of vascular reaction.   There was a marked dissociation between the circulatory changes in the myocardium and the heart rate: that is, a difference in the latent periods and an increased heart rate when the myocardial circulation rate was reduced and conversely, bradycardia with an increase of the coronary circulation rate.

Monkeys with experimental neurosis often suffer from coronary insufficiency, bradycardiac neurosis and minor myocardial necroses (Lagutina et al., 1970; Startsev, 1971).

The above data suggest that the neurovascular factor may play an important part in the etiology and pathogenesis of angina pectoris and myocardial infarction in man (Bykov and Kurtsin, 1960, 1966a).   At this point, we should again like to emphasize that vascular disturbances in an organ develop in parallel with changes in its intramural nerve supply.

The mechanism of such protracted and profound vascular disorders and of their relationship to cardiac contraction is extremely complex and only

---

* Since the thermoelectric recording of the volumetric circulation rate cannot be quantitatively calibrated, the magnitudes of the conditioned and unconditioned reactions were estimated in millimeters of the deviation of the recorded circulatory curve from the initial level.

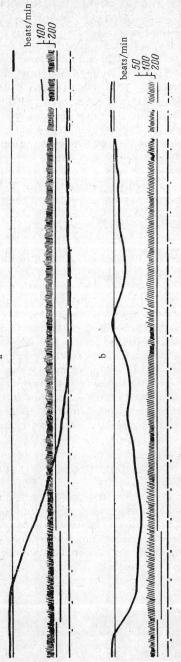

FIGURE 42. Conditioned-reflex changes in the coronary circulation in dogs exposed to an exceptionally strong acoustic stimulus (after Zakharzhevskii, 1966):

a) Kudryash;* b) Pirat.* From above down: circulation rate in coronary artery; mark of the initial level of the circulation rate; heart rate (the height of the vertical lines marks the interval between cardiac contractions); stimulation mark; time mark, 10 sec.

* [Name of dog].

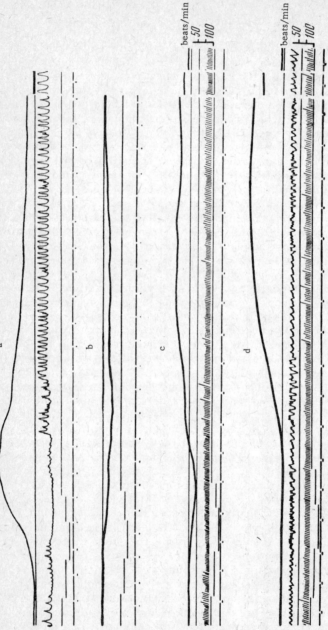

FIGURE 43. Variations in the coronary circulation of the dog Grom in conditioned and unconditioned alimentary reactions during experimental neurosis (after Zakharzhevskii, 1966):

a) before the conflict; b, c, d) 1, 3.5 and 5 months after conflict. From above down: circulation rate in the coronary artery; mark of the initial circulation rate; the two bottom marks: time and stimulus; on a and d (3rd curve) – respiration; on c (3rd and 4th curves) and on d (4th and 5th curves) – mark of the interval between cardiac contractions and heart rate.

partly understood. It is not limited to the higher divisions of the CNS, that is, to the higher vasomotor and cardiac cerebral centers, although the functional disturbance of these centers is one of the main causes of all the subsequent specific disorders of cardiac function of the blood supply of the heart. An important part is also played by disturbances of the feedback from the heart to the cerebral control centers, since the spasm of the walls of the myocardial vessels, which occurs from the very first moment of exposure to the exceptionally strong stimulus, gives rise to ischemia of the myocardium, nerve ganglia, conducting system and other cardiac structures. It is this which stimulates the cardiac receptors and results in the generation of intense, afferent impulsation to the cerebral centers which regulate the rhythm and amplitude of cardiac contraction, the blood supply to the myocardium and the trophic processes in the muscle cells. Such excessive impulsation from the organ still further aggravates the pathological state of the vasomotor and cardiac cerebral centers, resulting in their overactivity and creating dominant foci in the CNS, first of excitation and then of inhibition. At a certain point the increased afferent impulsation from the heart heightens the excitability of the cerebral vasomotor centers, still further intensifying their impulsation to the heart.

By reciprocally strengthening and weakening one another in this manner, the cerebral centers and the heart become caught up in a vicious circle which is responsible for the chronic nature of the disorders involving cardiac activity and the myocardial blood supply. We are apt to support this concept and not only because of the prolonged and severe disturbances which occur in experimental neurosis, such as the functional and even organic, degenerative-atrophic changes in the intracardiac nervous mechanism (Tsvetkova, 1971) or the vascular disorders, such as have been described above for the vessels of the internal organs. In experimental myocardial infarction (ligation of the left coronary artery) it has also been found that the blood supply to both the left and right sides of the heart is disrupted by a purely reflex mechanism, since the influence of the left heart receptors on the right heart is totally eliminated by severance of the vagus nerves.

Furthermore, this purely neurogenic pathogenesis of cardiac disorders is assisted, from the very first minutes of cerebral traumatization, by abnormal humoral reactions, particularly by the action of hormones such as the corticosteroids and catecholamines, the blood content of which is increased in neurosis (Sergeeva, 1969). A change in the reactivity of the substratum itself may also play a part. Special investigations by Zakharzhevskii (1966b) have shown that in neurosis following the functional traumatization of the cerebral cortex the reactions of the coronary circulation to sympathetic catecholamines already undergo a change on the 2nd day in some dogs and on the 4th to 6th day in others. These appear as the neurotic state develops in the nervous system and disappear as higher nervous activity returns to normal. Attention is drawn to the equalization and paradoxical effects in the coronary vessels in response, for example, to small (0.1 μg/kg), medium (1 μg/kg) and large (10 μg/kg) doses of catecholamines.

In this connection, it is also of interest to note the findings of Tsvetkova (1971) in experiments carried out together with our own laboratory. Using physiological (ECG) and neurohistological techniques, she carried out a

series of studies on dogs before and during a neurosis caused by electroconflict. The chief criterion was the effect of the administration of pituitrin, large doses of which induced coronary spasm with myocardial ischem
(Teplov, 1962). The intravenous administration of pituitrin produced more
severe and persistent disturbances in neurotic than in healthy animals. Th
was shown by the more rapid development of disturbances of the coronary
circulation; a significant rise of the S—T segment; a high, symmetrical T
wave; frequent ventricular extrasystoles against a background of marked
sinus bradycardia; and slowing of the atrioventricular conduction by at
least 0.05 sec, or even complete atrioventricular block. The pathological-
anatomical changes were correspondingly more marked, both in the coronar
vessels themselves and in the myocardium. In the controls (intact dogs)
there were no noticeable changes in the vessels or myocardium after the
administration of pituitrin for 16 months. The neurotic dogs already showe
organic changes in these structures after 3 months, in the form of local
hypertrophy of the arteriolar walls, sometimes with constriction of the
lumen, the extravasation of plasma, hyalinosis and fibrous plaques in the intima
as well as scarring of the myocardium. The occurrence in the myocardium
of earlier compensatory reactions, mainly affecting the afferent nerve endings
which developed perineural "coils" and free "neuromas," indicates that this
part of the heart was being subjected to a heavy functional load.

Thus, experimental physiology is producing an increasing number of
findings indicating that the following phenomena occur in neurosis: a) disturbances of the specific functions of an internal organ are associated with
severe and prolonged vascular disorders of the organ, which may assume
various pathological forms (inert, excitable, inhibitory, asthenic, undulatory
and inverted, or paradoxical); b) the normal relationship between the specific functions of the organ, such as secretion or motility, and its blood
supply is disturbed in such a manner that the vascular reaction does not
correspond to the amount of work performed by the organ; c) deviations
from the norm of the functional state and activity of an internal organ are
partly due to this disturbance in its blood supply.

The vascular factor also appears to play an essential part in maintaining the pathological state of the cerebral centers themselves (Kurtsin and
Pastukhov, 1970), as indicated by the following experimental findings obtained by Pastukhov (1970) in our laboratory. Flat thermoelectrodes were
implanted in the temporal area of the brain in dogs, for volumetric study of
the circulation rate in the auditory cortex (zones T_1 and T_3, according to the
atlas produced by Adrianov and Mering, 1959). The blood supply of this
region was studied after the animal was subjected to sonic, photic and alimentary unconditioned and conditioned stimuli. After conditioned vascular
positive and inhibitory reflexes were established and consolidated in a
stereotype, neurosis was induced by means of a conflict and the changes in
the blood supply of the auditory cortex on exposure to the same conditioned
and unconditioned stimuli were observed for several weeks. In our opinion,
the three most important findings resulting from this investigation were the
possibility of establishing a conditioned reflex to the blood supply of the
cerebral cortex, the possibility of involving the conditioned vascular reactio
of the cerebral cortex in the conflict and the development of neurotic disturbances in the blood supply of the cortical cells.

The first of these findings provides experimental confirmation of the possibility that conditioned-reflex changes may occur in the blood supply of the human brain, as previously established by one of our colleagues (Golovskii, 1966).   Moreover, it also extends the concept of the cortical regulation of autonomic activity, since it demonstrates that the blood supply of the cortex itself is controlled and regulated by its own cerebral centers.   Evidently, the activity of the latter is continually correlated with the rate of blood supply, and the vascular mechanism which implements this constantly adjusts itself to the needs of the cortical neurons.   The other two findings directly indicate a connection between the pathological state of the cortical cells and the disturbance in their blood supply. Indeed, such a disturbance in the blood supply of the auditory cortex during the experimental neurosis was indicated by a change in the latent periods in response to both uncon-ditioned and conditioned stimuli (Table 10).   The changes in the blood supply assumed an undulatory form ("play of the vasomotor nerves"), with patho-logical vascular reactions of the inert, paradoxical and inhibitory types. The most pronounced effect was the persistent damage to the conditioned-reflex mechanism for regulating the blood supply of the temporal cortex. All these vascular disturbances in the dogs disappeared 3—4 weeks after the conflict, without any special treatment.   The unconditioned reactions re-turned to normal earlier than the conditioned reactions.

TABLE 10.   Duration of the latent period of changes in the blood supply of the auditory cortex in response to different stimuli, in the normal state and at the height of experimental neurosis (after Pastukhov, 1970)

Stimulus	Latent period, sec (x ± S)		
	normal	neurosis	P
Tone (1,500—2,200 cps, 60 db), unconditioned	5.8 ± 4.0	11.6 ± 3.7	< 0.05
Milk, 600 ml	20.8 ± 8.7	56.4 ± 12.5	< 0.05
Conditioned positive tone	5.2 ± 2.7	18.8 ± 4.6	< 0.05
Differential conditioned tone	0	16.8 ± 7.4	< 0.01

The possibility that marked changes may occur in the cerebral blood supply in extreme experimental situations has also been confirmed by Bugaev (1971), again using dogs with implanted thermoelectrodes.

SIGNIFICANCE OF DAMAGE TO THE PERMEABILITY OF THE TISSUE-BLOOD AND BLOOD-BRAIN BARRIERS IN CORTICOVISCERAL DISTURBANCES

Damage to the tissue-blood barriers of the internal organs and the CNS is, in our opinion, one of the vascular factors which plays an important part in the development of corticovisceral disturbance, particularly in deter-mining their chronicity.   This conclusion is based on the following experi-mental findings obtained in our own laboratory and elsewhere.   Our colleague Ermolaeva (1958) has studied the permeability (absorption) of the skin capillaries in dogs: the criterion being the rate of loss of activity of a subcutaneously administered solution of radioactive phosphorus ($NaHP^{32}O_4$). The experimental neurosis was induced in the animals by overstraining the strength and mobility of the excitatory and inhibitory processes of the cerebral cortex.

TABLE 11. Changes in the permeability of the skin capillaries in experimental neurosis in dogs (after Ermolaeva, 1958)

Name of dog	before conflict	Absorption of radioactive phosphorus as % of the quantity absorbed during the first 6 min after administration									
		days following conflict									
		2–3	11–12	16–17	21–22	30–31	35–36	40–41	50–51	60–61	80–81
Sokol	32–37	50	56	63	50	53	38	40	35	37	38
Voron	40–55	70	77	75	70	65	30	32	40	30	40
Kudlash	49–62	72	35	60	30	50	33	37	53	57	52
Snezhok	50–53	72	65	70	60	52	30	45	55	50	54
Rozhok	57–59	42	31	35	40	42	45	38	42	45	45

The experiments showed that the capillary permeability underwent prolonged changes: rising by 10–18% or falling by 15–20%, especially in the first 6 min following administration of the radioactive phosphorus (Table 11) The increase and decrease of permeability usually alternated. This undulatory variation often coincided with fluctuations in the conditioned-reflex cerebral activity. The duration of the permeability changes coincided with that of the disturbances in higher nervous activity. The permeability generally returned to normal just before or after the disappearance of the neurotic state, which occurred 6 weeks to 3 months after four repeated conflicts. The control findings showed that this effect could not be explained by changes in the circulation rate in the vessels and confirmed that the neurosis had given rise to direct damage to the tissue-blood barrier. The question remains whether this finding also applies to the permeability of the vessels in the internal organs.

The answer depends on an understanding of the part played by the cerebral cortex in vascular-tissue permeability. From the studies carried out by Bykov's school (1942), it is known, for example, that the vascular-tissue permeability of the salivary gland is under the control of the cerebral cortex. This has been very convincingly demonstrated by Chernigovskii (1938), who showed that the extinction of a previously established conditioned reflex diminished the vascular-tissue permeability to iodine of the salivary gland. Our colleague Hua Kuang (1955) in long-term experiments on dogs by means of conditioned reflexes and radioisotope markers has shown that prolonged disturbances may occur in the permeability of cell membranes of the parotid gland in experimental neurosis.

Important findings on this matter have been obtained by Sultanov (1967) in studies of the changes in the vascular-tissue permeability in the internal organs of rats, which occurred on overheating the body. For this the animal was daily placed in a thermochamber at 45° over a period of 35 days. The degree of permeability was indicated by the passage and accumulation rates of acrichine hydrochloride which had been subcutaneously administered in solution. The first series of experiments showed that the heat alone produced changes in vascular-tissue permeability in many of the internal organs. In the second series, a conditioned reflex was established to the change of permeability to acrichine under the influence of heat. After several exposures to a combination of the high temperature and the general experimental situation, merely placing the animal in the thermochamber at room temperature (which normally had no effect on the permeability of the vascular-tissue barrier) induced the same changes in vascular-tissue permeability which had previously been produced by exposure to heat. There was increased permeability of the cells of the internal organs, particularly of the lungs. These experiments thus confirmed the dependence of the permeability of internal organs on the cortical regulatory mechanisms, but they did not demonstrate the part played by this disturbed permeability of the internal organs in the development of the pathological process. This has been provided by numerous findings regarding the prolonged and severe disorders of absorption in the small intestine and gallbladder which accompany derangement of higher nervous activity in dogs. The process of absorption is, of course, influenced not only by the cell membrane but also by the adjacent vascular network, through the walls of which the substances pass. In this regard there is much experimental evidence that neurosis gives rise to disturbances in the intestinal absorption of chemical substances and their passage into the blood (Rybnikova, 1955, 1966) and the same has been found for the gallbladder (Lindemann, 1957). These disturbances are severe and prolonged, persisting for months or even years, depending on the type of constitution of the nervous system. The rate of passage through the vessel wall may be increased or diminished, and in the case of certain substances, such as glucose, it may become inverted with regard to the passage of other substances, such as water. As this finding has been reported and discussed elsewhere (Bykov and Kurtsin, 1960, 1966a), it will not be dealt with here.

In discussing the part played by the vascular factor in pathological changes in an internal organ, it should not be assumed that the importance of vascular disorders is limited to the particular organ. Depending on the nature of the organ, the severity of the lesion and the functional state of its information mechanisms, there may be resonance to other organs. It is particularly important for an understanding of the mechanism of corticovisceral disturbances to realize that there may be resonance to the cerebral centers which govern autonomic activity. In the case of endocrine glands, such as the hypophysis, thyroid, adrenals, and sex glands, circulatory disturbances caused by disturbed vascular reactions and changes in the permeability of the tissue-blood barrier of the glands in neurosis, may significantly affect the synthesis of hormonal substances and the rate of their liberation into the bloodstream.

Damage to the permeability of the blood-brain barrier may play a part in maintaining the chronicity of corticovisceral disturbances. The main task of this barrier is to prevent substances liable to injure the cerebral tissue from entering the CNS from the blood. It thus performs a defense function as well as regulating the physical and chemical composition of the cerebrospinal fluid, thereby maintaining its constancy (Kassil', 1963). In our long-term experiments (Bykov and Kurtsin, 1960, 1966a; Kurtsin, 1960, 1971; Kurtsin and Kuzovkov, 1961; Kuzovkov, 1971a) on healthy dogs with an established stereotype of conditioned salivary reflexes, traces of radioactive phosphorus ($NaHP^{32}O_4$) could not be detected in the CSF obtained by cisternal puncture earlier than 10 min after the subcutaneous administration of this substance. The maximum passage of phosphorus across the blood-brain barrier occurred between 60 and 90 min after the administration. The mean radioactivity of the CSF varied between 6.2 and 11.2% of the blood radioactivity for the experiment in different dogs, depending on their particular type of nervous system.

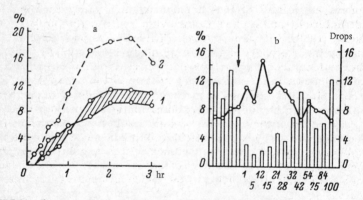

FIGURE 44. Changes in the permeability of the blood-brain barrier and in the conditioned reflexes in a dog affected by experimental neurosis (after Kurtsin, 1965b):

y-axis (left) — permeability of the barrier determined from the ratio of the percentage radioactivity of the CSF and the blood; bars — magnitude of conditioned reflexes in drops (right); x-axis: a) time since conflict, hr; b) day of experiment; 1) range of variation of barrier permeability on different days before the neurosis; 2) during the neurosis. Arrow — mental trauma.

Dogs with neurosis produced by a conflict displayed marked changes in their conditioned reflexes, such as lower values for positive conditioned reflexes, disinhibition of differentiation and the occurrence of hypnotic phases in the activity of the cortical cells. The conflict was followed on most days by a marked increase in the permeability of the blood-brain barrier, the time of maximum penetration of radioactive phosphorus shifting from 90 min after administration to a later period. However, on some days the permeability diminished down to or even below the initial level (the undulation phenomenon). Changes in the permeability of the blood-brain barrier occurred on the first day after the conflict in some dogs and a few days later in others, and it then persisted for a number of weeks or even months (Figure 44). These variations in the pattern and the different durations are probably related to the typological features of the nervous system of the individual animal, since in special studies on dogs our colleague Kuzovkov (1971a) has demonstrated a correlation between the type of nervous system and the permeability of the blood-brain barrier. Following these changes brought on by the neurosis, the normal permeability to radioactive phosphorus was restored once higher nervous activity had returned to normal.

Hence, to all that has been said above, concerning the importance of vascular disorders in the mechanism responsible for the onset and above all for the development of disturbances in the specific functions of an organ in neurosis, must be added the findings indicating the important functional damage which may be caused to the tissue-blood barriers, including those of the internal organs and the blood-brain barrier, often resulting in increased permeability. Changes in the normal permeability of the blood-brain barrier to many biological substances, for example, constitute a pathogenetic factor (Rosin, 1970).

This appreciable increase in the permeability of the blood-brain barrier suggests that during neurosis the cerebrospinal fluid receives from the blood huge quantities of various "slag" substances which are normally excreted by the kidneys, as well as various hormones which markedly affect the nervous structures (Kurtsin and Yaroslavtseva, 1960; Kurtsin and Nikolov, 1966; Nikolov, 1969; Kuzovkov, 1971a). This may be one of the factors accounting for the prolonged nature of the disturbances of the cerebral centers in corticovisceral pathology, but others are also of importance, such as disturbances in the circulatory system of the organ itself.

These experimental findings regarding disturbances of vascular activity in neurosis provide a physiological explanation of the etiology of certain functional disorders of the vascular system itself, from the point of view of the corticovisceral theory. Of particular importance in this case is the fact that they indicate the great importance of the vascular factor in the development of a pathological condition of the internal organs and in the maintenance of a pathological condition of the cerebral centers in corticovisceral disturbances.

Chapter 12

THE TRIPARTITE MORPHOFUNCTIONAL STRUCTURE
OF THE CEREBRAL CORTEX IN MAN AND HIGHER
MAMMALS ("MENTAL BRAIN," "SOMATIC BRAIN,"
"VISCERAL BRAIN")

Finally, we would like to discuss some fundamental conclusions which
stem directly from the above findings and which have been of great concern to several generations of scientists, and particularly to physiologists
and clinicians in recent years. The main aspects to be considered are
1) whether the psychosomatic findings obtained in experiments on animals
apply to man, in addition to the pathogenetic role of stimuli belonging
to the second signal system which is peculiar to man; 2) whether corticovisceral disorders can occur in man without mental disturbances.

In discussing mental trauma as the initial trigger mechanism in various
lesions of internal organs, we have repeatedly emphasized that experimental
corticovisceral disturbances in animals correspond in many ways to
various nervous, mental and somatic human syndromes and that in human
subjects, as in animals, they are produced by overstraining the strength and
mobility of excitation or inhibition. In every case the basic cause lies in
one of the following situations: the acute effect of an exceptionally strong
stimulus which cannot be borne by the cerebral cortical cells; the conflict
of a positive and an inhibitory (differential) stimulus occurring simultaneously;
frequent exposure to inhibitory stimuli; long-term, incessant overstrain of
the strength or mobility of nervous processes in the cerebral cortex; the
conflict of two innate, but biologically dissimilar reflexes, such as the
defense and alimentary reflexes; other conflicting and extreme stimuli
which exceed the functional limit of the working capacity of the cortical cell.
Various combinations and permutations of all these situations occur in
every sphere of life. In this connection, we recall a lecture delivered by
Pavlov on 10 May 1934 at the Leningrad Graduate Medical Institute,
entitled "The Experimental Pathology of Higher Nervous Activity." With
great passion and conviction, he told the physicians who packed the large
lecture hall that "the morbid nervous states produced by us, if transposed
to man, largely correspond to the so-called psychogenic diseases. The
same overstrain, the same conflict of stimulatory and inhibitory mechanisms
— all these also occur in our own lives. For example, if somebody were to
insult me very deeply, but I were unable, for some reason, to reply with
appropriate words, let alone take some action, but were forced to overcome
this struggle, this would represent a conflict of the stimulatory and inhibitory
processes within myself. And such a situation may occur more than once.
Or let us take another example: this time from the literature on

neuroses. A daughter witnesses the last days and hours of her dearly beloved father, yet is required to behave as if everything were alright, as if the family were expecting a recovery, although she is actually experiencing terrible anguish and depression. All this often leads to a derangement, to a neurosis. Indeed, in what way do such conflicts differ in actual physiological terms from the conflict of stimulatory and inhibitory processes to which our experimental animals are subjected?" (Pavlov, 1951, Vol. 3, book 2, p. 303).

However, while admitting that experimental neurosis may be transposed to human neurosis, Pavlov at once emphasized that, besides such general neuroses (neurasthenia), there also exist specifically human neuroses, among which he named psychasthenia and hysteria. In the course of this lecture he also cited a number of examples of experimental conditions which appear to lie on the borderline between neurosis and psychosis, such as isolated lesions of points on the cortex, paranoia, obsession and persecution mania. In conclusion, he said, "And now we are also making attempts, which appear to me to be legitimate, to apply this relationship to that sphere of higher nervous activity in man, which is usually known as the psyche" (ibid., p. 303). Now, 40 years later, we still seem to hear the thunderous applause with which the audience expressed its enthusiasm, respect and gratitude to the great physiologist. This was a historic lecture, summarizing some 30 years of research in the field of experimental neurosis* and suggesting ways of further study of the physiological mechanisms responsible for the onset and development of certain forms of human neurosis and psychosis.

The significance of mental trauma as the trigger mechanism in the development of psychosomatic diseases, particularly in peptic ulcer, hypertension, angina pectoris and myocardial infarction, disorders of gastrointestinal secretion and motility, endocrine disturbances and certain metabolic diseases, has been repeatedly emphasized by Soviet workers and others. Since, moreover, the physiological mechanisms involved in disturbances of mental reactions and of corticovisceral interactions are common to man and animals, it is clearly legitimate to extrapolate the experimental findings from animals to man. Thus we cannot refuse to apply the vast and mainly unique accumulation of experimental findings to the explanation and interpretation of clinical conditions. More complex, in our opinion, are the relations between mental and somatic factors in human corticovisceral disturbances resulting from mental trauma. While admitting that autonomic visceral disorders may follow such trauma, the clinicians also note that human corticovisceral disorders are not always accompanied by disorders in the mental sphere, even when the history features very severe mental trauma. A definite correlation cannot always be observed between the degree of autonomic and mental disturbances during the course of the disease and in the convalescent period (Kalyapin, 1966; Rozhdestvenskaya, 1966).

This question has been little discussed in the literature, although its theoretical and clinical significance is evident. In general, the psychosomatic disturbances which arise after a mental trauma, as described in the literature, can be divided into the three groups shown in Table 12.

* Pavlov delivered his paper on "Experimental psychology and psychopathology in animals" at the International Medical Congress in Madrid, in 1903.

TABLE 12. Possible types of involvement of human mental and autonomic
activity in corticovisceral pathology

Type of psychoso-matic disturbance	Mental (mental mechanism of the cerebral cortex)	Autonomic (autonomic visceral mechanism of the cerebral cortex)
1	+	+
2	+	-
3	-	+

The first group consists of cases with both mental and autonomic disorders (type 1); the second, cases with marked mental disorders, but no
autonomic disturbances (type 2); the third, cases with autonomic but no
mental disorders (type 3). Any such classification involves a certain
degree of abstraction and hypothesizing, and ours is no exception. Obviously, the three types of psychosomatic disturbance do not exhaust the
entire range of intermediate and transitional states encountered in medical
practice. The real picture is much richer, more fragmentary and varied.
Nevertheless, a definite starting point is needed in order to find a way
through this mosaic. In discussing the nature of the complex nervous
phenomena revealed by the method of conditioned salivary reflexes, Pavlov
has said that the phenomena were certainly much more complex than
presented experimentally, but that such schematization allowed progress
to be made in the objective study of the subject and this was its significance
and justification (Pavlov, 1951, Vol. 3, book 1, p. 55).

Our classification takes into account the following two factors. The
corticovisceral etiology of a disease cannot always be related to some
mental trauma and the so-called psychogenic conditions of the heart,
vessels, stomach, intestines and other organs are not always etiologically
related to some acute or chronic mental trauma. Clinical neurology and
psychiatry have produced sufficient evidence of the onset and development
of certain forms of neurosis (hysteria, neurasthenia and psychasthenia)
and psychosis in human subjects, in association with the development of a
pathological process, such as inflammation, or a tumor, in various internal
organs, such as the stomach, liver, uterus, intestine, urinary bladder and
kidney, or at various levels of autonomic innervation (Grinshtein, 1958).
This has already been discussed above (see Chapter 8), but it is now important to stress another aspect of the matter. The development of
corticovisceral pathology by this mechanism need not necessarily involve
the mental element within the pathological process, so that the effect may
be limited to a breakdown of the cortical mechanisms governing autonomic
and visceral activity. In some cases, however, the corticovisceral disturbances are accompanied by mental manifestations. In our opinion, the
large group of so-called iatrogenic diseases which have attracted much
attention from the clinicians and have often been classified with the psycho-
neuroses (Luriya, 1944), provides a vivid clinical illustration of this possibility. The onset of viscerocortical pathology in this manner is endorsed
by the findings of experimental physiology, which moreover provide an
explanation of the mechanism of its development (see Chapter 9). Even

when mental disturbances occur in man following mental trauma, they are not always accompanied by disturbances of visceral activity, just as the visceral-autonomic disorders caused by mental trauma or otherwise due to the mechanism of viscerocortical pathology, are not always accompanied by mental disturbances.

In his work substantiating the cortical theory of hypertension, Lang (1950) already noted that there was often a discrepancy between the mental state of the patient and the height of the blood pressure reported by the clinicians and remarked that in some clinics the diagnosis of the state of the nervous system of the patient is carried out in a most primitive and superficial manner, without any consideration of the state of higher nervous activity and without determining its type. Little has changed over the 20 years which have since elapsed, with respect to the evaluation of the mental state of the patient. Some physicians and even specialists in the field take no cognizance of functional disturbances of the cerebral cortex of patients with corticovisceral conditions, unless these manifest themselves in the form of restless behavior, numerous, varied and incessant complaints, weeping and garrulity; or, on the contrary, by reticence, a loss of touch with reality, hallucinations, loss of consciousness, or other mental phenomena. In the absence of these or similar manifestations, the patient is considered to be mentally normal and it is thus concluded that the ulcer or hypertension, angina pectoris, gastrointestinal dyskinesia, digestive or endocrine secretory disorders, or metabolic or other vegetative disturbances, bear no relation to mental trauma. Yet, the examination of such a patient by the method of conditioned reflexes or by the EEG often reveals a difficulty in the establishment of conditioned somatic and autonomic reflexes, particularly the inhibitory reflexes, a parabiotic state of the cortical cells, pathological findings in the EEG and other objective data which attest to the presence of a severe functional lesion in the cerebral cortex.

Hence, the main point at issue today is not the occasional inadequacy of the investigations of higher nervous activity, but our very imperfect knowledge of the morphofunctional structure of the human cerebral cortex and the absence of exact information on the dynamic localization and irradiation of the pathological process in the cortical formations in corticovisceral conditions. According to Pavlov (1951), the morphofunctional structure of the cerebral cortex is distinguished by two mechanisms: the closure of temporary connections and the analyzer systems. It is these which underlie a) cerebral mental activity; b) the relationships of the organism with the external environment; c) the mechanisms governing somatic activity; d) the mechanisms governing autonomic activity; e) integration of somatic-autonomic functions; and f) psychosomatic relationships. According to Pavlov all these highly complex functions must be located in specific cerebral structures. The subject has not yet been fully and comprehensively studied, so that these questions are not yet clarified. We thus dare to suggest that it would not be so sinful or improper if, to the numerous assumptions and guesses which have been applied to all such highly complex problems of modern natural science, another hypothesis be added — that of the tripartite morphofunctional structure of the cerebral cortex (Kurtsin, 1968a, 1970a, 1970b, 1971a). This hypothesis is based on a vast number of experimental and clinical findings obtained by scientists in many countries and it essentially constitutes the first attempt to systematize and generalize this body of knowledge from the point of view of corticovisceral pathology (psychosomatic medicine). The theory may be summarized as follows: Architectonic and clinical studies have demonstrated the utter untenability of the idea of equipotentiality (homogeneity) of cortical function in all parts of the brain, on the one hand, and of a narrow localization, the pinpointing of individual morphofunctional centers, on the other. Nor is there any doubt that the cerebral cortex functions as an integral unit together with the infracortical structures. Despite this, it would appear that the cortex can be divided into three groups of cerebral centers with strictly separated specific functions: the "mental brain," the "somatic brain" and the "visceral brain."

As a result of neurophysiological and neuropathological studies it has indeed long been known that the somatic innervation which governs voluntary muscle action is located in the motor area of the cerebral hemispheres. Its close relationship with the motor analyzer has recently been established, the analyzer being located in the sensimotor zone of the cerebral cortex.

The location of the cortical mechanism governing the autonomic innervation and autonomic visceral activity is daily becoming clearer (see Chapters 1 and 2). Our knowledge in this respect has been substantially advanced by the use of such methods as chemical stimulation, extirpation, coagulation, the pharmacological dissociation of individual structures and formations of the cerebral cortex, the method of evoked potentials and other electrophysiological techniques. Although by means of present-day short-term and long-term experimental techniques autonomic effects can be elicited from the greater part of the cerebral cortex, the most pronounced and as a rule, entirely vegetative effect is achieved by stimulation of the limbic cortex, orbital cortex, hippocampus, premotor area and amygdaloid complex. Clinical observations are in agreement with these architectonics of the cortical autonomic centers. For example, a pathological focus in the precentral area of the cortex gives rise to significant morphofunctional changes in the skin, subcutaneous tissue and fascia, muscles and bones, but to only minor changes in the activity of internal organs. By contrast, pathological lesions of the inner and basal surfaces of the temporal cortex, the cortex of the basal surface of the frontal lobe and the gyrus cinguli produce marked and considerable disorders in the activity of the internal organs, with only insignificant resonance in organs and tissues innervated by the somatic nervous system.

Our knowledge is also increasing with regard to the location of the mechanisms of cortical integration of somatic-vegetative functions. The principle of dynamic localization is widely applied in this field, also at both the cortical and subcortical levels. Important findings have been made regarding the existence of special associative centers and a wide network of associative fibers in the cerebral cortex. We are now in possession of more definite, though as yet incomplete, knowledge of the structure of the analytical-synthetic function of the cerebral cortex, including the structural localization of the afferent-efferent part of the mechanism which governs the organs and both the somatic (voluntary) and autonomic (involuntary) nervous systems. According to Anokhin (1958a), the clue to the function of the visceral cortex lies in the structure of every integrated reaction of the body. The relative participation of the somatic and vegetative components, both of which are always present at the effector end, is determined at the level of the cerebral cortex. This notion is supported by the presence of autonomic fibers in the pyramidal tract. Obviously, an association of the somatic and autonomic innervation at cortical level would constitute the most efficient and economical way of ensuring an integrated adaptive reaction by the organism. It is brought about by both the functional and the anatomical cooperation of these two major divisions of the nervous system. Nevertheless, the human cerebrum is the primary organ of cerebration and, according to Pavlov, mental activity is the result of the physiological activity of a certain brain-mass. Pavlov presumed that the frontal lobes constituted the organ of cerebration in man (Vol. 3, book 2, p. 233). It is now possible to determine more specifically the cortical areas (fields) responsible for human mental activity, thought and consciousness.

Current ideas of the morphofunctional structure of the human cerebral cortex are as follows: The posterocerebral regions, with the cortical termini of the auditory, visual, dermokinesthetic and vestibular analyzers, analyze the information arriving in the brain from the external environment and produce those highly complex forms of spatial and temporal syntheses which underlie cognitive activity (Luriya, 1964). The anterocerebral regions assess the information received by the brain, adjust it to the needs of the organism, and use it in compiling programs for the actions required. Although different cortical areas play different parts in shaping behavior, the entire cerebral cortex is involved in the implementation of complex forms of mental activity.   The projection zones of the analyzers provide the most detailed analysis of incoming information (primary fields), followed by synthesis of the response (secondary fields). It is known from clinical observation that destruction of these analyzer fields results in characteristic disturbances of analyzer activity. For example, destruction of the visual analyzer nucleus (occipital area) eliminates complex visual sensations (visual agnosia); destruction of the auditory analyzer nucleus (temporal area) disrupts the analysis and synthesis of acoustic stimuli, and in the case of the left cerebral hemisphere, it disrupts the auditory perception of speech sounds; destruction of the dermokinesthetic analyzer nucleus (infraparietal area) results in astereognosis. Destruction or a lesion of the temporal area and of the closely allied infraparietal and posterofrontal areas responsible for the analysis and synthesis of speech sounds gives rise to sensory aphasia: a disorder of phonematic hearing. Destruction of the inferior part of the cortex of the postcentral region in the left hemisphere, which is responsible for the finest kinesthetic analysis for speech, results in motor aphasia. The same effect is brought about by a lesion in the posterior portion of the inferior frontal gyrus of the left hemisphere (Broca's area). A lesion of the parietal-temporal-occipital area of the cortex of the left hemisphere disrupts the complex logico-grammatical codes (semantic aphasia).

All these components which together constitute the speech areas of the cerebral cortex, constitute the substratum of the second signal system situated in the frontal, temporal, occipital and part of the parietal lobes.

The frontal divisions are responsible for the synthesis and analysis of kinesthetic perception of speech and writing; the temporal divisions, for the synthesis and analysis of auditory reception of speech; the occipital divisions, for the visual synthesis and analysis of written communications.

Hence, the second signal system is coextensive with the speech region, but is extended by its connections with other regions. Thus, according to present concepts, the higher cortical centers include an extensive speech region, in contrast to the earlier notion of sharply demarcated speech centers in the region of the second and third frontal gyri (for right-handed persons) in the left hemisphere (Broca's motor-kinesthetic center) and in the region of the superior temporal gyrus (Wernicke's sensory speech center, reading center, writing center). Now it can be more precisely stated that the second signal system (for words "spoken, heard and seen," according to Pavlov) is located mainly in areas 44 and 45 of the frontal region, areas 21 and 22 of the temporal region and areas 37, 39 and 40 of the parieto-occipital region of the cerebral cortex, while the first signal system is located in parts of the cortex lying beyond the speech area (Ivanov-Smolenskii, 1971). However, there are grounds for maintaining that the decisive role in the programming and control of actions is played by the nervous mechanisms of the frontal areas of the brain, which are super-structures over the cortical divisions of the motor analyzer (Luriya, 1963). The frontal lobes are closely associated with the posterior part of the cortex and with the parts of the fore-brain which shape the acts of external and internal verbalization. For this reason, lesions of these lobes result in manifest disturbances of behavior programming and of the critical attitude to committed actions, without any appreciable effect on the performance of the external and internal analyzers. A person with damaged frontal lobes loses the higher intellectual qualities while retaining the primitive everyday skills (Woolridge, 1963). Extirpation of these lobes in animals disrupts the most complex forms of higher nervous activity.

According to observations made by Penfield (1957), the well-known Canadian neurosurgeon, on human subjects during brain operations, electrical stimulation of the lateral surface of the temporal cortex brought back to the patient's memory (consciousness) certain past events. Following unilateral extirpation of the temporal cortex stimulation of the other side still brought back to the patient's consciousness previously seen objects and past events.

Thus, a review of the numerous findings regarding the structure and functions of the human cerebral cortex reveals the extraordinary complex, neuronal organization of a hierarchic system consisting of at least three complexes of major zones: 1) a complex of primary, or projection zones responsible for the primary, specific, analytical and synthetic processing of information arriving at the cortical terminal of an analyzer; 2) a complex of secondary, or projective and associative zones responsible for the most detailed analysis of stimuli and above all for their orderly arrangement, systematization and synthesis; 3) a complex of tertiary, projective and associative zones (associative zones according to the terminology used by earlier authors; inner zones, by the terminology of certain present-day workers) responsible for the most complex types of analysis, synthesis and association of the activities of a number of analyzers, such

as the visual, auditory, vestibular and tactile analyzers or the dermokinesthetic, visceral and visual analyzers.

To conclude our brief review of present concepts of the morphofunctional structures of the cortex responsible for the mental activity of the
brain, we should like to emphasize two particular aspects. Mental activity
arises not only from the activity of certain groups of cortical cells, but
also from the continuous influences exerted on the higher cortical divisions
by the mediobasal regions, mainly limbic and hippocampal, as well as by
certain infracortical structures, such as the reticular formation of the
thalamus and brain stem and the hypothalamus. It is these which ensure
the cortical tone necessary for vital activity, the prolonged fixation of
stimulus traces and the participation in elementary forms of inclinations
and emotions.

The mechanisms of the mental, somatic and visceral brain are closely
interconnected by anatomical and functional ties; the mental brain being
associated more with the somatic than with the visceral brain. This
follows from the well-known fact that a person can produce a contraction
of striped muscle by desire or by an effort of will; that is, he can perform
a motor act which is often very complex and prolonged, although few are
able to increase or decrease their heart rate, or the movements of their
stomach or intestine at will. Yet, the ability of certain persons to produce
at will autonomic reactions which were originally involuntary (see the
review by Valueva, 1967) shows that there must also be a close, if weak
connection between the mental and the visceral brain. This is why some
pathological syndromes constitute combinations of psychosomatic disorders
in which disturbances in the somatic and autonomic spheres are not accompanied by mental disturbances, while in other cases the latter are
associated only with somatic or only with viscero-autonomic disturbances.
With the recognition of this tripartite morphofunctional structure of the
cerebral cortex, it becomes clear that mental trauma may cause damage
to all three brain formations, or may lead to the development of corticovisceral disturbances only in the mental, or only in the somatic (animal),
or only in the visceral (autonomic) sphere. The existence of bilateral
anatomical-functional connections between the neocortex and the paleocortex and archicortex and with numerous infracortical formations and
structures suggests that the mental brain may influence the visceral brain.
Yet, much is still obscure in this respect. If mental trauma is inflicted
via the auditory analyzer, one would expect primary damage to the cells of
the nucleus of this analyzer. However, how does the damage spread and
reach the mechanisms governing autonomic activity? Is an excessively
strong stimulus transmitted directly from the auditory area of the cortex
to the limbic or orbital cortex? Or is this perhaps achieved with the
participation of associative mechanisms which are also likely to sustain
damage under such a strong stress? In short, a number of points still remain to be elucidated.

The concept of the dynamic localization of centers, however labile and
swiftly operative, still requires that these be based on specific neural sub-
strata (although their location may vary), in view of the widely scattered
peripheral elements of each analyzer, apart from the nucleus. The problem
is difficult because any mental trauma — whatever its nature, intensity and
duration — has an emotional accompaniment, and in human emotional stress

one must reckon not only with the biological and physiological effects related to the high or low emotional excitability and mobility of the mental processes, but also with the psychological component, with its highly complicated content and structure (the subcortical and cortical centers of the emotions).

In man a very important part is played by the subject's estimate of the degree of menace constituted by the acting stress factor. This intellectual aspect of the process possesses individual features for each subject, depending on his personality structure, upbringing, education, life experience, age, sex, occupation and conditions of life and work. These are liable to leave their imprint on the response which may take the form of anger and rage in some persons, of satisfaction and joy in others, or may evoke no emotion whatsoever. It should be emphasized that physical stressors, such as sound or light exert a weaker autonomic effect, as shown, for example, by the quantity of catecholamines released (Levi, 1970b), than the intellectual factor, the attitude of the subject toward the events and the situation.

Hence the impression that mental trauma may in some cases affect mental function and the mechanism governing autonomic activity, while in other cases it affects only the former, or only the latter. Since the emotional factor acts, as it were, as the connecting link between the organ of the mental life and the organs of the visceral-autonomic sphere, it is not surprising that mental trauma often appears to produce simultaneous mental and somatic disturbances, particularly of an autonomic and endocrine nature. At present this is just a general impression. Our assessment will only become more precise and specific when we have extended our knowledge of the dynamic localization of the mechanisms of mental activity and of their relationships and interaction with the mechanisms connecting the cerebral cortex with the somatic and autonomic nervous systems. Much is still obscure and contradictory in this field. Nevertheless, despite these and other difficulties which are inevitable in the study of such highly complex problems, certain pathological conditions of the cerebral cortex can already be explained by means of the hypothesis of the tripartite morphofunctional structure of the human cerebral cortex. Thus, for example, in psychosomatic conditions unaccompanied by any perceptible mental disorder, the pathological process is probably confined to the visceral areas of the cortex, or to the areas associated with the regulation of visceral-autonomic activity (see Chapters 1 and 2). When the pathological lesion is located in the cortical area containing the mechanism of mental activity, the morbid manifestations may be confined to this activity without involvement of the cortical centers responsible for regulating the activity of the internal organs. Only in 3 dogs out of 400 were we able to create an experimental model of this kind. In these few dogs, the derangement of higher nervous activity was followed by persistent changes in the conditioned reflexes without autonomic disturbances.

Of decisive importance in this field are clinical observations and medicopsychological studies. The psychologists have accumulated extensive information on the mental reactions of healthy persons. The neuropathologists and the clinicians, particularly the psychiatrists, have made many significant observations on the relationship between mental activity and certain structures of the cerebral cortex. The widespread use of electro-encephalography has served as a mine of information on the dynamics of electrical phenomena in the human brain in a great variety of mental re-actions. True, it is not always clear which changes can be attributed to the brain itself and which to the skin, muscles, cranial bones and the changes in the cerebral blood volume. Moreover, no differentiation is ever made between the bioelectric phenomena in the cerebral cortex and those in the subcortical neural structures. The difficulties are especially great when the same conditioned stimulus causes desynchronization in some subjects but an increase of EEG synchronization in others. Never-theless, EEG studies on healthy and sick persons have increased our know-ledge of the part played by different areas of the cortex in different kinds of mental activity and in the integration of highly complex mental activities.

Substantial progress in this field is also due to the clinical use of elec-trical stimulation of the cerebral cortex (electrocorticograms) and especi-ally to the implantation of electrodes in human subjects for purposes of diagnosis and treatment.

These valuable methods have demonstrated the relationships between mental and autonomic reactions and the stimulation of cerebral structures, as well as the electrical reaction of various nervous structures to verbal signals with a specific significance. Both types of findings are equally interest-ing. A major outcome of this type of neurophysiological investigation was the confirmation of Pavlov's view of cerebration: consciousness being a reflection of the creative activity of cortical neurons. Pavlov, starting from the concept of the dynamic localization of cerebral function, repre-sented such activity as a pattern of "glowing" and "extinguished" cortical areas; the state of flux being the result of the continuous analysis of the state of the external environment. Similarly, the electrophysiologists have succeeded in establishing the part played by many points on the cerebral cortex in the realization of mental reactions. Moreover, this participation is not confined to the cortex. The development of a mental reaction is ensured by deeper cerebral structures, although their cells are devoid of thought or consciousness, that extremely complex property of highly organized matter, which is found only in the cells of the cerebral cortex. In both form and content the manifestations of the cerebral cortex in mental reactions are entirely different from thought processes, such as speech, conceptualization, or abstraction. The former are biological, whereas the latter are spiritual and nonmaterial, although in both cases the brain constitutes the material substrate.

One must not forget that the action of a mental stimulus, as many other stimuli, is realized through systems of analyzers, the cortical termini of which are in a constant state of interaction with other areas and structures of the cerebral cortex and subcortex, with their powerful activizing systems. Any conditioned reflex is realized in a complex manner, with the participa-tion of various cortical and subcortical areas. Nevertheless, all these elements become incorporated in the realization of the mental reaction, in order to produce the optimal excitability level of the material substratum of the mental reaction and their role is terminated at this point. Thought, consciousness and other mental phenomena are the province of cortical cells. The proliferation and diversity of the cortical and subcortical structures which bring about a mental reaction introduce a kaleidoscopic quality into the electrophysiological pattern, although a distinction must be made between the (rigid) links of the integrated morphofunctional system and those (flexible) links which are periodically connected and disconnected.

Yet, neither individually nor in combination are psychology, clinical medicine, or neurophysiology (by recording the biocurrents at different points in the brain) able to answer the question whether the processes revealed in an experiment are identical with those taking place under natural conditions, in human life. Most important, they do not provide a final answer to the fundamental question of the specific cerebral structures responsible for the reproduction of thought, logical speech, abstract ideas and other mental phenomena.

The following is a recent comment on this concept of the structural-functional substratum of mental activity: "Numerous experimental findings have convincingly demonstrated that the structural-functional substratum which supports mental activity is the cerebral system, consisting of links of different degrees of rigidity, or, to put it schematically, of rigid and flexible links. It is this property of the system in question which ensures not only the economic operation of the brain, but also its reliability under varying environmental conditions" (Bekhtereva and Grechin, 1970, p. 148).

Thus, "rigidity" and "reliability" is, as yet, all that can be said of the structural-functional substratum of human mental activity. It may be added that "it is as yet difficult to say anything about the degree of stability of the zones of rigid and flexible functional and structural connections in different persons. Individual anatomical variations in the brain, the extraordinary fragmentation of cerebral function and the fact that most of the data concerns pathological conditions of the brain, only constitute a partial list of the limitations which prevent us from reaching final conclusions" (ibid., p. 149).

The solution of this problem, or at least the achievement of some degree of progress in this direction, is essential before the trigger mechanisms of psychogenic stress can be determined. It is also desirable from the general biological point of view, quite apart from its philosophical significance. It is only natural, therefore, that scientists have always been concerned with the problem of the material basis of psychological phenomena. The difficulty of its solution and the obscurity of its fundamental aspects give rise to erroneous interpretations and to methodological "zigzagging" in the attempt to correlate the physiological and mental aspects. Obviously the findings obtained so far must be regarded as initial steps in the study of the material basis of the higher forms of reflection of the ambient world in human consciousness. An adequate knowledge of this structural-functional basis is a prerequisite for an understanding of the manner in which the ambient world is refracted through the prism of our consciousness and of the laws which govern this refraction. Yet, one can understand why researchers maintain that the day will come when we shall be thoroughly familiar with the material basis of consciousness, but man will still stand perplexed by the final riddle: the location of the bridge between the nerve impulse and consciousness and the manner of transformation of the nerve impulse into thought and of thought into the nerve impulse (Pavlov, 1951;

Penfield, 1957;   Gellhorn and Loofbourrow, 1963; Delgado, 1971). Investigations of this aspect have yielded much valuable information, particularly
with regard to the part played by numerous subcortical nervous structures
in the realization of complex mental phenomena.   However, the interpretation of this information calls for caution, as has rightly been exercised
by Bekhtereva and Grechin (1970) in their analysis of their own observations
and of those of other investigators.   For a final understanding of the structural and functional nature of mental activity, incomparably more information of a more diversified nature is required than is now available in the
fields of neurophysiology and neuropathology.   The tendency to increase
the number of electrode points in contact with the brain would appear to
be reasonable.   Yet, one must not forget that the EEG does not record
mental phenomena but only their physiological basis.   Thus, the fact that
stimulation of a point or a group of points in the human brain evokes a
mental reaction does not necessarily mean that these cerebral points
actually engender the mental reaction.   This process may take place at
points which have not been subjected to the stimulus but which are morphologically or functionally connected with the stimulated points (Penfield, 1957).

It is obvious that the same applies to mental reactions evoked by the
stimulation of various points in subcortical structures, particularly the
reticular formation of the thalamus, the hypothalamus and striopallidal structures connected with the neocortex directly, as well as indirectly via the
paleocortex (Umbach, 1964).   It would be erroneous to assume that any
single point in the cerebral cortex, composed of a small group of neurons,
is responsible for any single mental or emotional reaction.   Quite
obviously, the formation of a mental or emotional reaction proceeds through
numerous intracortical and cortical-subcortical channels, involving a huge
number of both cortical and subcortical points, all of which interact among
themselves, creating reciprocally amplifying and inhibiting systems of
closed cycles of impulsation.   A mental or an emotional reaction is not the
simple sum of the activities of all the points participating in the cyclic
integration.

Nevertheless, the above considerations do not preclude the possibility
that mental disorders may exist without somatic disturbances, as has been
confirmed by pharmacological tests on human subjects.   Substances such
as the amphetamines and adrenocortical hormones give rise to severe
stress changes in both psyche and soma, but others, from the same psychotropic group, are capable of producing grave mental disorders without
somatic effects (Hormsberg, 1970).

Furthermore, the activity of the cerebral cortex is not confined to the
temporary connection mechanism but also includes the mechanism of inborn,
unconditioned reflexes.   According to Asratyan (1970), the cerebral cortex
is the supreme stage in the multilevel structure of unconditioned reflexes.
Consequently, mental trauma and strong interoceptive stimuli reaching the
cerebral cortex may also produce corticovisceral disturbances via the
mechanism of unconditioned reflexes.   However, in this case, too, it may act
as the trigger mechanism of a psychosomatic disorder with simultaneous
damage to the mental mechanism and to the mechanism governing the
visceral-autonomic system; or it may trigger off corticovisceral disturbances alone, without any mental overlay, with relatively normal mental

activity. In the latter case, however, one must take into consideration the possibility that some latent mental disorder may exist, which only reveals itself under special conditions of functional stress. It is also obviously necessary to test the functional state of the cerebral cortex not only by means of conditioned reflexes but also by its innate reactions; moreover, a number of different qualitative aspects of the conditioned reflexes require to be tested. In our experiments, we have repeatedly encountered a situation in which the pathological state of the cerebral cortex was only clearly revealed by the method of conditioned alimentary reflexes, whereas the performance of the cortical cells appeared normal when tested by the antacid-defense reflex. Such a division of cerebral cortical function has been clearly observed in dogs subjected to total irradiation with penetrating radiation (Kurtsin, 1961). Phenomena of this kind have also been described by other authors. For example, in Pshonik's laboratory the conflict and the disturbances in the stereotype of conditioned stimulation in dogs were followed by periods when certain reflexes indicated a pathological condition of the cortex, while others did not (Grushevskii, 1969).

Thus, in this aspect too, one encounters the problem of the localization of cortical activity. A final solution of the problem of the trigger mechanisms of corticovisceral disturbances will therefore only be achieved when we possess more detailed knowledge of the material location of the mental, somatic and vegetative brain in the cerebral cortex and of the physical basis of the direct and indirect connections between the mental and somatic-autonomic mechanisms and those subcortical nervous structures which are in direct neurohumoral connection with the internal organs and bodily systems.

Hence, the visceral brain is not just an assemblage of the cortical and subcortical nerve centers which regulates autonomic visceral activity within the framework of the limbic system, as visualized by MacLean (1955) who initiated the concept of the visceral brain. The regions of analysis and synthesis of visceral (interoceptive) signalization must also be included within it. Again, the visceral brain is not merely an assemblage of the cortical and subcortical portions of the visceral (interoceptive) analyzer, as claimed by Airapet'yants and Sotnichenko (1967). In our view, the visceral brain is an association of nerve centers (graphically described by Ukhtomskii as a "constellation of centers"), with an integrated pattern of efferent and afferent structures for the central control of visceral systems and with special apparatus for the analysis and synthesis of visceral information reaching the brain via the feedback mechanisms.

It would thus appear that psychosomatic disorders always involve corticovisceral disturbances, but may or may not be accompanied by mental manifestations. The crucial point is whether the pathological process is confined to the visceral brain or has also spread to the mental brain, involving various nervous structures of mental activity. In principle, this also applies to the somatic brain which is of an analogous design, being an integrated efferent-afferent system which possesses bilateral connections with the mental brain.

The consistent incorporation of the autonomic component, such as the blood supply and metabolic processes, in the somatic activities of the organs and tissues under normal conditions, suggests that the visceral brain may also be involved in disorders of function within the sphere of the somatic brain, with corresponding autonomic resonance in the viscera. Again, pathological processes of this kind may or may not involve the participation of the mental brain, depending on the intensity and extent of the pathological process and the degree to which it involves the various elements of the mental brain.

Chapter 13

THEORETICAL PRINCIPLES OF PSYCHOSOMATIC MEDICINE: PAST FINDINGS AND FUTURE RESEARCH TRENDS

Any research on a medical subject in the natural sciences must be firmly rooted in scientifically validated theory if it is to justify its existence and to develop in a scientific manner. This statement also applies to psychosomatic medicine, the beginnings of which go back to antiquity, when the question first arose as to the part played by mental factors in somatic disease and the significance of the latter in mental disorders. However, for a long time psychosomatic medicine was devoid of those specific elements which are essential to any branch of knowledge. It lacked sharply defined targets and tasks, specific diagnostic and therapeutic methods and any scientifically substantiated theories of the onset, pathogenesis and therapy of these conditions. All these circumstances led to muddled theoretical considerations and created difficulties in everyday clinical work.

It was only in the 1930's that psychosomatic medicine "came of age" and began to develop independently. By that time, the natural sciences were already in possession of the two fundamental theories of mental and cerebral activity. One of these was the creation of the Austrian psychiatrist, neuropathologist and psychologist, Sigmund Freud; the other was initiated by the Russian physiologist, Ivan Pavlov.

Freud's theory was based on abstract, experimentally unsubstiantiated ideas of the mind and on a mythologized structure of the mental apparatus ("Ego," "Id," "Superego"). His principal tool for research into pathological cerebral phenomena was the subjective method of psychoanalysis.

Pavlov's theory was based on precise, scientific facts and ideas on the subject of cerebral activity, objectively determined by the method of conditioned reflexes.

The introduction of these theories into the field of psychosomatic medicine proceeded in different ways in different countries. Pavlov's ideas and principles were adapted to psychosomatic medicine in the Soviet Union and in certain East European countries, whereas the theoretical basis of psychosomatic medicine in the U.S.A., Germany and other American and West European countries became deeply imbued with Freudian ideas and principles This sharp polarization of the underlying theoretical principles, which occurred at the very headspring of modern psychosomatic medicine, has persisted to this day.

As a result of the development of the Pavlovian theory, especially as it concerns the functional relationships between the cerebral cortex and the internal organs (Bykov, 1942), corticovisceral pathology has come to constitute the theoretical basis of psychosomatic medicine in the Soviet Union, so that ideas of the etiology, pathogenesis, therapy and prevention of psychosomatic disorders are all based on the corticovisceral theory.

The adoption of Freudianism by psychosomatic medicine, particularly in the U.S.A., has resulted in a multitude of theories differing in concept and terminology. Concepts which have become widespread among Western psychosomatists include "conversion to the organ"; physiological regression, or "vegetative retreat"; the symbolic language of an organ ("the organ's voice"); and the personal profile or "personality constellation," which produced the idea of ulcerative, hypertonic, bronchial and migrainous personality types. Clinicians have also been attracted by the concept of the maternal personality profile, whereby the origin of psychosomatic disorders in the child is related to the features of the mother's personality. These ideas have much in common with the constitutional-hereditary theory and the theory of emotional specificity.

All these views have been severely criticized. It has been pointed out that they do not provide useful or correct information and that they were formulated only for the sake of a new terminology which is often ambiguous and essentially highly contradictory. It has been unequivocally noted that the main problems of psychosomatic medicine will remain unsolved until all attempts at studying them through the medium of Freud's theory of psychoanalysis have been abandoned (Mendelson et al., 1956). Significantly, this criticism appeared in the journal "Psychosomatic Medicine" which is the mouthpiece of the American psychosomatic school, and it was advanced by the Americans themselves.

Wittkower (1960), a former president of the American Psychosomatic Society and now professor of psychiatry at the University of Montreal, has stated outright that the theory of psychogenesis, inasmuch as it is represented by the psychoanalysts, has been dethroned; that the theory of emotional specificity is being seriously doubted; that the theory of the personality profile has been refuted; that the theory of correlation of the psychodynamic model has likewise been seriously criticized and that in general, "psychosomatic medicine has entered a crisis threatening its very existence" (p. 315). The American clinician F. Brown (1958) says that the theoreticians of Western psychosomatic medicine promise much, but deliver little; that psychosomatic research as a whole is either bogged down in routine, or else is increasingly turning toward the actual physical basis of human behavior and away from the untenable postulates of psychodynamics (p. 174). He says that the Freudian psychoanalytical techniques are so abstract and imperfect that, after applying them, the experimenter, figuratively speaking, leaves by the same door by which he entered.

In his book "The Downfall of Psychoanalysis," the prominent American scientist and publicist H. Wells (1968) maintains that Freudian psychoanalysis is not a science by the criteria of the exact sciences; that Freudian speculations are unilateral, far-fetched and utterly fictitious, that is, devoid of reality, while the Freudian approach itself interferes with the correct understanding of mental activity. He further says that not only orthodox Freudian psychoanalysis, but even the recent reform movements play a disorientating role in the approach to the truth.

In other countries the same criticism is voiced as in the U.S.A. The psychiatrist L. Michaux (1961), writing in the French journal "Revue de Médicine Psychosomatique," states that the views of the proponents of psychosomatic medicine constitute a cacophony of opinions. The Parisian psychiatrist K. Koupernik (1961) has written that in France psychosomatic medicine is an antiscientific specialty, because it makes little use of the principles of objective analysis of phenomena and relies excessively on speculative concepts of psychogenesis to explain organic disease. Sharp criticism has also been advanced by the French physician Marie Bonaparte (1954).

Opposition to Freudianism in medicine can be noted in the "Zeitschrift der psychosomatischen Medizin" published in the German Federal Republic since 1954 and in the British journal "Psychosomatic Research" which has appeared since 1956. Criticism of Freudian principles in psychosomatic medicine is also to be found in the writings of Soviet, Czechoslovak, Bulgarian, Hungarian and German scientists (Völgyesi, 1964; Dimitrov, 1965; Kurtsin, 1965b; Lisitsyn, 1968). Recently, the problem of the "subconscious" has been examined by Bassin (1968), while Biryukov and Smirnov (1968) have discussed "Freudianism and psychosomatic medicine."

At present, scientists outside the USSR are divided on the subject. Some specialists in psychosomatic disease are trying to veil Freudian psychoanalytical interpretations with more progressive ideas and modern physiological concepts, while others are entirely discarding Freudian postulates. In this connection, the prominent U.S. physiologist and psychiatrist Corson (1967) voices his surprise that certain laboratory workers and clinicians are still stubbornly striving to preserve Freud's unconfirmable postulates, instead of testing them in controlled experiments. On the other hand, he remarks that due to their speculative nature Freudian postulates are impossible to check and he maintains that this is one reason for the dwindling interest in Freud's ideas. However, in his opinion, the main cause of the downfall of Freudianism in medicine is that Freud committed a grave error in concentrating his entire attention on sexual and anal factors, particularly the Oedipus and castration complexes, disregarding the multifactorial interaction between the organism and its environment. Far from correcting this mistake, Freud's disciples have even aggravated it. For example, in his book "Psychosomatic Medicine" (1953), F. Alexander, the leader of the American school of medical psychoanalysis advanced the idea of integrated medicine but did not furnish any convincing and reliable facts in its support and even did not mention the classical causality of physiological phenomena and processes, nor did he refer to the well-known work of Pavlov, Bykov, Kurtsin, Skinner, Gantt and Liddell, all of whom have made important contributions to the development of methods of research into the integrative behavioral and physiological responses of the integral organism of man and higher animals.

Corson's statements are quite characteristic, since many scientists outside the USSR regard the Pavlovian theory as the only force capable of solving the problem of the relationship of mind and body, which has been discussed for many centuries. According to the American psychiatrist Razran (1963) and the Norwegian clinician Astrup (1968), research into the behavior of man and animals is altogether impossible without acceptance of the Pavlovian conditioned reflex and the resort to Pavlovian concepts. The Swiss neurologist Brun (1954) has utterly rejected Freudian concepts in his treatment of the early stages of psychosomatic disorders and considers it now in the light of Pavlov's teachings.

It is not an accident that voices in favor of merging Freudian theory and Pavlovian physiological theory are being increasingly heard amidst the enormous number of writings on psychosomatic medicine which are appearing outside the USSR. Summarizing the discussion on this subject at the Second International Congress of Psychosomatic Medicine, Völgyesi (1964) emphasized that the neo-Freudian specialists in psychosomatic medicine are trying to bring about a compromise between the teachings of Freud and Pavlov. This is noted even in the title of the theme itself; whereas formerly it would have appeared as "Freud or Pavlov," now it was "Freud and Pavlov." The papers themselves and the discussions demonstrated the obvious superiority of Pavlov's teachings over the misconceptions of Freud. Moreover, some orthodox Freudians and neo-Freudians openly confessed to the errors of their psychoanalytical theories and to the ineptness of their therapeutic techniques. One of the participants in the congress said that "the Western school (meaning the European and American psychosomatic school. – I.K.) has until now drawn its ideas only from Freud and has confined its clinical practice exclusively to Freudian psychoanalysis. The Eastern school (meaning Soviet psychosomatic medicine, or corticovisceral pathology. – I.K.), on the contrary, is based on Pavlov's doctrines."

This subject was also discussed at the Second International Symposium on Corticovisceral Physiology and Pathology, sponsored by the German Academy of Sciences and the Institute of Corticovisceral Pathology and Therapy in Berlin (German Democratic Republic) in November, 1964. The paper delivered by Wittkower (Wittkower and Solyom, 1964) again emphasized the great difference of opinion between the scientists of East and West European countries with regard to psychosomatic disturbances; the controversy between Eastern corticovisceral medicine and Western psychosomatic medicine. The author attributed the cause of this divergence to the fact that Pavlov was an experimental physiologist, with a purely laboratory approach to mental problems, while Freud was a clinician, so that his approach, like the psychoanalytical method, was subjective. He further mentioned the notable advances in determining the part played by exteroceptive and interoceptive connections in the normal and pathological activity of the internal organs, which have been achieved by the experimental investigations of Bykov, Kurtsin, Usievich and their colleagues. These findings and the theories based on them were then successfully used in Myasnikov's and Myasishchev's work on hypertension, in Chernorutskii's work on peptic ulcer and in Bulatov's work on bronchial asthma. However, notwithstanding these important discoveries and interesting research projects, Pavlovian corticovisceral pathology has concentrated on experimental investigations on animals, whereas Western psychosomatic medicine has mainly dealt with human subjects. Hence, in Wittkower's opinion, the difference between the proponents of Freudian psychosomatic medicine, who attribute decisive importance to the question why such psychosomatic disturbances occur, and the Pavlovian school of psychosomatic medicine, which is concerned with how the corticovisceral disturbances are initiated and develop. Thus, the former emphasize the etiology; the latter the pathogenesis of psychosomatic disease. Furthermore, the former pay much attention to the problem of emotional conflict, whereas the latter tend to neglect it.

Nevertheless, Wittkower concluded that the corticovisceral and psychosomatic methods, as they have developed in Eastern and Western Europe, are by no means mutually exclusive, but being different aspects of the same problem are, therefore, scientifically compatible. It should thus be possible to merge the two methods and trends. Wittkower also used a similar approach to these problems at a meeting of the Expert Committee of the World Health Organization in 1963.

Wittkower's statements faithfully mirror the opinion of many Western scientists and the questions which he poses are of some urgency. The papers presented by Wittkower and myself at the Berlin symposium were followed by an extensive discussion with the participation of scientists from the Soviet Union (Asratyan, Biryukov, Volokhov, Kogan, Chernigovskii) and from the U.S.A. (Corson and others), as well as from France (Chertoc), Czechoslovakia (Michalova, Horvath, and others), the German Democratic Republic (Miller-Hegemann, Baumann), Britain (Walter, Leigh) and elsewhere. At the request of Chertoc, a psychiatrist and the secretary of the French Psychosomatic Society, the two papers were published in "Revue de Médecine Psychosomatique" in 1965 and became the subject of further discussion in the "International Journal of Psychiatry" in 1967.

However, not all of Wittkower's opinions are incontrovertible. Indeed one could hardly expect a consensus of opinion on all aspects of the subject, since some of these opinions reflect basically dissimilar approaches even to the methodology of the subject under discussion, so that the differences are of an ideological and theoretical nature, as we ourselves have previously pointed out (Kurtsin, 1965b). At this point, two further aspects must be examined.

The first of these is the question of the national, state, or geographical division of psychosomatic medicine. In our opinion, such a division is not justified, since the psychosomatic medicine of the Soviets, the Americans, or of any other nation, are only branches of an integral, indivisible psychosomatic medicine, while corticovisceral pathology is the theoretical foundation of psychosomatic medicine in general, irrespective of the particular country or continent in which it has been developed. Moreover, human corticovisceral disturbances are often evoked by the word, that is through the second signal system, so that this type of pathology should be classified with psychosomatic medicine.

Thus, one may only speak of different ideological and theoretical trends within psychosomatic medicine in a given country and this is the probable meaning of the discussions concerned with the integration of the corticovisceral and psychosomatic points of view. In our opinion, the proponents of corticovisceral theory can hardly object to cooperation with representatives of Western psychosomatic medicine, since the object of their studies, the scientific targets and the subjects of research are indeed common to both. Such integration, however, is only possible on the ideological, theoretical foundation provided by Pavlov's teachings (Kurtsin, 1965b, p. 245).

The other aspect is concerned with Wittkower's claim (Wittkower and Solyom, 1964) that emotional conflicts and emotional states can be studied only in human subjects. In our opinion, this is basically incorrect. Pavlov (1951) emphasized the common basis of nervous activity in man and higher animals (Vol. 4, p. 415).   The same applies to the physiological basis of the emotions.   The differences are limited to the evocative, etiological factors and to their emotional "coloring."   In man, the dominant part is played by the word with its complex meanings, but its realization in the emotional sphere proceeds via the same channels and emotional mechanisms (see Chapters 4 and 7).

Thus, studies of emotions and emotional conflicts and stresses by experiments on animals are not merely justified but absolutely necessary. Incidentally, the classical treatise, "The Physiology of the Emotions" by the eminent American biologist, W. B. Cannon (1923), often cited by the proponents of Western psychosomatic medicine in recent years, is based on animal experiments.   Furthermore, one should not forget that our present knowledge of the emotions has been considerably extended by the remarkable studies carried out by the American physiologists Olds (1958) and Delgado (1967) on rats, monkeys and bulls with electrodes implanted in their brains.   Consequently, research into emotional conflict need not be confined to man.

Similar objections may be voiced against Wittkower and his colleagues, when they contrast the clinician Freud with the experimenter Pavlov in their discussion of the problems of psychosomatic medicine.   The juxtaposition of clinical methods and physiological thinking and methods of investigation cannot be accepted without objection, since physiology and medicine are fundamentally inseparable, as Pavlov himself has stated. Psychosomatic medicine must be based on an alliance of physiology and clinical practice, on the profound penetration of physiological thought into clinical practice and of clinical thought into the theoretical concepts of physiology.

In our opinion, this requirement is satisfied by the corticovisceral theory (Bykov and Kurtsin, 1948, 1960, 1966a, 1966b, 1968) which has succeeded in integrating clinical and experimental findings.

Starting from the corticovisceral theory, experimental models have been created of the autonomic neuroses affecting the heart, blood vessels, stomach and intestine, of coronary insufficiency, of angina pectoris and cardiospasm, biliary and gastrointestinal dyskinesia and of such conditions as diabetic hyperglycemia, amenorrhea, gastric achylia, adenomatosis, gastric polyposis, gastric ulcer, certain forms of myocardial infarction and atherosclerosis. These conditions are based on a primary disturbance of the cortical mechanism governing the visceral organs and systems, due to an overstrain of the excitatory and inhibitory mechanisms in the cerebral cortex.

The corticovisceral theory thus solves one of the principal and fundamental problems of the etiology of psychosomatic disorders.

According to this theory, the term psychosomatic medicine covers all disorders associated with a primary functional disturbance in the cerebral cortex (a neurosis or a psychosis) and with a secondary disturbance in the somatic (visceral-autonomic) sphere (Kurtsin, 1971a).   The onset and development of psychosomatic disorders are determined by both external, environmental factors (which in the case of man are mainly social factors) and internal factors, particularly interoceptive stimuli, which, like the exteroceptive stimuli, are capable of producing a conflict between excitation and inhibition in the cerebral cortex and subcortical structures.   A combined effect of these two kinds of trauma may also be manifested; the psychogenic trauma often constituting a trigger mechanism which is followed by other mechanisms (including interoceptive stimuli) which sustain and exacerbate the primary trauma to the cerebral cortex.

The corticovisceral theory has thus added to the number of trigger mechanisms which help initiate a pathological process of cortical origin, thereby facilitating the interpretation of the nature (etiology) and development (pathogenesis) of psychosomatic disorders.

Numerous experiments on animals have demonstrated that cortical stress gives rise to protracted disturbances of cerebral activity, of the autonomic visceral systems of the body, and moreover of such general biological processes as the permeability of cell membranes, the absorption and metabolism of various substances and the synthesis of enzymes and hormones. Ultrastructural changes in the cells have been revealed by electron microscopy. All these findings demonstrate the widespread resonance to functional trauma of the cerebral cortex, which takes place in the body at the systemic, organ, cellular and subcellular level and possibly at the molecular level.

The corticovisceral theory is thus nearing the solution of one of the most immediate problems of the pathogenesis of psychosomatic disorders: the way in which functional disturbances are transformed into organic disorders.

Experiments have shown the significance of a typology of higher nervous activity with regard to the onset, development and outcome of corticovisceral disturbances. Extrapolating the laboratory results to man, it may be said that the overwhelming majority of the "carriers" of psychosomatic disorders are those whose nervous system is of the weak, or unbalanced, strong types.

The corticovisceral theory has thus helped solve a centuries' old problem of psychosomatic medicine: the significance of constitutional, hereditary factors in the etiology and pathogenesis of psychosomatic disorders.

Experimental studies have shown that the predominant, or selective, localization of a morbid process in an organ in a general neurosis depends on the functional state of the organ and its afferent signaling system at the moment of traumatization of the cerebral cortex. Following a disease process (inflammation), or excessive and frequent stimulation of the interoceptive mechanism, an organ enters a state of increased reactivity (locus majoris reactivae) and of lowered resistance (locus minoris resistentio). There is also the possibility that selective damage can be inflicted on an organ by means of conditioned reflexes, as has been noted in animal experiments and in observations on human subjects. Hence, the nature of the selective damage to an organ is not determined exclusively by the genetic code, as is presumed by many specialists in psychosomatic medicine, but is also affected by the action of exteroceptive and interoceptive factors on the organ after birth.

The corticovisceral theory has thus shed light on one of the major problems of psychosomatic medicine: the reason for the selective localization of the pathological process in an organ or a visceral system following mental trauma and the development of cortical stress.

Simultaneous studies of higher nervous activity and autonomic visceral activity have revealed that pathological function in an organ (hyperfunction, hypofunction) depends on the interplay of the excitatory and inhibitory processes in the cortical and subcortical structures. They have demonstrated the chain nature of the reaction, which proceeds with the participation of both neural and hormonal-mediator components. They have also shown that the chronic course of corticovisceral disturbances may be due to a large number of factors the most important of which is the degree of overstrain of the excitatory and inhibitory processes with exhaustion of the cortical neurons. Other factors are disordered relationships between the neocortex and the nerve centers of the limbic and striopallidal systems, the thalamo-hypothalamic region and the reticular formation of the brain stem; the location of foci of stagnant excitation and inhibition, formed at different levels of the CNS; the stability of the "vicious circles" which are set up between the nerve centers and also between them and the internal organs, the endocrine glands and the blood vessels; the degree of disorientation between the neural and hormonal regulatory systems; the degree of involvement in the pathological process of broad-spectrum hormones, such as ACTH, corticosteroids and thyroxin and strictly specialized hormones, such as gastrointestinal gastrin, secretin and cholecystokinin; the degree of disturbance of the blood supply to the cells of the brain and of the internal organs, with particular regard to the vascular tone and the permeability of the blood-brain and tissue-blood barriers; the intensity of trophic disturbances at the cellular and subcellular levels; and the intensification, attenuation and even complete dissociation of the afferent impulsation between the pathologically altered organ and the cerebral centers (Kurtsin, 1971a).

The corticovisceral theory has thus made an important contribution to our knowledge of the pathogenesis of psychosomatic disorders.

It may thus be asserted that the corticovisceral theory has already yielded much valuable information which is of great importance for an understanding of the nature and the development, course and outcome of psychosomatic disorders, as well as for their efficient treatment and prevention. There is now every reason to regard the corticovisceral theory as the true physiological basis of psychosomatic medicine.

BIBLIOGRAPHY

Abolenskaya, A.V. The Experimental Study of Indices of Higher Nervous Activity and their Practical
   Utilization in the Care of the Healthy and Sick Child. Handbook. — Arkhiv Nauchno-Issled. Pediatr.
   Inst. of the Ministry of Public Health of the Russian Soviet Federative Socialist Republic (MZRSFSR).
   Gorki, 1967. (Russian)
Abraham, A. Die mikroskopische Innervation des Herzens und der Blutgefässe von Vertebraten. — Budapest,
   1964.
Abrahams, V.S., M.Hilton, and A.W.Zbrozyna. The Role of Active Muscle Vasodilation in the
   Alerting Stage of the Defense Reaction. — J. Physiol., Lond., Vol.171 (1964), 189.
Adolph, E.F. Origin of Physiological Regulations.— New York, Acad. Press, 1968.
Adrianov, O.S. and T.A.Mering. An Atlas of the Dog's Brain. — Moscow, 1959. (Russian)
Airapet'yants, E.Sh. Higher Nervous Activity and the Visceral Receptors. — Moscow—Leningrad, 1952.
   (Russian)
Airapet'yants, E.Sh. The Localization of the Visceral Cortex. — Proceedings of the Conference on the
   Functional Relationships between Different Bodily Systems in the Normal and Pathological State,
   pp.503—510. Ivanovo, 1962. (Russian)
Airapet'yants, E.Sh. The Mechanism of the Brain and the Internal Analyzers. — In: Kortiko-vistseral'nye
   vzaimootnosheniya v fiziologii, biologii i meditsine, pp.29—41. Leningrad, 1971. (Russian)
Airapet'yants, E.Sh. and T.S.Sotnichenko. The Limbic System. — Leningrad, 1967. (Russian)
Aleshin, B.V. The Histophysiology of the Hypothalamus and Hypophyseal System. — Moscow, 1971.
   (Russian)
Alexander, F. Psychosomatic Medicine: its Principles and Applications. — New York, 1953.
Alexander, F., G.W.Flagg, S.Foster, T.Clemens, and W.Bladh. Experimental Studies of
   Emotional Stress and Hyperthyroidism. — Psychosom. Med., Vol. 23 (1961), 104—114.
Aliev, M.A. Conditioned Reflex Hypotension Induced on the Basis of a Chloropromazine Unconditioned-
   Pressor Reaction. — Synopses of Reports to the Eighth Conference on Corticovisceral Relationships
   in Physiology, Medicine and Biology, No.1, p.7. Leningrad, 1967. (Russian)
Allikmets, L.Kh. Is the Hypothalamic Trigger Mechanism of Aggression Cholinergic?— Proceedings of the
   All-Union Symposium on the Structural, Functional and Neurochemical Mechanisms of Emotions,
   pp.144—147. Leningrad, 1971. (Russian)
Alvarez, W.C. The Neuroses. — Philadelphia, 1951.
Amiragova, M.G. The Functional Relationships of the Cerebral Cortex and Endocrine Glands. —Proceedings
   of the Symposium on Perspectives in the Experimental and Clinical Study of Corticovisceral Relation-
   ships, pp.4—5. Leningrad, 1968. (Russian)
Amiragova, M.G. The Cerebral Cortex and Thyroid Gland. — In: Mekhanizmy regulyatsii fiziologicheskikh
   funktsii, pp.115—124. Leningrad, 1971. (Russian)
Anand, B.K. The Functional Importance of the Limbic System of the Brain. — Indian J. Med. Res., Vol.51
   (1963), 175.
Andreeva, V.A. The Excretory Function of the Stomach in Pathological States of Higher Nervous Activity. —
   Author's Summary of Thesis. Leningrad, 1955. (Russian)
Andreeva, V.A. and I.T.Kurtsin. Changes in Higher Nervous Activity in Experimental Proctitis. — Trudy
   Inst. Fiziol. im. I.P.Pavlova, Vol.7 (1958), 400—404. (Russian)
Anichkov, S.V., I.S.Zavodskaya, and E.V.Moreva. Neurogenic Dystrophy of the Viscera Caused by
   Irritation of the Hypothalamus. — Proceedings of the Eighth All-Union Conference on Corticovisceral
   Physiology, pp.16—17, Baku, 1971. (Russian)
Anokhin, P.K. Internal Inhibition as a Physiological Problem. Moscow, 1958. (Russian)
Anokhin, P.K. The Emotions. — Bol'shaya Med. Entsikl. (BME), Vol.35, pp.339—357. Moscow, 1964.
   (Russian)

Anokhin, P.K. The Biology and Neurophysiology of the Conditioned Reflex. — Moscow, 1968. (Russian)

Anokhin, P.K. An Outline of the General Theory of Functional Systems. — Moscow, 1971. (Russian)

Antal, J. Conditioned Reflex Preparation of the Organism for Muscular Activity. — Activitas nerv. sup., Vol.4, pp.284—293. Praha, 1962.

Apter, I.M. The Pathophysiological Basis of the Mechanisms of Development of Systematic Neurotic Disorders in Man. — Proceedings of the Fourth Conference of the West Siberian Society of Physiologists, Biochemists and Pharmacologists, Vol.1, pp.3—6. Krasnoyarsk, 1969. (Russian)

Apter, I.M. Experimental Neurosis of Animals under Free Conditions. — In: Problemy fiziologii i patologii vysshei nervnoi deyatel'nosti, No.4, pp.126—137. Leningrad, 1970. (Russian)

Arkhipenko, V.I. The Thyroid Gland in Experimental Neurosis. — Problemy Endokr. Gormonoter., Vol.1 (1956), 42—50. (Russian)

Asratyan, E.A. Papers on the Physiology of Conditioned Reflexes. — Moscow, 1970. (Russian)

Asratyan, E.A. and P.V.Simonov. A Review of Neurophysiological Studies in 1964, Including Studies Carried out in Other Countries. — Inform. Mater. Ob"edinennyi Nauchn. Sovet: Fiziol. Cheloveka i Zhivotnykh, Vol.1, pp.4—28. Leningrad, 1965. (Russian)

Astrup, C. Pavlovian Concepts of Abnormal Behavior in Man and Animal. — In: Abnormal Behavior in Animals. Edited by M.W.Fox and W.B.Saunders Company, pp.117—128. Philadelphia—London—Toronto, 1968.

Azhina, Ya.I. The Part Played by Hormones in the Development of Neurogenic Dystrophy. — 10 s"ezd Vses. fiziol. obshch. im. I.P.Pavlova, Vol.1, pp.70—71. Abstracts, Reports on Symposium. Moscow—Leningrad, 1964. (Russian)

Badikov, V.I. The Radiation of Stimuli from the Emotional Centers of the Hypothalamus to the Cerebral Cortex. — Proceedings of the Ninth All-Union Conference on Corticovisceral Physiology, p.19. Baku, 1971. (Russian)

Bailey, N.T.J. The Mathematical Approach to Biology and Medicine. — London, Wiley, 1967.

Bakhtadze, G.G. The Pathology and Clinical Aspects of Chronic Arterial Hypotension. — Author's Summary of Thesis. Tbilisi, 1967. (Russian)

Baklavadzhyan, O.G. An Electrophysiological Study of the Representation of Visceral and Somatic Afferent Systems in the Hypothalamus.— 11 s"ezd Vses. fisiol. obshch. im. I.P.Pavlova, Vol.1, pp.209—212. Abstracts of Reports to Symposium. Leningrad, 1970. (Russian)

Bakuradze, A.N. and T.M.Nikolaeva. The Effect of the Electrical Stimulation of Certain Cerebral Structures on Gallbladder Motility. — In: Fiziologiya i patologiya pishchevareniya, pp.9—12. Summary of Reports to the Conference. L'vov, 1965. (Russian)

Baladzhaeva, S.S. The Physiological Basis of the Treatment of Peptic Ulcer with Naphthene. Hydrocarbons from Naphthalene Oil (Petroleum). — Author's Summary of Thesis. Baku, 1968. (Russian)

Baladzhaeva, S.S. Changes in Gastric Activity after Interference of the Food and Defense Reflexes. — Proceedings of the Ninth All-Union Conference on Corticovisceral Physiology, pp.21—22. Baku, 1971. (Russian)

Balakshina, V.L. The Function of the Urinary System in Pathological States of Higher Nervous Activity. — Trudy Inst. Fiziol. im. I.P.Pavlova, Vol.3 (1954), 463—474. (Russian)

Balakshina, V.L. The Role of the Hormonal Link in the Reflex Activity of the Kidneys in Corticovisceral Pathology. — 10 s"ezd Vses. fiziol. obshch. im. I.P.Pavlova, Vol.1. Scientific Communications, No.1, p.72. Moscow—Leningrad, 1964. (Russian)

Balakshina, V.L. The Mechanism of Functional Asymmetry in Kidney Function in Dogs with Corticovisceral Pathology. Proceedings of the Ninth All-Union Conference on Corticovisceral Physiology, pp.22—23. Baku, 1971. (Russian)

Balakshina, V.L., K.F.Britikova, N.K.Gaza, L.N.Gulyaeva, M.Lindemann, M.A.Obukhova, N.M.Rybnikova, I.V.Sergeeva, and L.D.Tikhomirova. Normal and Pathological Manifestations of Higher Nervous Activity and Autonomic Function in Dogs in Estrus. — Proceedings of the Conference on Mechanisms of Corticovisceral Relationships, pp.26—28. Baku, 1960. (Russian)

Balakshina, V.L., K.F.Britikova, and O.G.Onisko. The Formation and Course of the Conditioned Antidiuretic Reflex. — In: Kortikal'nye mekhanizmy regulyatsii deyatel'nosti vnutrennikh organov, pp.20—27. Moscow—Leningrad, 1966. (Russian)

Balakshina, V.L., K.F.Britikova, and O.G.Onisko. The Effect of Chlorpromazine on the Osmoregulatory Function of the Liver and Kidneys in Corticovisceral Pathology. — Synopses of Reports to the Eighth Conference on Corticovisceral Relationships in Physiology, Medicine and Biology, No.1, pp.17—18. Leningrad, 1967. (Russian)

Balakshina, V.L. and K.F.Britikova. The Role of the Hormone Factor in the Regulation of Corticoviscera? Relations. — In: Tsepnye neirogormonal'nye reaktsii i simpato-adrenalovaya sistema, pp.38—42. Leningrad, 1968. (Russian)

Ban, T. The Septal-Preoptic-Hypothalamic System. — 23rd Intern. Congr. Physiol. Sci., Abstracts of Papers, p.473. Tokyo, 1965.

Barenne, J.G. de and W.S.McCulloch. The Direct Functional Interrelation of Sensory Cortex and Optic Thalamus. — J. Neurophysiol., Vol.1 (1938), 176—186.

Barraquer-Bordas,L. Aportaciones fisiologicas y clinicas recientes sobre la region temporolimbica. — Med. clin., Barcelona, Vol.30 (1958), 83.

Bassin, F.V. The Problem of the "Subconscious." — Moscow, 1968. (Russian)

Batrak, G.E. The Role of the Cerebral Hemispheres in Regulating the Adaptation Reactions of the Organism.— Textbook for Students, Lecturers and Practitioners. Dnepropetrovsk, 1970. (Russian)

Bayandurov, B.I. The Trophic Function of the Brain. — Moscow, 1949. (Russian)

Bekhtereva, N.P. and V.B.Grechin. Physiological Aspects of Mental Activity in Man. — In: Problemy fiziologii i patologii vysshei nervnoi deyatel'nosti, pp.138—149. Leningrad, 1970. (Russian)

Belenkov, N.Yu. Conditioned Reflexes and the Subcortical Structures of the Brain. — Moscow, 1965. (Russian)

Belenkov, N.Yu. The Neocortex (Neopallium) and the Mechanism of the Emotions. — Proceedings of the All-Union Symposium on Structural, Functional and Neurochemical Aspects of the Emotions, pp.27—31. Leningrad, 1971. (Russian)

Beller, N.N. The Specific Effect of the Afferent Area of the Anterior Limbic Cortex on Intestinal Activity and Blood Pressure. — Proceedings of the Ninth All-Union Conference on Corticovisceral Physiology, pp.26—27. Baku, 1971. (Russian)

Beritov, I.S. The Structure and Function of the Cerebral Cortex. — Moscow, 1969. (Russian)

Berko, V.D. The Effect of Novocaine on Viscerocerebral Relationships in Pluriglandular Insufficiency. — Proceedings of the 17th Conference of Physiologists of the Southern Part of the Russian Soviet Federative Socialist Republic (RSFSR), Vol.1, pp.48—50. Stavropol', 1969. (Russian)

Berko, V.D. and V.K.Trofimov. Experimental Neuroses of Endocrine Origin. — Proceedings of the Ninth All-Union Conference on Corticovisceral Physiology, pp.29—30. Baku, 1971. (Russian)

Berkovich, E.M., K.V.Sekretaryuk, and M.D.Ganin. The Effect of the Functional State of the Central Nervous System on Energy Metabolism. — Proceedings of the All-Union Conference on Corticovisceral Relationships in Physiology, Medicine and Biology, pp.19—20. Tselinograd, 1967a, (Russian)

Berkovich, E.M., R.M.Stupnitskii, N.F.Kislenko, and M.D.Il'chenko. The Effect of the Functional State of the Cerebral Cortex on the Tissue Permeability of the Mammary Gland and Diffusion of Certain Substances into the Milk. — Synopses of Reports to the Eighth Conference on Corticovisceral Relationships in Physiology, Medicine and Biology, No.1, pp.21—22. Leningrad, 1967b. (Russian)

Bichat, M.F. Anatomie générale. — Paris. 1801.

Biryukov, D.A. and L.S.Bachurikhina. The Comparative Pathology of Higher Nervous Activity. — In: Problemy fiziologii i patologii vysshei nervnoi deyatel'nosti, pp.82—94. Leningrad, 1970. (Russian)

Biryukov, D.A. and V.M.Smirnov. Freudianism and Present-Day Science. — Meditsinskaya Gazeta, 4 oktyabrya, p.3, 1968. (Russian)

Bochorishvili, G.B. The Effect of the Central Nervous System on the Regeneration of Bony Tissue. — Tbilisi, 1958. (Russian)

Bogach, P.G. The Nervous System and Gastric Secretion. — Proceedings of the Symposium on Gastric Secretion, pp.3—6. Tallin, 1968. (Russian)

Bogach, P.G. The Humoral Link in the Hypothalamic Regulation of Gastrointestinal Function. — In: Gormonal'noe zveno kortikovistseral'nykh vzaimootnoshenii, pp.27—37. Leningrad, 1969 (Russian)

Bogach, P.G. The Role of the Hypothalamus and the Limbic System in the Regulation of Gastrointestinal Motility and Secretion. — In: Kortikovistseral'nye vzaimootnosheniya v fiziologii, biologii i meditsine, pp.41—50. Leningrad, 1971. (Russian)

Bogomolets, A.A. Arterial Hypertension. — Moscow—Leningrad, 1929. (Russian)

Bolondinskii, V.K. The Blocking of Corticovisceral Disorders by Chlorpromazine in Dogs. — Proceedings
    of the Conference on the Physiology and Pathology of Corticovisceral Relationships and the
    Physiological Systems of the Body, Vol.1, pp.144—149. Ivanovo, 1965. (Russian)
Bolondinskii, V.K. and N.K.Gaza. The RNA and DNA Content of the Liver in Dogs with Experimental
    Neurosis. — Synopses of Reports to the Eighth Conference on Corticovisceral Relationships in
    Physiology, Medicine and Biology, No.1, pp.24—25. Leningrad, 1967. (Russian)
Bolondinskii, V.K. and L.N.Gulyaeva. The Nucleic Acid Content of the Gastric Mucosa in Normal
    Dogs, and in Experimental Neurosis. — Proceedings of the Ninth All-Union Conference on Cortico-
    visceral Physiology, pp.248—249. Baku, 1971. (Russian)
Borodkin, Yu.S. An Electrophysiological and Pharmacological Study of Central Relationships between
    Various Structures of the Limbic System and the Formatio reticularis of the Midbrain
    (Mesencephalon). — Proceedings of the Conference on the Physiology and Pathology of Cortico-
    visceral Relationships and the Physiological Systems of the Body, Vol.1, pp.153—157. Ivanovo,
    1965. (Russian)
Borodkin, Yu.S. A Study of the Central Interrelationships on Stimulation of Various Structures of the Brain.—
    Proceedings of the All-Union Symposium on the Structural, Functional and Neurochemical
    Mechanisms of the Emotions, pp.67—71. Leningrad, 1971. (Russian)
Bratus', N.V. The Cerebellum and the Visceroceptors. — Leningrad, 1969. (Russian)
Britikova, K.F. Changes in the Relationships of the Osmoregulatory Activity of the Liver and the Kidneys
    in Corticovisceral Pathology. — Kortikal'nye mekhanizmy regulyatsii deyatel'nosti vnutrennikh
    organov, pp.35—44. Moscow—Leningrad, 1966. (Russian)
Britikova, K.F. Corticovisceral Disorders of the Water Excretion by the Liver and Kidneys on Inhibition of
    the Hormonal Regulatory Link. — Proceedings of the Ninth All-Union Conference on Corticovisceral
    Physiology, pp.32—33. Baku, 1971. (Russian)
Britikova, K.F. and V.L.Balakshina. The Part Played by the Adrenals in the Corticovisceral Mechanisms
    of Disorders of Hepatic and Renal Osmoregulation. — In: Gormonal'noe zveno kortiko-vistseral'nykh
    vzaimootnoshenii, pp.32;37. Leningrad, 1969. (Russian)
Brodal, A. The Reticular Formation of the Brain Stem. — Springfield, Thomas, C.C., 1958.
Brown, F. A Clinical Psychologist's Perspective. — Psychosom. Med. Monogr. Suppl., Vol.20, No.3 (1958),
    174.
Brun, R. Allgemeine Neurosenlehre, Psychoanalyse und Psychohygiene leib-seelischer Störungen. — Basel,
    1954.
Budylin, V.G. Findings with Regard to the Reflection of the Corticovisceral Relationships. — Proceedings of
    the 17th Conference of Physiologists of the Southern Part of the Russian Soviet Federative Socialist
    Republic (RSFSR), Vol.1, pp.33—34. Stavropol', 1969. (Russian)
Budylin, V.G. Corticovisceral Activity after Pathological Interception. — 11 s"ezd Vses. fiziol. obshch. im.
    I.P.Pavlova, Vol.2, p.168, Scientific Communications. Leningrad, 1970. (Russian)
Budylin, V.G. and G.P.Zinchenko. Bioelectric Activity of the Cortex and Subcortical Structures in
    Experimental Cholecystitis. — Proceedings of the 17th Conference of Physiologists of the Southern
    Part of the Russian Soviet Federative Socialist Republic (RSFSR), Vol.1, pp.74—75. Stavropol', 1969.
    (Russian)
Bugaenko, P.A. The Hormonal Regulation of Nervous Activity. — In: Kortiko-vistseral'nye vzaimootno-
    sheniya i gormonal'naya regulyatsiya. Reports to the Conference, pp.23—26. Kharkov, 1963.
    (Russian)
Bugaev, S.A. Changes in the Brain and in the Coronary Circulation on Extreme Stimulation. — Proceedings
    of the Conference on Neurohumoral Mechanisms of Disease and Recovery, pp.120—121. Moscow,
    1971. (Russian)
Bulekbaeva, L.E. Bioelectric Reactions of the Cerebral Cortex on Irritation of the Thoracic Duct. —
    Synopses of Reports to the Eighth Conference on Corticovisceral Relationships in Physiology,
    Medicine and Biology, Vol.1, pp.26—27. Leningrad, 1967. (Russian)
Bulygin, I.A. Chain and Annular Neurohumoral Mechanisms of Visceral Reflex Reactions. — Minsk, 1970.
    (Russian)
Bulygin, I.A. The Afferent Link in Interoceptive Reflexes. — Minsk, 1971. (Russian)
Busalov, A.A. The Physiological Basis of Certain Surgical Problems. — Moscow, 1958. (Russian)
Bykov, K.M. The Effect of the Cerebral Cortex on Visceral and Tissue Activity. — Izbran. Proizved.,
    Vol.1, pp.141—156. Moscow, 1937, 1953. (Russian)

Bykov, K.M. The Cerebral Cortex and the Viscera. — Izbran. Proizved., Vol.2, pp.5—415, Moscow, 1942, 1954. (Russian)

Bykov, K.M. Pavlovian Theory and the Natural Sciences Today. — Izbran. Proizved., Vol.1, pp.376—397. Moscow, 1952, 1953. (Russian)

Bykov, K.M. The Cerebral Cortex. — Bol'sh. Medits. Entsikl. (BME), Vol.13, pp.1015—1020. Moscow, 1959. (Russian)

Bykov, K.M. and I.A.Alekseev-Berkman. The Formation of Micturition Conditioned Reflexes. — Trudy Vses. s"ezda fiziologov, p.134. Leningrad, 1926. (Russian)

Bykov, K.M., I.A.Alekseev-Berkman, E.S.Ivanova, and E.P.Ivanov. The Formation of Conditioned Reflexes on Automatic and Interoceptive Stimulation. — Trudy III Vses. s"ezda fiziologov, p.263. Leningrad, 1928. (Russian)

Bykov, K.M., S.M.Gorshkova, I.T.Kurtsin, A.V.Rikkl', A.A.Rogov, and A.V.Solov'ev. The Chemical Transmission of Excitation in the Nerve Centers. — In: Sb. dokl. VI Vses. s"ezda fiziologov, biokhimikov i farmakologov, p.186. Tbilisi, 1937. (Russian)

Bykov, K.M. and I.T.Kurtsin. The Physiological Basis of the Corticovisceral Theory of the Pathogenesis of Peptic Ulcer. — Novosti Meditsiny, No.10 (1948), 1. (Russian)

Bykov, K.M. and I.T.Kurtsin. The Corticovisceral Theory of the Pathogenesis of Peptic Ulcer (1st edition) Moscow, 1949; (2nd edition) Moscow, 1952. (Russian)

Bykov, K.M. and I.T.Kurtsin. Normal and Pathological Corticovisceral Relationships. — Klinich. Med., Moscow, Vol.29, No.9 (1951), 12. (Russian)

Bykov, K.M. and I.T.Kurtsin. Problems of Corticovisceral Physiology and Pathology. — Klinich. Med., Moscow, Vol.32, No.9 (1954), 3. (Russian)

(Bykov, K.M. and I.T.Kurtsin). Bykow, K.M. and I.T.Kurtzin. Teoria corticovisceral de la patogenia de la enfermedad ulcerosa. — Buenos Aires, 1955.

Bykov, K.M. and I.T.Kurtsin. Corticovisceral Relationships. — Bol'sh. Medits. Entsikl. (BME), Vol.13, pp.1021—1036. Moscow, 1959. (Russian)

Bykov, K.M. and I.T.Kurtsin. Corticovisceral Pathology. — Leningrad, 1960. (Russian)

Bykov, K.M. and I.T.Kurtsin. Corticovisceral Pathology, Vol.1. Athens, 1962. (Greek)

Bykov, K.M. and I.T.Kurtsin. Corticovisceral Pathology, Vol.2. Athens, 1963 (Greek)

(Bykov, K.M. and I.T.Kurtsin). Bykow, K.M. and I.T.Kurzin. Kortiko-viscerale Pathologie. — Berlin, 1966a.

(Bykov, K.M. and I.T.Kurtsin). Bykow, K.M. and I.T.Kurtsin. The Corticovisceral Theory of the Pathogenesis of Peptic Ulcer. — Oxford, 1966b.

(Bykov, K.M. and I.T.Kurtsin). Bykow, K.M. and I.T.Kurtsin. Patologia Cortico-Visceral. — Madrid, 1968.

Cannon, W.B. Bodily changes in pain, hunger, fear and rage, on account of recent researches into the function of emotional excitement. 2nd ed. Boston, C.T.Branford. 1953.

Cannon, W.B. The Wisdom of the Body, 1932. 6th edition. Norton, 1963.

Chachanidze, A.I. Wound Healing in Experimental Neurosis. — Author's Summary of Thesis. Tbilisi, 1965. (Russian)

Chechulin, A.S. Pathophysiological Mechanisms of Secretory Disorders of the Stomach and of Certain Other Bodily Functions in Cortical and Subcortical Neurosis. — Synopses of Report to the Conference on the Digestive Physiology and Pathology and Problems of Health Resorts and Physiotherapy, pp.188—189. Tbilisi, 1963. (Russian)

Chereshnev, I.A. Corticovisceral Disturbances in Animals in Disorders of the Hypothalamic Region. — Proceedings of the Ninth All-Union Conference on Corticovisceral Physiology, pp.236—237. Baku, 1971. (Russian)

Cherkes, V.A. The Compensatory Ability of Subcortical Structures after Gradual Excision of the Neocortex in Cats. — Proceedings of the Symposium on the Cortical Regulation of Subcortical Activity of the Brain, pp.325—334. Tbilisi, 1968. (Russian)

Chernigovskii, V.N. The Influence of the Cerebral Cortex on Iodine Excretion by the Salivary Glands on Extinction of the Conditioned Reflex. — Fiziol. Zh. SSSR, 25, No.6 (1938), 865—870. (Russian)

Chernigovskii, V.N. Afferent Visceral Mechanisms. — Kirov, 1943. (Russian)

Chernigovskii, V.N. Interoceptors. — Moscow, 1960. (Russian)

Chernigovskii, V.N. The Importance of the Interoceptive Signals in the Behavior of Animals towards Food. — Moscow—Leningrad, 1962. (Russian)

Chernigovskii, V.N. Neurophysiological Study of the Corticovisceral Reflex. — Arch. Leningrad, 1967. (Russian)

Chernigovskii, V.N. Present Concepts of Corticovisceral Relationships. — Fiziol. Zh., 55, No.8 (1969), 904—911. (Russian)

Chernigovskii, V.N. Academician Konstantin Mikhailovich Bykov. A Short Essay on his Life and Works. — In: Kortiko-vistseral'nye vzaimootnosheniya v fiziologii, biologii i meditsine, pp.3—19. Leningrad, 1971. (Russian)

Chernigovskii, V.N., S.Yu. Shekhter, and A.Ya.Yaroshevskii. The Regulation of Erythropoiesis. — Leningrad, 1967. (Russian)

Chernigovskii, V.N. and A.Ya.Yaroshevskii. Aspects of the Nervous Regulation of the Blood. — Moscow, 1953. (Russian)

Chernogorov, I.A. Vvedenskii—Ukhtomskii's Theory Regarding the Diagnosis of Internal Diseases. — Moscow, 1956. (Russian)

Chernorutskii, M.V. Peptic Ulcer and Hypertension as Manifestations of Corticovisceral Pathology. — In: Problemy kortiko-vistseral'noi patologii, pp.15—20. Moscow-Leningrad, 1952. (Russian)

Chintaeva, F.Kh. The Influence of the Hippocampus on the Lymphatic Circulation. — Author's Summary of Thesis. Alma Ata, 1971. (Russian)

Chumburidze, O.G. Gastric Ulcer of Corticovisceral Origin. — Tbilisi, 1970. (Russian)

Cobbs, S. Emotions and Clinical Medicine. — New York, 1950.

Corson, S.A. Conditioning of Water—Electrolyte Excretion. — Endocrines and the Central Nervous System, Vol.43 (1966), 140—199.

Corson, S.A. The Cerebrovisceral Theory — a Physiologic Basis for Psychosomatic Medicine. — Int. J. Psychiat., Vol.4 (1967), 234—241.

Danilov, N.V. and N.N.Makarovskaya. Some Aspects of the Regulation of the Blood Supply in Digestion. — In: Problemy sovremennoi fiziologii, pp.75—86. Kishinev, 1969. (Russian)

Danilova, L.K. Prolonged Hypertension of Cortical Origin. — Proceedings of the Conference on the Physiology and Pathology of Corticovisceral Relationships and the Physiological Systems of the Body, Vol.1, pp.344—347. Ivanovo, 1965. (Russian)

Danilova, L.K. and P.K.Klimov. The Role of the Amygdaloid Nucleus in the Secretion of Bile by the Liver. — Synopses of Reports to the Eighth Conference on Corticovisceral Interrelationships in Physiology, Medicine and Biology, No.1, p.47. Leningrad, 1967. (Russian)

Dan'ko, Yu.I. The Corticovisceral Mechanism of Cardiac Regulation in Human Muscular Activity. — Synopses of Reports to the Eighth Conference on Corticovisceral Relationships in Physiology, Medicine and Biology, No.1, p.48. Leningrad, 1967. (Russian)

Darovskaya. T.G. Some Cortico-Cardiac Parallels in Children at the Age of Puberty. — Synopses of Reports to the Eighth Conference on Corticovisceral Relationships in Physiology, Medicine and Biology, No.1, pp.50—51. Leningrad, 1967. (Russian)

Delgado, J.M.R. Free Behavior and Brain Stimulation. — Int. Rev. Neurobiol., Vol.6 (1964), 349—449.

Delgado, J.M.R. Emotions. — In: Introduction to General Psychology; a Self-Selection Textbook, 1. Iowa, 1966.

Delgado, J.M.R. Structure and Function of the Limbic System. — In: Progress in Brain Research, Vol.27 (1967), 48.

Delgado, J.M.R. Physical Control of the Mind, New York, Harper and Row, 1969.

Delov, V.E., N.A.Adamovich, and A.N.Borgest. The Influence of Afferent Impulses from Receptors of Internal Organs on the Bioelectric Activity of the Limbic Cortex. — Fiziol. Zh. SSSR, 47, No.9 (1961), 1083—1086. (Russian)

Denisenko, M.M. Cortical Regulation of the Stability of the Internal Environment. — Proceedings of the Conference on Mechanisms of Corticovisceral Relationships. Synopses of Reports, pp.103—105. Baku, 1960. (Russian)

Devyatkina, O.V. The Influence of the Limbic Cortex and Thalamus on Gastrointestinal Motility in Ruminants. — Author's Summary of Thesis. Alma-Ata, 1971. (Russian)

Dimitrov, Kh. Psychoanalysis and Neuro-Variability. — Sofia, 1965. (Bulgarian)

Dmitrieva, N.A. and I.T.Kurtsin. Changes in Phosphorus Metabolism in the Brain and Viscera of Rats under the Influence of a Powerful Sound Stimulus. — Proceedings of the Conference on the Mechanisms of Corticovisceral Relationships. Synopses of Reports, pp.112—116. Baku, 1960. (Russian)

Dobrovol'skaya, Z.A. The Hypothalamic Regulation of Absorption by the Small Intestine. — Proceedings of the Fourth Conference of the West Siberian Physiology, Biochemistry and Pharmacology Society, Vol.1, pp.102—104. Krasnoyarsk, 1969. (Russian)

Dolgo-Saburov, B.A. The Neuronal Theory as the Basis of Present Concepts of the Structure and Function of the Nervous System. — Leningrad, 1956. (Russian)

Dolin, A.O. The Pathology of Higher Nervous Activity. — Moscow, 1962. (Russian)

Doty, R. The Subcortical Structures and their Role in the Formation of Conditioned Reflexes. — In: Vysshaya nervnaya deyatel'nost'. Proceedings of the North American Conference in Memory of Pavlov, p.121. (Russian translation, 1963)

Drischel, H. The Regulation of Autonomic Activity. — In: Protsessy regulirovaniya v biologii, pp.125—157. Moscow, 1960. (Russian)

Dubarry, I.I., Ch.Pissot, and J.Duhmel. The Hereditary Factor in Peptic Ulcer. — Proceedings of the World Congr. Gastroenterol., Vol.1, p.386. Baltimore, 1959.

Durinyan, R.A. The Central Apparatus of Afferent Systems. — Moscow, 1965. (Russian)

Durmish'yan, M.G. Stress and Nervousness (Preface). — In:Selye,H.Ocherki ob adaptatsionnom sindrome, pp.5—34. Moscow, 1960. (Russian)

Dzidziguri, T.D. Gastrointestinal Motility in Pathological States of Higher Nervous Activity. — Author's Summary of Thesis. Leningrad, 1953. (Russian)

Dzidziguri, T.D. Quantitative Aspects of Gastrointestinal Motility. — Author's Summary of Thesis. Leningrad, 1968. (Russian)

Efimova, E.K. The Effect of Corticosteroids on the Bioelectric Activity of Areas of the Brain. — In: Gormony i golovnoi mozg, pp.50—54. Kiev, 1968. (Russian)

Emel'yanova, E.A. and V.K.Trofimov. The Dynamics of Conditioned Reflex Activity, Bioelectric Activity of the Brain and Phagocytic Activity of the Leucocytes in Neuroses of Interoceptive Origin. — XI s"ezd Vses. fiziol. obshch. im. I.P.Pavlova, Vol.2. p.173. Scientific Communications. Leningrad, 1970. (Russian)

Ermolaeva, V.Yu. Changes in the Capillary Permeability of the Skin in Disorders of Higher Nervous Activity. — Author's Summary of Thesis. Leningrad, 1958. (Russian)

Ermolaeva, V.Yu. Interneuronal Relationships of Somatic Areas of the Cerebral Cortex of a Cat. — Author's Summary of Thesis. Leningrad, 1969. (Russian)

Esipenko, B.E. The Role of Gastrointestinal Secretion in Water Regulation. — Author's Summary of Thesis. Kiev, 1965. (Russian)

Eskin, I.A., Yu.B.Skebel'skaya, and N.V.Mikhailova. The Role of the Nervous System in the Formation and Function of Pituitary Hormones. — In: Mekhanizm deistviya gormonov, pp.70—74. Kiev, 1959. (Russian)

Faitel'berg, R.O. The Regulatory Mechanisms of Absorption. — In: Kortiko-vistseral'nye vzaimootnosheniya v fiziologii, biologii i meditsine, pp.175—182. Leningrad, 1971. (Russian)

Fedorovich, G.I. Functional Relationships of the Hypothalamus and the Cerebral Cortex. — XI s"ezd Vses. fiziol. obshch. im. I.P.Pavlova, Vol.2, p.118. Scientific Communications. Leningrad, 1970. (Russian)

Fessard, A.E. A Study of the Closure of Temporary Connections at the Neuron Level. — In: Elektroentsefalograficheskoe izuchenie vysshei nervnoi deyatel'nosti (Russian translation from the French, 1962).

Filatov, A.T. The Possibility of Forming Conditioned Reflex Connections in Man: a Critical Point of View. — X s"ezd Vses. fiziol. obshch. im. I.P.Pavlova, Vol.2, No.2, pp.356—357,. Scientific Communications. Moscow—Leningrad, 1964. (Russian)

Filippova, A.G. and T.K.Valueva. The Dynamics of Conditioned Reflex Activity in Dogs after Total Adrenalectomy. — X s"ezd Vses. fisiol. obshch. im. I.P.Pavlova, Vol.2, No.2, pp.358—359. Scientific Communications. Moscow—Leningrad, 1964. (Russian)

French, J.D. Corticofugal Connections with the Formatio reticularis. — In: Retikulyarnaya formatsiya mozga, pp.433—445. (Russian translation, 1962)

Frol'kis, V.V., K.I.Kul'chitskii, V.I.Mil'ko, and U.A.Kuz'minskaya. The Coronary Circulation and Experimental Myocardial Infarction. — Kiev, 1961. (Russian)

Fulton, J.F. The Limbic System: a Study of the Visceral Brain in Primates and Man. — Yale J. Biol. Med., Vol.26 (1953), 107.

Gaito, J. Molecular Psychobiology: A Chemical Approach to Learning and Other Behavior. — C.C.Thomas, 1966.

Gal'perin, S.I. The Importance of Interception (Sensitivity of Internal Organs) in the Regulatory Activity of the Higher Divisions of the Nervous System. — Leningrad, 1937. (Russian)

Ganelina, I.E. Some Problems of Corticovisceral Pathology as Exemplified by Ischemic Heart Disease. — Proceedings of the Symposium on Perspectives in the Experimental and Clinical Study of Corticovisceral Relationships, pp.6—8. Leningrad, 1968. (Russian)

Gantt, W.H. Experimental Basis for Neurotic Behavior. — New York, 1969.

Gantt, W.H. The Principles of Nervous Breakdown — Schizokinesis and Autokinesis. — Ann. N.Y.Acad. Sci., Vol.156 (1953), 142—163.

Gantt, W.H. The Use of Pharmacological Agents in the Study of Higher Nervous Activity. — In: Problemy fiziologii tsentral'noi nervnoi sistemy, pp.180—184. (Russian translation, 1957)

Gantt, W.H. Autonomic Conditioning. — Ann. N.Y. Acad. Sci., Vol.117 (1964), 117—132.

Gantt, W.H., F.W. Baker, and A. Livingston. Hormonal Factors in Conditioned Reflex Diuresis. — XXII Intern. Congr. Physiol. Sci., p.26. Abstracts of papers, Tokyo, 1965.

Gasanov, G.G. Interoceptive Glycemic Reflexes: their Cortical Localization and Mechanisms of Nervous Regulation. — Baku, 1970. (Russian)

Gastaud, H. and A. Roger. The Participation of the Main Cerebral Structures in the Mechanisms of Higher Nervous Activity. — In: Elektroentsefalicheskie issledovaniya vysshei nervnoi deyatel'nosti, p.18. (Russian translation, 1962)

Gaza, N.K. Changes in Higher Nervous Activity and Bile Formation in Dogs with Experimental Cholecystitis.— Byull. Eksp. Biol. Med, 43, No.4 (1957), 45—49. (Russian)

Gaza, N.K. Changes in Bile Formation by the Liver and the Level of the Blood Pressure in Dogs after Excitation of the Anterior Part of the Limbic Cortex. — Proceedings of the Conference on Normal and Pathological Functional Relationships between Various Systems of the Body, pp.384—386. Ivanovo, 1962. (Russian)

Gaza, N.K. Bile Formation by the Liver in the Presence of an Organic Lesion of the Cerebral Cortex. — In: Fiziologiya i patologiya zhelcheobrazovaniya i zhelchevydeleniya. Proceedings of the Symposium in L'vov, pp.14—22. Leningrad, 1965a. (Russian)

Gaza, N.K. Bile Formation by the Liver and the Blood Pressure in Dogs after a Cortical Conflict Following the Administration of Chlorpromazine. — Proceedings of the Conference on the Physiology and Pathology of Corticovisceral Relationships and the Physiological Systems of the Body, Vol.1, pp.266—269. Ivanovo, 1956b. (Russian)

Gaza, N.K. Bile Formation and Blood Pressure in Experimental Neurosis in Dogs after Trauma to the Limbic Cortex. — In: Kortikal'nye mekhanizmy regulyatsii deyatel'nosti vnutrennikh organov, pp.45—50. Moscow—Leningrad, 1966. (Russian)

Gaza, N.K. Changes in Higher Nervous Activity and Hepatic Secretion of the Liver after the Direct Injection of Acetylcholine into the Limbic Cortex. — Synopses of Reports to the 22nd All-Union Conference on Higher Nervous Activity (VND) to Mark the Hundred and Twentieth Anniversary of Pavlov's Birth, p.60. Ryazan, 1969, (Russian)

Gaza, N.K. Bile Secretion after the Injection of Acetylcholine, Norepinephrine (Arterenol) and Serotonin into the Limbic Gyrus of a Dog. — Synopses of Reports to the 11th Conference on the Physiology and Pathology of Digestion, pp.130—131. Lvov, 1971. (Russian)

Gaza, N.K. and G.D. Guseinova. The Functional Ultrastructure of the Liver in Experimental Neurosis. — Proceedings of the Ninth All-Union Conference on Corticovisceral Physiology, pp.48—49. Baku, 1971. (Russian)

Gaza, N.K. and G.A. Nechaeva. Changes in the Ribonuclease Activity of Liver and Brain Tissues in Dogs with Experimental Neurosis. — Proceedings of the Fourth Inter-University Conference of Physiologists and Histologists at Teaching Institutes, pp.93—94. Yaroslavl', 1970. (Russian)

Gellhorn, E. and G.N. Loofbourrow. Emotions and Emotional Disorders. — New York, Hoeber, 1963.

Genes, V.S. and B.Ya. Rashap. The Use of Cybernetic Methods for the Evaluation of Corticovisceral Relationships. — In: Kortiko-vistseral'nye vzaimootnosheniya i gormonal'naya regulyatsiya, pp.68—74. Reports to the Conference. Kharkov, 1963. (Russian)

Gilinskii, E.Ya. Morphological Aspects of the Receptor Apparatus of the Vertebrate Stomach. — Moscow— Leningrad, 1958. (Russian)

Ginetsinskii, A.G., L.I. Kurduban, and B.F. Tolkunov. Conditioned Reflex Hydremia. — In: Problemy obshchei neirofiziologii i vysshei nervnoi deyatel'nosti, pp.310—317. Moscow, 1961. (Russian)

Golovacheva, D.A., S.M. Oplavin, N.V. Sysoev, and V.M. Frolov. Physiological and Psychological Changes in Persons under Prolonged Physical and Neuropsychical Stress. — Abstracts of Reports to the 21st Conference on Higher Nervous Activity, p.93. Moscow—Leningrad, 1966. (Russian)

Golovskii, A.D. The Temporary Connection Mechanisms in the Regulation of the Cerebrovascular System. — Abstracts of Reports to the 21st Conference on Higher Nervous Activity, pp.93—94. Moscow—Leningrad, 1966. (Russian)

Golovskii, A.D. and I.T.Kurtsin. Mechanisms of Vascular and Secretory Reactions of the Stomach. — Proceedings of the Conference on the Physiology and Pathology of Digestion, in Memory of K.M.Bykov, pp.169—174. Ivanovo, 1960. (Russian)

Golovskii, A.D., I.T.Kurtsin, and A.A.Fadeeva. Normal and Pathological Secretory and Vascular Reactions of the Stomach. — Trudy Inst. Fiziol. im. I.P.Pavlova, Vol.9 (1960), 42—49. (Russian)

Gorizontov, P.D. and T.N.Protasova. The Role of Adrenocorticotropic Hormone (ACTH) and Corticosteroids in Pathological States: the Problem of Stress. — Moscow, 1968. (Russian)

(Gorshkova, S.M. and I.T.Kurtsin). Gorshkowa, S.M. and I.T.Kurtsin. The Chemical Reflex in the Regulation of Bile Secretion and Excretion. — Third National Conference of the Bulgarian Society for Physiol. Sciences, Varna, p.30, 1967a.

Gorshkova, S.M. and I.T.Kurtsin. Mechanisms of Secretion of Bile. — Moscow—Leningrad, 1967b. (Russian)

Graham, B.F. Neuroendocrine Components in the Physiological Responses to Stress. — In: Comparative Conditioned Neuroses. Ann. N.Y. Acad. Sci., Vol.56 (1953), 184.

Granit, R. Receptors and Sensory Perception, a Discussion of Aims, Means, and Results of Electrophysiological Research into the Process of Reception. — New York. Yale Univ. Press, 1956.

Grashchenkov, N.I. The Hypothalamus: its Role in Physiology and Pathology. — Moscow, 1965. (Russian)

Grashchenkov, N.I. and G.N.Kassil'. A Review of Neurohormonal Studies in 1964. — Inform. Mater. Ob"ed. Nauch. Sovet.: In: Fiziologiya cheloveka i zhivotnykh, No.1, pp.29—45. Leningrad, 1965. (Russian)

Grigor'eva, T.A. Innervation of Blood Vessels. — Moscow, 1954. (Russian)

Grinshtein, A. Diseases of the Autonomic Nervous System. — Bol'sh. Med. Entsikl. (BME), Vol.4, pp.1149—1155 and 1167—1179. Moscow, 1958. (Russian)

Grodins, F. Control Theory and Biological Systems. — Columbia Univ. Press, 1963.

Groza, P. Secreția și motalitatea stomacului. — București. 1964 (Rumanian)

Grushevskii, E.F. The Site of Conditioned Excitation and Inhibition and the Effect of Psychotropic Substances on these Processes. — Proceedings of the Fourth Conference of the West Siberian Society of Physiology, Biochemistry and Pharmacology, Vol.2, pp.765—768. Krasnoyarsk, 1969 (Russian)

Gubergrits, A.Ya. Diseases of the Biliary Tract. — Moscow, 1963. (Russian)

Gubler, E.V. Computing Methods for the Diagnosis of Pathological Processes. — Leningrad, 1970. (Russian)

Gulyaeva, L.N. Gastric Secretion in Disorders of Higher Nervous Activity. — Author's Summary of Thesis. Leningrad, 1956. (Russian)

Gulyaeva, L.N. Gastric Secretion, Blood Pressure and Diuresis in Dogs after Bilateral and Partial Disruption of the Anterior and Posterior Parts of the Limbic Cortex. — Proceedings of the Conference on Normal and Pathological Relationships of the Systems of the Body, Vol.1, pp.392—397. Ivanovo, 1962. (Russian)

Gulyaeva, L.N. The Importance of the Reticular Formation in the Etiology of Corticovisceral Disorders. — Proceedings of the Conference on Corticovisceral Relationships and Physiological Systems of the Body in Normal and Pathological States, Vol.1, pp.327—331. Ivanovo, 1965. (Russian)

Gulyaeva, L.N. Corticovisceral Disorders in Neurosis in Dogs with Partial Disruption of the Limbic Cortex.— In: Kortikal'nye mekhanizmy regulyatsii deyatel'nosti vnutrennikh organov, pp.51—58. Moscow— Leningrad, 1966. (Russian)

Gulyaeva, L.N. Hormonal Regulation of the Gastric Glands in Dogs in the Normal State and in Experimental Neurosis. — In: Gormonal'noe zveno kortiko-vistseral'nykh vzaimootnoshenii, pp.59—66. Moscow—Leningrad, 1969. (Russian)

Gulyaeva, L.N. and T.A.Agadzhanova. Functional and Ultrastructural Changes in the Gastric Mucosa.— Proceedings of the All-Union Conference on the Electron-Microscopic Study of Cells and Tissues, pp.105—106, Leningrad, 1968. (Russian)

Gulyaeva, L.N., V.A.Andreeva, and V.N.Shvalev. Morphological Changes in the Gastric Mucosa in Experimental Neurosis and its Relationship to Secretory Activity. — In: Fiziologiya i patologiya pishchevareniya. Abstracts of Reports to the Scientific Conference in L'vov, pp.59—62, 1965. (Russian)

Gulyaeva, L.N., S.A.Geller, I.T.Kurtsin, and G.I.Chipens. The Effect of Synthetic Analogs of Gastrin on the Gastric Secretion in the Normal State and in Experimental Neurosis. — Proceedings of the Ninth All-Union Conference on Corticovisceral Physiology, pp.67—68. Baku, 1971a. (Russian)

Gulyaeva, L.N., I.T.Kurtsin, D.Yu.Guseinov, and S.R.Rustambekov. The Ultrastructure of the
    Stomach in Experimental Neurosis. — Proceedings of the Ninth All-Union Conference on Cortico-
    visceral Physiology, pp.68—69. Baku, 1971b. (Russian)
Gulyaeva, L.N. and M.S.Seregin. The Blood Corticosteroid Level and Gastric Secretion in Dogs with
    Experimental Neurosis. — In: Gormonal'noe zveno v kortikovistseral'nykh vzaimootnosheniyakh,
    pp.67—74. Leningrad, 1969. (Russian)
Gurevich, M.I. and G.Kh.Bykhovskaya. The Architectonics of the Cerebral Cortex (Isocortex) of the
    Dog. — Med. Biol. Zh., No.2 (1927), 58. (Russian)
Gurskaya, L.I. Types of Gastric Secretion and their Diagnostic Importance. — Moscow, 1964. (Russian)
Guseva, E.G. The Influence of the Healthy and Functionally Weakened Cerebral Cortex on the Healing
    of Burns in Dogs. — Abstracts of Reports to the 16th Conference on Higher Nervous Activity, pp.68—69.
    Moscow—Leningrad, 1953. (Russian)
Guseinov, D.Yu. and I.T.Kurtsin. The Ultrastructure and Function of Certain Internal Organs in Experi-
    mental Neurosis. — Proceedings of the Ninth All-Union Conference on Corticovisceral Physiology,
    pp.71—72. Baku, 1971. (Russian)
Guseinova, G.D. and I.V.Sergeev. The Ultrastructural Basis of Kidney Function in Experimental
    Neurosis. — Proceedings of the Ninth All-Union Conference on Corticovisceral Physiology, pp.72—73.
    Baku, 1971. (Russian)
Hamberger, C. and H.Hyden. Cytochemical Changes in the Cochlear Ganglion Caused by Acoustic
    Stimulation and Trauma. — Acta otolar., Suppl., Vol.61 (1945), 1—89.
Harris, G. The Reticular Formation Reaction to Stress and Endocrine Activity. — In: Retikulyarnaya for-
    matsiya mozga, p.191. Moscow, 1962. (Russian translation)
Harvát, I. The Neurohumoral Concept in Endocrinology. — Klinich. Med., Vol.33 (1955), 10—21.
    (Russian translation)
Havlíček, V. Conditioned Defense Dominance as a Model of the Hypertensive Stage. — Moscow, 1962.
    (Russian translation)
Hess, W.R. Hypothalamus und Thalamus. — Stuttgart, 1956.
Heymans, C. and E.Nell. Reflexogenic Areas of the Cardiovascular System. — London, 1958.
Holmberg, G. Pharmacology and Stress Reactions. — In: Emotional Stress, edited by L.Levi. Basel—New York,
    S.Karger. 1967.
Horvath, M.E., E.Frantík, E.Grosmanová, and H.Mikisková. Central Nervous and Autonomic
    Activity in Animal Toxicity Studies. — Symposium on Higher Nervous Activity and Occupational
    Health, pp.22—23. Prague, 1966.
Hua Kuang. The Permeability of Glandular Tissue in Disorders of Higher Nervous Activity. — Author's
    Summary of Thesis. Leningrad, 1955. (Russian translation)
Ibragimova, B.I. Gastric Function and the Blood Biochemistry in Patients with Gastric Ulcer and Chronic
    Gastritis after Conservative Treatment. — Author's Summary of Thesis. Baku, 1968. (Russian)
Il'inskii, O.B. Mechanoreceptors: their Mode of Action and Sensory Systems (Review). — Leningrad, 1967.
    (Russian)
Il'inskii, O.B., G.N.Akoev, N.K.Volkova, and T.L.Krasnikova. Some Features of Mechano- and
    Electroceptor Structures. — XI s"ezd Vses. fiziol. obshch. im. I.P.Pavlova, Vol.1, pp.107—110.
    Reviews and Reports on the Symposium. Leningrad, 1970. (Russian)
Il'yuchenok, R.Yu. Neurohumoral Mechanisms of the Reticular Formation of the Brain Stem. — Moscow,
    1965. (Russian)
Istamanova, T.S. Disorders of Visceral Function in Neurasthenia. — Moscow, 1958. (Russian)
Ivanov-Smolenskii, A.G. A Survey of Experimental Studies of Higher Nervous Activity in Man. —
    Moscow, 1971. (Russian)
Jacobson, E.O. Progress in Gastroenterology: The Circulation of the Gastrointestinal Tract. — Gastro-
    enterology, Vol.52 (1967), 98—112.
Jefferson, J. The Reticular Formation and Clinical Neurology. — In: Retikulyarnaya formatsiya mozga,
    p.636. Moscow, 1962. (Russian)
John, E.R., D.S.Ruchkin, A.Leiman, E.Sachs, and H.Ahn. Electrophysiological Studies of
    Generalization Using Both Peripheral and Central Conditioned Stimuli. — Abstr. XXIII Intern. Congr.
    Physiol. Sci., Tokyo, p.23, 1965.
Kaada, B.R. Somato-Motor, Autonomic and Electrocorticographic Responses to Electrical Stimulation of
    "Rhinencephalic" and Other Structures in Primates, Cat and Dog. — Acta physiol. scand., Vol.24
    (1951), 1—285.

K a a d a, B.R. Cingulate, Posterior Orbital, Anterior Insular and Temporal Pole Cortex. Handbook of
    Physiology, Sect. 1. — Neurophysiology, Vol.2 (1960), 1345—1372.
K a d a n o f f, D. and D.Gürowski. Morphologie der Rezeptoren des Atmungs- und Verdauungssystems beim
    Menschen. — Jena, 1963.
K a k h a n a, M.S. The Pathophysiology of Thyrotoxicosis. — Kishinev, 1959. (Russian)
K a k h a n a, M.S. The Corticovisceral Regulation of Activity of the Thyroid Gland.— Kishinev, 1960.
    (Russian)
K a k h a n a, M.S. The Role of the Hypothalamus in the Endocrine Mechanism of Homeostasis. — In:
    Gipotalamoendokrinnye vzaimootnosheniya, Vol.2, pp.3—48. Kishinev, 1970. (Russian)
K a l y a p i n, A.G. Clinical and Experimental Tests of Higher Nervous Activity in Patients with Hypertension
    and Mental Disorders. — Abstracts of Reports to the 21st Conference on Higher Nervous Activity,
    p.139. Moscow—Leningrad, 1966. (Russian)
K a n, E.L. The Nervous Regulation of Erythrocytic Equilibrium. — Author's Summary of Thesis. Leningrad,
    1971. (Russian)
K a r a e v, A.I. The Reticular Formation and Corticovisceral Relationships. — In: Kortiko-vistseral'nye
    vzaimootnosheniya v fiziologii, biologii i meditsine, pp.76—80. Leningrad, 1971. (Russian)
K a r a e v, A.I. and A.A.Loginov. Interoceptive Metabolic Reflexes. — Baku, 1960. (Russian)
K a r a m y a n, A.I. Functional Evolution of the Vertebrate Brain. — Leningrad, 1970. (Russian)
K a r a p e t y a n, S.K. The Neurohumoral Regulation of Reproductive Activity in Farm Animals. — X s"ezd
    Vses. fiziol. obshch. im. I.P.Pavlova, Vol.1, pp.168—169. Reports on the Symposium. Moscow—
    Leningrad, 1964. (Russian)
K a s s i l', G.N. The Blood Brain Barrier. — Moscow, 1963. (Russian)
K a s s i l', G.N. Action at a Distance of Biologically Active Substances in Normal and Pathological Conditions.—
    Proceedings of the Fourth Conference of the West Siberian Society of Physiology, Biochemistry and
    Pharmacology, Vol.1, pp.147—150. Krasnoyarsk, 1969. (Russian)
K a s s i l', V.G. The Gastrointestinal Tract and Behavior towards Food. — Author's Summary of Thesis,
    Leningrad, 1968. (Russian)
K a s s i r s k i i, I.A. Problems and Doubts Regarding Treatment. — Moscow, 1970. (Russian)
K a s' y a n o v, V.M. Physiological Significance of the Limbic Area of the Dog's Brain. — In: Problemy
    vysshei nervnoi deyatel'nosti, pp.223—245. Moscow, 1949. (Russian)
K h a i k i n a, B.I. Changes in Carbohydrate-Phosphorus Metabolism in Brain and Liver Tissue in Disorders of
    Higher Nervous Activity. — Zhurn. Vyssh. Nerv. Deyat. I.P.Pavlova 8, No.5 (1958), 766. (Russian)
K h a l e e v a, L.D. and N.N.Petrenko. Experimental Neurosis and the Tone of the Renal Vessels. — Pro-
    ceedings of the Ninth All-Union Conference on Corticovisceral Physiology, pp.227—228. Baku, 1971.
    (Russian)
K h a n a n a s h v i l i, M.M.   The Physiology and Pathology of Higher Nervous Activity in Animals and Man. —
    In: Problemy teoreticheskoi meditsiny, pp.5—37. Leningrad, 1968. (Russian)
K h a n a n a s h v i l i, M.M. Mechanisms of Closure of the Temporary Connection in Conditioned-Reflex
    Activity. — In: Problemy fiziologii i patologii vysshei nervnoi deyatel'nosti, pp.16—39. Leningrad,
    1970. (Russian)
K h a n a n a s h v i l i, M.M. and I.A.Lapina. The Structural Basis of Emotional Excitation in Dogs during
    Sexual and Digestive Activity. — Proceedings of the All-Union Symposium on the Structural,
    Functional and Neurochemical Mechanisms of the Emotions, pp.32—35. Leningrad, 1971. (Russian)
K h a r c h e n k o, P.D. and N.M.Myznikov. The Interrelationships of the Cerebral Cortex and Hypothalamus.—
    Synopses of Reports to the Eighth Conference on Corticovisceral Relationships in Physiology, Medicine
    and Biology, Vol.1, pp.156—157. Leningrad, 1967. (Russian)
K i b y a k o v, A.V. The Mechanism of Continuous Nervous Control over the Autonomic Nervous Activity of
    the Internal Organs. — X s"ezd Vses. fiziol. obshch. im. I.P.Pavlova, Vol.1, p.56. Reviews and
    Reports on the Symposium. Moscow—Leningrad, 1964. (Russian)
K l i m o v, P.K. Regulatory Mechanisms of the Bile-Secreting (Cholagogic) System. — Leningrad, 1969.
    (Russian)
K o h o u t, G. and L.Korobova. The Formation of a Conditioned Secretory Reflex of the Stomach on
    Administration of Histamine. — In: Gormonal'noe zveno kortiko-vistseral'nykh vzaimootnoshenii,
    pp.103—105. Leningrad, 1969. (Russian)

Kolesnikov, M.S. and V.M.Borisov. The Correlation between the Typological Characteristics of the Nervous System, Thyroid Activity and Spermatogenesis. — Synopses of Reports to the Eighth Conference on Corticovisceral Relationships in Physiology, Medicine and Biology, No.1, pp.71—72. Leningrad, 1967. (Russian)

Kolosov, N.G. The Innervation of the Human Alimentary Tract. — Moscow—Leningrad, 1962. (Russian)

Kolosov, N.G. Perspective in Soviet Neurohistology. — In: Morfologicheskie issledovaniya kortiko-vistseral'-nykh svyazei, pp.7—16. Leningrad, 1970. (Russian)

Kolosov, N.G. and A.A.Milokhin. The Sensory Innervation of Vegetative Ganglia and their Neurons. — XI s"ezd Vses. fiziol. obshch. im. I.P.Pavlova, Vol.1, pp.227—232. Reviews and Reports to the Symposium. Leningrad, 1970. (Russian)

Komarov, F.I. The Secretory Activity of the Digestive Glands in Man during Sleep. — Leningrad, 1953. (Russian)

Konradi, G.P. Some Further Consideration of Corticovisceral Relationships. — Proceedings of the Symposium on Perspectives in the Clinical and Experimental Study of Corticovisceral Relationships, pp.11—13. Leningrad, 1968. (Russian)

Konradi, G.P. Some Present Problems of Corticovisceral Relationships. — Proceedings of the Ninth All-Union Conference on Corticovisceral Physiology, pp.117—119. Baku, 1971. (Russian)

Korobkina, A.G. and I.T.Kurtsin. Changes in Cell Respiration in the Brain and Viscera of Rats Exposed to Supersonic Stimuli. — Proceedings of the Conference on Mechanisms of Corticovisceral Relationships, pp.153—155. Baku, 1960. (Russian)

Korzhova, V.V. The Influence of Experimental Neurosis in the Course of Pregnancy and on the Newborn. — Synopses of Reports to the Eighth Conference on Corticovisceral Relationships in Physiology, Medicine and Biology, No.1, p.74. Leningrad, 1967. (Russian)

Kosenko, A.F. Mechanisms of the Hypothalamic Regulation of Salivary and Gastric Secretion. — Author's Summary of Thesis. Kiev, 1971. (Russian)

Kosenko, Z.V. and E.G.Paramonova. The Mental State and Coronary Disease. — Moscow, 1967. (Russian)

Kositskii, G.I. and V.M.Smirnov. The Nervous System and "Stress." — Moscow, 1970. (Russian)

Kositskii, G.I. and I.A.Chervova. The Heart as a Self-Regulating System. — Moscow, 1968. (Russian)

Kosmolinskii, F.P. The Influence of Emotions on the Neuroendocrine Regulation of Activity of the Body during a Flight. — X s"ezd Vses. fiziol. obshch. im. I.P.Pavlova, Vol.2, No.1, p.415. Summaries of Scientific Communications, Moscow—Leningrad, 1964. (Russian)

Koupernik, C. Psychoanalysis in Recent French Psychiatry. — Zhum. Nevropatol. i Psikhiatr. 61, No.8 (1961), 1255. (Russian translation)

Kourtsine, I.T. Principes fondamentaux de la physiologie et de la pathologie corticoviscérales. — XIX Intern. Congr. de Physiologie, pp.529—530. Resumés des Communications, Montreal, 1953.

Kourtsine, I.T. La conception Pavlovienne des névroses experimentales basée de la psychopathologie des animaux. — Psychiatrie Animale, pp.205—210. Paris, 1965a.

Kourtsine, I.T. Quelques problèmes actuels de la pathologie corticoviscérale. — In: Revue de Médecine Psychosomatique, Vol.7 (1956b), 117—129.

Kourtsine, I.T. Les méchanismes intéroceptifs des troubles corticoviscéraux. — Eighth Intern. Congr. of Gastroenterology (Prague), pp.1721—1725. Stuttgart—New York, 1969.

Kozenko, T.M. Materials for the Study of Cortical Regulation of the Cardiovascular System. — Author's Summary of Thesis. Moscow, 1961. (Russian)

Kozlovskaya, M.M. The Emotional State and Emotional Responses on Activation of Deep Structures of the Brain. — Proceedings of the All-Union Symposium on the Structural, Functional and Neurochemical Mechanisms of the Emotions, pp.99—104. Leningrad, 1971. (Russian)

Kozlovskaya, M.M. and A.V.Val'dman. A Study of the Effect of Neurotropic Substances on Behavioral Reactions at the Diencephalic Level. — In: Aktual'nye problemy farmakologii retikulyarnoi formatsii v sinapticheskoi peredache, pp.116—164. Leningrad, 1963. (Russian)

Krauklis, A.A. The Self-Regulation of Higher Nervous Activity. — Riga, 1964. (Russian)

Kruchinina, N.A. and Ya.M.Kraevskii. The Influence of Neuroses on the Development of Hypertension and Ischemic Heart Disease. — Proceedings of the Ninth All-Union Conference on Corticovisceral Physiology, pp.123—124. Baku, 1971. (Russian)

Kryazhev, V.Ya. The Trophic Role of the Emotional, Thalamic and Hypothalamic Conditioned Reflex Complex in Corticovisceral Pathology. — In: Problemy kortiko-vistseral'noi patologii, p.312. Moscow—Leningrad, 1952. (Russian)

Kubie, L.S. The Problem of Specificity in the Psychosomatic Processes. — In: Recent Developments in Psychosomatic Medicine. London, 1954.

Kullanda, K.M. Electrophysiological Studies of the Central Nervous Mechanisms Regulating Visceral Functions. — XI s"ezd Vses. fiziol. obshch. im. I.P.Pavlova, Vol.1, pp.242—247. Reviews and Reports on the Symposium, Leningrad, 1970. (Russian)

Kupalov, P.S. Some Aspects of the Physiology of Higher Nervous Activity. — Report to the 20th International Congress of Physiology, Brussels, pp.34—56. Moscow, 1956. (Russian)

Kupalov, P.S. Experimental Neuroses. — Bol'sh. Med. Entsikl., Vol.20, pp.238—245. Moscow, 1961. (Russian)

Kurcin, I.T. The Mechanism of Corticovisceral Relationships. — Folia med., Plovdiv 7, No.1 (1965), 8—13.

Kurtsin, I.T. The Influence of Afferent Impulses from the Alimentary Tract on Cortical Activity. — Fiziol. Zh. SSSR, 25, No.6 (1938), 885—905. (Russian)

Kurtsin, I.T. The Mechanoreceptors of the Stomach and Digestive Activity. — Moscow—Leningrad, 1952. (Russian)

Kurtsin, I.T. A New Test of Gastric Function for the Diagnosis of Gastric Disease in Man. — Moscow, 1953. (Russian)

Kurtsin, I.T. The Principles of Corticovisceral Physiology and Pathology. — Leningrad, 1954. (Russian)

Kurtsin, I.T. The Undulatory Nature of Autonomic Disorders in Experimental Neurosis. — Trudy Inst. Fiziol. im. I.P.Pavlova, Vol.8 (1959), 261—267. (Russian)

Kurtsin, I.T. The Corticovisceral Theory in Medicine. — Leningrad, 1960. (Russian)

Kurtsin, I.T. Ionizing Radiation and Digestion. — Leningrad, 1961. (Russian)

Kurtsin, I.T. Cardiovascular Pathology in the Light of the Corticovisceral Theory, — Activitas nerv. sup. (Praha) 13, No.4 (1962a), 277—293.

Kurtsin, I.T. Mechanisms of Corticovisceral Relationships. — XXII Intern. Congr. Physiol. Sci., II, Leiden, p.1146, 1962b.

Kurtsin, I.T. The Digestive Enzymes. — Leningrad, 1962e. (Russian)

Kurtsin, I.T. The Study of the Organism as a Whole at the Cellular, Subcellular and Molecular Levels. — In: Fiziologiya a patologiya pishchevareniya i voprosy kurortologii i fizioterapii, pp.103—107. Tbilisi, 1963. (Russian)

Kurtsin, I.T. Cortical Pathology and Intestinal Absorption. — Proceedings of the Symposium on the Physiology and Pathology of Gastrointestinal Absorption pp.53—66. Odessa, 1964. (Russian)

Kurtsin, I.T. The Elective Visceral Lesion in Experimental Neurosis. — Zhurn. Vyssh. Nerv. Deyat. I.P.Pavlova 15, No.2 (1965a), 414. (Russian)

Kurtsin, I.T. A Critique of Freudian Ideas in Medicine and Physiology. — Leningrad, 1965b. (Russian)

Kurtsin, I.T. Present Ideas on the Cortical Regulation of Bile Formation and Excretion. — In: Fiziologiya i patologiya zhelcheobrazovaniya i zhelchevydeleniya. Proceedings of the Symposium, pp.72—91. (L'vov), Leningrad, 1965c. (Russian)

Kurtsin, I.T. Hormones in the Pathogenesis of Corticovisceral Disorders. — Synopses of Reports to the Inter-University Conference on Neurohumoral Regulation under Normal and Pathological Conditions, pp.32—34. Uzhgorod, 1965d. (Russian)

Kurtsin, I.T. The Hormonal Link in Corticovisceral Relationships. — 23rd Intern. Congr. Physiol. Sci., Abstracts of Papers, p.251. Tokyo, 1965e.

Kurtsin, I.T. Conditioned Reflex and Autonomic Reactions of the Organism in Psychogenic Stress. — XV Intern. Congr. of Occupational Health, Vienna Symposium on Higher Nervous Activity and Occupational Health. Abstr. Prague, p.30, 1966a.

Kurtsin, I.T. Interoceptive Mechanisms of Corticovisceral Disorders. — Proceedings of the Symposium on Mechanisms of Interoception, pp.50—59. Ivano-Frankovsk, 1967a. (Russian)

Kurtsin, I.T. The Cortical Etiology of Functional Dyskinesia of the Alimentary Tract. — In: Funktional'-naya neprokhodimost' pishchevaritel'nogo trakta. Proceedings of the Symposium, pp.9—16. Moscow. 1967b. (Russian)

Kurtsin, I.T. Unsolved Problems of Cortical Influence on Visceral Activity. — Proceedings of the Symposium on Perspectives in the Experimental and Clinical Study of Corticovisceral Relationships, pp.14—15. Leningrad, 1968a. (Russian)

Kurtsin, I.T. Pavlov's Concept of Experimental Neurosis and Abnormal Behavior in Animals. — In: Abnormal Behavior of Animals, Vol.6, pp.77—106. Philadelphia—London—Toronto, 1968b.

Kurtsin, I.T. Physiological Mechanisms of Behavior Disturbances and Corticovisceral Interrelations. — In: Abnormal Behavior in Animals, Vol.7, pp.107—116. Philadelphia, 1968c.

Kurtsin, I.T. Hormones of the Digestive System and their Participation in the Functional Relationships between the Digestive Organs. — In: Vzaimodeistvie organov pishchevaritel'noi sistemy, pp.45—59. Leningrad, 1968d. (Russian)

Kurtsin, I.T. Hormones of the Gastrointestinal Tract and their Role in Disorders of the Digestive Tract. — Address to the Republican Conference on Experimental and Clinical Gastroenterology: The Care of Patients with Diseases of the Digestive System, pp.115—116. Chernovtsy, 1968e. (Russian)

Kurtsin, I.T. Mental Trauma and its Physiological Mechanisms. — Proceedings of the Fourth Scientific Conference of the West Siberian Society of Physiology, Biochemistry and Pharmacology, Vol.1, pp.211—214. Krasnoyarsk, 1969a. (Russian)

Kurtsin, I.T. Causes of the Chronicity of Gastrointestinal Disorders of Corticovisceral Origin. — Proceedings of the Conference on the Prevention, Diagnosis and Treatment of Digestive Disorders, pp.54—56. Dnepropetrovsk, 1969b. (Russian)

Kurtsin, I.T. The Hormones of the Gastrointestinal Tract and the Gastro-Hepato-Pancreaticoduodenal System. — In: Voprosy patologii pecheni i podzheludochnoi zhelezy, pp.7—19. Smolensk, 1969e. (Russian)

Kurtsin, I.T. The Levels of Influence of the Cerebral Cortex on Vegetative Activity. — Proceedings of the Fourth Conference on Physiology of the Republics of Soviet Central Asia and Kazakhstan, Vol.1, pp.188—192. Alma-Ata, 1969d. (Russian)

Kurtsin, I.T. Psychogenic Stress and its Physiological Mechanisms. — Proceedings of the 17th Conference of Physiologists of the South of the Russian Soviet Federative Socialist Republic (RSFSR), Vol.1, pp.34—35. Stavropol', 1969e. (Russian)

Kurtsin, I.T. The Nervous System and Hormones. — VI Congr. of Yugosl. Physiol. Soc. Abstr. of Volunteer Papers, p.69. Ohrid, 1969f.

Kurtsin, I.T. The Cortical Regulation of Visceral Activity. — Fiziol. Zh. SSSR 6, No.10 (1970a), 1350—1359. (Russian)

Kurtsin, I.T. Theoretical Problems of the Cortical Regulation of Visceral Activity. — XI s"ezd Vses. fiziol. obshch. im. I.P.Pavlova, Vol.1, pp.247—254. Reviews and Reports to the Symposium, Leningrad, 1970b. (Russian)

Kurtsin, I.T. The Corticovisceral Theory — the Physiological Basis of Psychosomatic Medicine. — Proceedings of the Ninth All-Union Conference on Corticovisceral Physiology, pp.127—129. Baku, 1971a. (Russian)

Kurtsin, I.T. Studies in the Field of Corticovisceral Pathology. — In: Mekhanizmy regulyatsii fiziologicheskikh funktsii, pp.77—89. Leningrad, 1971b. (Russian)

Kurtsin, I.T. Interoceptive Signals in the Mechanism of Corticovisceral Disorders. — Activitas nerv. sup. (Praha), Vol.13 (1971c), 277—293. (Russian)

Kurtsin, I.T. Mechanisms of Corticovisceral Relationships. — In: Kortikovistseral'nye vzaimootnosheniya v fiziologii, biologii i meditsine, pp.99—120. Leningrad, 1971d. (Russian)

Kurtsin, I.T. and V.K.Bolondinskii. Corticovisceral Biochemistry as a Further Stage in the Development of the Physiology and Pathology of Corticovisceral Relationships. — Uspekhi Sovr. Biol. 63, No.2 (1967), 184—204. (Russian)

Kurtsin, I.T. and N.I.Chubarova. Corticovisceral Disorders in "Psychogenic" Stress in Hypophysectomized Dogs. — In: Tsepnye neiro-gormonal'nye reaktsii simpato-adrenalovaya sistema, pp.120—126. Leningrad, 1968. (Russian)

Kurtsin, I.T., N.I.Chubarova, and V.A.Andreeva. The Role of Preliminary Traumatization of the Stomach in the Production of Experimental Gastric Ulcer. — Proceedings of the Conference on the Physiology and Pathology of Corticovisceral Relationships and the Physiological Systems of the Body, Vol.1, pp.534—537. Ivanovo, 1965. (Russian)

Kurtsin, I.T. and N.K.Gaza. The Chemical Nature of Neurosis and Corticovisceral Pathology. — Proceedings of the Fourth Inter-University Conference of Physiologists and Histologists at Teaching Institutes, pp.180—183. Yaroslavl', 1970. (Russian)

Kurtsin, I.T. and N.K.Gaza. Central Mechanisms of the Development of Neuroses and Corticovisceral Disorders. — Proceedings of the Ninth All-Union Conference on Corticovisceral Physiology, pp.129—130. Baku, 1971. (Russian)

Kurtsin, I.T. and L.N.Gulyaeva. Hormonal Excitation of the Gastric Secretory Cells in Disorders of Higher Nervous Activity. — Proceedings of the Conference on Normal and Pathological Digestive Activity and its Regulation, pp.95—98, Moscow, 1969. (Russian)

Kurtsin, I.T. and T.D.Dzidziguri. The Types of Gastric Motility and their Quantitative Differentiation. — In: Motornaya funktsiya zheludochno-kishechnogo trakta. Reports to the Symposium, pp.111—125. Kiev, 1965. (Russian)

Kurtsin, I.T. and A.G.Kuzovkov. Permeability of the Blood-Brain Barrier in Dogs with Neurosis and Radiation Sickness. — In: Gisto-gematicheskie bar'ery, pp.190—202. Moscow, 1961. (Russian)

Kurtsin, I.T., V.V.Nikolaeva, L.N.Gulyaeva, and V.A.Andreeva. The Oxidation Processes in the Gastric Mucosa in Relation to Secretion in Normal and Pathological Nervous Activity. —In: Fiziologiya i patologiya pishchevareniya. Abstract of Papers to the Conference, pp.143—146. L'vov, 1965. (Russian)

Kurtsin, I.T. and V.V.Nikolaeva. The Influence of the Thyroid Gland on Gastric Secretion in Dogs with Experimental Neurosis. — In: Kortikal'nye mekhanizmy regulyatsii deyatel'nosti vnutrennikh organov, pp.89—94. Moscow—Leningrad, 1966. (Russian)

Kurtsin, I.T. and N.A.Nikolov. The Corticovisceral Theory of Medicine and Hormonal Regulation. — Plovdiv, 1966. (Bulgarian)

Kurtsin, I.T. and V.A.Pastukhov. The Blood Supply of the Cerebral Cortex under Normal Conditions and in Experimental Neurosis. — Proceedings of the Fourth Inter-University Conference of Physiologists and Histologists at Teaching Institutes, pp.170—172. Yaroslavl', 1970. (Russian)

Kurtsin, I.T. and I.V.Sergeeva. Changes of the Hypothalamic Mechanisms Regulating Micturition in Functional Disorders of the Cerebral Cortex. — Proceedings of the Third All-Union Conference on Water and Salt Metabolism and Kidney Function, pp.37—39. Ordzhonikidze, 1971. (Russian)

Kurtsin, I.T. and N.T.Suplyakov. The Central Regulation of Hormonal Stimulation of the Pancreas. — X s"ezd Vses. fiziol. obshch, im. I.P.Pavlova, Vol.1, pp.150—151. Reviews and Reports to the Symposium. Moscow—Leningrad, 1964. (Russian)

Kurtsin, I.T. and N.A.Yaroslavtseva. The Effects of Adrenocorticotropic Hormone (ACTH) and Cortisone on Higher Nervous Activity and Gastric Secretion. — Synopses of Reports to the 13th Conference of Physiologists of the South of the Russian Soviet Federative Socialist Republic (RSFSR), pp.79—80. Rostov-on-Don, 1960. (Russian)

Kurtsin, I.T., V.N.Zvorykin, I.K.Kurpatov, and F.M.Lebedev. An Experimental Study of Gastric Function in Clinical Practice by the Method of Bykov and Kurtsin. — Terapevticheskii Arkhiv, Vol.3, (1960), 60—67. (Russian)

Kurzin, I.T. Normale und pathologische kortikoviszerale Wechselbeziehungen. — Pavlow-Tagung, pp.59—82. Berlin, 1953.

Kurzin, I.T. Einige aktuelle Probleme der kortikoviszeralen Pathologie. — In: Abhandlungen der deutschen Akad. der Wissenschaften zu Berlin. 2. Kortikoviszerale Physiologie, Pathologie und Therapie. Intern. Sympos., pp.125—132. Berlin, 1966.

Kuznetsov, V.A. The Role of the Cortical and Subcortical Divisions of the Auditory Analyzer in the Inhibitory Influence of Sound Stimuli on the Healing of Flesh Wounds. — 21st Conference on Higher Nervous Activity. Summaries and Abstracts of Papers, p.165. Moscow—Leningrad, 1966. (Russian)

Kuznetsova, E.K. The Secretory and Vascular Reactions of the Pancreas in Various Functional States of the Cerebral Cortex. — Proceedings of the Ninth All-Union Conference on Corticovisceral Physiology, pp.124—125. Baku, 1971. (Russian)

Kuzovkov, A.G. The Functional State of the Blood—Brain Barrier and the Central Nervous System when Exposed to Certain Very Powerful Stimuli. — Author's Summary of Thesis. Leningrad, 1971a. (Russian)

Kuzovkov, A.G. Cholinesterase Activity in the Tissues of the Brain, Stomach and Liver in Rats on Exposure to Very Powerful Sound Stimuli. — Proceedings of the Ninth All-Union Conference on Corticovisceral Physiology, pp.125—127. Baku, 1971b. (Russian)

Lagutina, N.I., A.A.Fufacheva, and I.T.Dzheliev. The Relationships of the Different Formations of the Limbic System in the Brain of Lower Monkeys. — X s"ezd Vses. fiziol. obshch. im. I.P.Pavlova, Vol.2, No.2, p.5. Summaries of Scientific Communications, Moscow—Leningrad, 1964. (Russian)

Lagutina, N.I., L.N.Norkina, and A.F.Sysoeva. Experimental Neurosis in Lower Monkeys. — In: Problemy fiziologii i patologii vysshei nervnoi deyatel'nosti, No.4, pp.94—110. Leningrad, 1970. (Russian)

Lang, G.F. Hypertension. — Leningrad, 1950. (Russian)

Langley, J.N. The Autonomic Nervous System. — Cambridge, W.Heffer and Sons, 1921.

Larin, E.F., V.D.Sukhodolo, A.V.El'kina, and M.A.Medvedev. The Effect of Viscerocerebral Relationships on the Interoceptors of the Gastrointestinal Tract. — Proceedings of the Ninth All-Union Conference on Corticovisceral Physiology, pp.132—133. Baku, 1971. (Russian)

Latmanizova, L.V. Lectures on the Physiology of the Nervous System. — Moscow, 1965. (Russian)

Lavrent'ev, B.I. The Sensory Innervation of the Internal Organs. — In: Morfologiya chuvstvitel'noi innervatsii vnutrennikh organov, pp.5—21. Moscow, 1948. (Russian)

Lazarus, R.S. Stress Theory and Psychophysiological Research. — In: Emotional Stress, edited by L.Levi. Basel—New York, S.Karger, 1967.

Lebedeva, V.A. Mechanisms of Chemoreception. — Moscow—Leningrad, 1965. (Russian)

Levi, L. Endocrine Reactions during Emotional Stress. — In: Emotional Stress. New York, Am. Elsevier, 1967.

Levi, L. Stressors, Stress Tolerance, Emotions and Performance in Relation to Catecholamine Secretion. — In: Emotional Stress. New York, Amsterdam, Elsevier, 1967.

Levshunova, N.A. The Role of Pathological Dominance in Disorders of Higher Nervous Activity and of the Electrical Activity of the Brain. — Proceedings of the Conference of Physiologists of the South of the Russian Federative Socialist Republic (RSFSR), Vol.1, pp.38—39. Stavropol', 1969. (Russian)

Linar, E.Yu. Normal and Pathological Acid Secretion by the Stomach. — Riga, 1968. (Russian)

Linar, E.Yu. Measurement of the Force of the Mechanical Stimulus and the Reciprocal Reaction of Muscular Gastric Motility. — Synopses of Reports to the 11th Conference on the Physiology and Pathology of Digestion, pp.451—452. L'vov, 1971. (Russian)

Lindemann, M. Absorption by the Gallbladder in Normal and Pathological States of the Cerebral Cortex. — Author's Summary of Thesis. Leningrad, 1957. (Russian translation)

Lindenbraten, L.D. Preface. — In: Rentgenofiziologiya i funktional'naya patologiya zhelchnogo puzyrya, pp.5—6. Moscow, 1965. (Russian)

Lisitsyn, Yu.P. Modern Theories of Medicine. — Moscow, 1968. (Russian)

Lissak, K. and E.Endröczi. The Neuroendocrine Control of Adaptation. — Oxford, Pergamon Press Inc., 1965.

Lobanova, L.V. Reflex Reactions in Decorticated Mammals. — In: Fiziologiya i patologiya vysshei nervnoi deyatel'nosti, p.103. Leningrad, 1965. (Russian)

Lukashin, V.G. The Structure of Local Receptor Neurons and their Nervous Connections in the Wall of the Large Intestine in Mammals. — Author's Summary of Thesis. Leningrad, 1970. (Russian)

Luriya, A.R. The Human Brain and Psychological Processes, Vol.1. — Moscow, 1963. (Russian)

Luriya, A.R. The Internal Representation of Illness and Iatrogenic Disease. — Moscow, 1974. (Russian)

McIntosh, F.C. and P.E.Oborin. The Release of Acetylcholine from the Intact Cerebral Cortex. — 19th Intern. Physiol. Congr., Abstracts of Communications, pp.580—581. Montreal, 1953.

McLean, P.D. The Limbic System ("Visceral Brain") in Relation to the Central Gray Matter and the Reticulum of the Brain Stem. — Psychosom. Med., Vol.17 (1955), 355—367.

McLean, P.D. The Limbic System with Respect to Two Basic Life Principles. — In: The Central Nervous System and Behavior. New York, 1959.

Maevskaya, I.P. The Relationship between Various Functional States of the Adrenal Cortex and the Noradrenalin Content of the Human Brain. — Synopsis of Reports to the Conference on Hormones and the Human Brain, pp.125—127. Kiev, 1968. (Russian)

Magoun, H.W. The Waking Brain. 2nd edition. — C.C.Thomas, Springfield, 1963.

Maiorov, F.P. Pavlov's Reply to American Reviewers. — Moscow, 1949. (Russian)

Maiorov, F.P. A History of the Theory of Conditioned Reflexes. — Moscow—Leningrad, 1954. (Russian)

Maisuradze, N.Z. Uterine Contractions in Experimental Neurosis. — Proceedings of the Ninth All-Union Conference on Corticovisceral Physiology, pp.138—139. Baku, 1971. (Russian)

Makarchenko, A.F. and A.D.Dinaburg. The Midbrain (Diencephalon) and the Autonomic Nervous System. — Kiev, 1971. (Russian)

Makarychev, A.I. and O.Ya.Kurtsin. Experimental Hypertension of Cortical Origin. – Zhurn. Vyssh. Nerv. Deyat. I.P.Pavlova 1, No.2 (1951), 199–212.

Malyshenko, N.M. Hormonal and Interoceptive Influences of the Adrenal Cortex on the Bioelectrical Activity of the Human Brain. – Proceedings of the Ninth All-Union Conference on Corticovisceral Physiology, pp.146–147. Baku, 1971. (Russian)

Manina, A.A. Ultrastructural Changes and Reparative Processes in the Central Nervous System under Different Conditions. – Leningrad, 1971. (Russian)

Manina, A.A., N.I.Zaskal'ko, L.N.Gulyaeva, and T.A.Agadzhanova. Ultrastructural and Functional Changes in the Gastric Mucosa under Various Conditions. – Proceedings of the All-Union Conference on Electron-Microscopic Studies of Cells and Tissues, pp.124–125. Leningrad, 1968. (Russian)

Margolin, L.B. The Role of Toxic Interoceptive Stimuli in Alimentary Activity. – Proceedings of the All-Union Conference on Corticovisceral Relationships in Physiology, Medicine and Biology, pp.148–149. Tselinograd, 1967. (Russian)

Marits, A.M., G.N.Rotaru, N.A.Andronatii, and D.P.Postolake. Nervous Mechanisms of the Emotions Connected with the Sense of Hunger and Fullness. – Proceedings of the All-Union Symposium on the Structural, Functional and Neurochemical Mechanisms of the Emotions, pp.171–174. Leningrad, 1971. (Russian)

Masserman, J.H. Behavior and Neurosis. – Chicago, 1944.

Masserman, J.H. and C.Pechtel. Neuroses in Monkeys: a Preliminary Report on Experimental Observations. – Ann. N.Y. Acad. Sci., Vol. 56 (1953), 253–265.

Melikova, T.G. Coupling in Interoceptive Metabolic Reflexes in Experimental Neurosis. – XI s"ezd Vses. fiziol. obshch. im. I.P.Pavlova, Vol.2. Opening Papers of Scientific Communications, p.101. Leningrad,1971. (Russian)

Mel'man, E.P. The Functional Morphology of the Innervation of Digestive Organs. – Moscow, 1970. (Russian)

Mendelson, M., S.Hirsch, and C.S.Webber. A Critical Examination of Some Recent Theoretical Models in Psychosomatic Medicine. – Psychosom. Med. 18, No.5 (1956), 363.

Mendelson, M. and W.R.Loewenstein. Mechanisms of Receptor Adaptation. – Science, Vol.144 (1964), 554–555.

Merkulova, O.S. Interoceptors and the Skeletal Muscles. – Moscow–Leningrad, 1959. (Russian)

Merkulova, O.S. Structural and Functional Changes in the Synapses of Central Neurons on the Activation of Afferent Nerves. – XI s"ezd Vses. fiziol. obshch. im. I.P.Pavlova, Vol.1, pp.19–24. Reviews and Reports to the Symposium. Leningrad, 1970. (Russian)

Michaux, L. Possibilités et limites de la médecine psychosomatique. – Presse méd., Vol.69 (1961), 1075.

Mikaelyan, N.G. The Evolution of the Central Nervous Control of Reproductive Function in Vertebrates. – X s"ezd Vses. fiziol. obshch. im. I.P.Pavlova, Vol.2, No.2, p.87. Summaries of Scientific Communications, Moscow–Leningrad, 1964. (Russian)

Mikhailov, B.N., L.B.Andreev, and R.A.Trapezontseva. The Role of Bromine in the Mechanism of Corticovisceral Disorders. – Proceedings of the Joint Conference on the Mechanisms of Corticovisceral Relationships, pp.69–73. Baku, 1962. (Russian)

Milenov, K. The Bioelectrical Activity of Some Cortical and Subcortical Formations in Cats with Experimentally Induced Gastric Ulcer. – In: Kortikal'nye mekhanizmy regulyatsii deyatel'nosti vnutrennikh organov, pp.95–102. Moscow–Leningrad, 1966. (Russian)

Milokhin, A.A. Interoceptors of the Alimentary Tract in Some Lower Vertebrates. – Moscow–Leningrad, 1963. (Russian)

Milokhin, A.A. The Sensory Innervation of Vegetative Neurons. – Leningrad, 1967. (Russian)

Milsum, J.H. Biological Control Systems Analysis. – New York, McGraw-Hill, 1966.

Mirzoev, B.M. The Influence of Disorders of Higher Nervous Activity on the Blood Circulation and Respiration before and after Castration. – Synopses of Reports of the 18th Conference on Higher Nervous Activity, No.3, pp.31–32. Leningrad, 1958. (Russian)

Mityushov, M.I. The Activity of the Cerebral Hemispheres and the Blood Sugar Level. – Leningrad, 1964. (Russian)

Mityushov, M.I., T.S.Bogdanova, I.A.Garina, A.D.Nozdrachev, T.T.Podvigina, E.V.Sokolova, V.V.Rakitskaya, L.D.Fedorova, and V.G.Shakyapina. Hormones of the Adrenal Cortex and the Central Nervous System. – Leningrad, 1970. (Russian)

Mogendovich, M.R. and I.B.Temkin. Analyzers and the Internal Organs. — Moscow, 1971.(Russian)

Moruzzi, G. and H.W.Magoun. The Reticular Formation of the Brain Stem and its Effect on the EEG. — Electroenceph. Clin. Neurophysiol. Vol.1 (1949), 455—473.

Motorina, M.V. The Structure of the Hypothalamic-Cortical Connections in Reptiles and Lower Mammals. — Author's Summary of Thesis. Leningrad, 1966. (Russian)

Muravieva, M.S. The Effect of Light and Sound on the External Secretion of the Pancreas. — Synopses of Reports to the Eighth Conference on Corticovisceral Interrelations in Physiology, Medicine and Biology, No.1, p.108. Leningrad, 1967. (Russian)

Muravieva, N.P. Experimental Neurosis in Systemic Activity. — In: Problemy fiziologii i patologii vysshei nervnoi deyatel'nosti, No.4, pp.110—126. Leningrad, 1970. (Russian)

Myasishchev, V.N. Preface to the Russian Publication. — In: Emotsional'nyi stress, pp.7—18. Leningrad, 1970. (Russian)

Myasnikov, A.L. Forty Years of Soviet Cardiology. — Proceedings of the Ninth All-Union Conference of Therapeutists, pp.31—34. Leningrad, 1958. (Russian)

Narikashvili, S.P. The Nonspecific Structures of the Human Brain and the Receptor Function of the Cerebral Hemispheres. — Tbilisi, 1962. (Russian)

Nasonov, D.H. Local Protoplasmic Reactions and the Diffusion of Excitation. — Moscow—Leningrad, 1959. (Russian)

Naumenko, E.V. The Central Chemoreactive Structures in the Hypothalamic Regulation of the Pituitary-Adrenal System. — Author's Summary of Thesis. Leningrad, 1968. (Russian)

Nauta, W.J. Limbic System and Hypothalamus; Anatomic Aspects. — Physiol. Rev., Vol.40 (1960), 102—104.

Nauta, W.J. Some Connections of the Limbic System. — In: Mechanisms of the Human Brain as an Entity. (Russian translation, 1963)

Nauta, W.J. A Survey of the Anatomic Connections of the Prefrontal Cortex. — In: The Localization of Function in the Human Brain. (Russian translation, 1968)

Nazaryan, M.B. Changes in the Amino Acid and SH Group Content in the Reproductive Organs, Hypophysis and Thyroid Glands in Birds Following Decerebration. — X s"ezd Vses.fiziol.obshch.im.I.P.Pavlova, Vol.2, No.2, p.118. Summaries of Scientific Communications, Moscow, 1964, (Russian)

Nichkov, S. and G.N.Krivitskaya. Acoustic Stress and Cerebrovisceral Disorders. — Moscow, 1969. (Russian)

Nikolaeva, V.V. The Effect of Experimental Neurosis on the Resistance of Higher Nervous Activity and of Certain Autonomic Functions in Dogs with the Weak Type of Nervous System. — Proceedings of the Conference on the Physiology and Pathology of Corticovisceral Relationships and the Physiological Systems of the Body, Vol.2, pp.110—114. Ivanovo, 1965. (Russian)

Nikolaeva, V.V. Changes of the Oxidation Processes in Dogs in Relation to the Restoration of Normal Cerebrocortical Function in Experimental Neurosis. — In: Kortikal'nye mekhanizmy regulyatsii deyatel'nosti vnutrennikh organov, pp.103—109. Moscow—Leningrad, 1966. (Russian)

Nikolaeva, V.V. The Role of the Thyroid Gland in the Development of Corticovisceral Pathology. — Proceedings of the Ninth All-Union Conference on Corticovisceral Physiology, pp.161—162. Baku, 1971. (Russian)

Nikolaeva, V.V. and A.S.Denisova. Functional Relationships of the Higher Autonomic Centers and Cerebral Cortex in Dogs with Weak and Strong Types of Nervous System. — In: Tsentral'nye mekhanizmy vegetativnoi i nervnoi sistemy, pp.309—315. Erevan, 1969. (Russian)

Nikolaeva, V.V. and E.A.Loskutova. Structural Changes in the Thyroid Gland of Dogs after Prolonged Functional Traumatization of the Central Nervous System. — In: Gormonal'noe zveno kortiko-vistseral'nykh vzaimootnoshenii, pp.118—123. Moscow—Leningrad, 1969. (Russian)

Nikolaichuk, S.P. The Influence of the Cerebral Cortex on the Production and Discharge of 17-Keto-steroids by the Adrenal Cortex. — Synopses of Reports to the Joint Session of the All-Union and Ukrainian Institutes of Experimental Endocrinology, pp.73—74. Moscow, 1954. (Russian)

Nikolaichuk, S.P. The Participation of Adrenocorticotropic Hormone (ACTH) in the Transmission of Nervous Impulses from the Brain to the Adrenal Cortex. — In: Kortiko-vistseral'nye vzaimootno-sheniya i gormonal'naya regulyatsiya. Reports to the Conference, pp.207—209. Kharkov, 1963. (Russian)

Nikolov, N.A. The Influence of Glucocorticoid Hormones and Adrenocorticotropic Hormone (ACTH) on Normal and Pathological Corticovisceral Relationships. — Author's Summary of Thesis. Leningrad, 1964. (Russian)

Nikolov, N.A. Corticovisceral Relationships and the Pituitary-Adrenal System. — In: Gormonal'noe zveno kortiko-vistseral'nykh vzaimootnoshenii, pp.124—132. Leningrad, 1969. (Russian)

Nikulin, K.G. Clinical Problems with Regard to the Theory of Corticovisceral Pathology. — Klinich. Med. 32, No.9 (1954), 19. (Russian)

Nozdrachev, A.D. Corticosteroids and the Sympathetic Nervous System. — Leningrad, 1969. (Russian)

Obraztsova, G.A. The Ontogeny of Higher Nervous Activity. — Moscow—Leningrad, 1964. (Russian)

Odinets, E.A. The Cortical Regulation of the Secretion and Discharge of Bile. — In: Fiziologiya i patologiya pishchevareniya. Abstracts of Papers to the Conference, pp.205—207. Lvov, 1965. (Russian)

Olds, J. Self-Stimulation of the Brain: its Use to Study the Local Effects of Hunger, Sex and Drugs. — Science, Vol.125 (1958), 315.

Ol'nyanskaya, R.P. Papers on the Regulation of Metabolism. — Moscow—Leningrad, 1964. (Russian)

Ol'nyanskaya, R.P. and A.D. Slonim. The Cortical Regulation of Metabolism and of the Effector Systems in the Adaptation Process. — In: Kortiko-vistseral'nye vzaimootnosheniya v fiziologii, biologii i meditsine, pp.120—130. Leningrad, 1971. (Russian)

Orbeli, L.A. The Adaptive-Trophic Function of the Nervous System. — Izbran. Trudy, Vol.2, Leningrad, 1962. (Russian)

Ordzhonikidze, Ts.A and L.D. Pkhakadze. Variations of Cardiac Rhythm in Different Emotional States in Decorticate and Normal Cats. — Proceedings of the All-Union Symposium on the Structural, Functional and Neurochemical Mechanism of the Emotions, pp.134—137. Leningrad, 1971. (Russian)

Orlov, I.V. The Limbic System. — Bol'sh. Med. Entsikl. (BME), Ezhegodnik, Vol.2, p.544. Moscow, 1969. (Russian)

Orlov, V.V. Corticovisceral Relationships and their Effect on the Cardiovascular System. — Proceedings of the Symposium on Perspectives in the Experimental and Clinical Study of Corticovisceral Relationships, pp.20—22. Leningrad, 1968. (Russian)

Orlov, V.V. Cortical Influences on the Circulation of the Blood. — Leningrad, 1971a. (Russian)

Orlov, V.V. Corticovisceral Relationships and their Effect on the Circulation of the Blood. — Proceedings of the Ninth All-Union Conference on Corticovisceral Physiology, pp.167—168. Baku, 1971b. (Russian)

Orlova, T.E. Problems of Noise Control in Industry. — Moscow, 1965. (Russian)

Ovcharova, V.F. On Coupled Changes in Higher Nervous Activity and General Respiratory Exchange. — Synopses of Reports to the 21st Conference on Higher Nervous Activity, p.219. Moscow—Leningrad, 1966. (Russian)

Papasova, M. An Electrophysiological Study of the Peristaltic Activity of the Stomach. — Sofia, 1971. (Bulgarian)

Papez, J.W. A Proposed Mechanism of Emotion. — Archs. Neurol. Psychiat., Lond., Vol.38 (1937), 725—734.

Papez, J.W. The Visceral Brain, its Structure and Connections. — In: The Reticular Formation of the Brain. International Symposium. (Russian translation, 1962)

Papoyan, E.V. Evoked Potentials of the Cerebral Cortex on the Cerebellar Nuclei in a Normal Cat. — Fiziol. Zh. SSSR 57, No.1 (1971), 3—9.

Pastukhov, V.A. The Blood Supply of Organs in Relation to their Activity and to the General Hemodynamics of the Circulation in Normal and Pathological Conditions of the Higher Divisions of the Brain. — Author's Summary of Thesis. Leningrad, 1970. (Russian)

Pátkai, P. Catecholamine Excretion and Performance. — In: Emotional Stress, pp.49—52, Basel. 1967.

Pavlov, I.P. Complete Collected Works (Poln. sobr. soch.), Vol.2, Nos.1 and 2, Vol.3, Nos.1—2; Vol.4. Moscow—Leningrad, 1951. (Russian)

Peleshchuk, A.P. The Effect of Sleep on Gastric Secretory Activity and Motility. — Author's Summary of Thesis. Kiev, 1962. (Russian)

Penfield, W. Some Observations on the Human Brain. — In: The Physiology of the Central Nervous System. (Russian translation, 1957)

Penfield, W. and H. Jaspar. Epilepsy and the Functional Anatomy of the Human Brain. — Beaton, Little, Brown. 1954.

Petrova, E.G. Afferent and Efferent Connections of the Heart with the Limbic Region of the Cerebral Cortex. — In: Kortikal'nye mekhanizmy regulyatsii deyatel'nosti vnutrennikh organov, pp.126—130. Leningrad, 1966. (Russian)

Petrova, M.K. The Role of the Functionally Weakened Cerebral Cortex in the Production of Various Pathological Processes in the Body. — Moscow—Leningrad, 1946. (Russian)

Plakhotina, L.S. The Influence of Experimental Neurosis on the Hypothalamus and the Course of Pregnancy.— Proceedings of the Ninth All-Union Conference on Corticovisceral Physiology, pp.175—176. Baku, 1971. (Russian)

Polenov, A.L. Hypothalamic Neurosecretion. — Leningrad, 1968. (Russian)

Poltyrev, S.S. The Pathogenesis and Treatment of Some Visceral Disorders. — Moscow, 1962. (Russian)

Poltyrev, S.S. Perspectives in the Study of Pathological Interoceptive Reflexes. — In: Kortiko-vistseral'nye vzaimootnosheniya v fiziologii, biologii i meditsine, pp.130—137. Leningrad, 1971. (Russian)

Popov, N.F. Studies in the Physiology of the Cerebral Cortex in Animals. — Moscow, 1953.

Portis, S.A. Diseases of the Digestive System. — Philadelphia, 1953.

Preobrazhenskaya, I.N. and P.I.Bul'. The Influence of Verbal Suggestion on the Shape of the Gall-bladder. — Vrachebnoe Delo, No.2 (1959), 197. (Russian)

Pressman, A.P. and P.P.Pressman. Disorders of Central Nervous Regulation in Cardiovascular Diseases. — Moscow, 1968. (Russian)

Prikhod'kova, E.K. and G.M.Omel'chuk. Disorders of the Regulation of Blood Pressure and of Biliary Secretion by the Liver as a Result of Experimental Neurosis. — In: Fiziologiya nervnykh protsessov, pp.210—218. Kiev, 1955. (Russian)

Pronin, L.A. The Effect of the Formation of Defensive Conditioned Reflexes and of the Disruption of Higher Nervous Activity on the State of Reactivity in Rabbits. — Problemy reaktivnosti v patologii, pp.217—225. Moscow, 1954. (Russian)

Pronina, N.N. The Hormonal Link in the Regulation of Water and Salt Metabolism. — In: Gormonal'noe zveno kortiko-vistseral'nykh vzaimootnoshenii, pp.133—138. Leningrad, 1969. (Russian)

Pronina, N.N. The Action of Hormones in the Regulation of Salt and Water in the Body to Maintain the Fluid Balance. — Scientific Communications to the Third All-Union Conference on Water and Salt Metabolism and Kidney Function, pp.53—54. Ordzhonikidze, 1971. (Russian)

Prosvirina, N.N. Higher Nervous Activity and Functional Sexual Disorders in Man. — Synopses of Reports to the 21st Conference on Higher Nervous Activity, p.245. Moscow—Leningrad, 1966. (Russian)

Pshonik, A.T. The Cerebral Cortex and the Receptor Activity of the Body. — Moscow, 1952. (Russian)

Pshonik, A.T. Pathological States of Higher Nervous Activity. — Proceedings of the Fourth Conference of the West Siberian Society of Physiology, Biochemistry, and Pharmacology, Vol.1, pp.383—386. Krasnoyarsk, 1969. (Russian)

Pshonik, A.T. The Cortical Regulation of Internal Organs in Normal and Pathological States. Manuscript.— Arkhiv Orgkomiteta XI s"ezda Vses. fiziol. obshch. im.I.P.Pavlova. Leningrad, 1970. (Russian)

Putilin, N.I. Energy Manifestations in Trophic Changes in the Gastric Mucosa. — In: Vzaimodeistvie organov pishchevaritel'noi sistemy, pp.102—110. Leningrad, 1968. (Russian)

Putintseva, T.G. The Peripheral Connections between the Different Parts of the Autonomic Nervous System and Self-Regulation of the Mediator Processes. — Author's Summary of Thesis. Leningrad, 1970. (Russian)

Rabinovich, P.D. and L.A.Kublanov. The Role of a Hereditary Predisposition to Gastric and Duodenal Ulcer. — Terapevtich. Arkhiv 35, No.3 (1963), 12. (Russian)

Rafikov, M.Z. Changes in the Peripheral Organs (Tissues) after Lesions of the Cerebral Cortex and Cerebellum. — X s"ezd Vses. fiziol. obshch. im. I.P.Pavlova, Vol.2, No.2, p.218. Summaries of Scientific Communications, Moscow—Leningrad, 1964. (Russian)

Raitses, V.S. Relationships of Various Conditioned Reflexes in Visceral Pathology. — Synopses of Reports to the 21st Conference on Higher Nervous Activity, pp.250—251, Moscow—Leningrad, 1966. (Russian)

Raitses, V.S. A Contribution to the Study of the Central Mechanism of Convergence of Afferent Systems. — Proceedings of the Ninth All-Union Conference on Corticovisceral Physiology, pp.183—184. Baku, 1971. (Russian)

Rakhmatova, M.R. The Influence of Disorders of Higher Nervous Activity (Experimental Neurosis) on Blood Regeneration after Hemorrhage. — Proceedings of the Ninth All-Union Conference on Corticovisceral Physiology, pp.184—185. Baku, 1971. (Russian)

Rashap, B.Ya. A Clinical and Physiological Study of the Nervous Mechanism in Regulating the Stomach in Peptic Ulcer. — Author's Summary of Thesis. Kiev, 1966. (Russian)

Razenkov, I.P. New Findings with Regards to the Physiology and Pathology of Digestion. — Moscow, 1948. (Russian)

Razran, G. Introductory Comments. — In: Higher Nervous Activity. Proceedings of the American Conference in Memory of Pavlov. (Russian translation, 1963)

Richter, C.P. The Neurological Basis of Responses to Stress. — In: The Neurological Basis of Behavior, pp.204—217. London, 1958.

Rikkl', A.V. The Nervous Regulation of Reciprocal Autonomic Activity. — Leningrad, 1961. (Russian)

Rikkl', A.V. The Functional Relationship of Growth and Activity in the Viscera. — In: Kortiko-vistseral'nye vzaimootnosheniya v fiziologii, biologii i meditsine, pp.137—148. Leningrad, 1971. (Russian)

Robertis, E.D.P. de. Histophysiology of Synapses and Neurosecretion. — New York, 1964.

Rogov, A.A. On Vascular Conditioned and Unconditioned Reflexes in Man. — Moscow—Leningrad, 1951. (Russian)

Romanov, S.N. The Reaction of Nerve Cells to Inadequate and Adequate Stimuli. — Author's Summary of Thesis. Leningrad, 1956. (Russian)

Rosin, Ya.A. The Physiology of the Autonomic Nervous System. — Moscow, 1965. (Russian)

Rosin, Ya.A. The Tissue—Blood Barriers and Neurohumoral Regulation. — XI s"ezd Vses. fiziol. obshch. im. I.P.Pavlova, Vol.2, p.204. Summaries of Scientific Communications, Leningrad, 1970. (Russian)

Rossi, G.F. and A.Zanchetti. The Reticular Formation of the Brain Stem. (Russian translation, 1957)

Rozhdestvenskaya, G.G. On the State of Higher Nervous Activity in Patients with Hypertensive Psychosis.— 21st Conference on Higher Nervous Activity, pp.254—255. Summaries and Abstracts of Reports, Leningrad, 1966. (Russian)

Rusinov, V.S. Electrophysiological Studies of Dominance. — Moscow, 1969. (Russian)

Rybnikova, N.M. Changes in the Intestinal Absorption of Glucose and Water in Various Functional States of the Cerebral Cortex. — Author's Summary of Thesis. Leningrad, 1955. (Russian)

Rybnikova, N.M. The Importance of the Reticular Formation in the Cortical Production of Disorders of Intestinal Absorption. — In: Kortikal'nye mekhanizmy regulyatsii deyatel'nosti vnutrennikh organov, pp.131—134. Moscow—Leningrad, 1966. (Russian)

Ryvkin, I.A. The Role of Heredity in the Etiology of Hypertension. — Klinich. Med. 38, No.12 (1960), 24. (Russian)

Safarov, R.I. The Effect of Afferent Impulses from the Abdominal Organs on the Functional State of the Intestinal Receptors and Nerve Centers. — Proceedings of the Conference on the Physiology and Pathology of Corticovisceral Relationships and Physiological Systems of the Body, Vol.2, pp.247—253. Ivanovo, 1965. (Russian)

Sager, O. The Midbrain. — Bucharest, 1960. (Russian translation)

Sakai, A., T.Ban, and T.Kurotsu. The Limbic System and the Autonomic Reaction. — Med. J. Osaka Univ., Vol.11 (1960), 69.

Samoilov, M.O. The Relationships between the Neocortex and the Hypothalamus in Cats. — Author's Summary of Thesis. Leningrad, 1971. (Russian)

Samson, E.I. The Functional Relationships between Higher Divisions of the Central Nervous System and the Viscera in Peptic Ulcer. — Proceedings of the Joint Conference on Mechanisms of Corticovisceral Relationships, pp.86—92. Baku, 1962. (Russian)

Saragea, M. and I.Foni. The Location of Visceral Disturbances in Neuroses. — Activitas nerv. sup., Vol.4 (1962). 313—321.

Schreiber, V. The Hypothalamic-Hypophyseal System. — Prague, 1963.

Selye, H. Stress. The Physiology and Pathology of Exposure to Stress. — Montreal, 1950.

Selye, H. The Story of the Adaptation Syndrome. 1952.

Selye, H. Perspectives in Stress Research. — Perspect. Biol. Med., Vol.11 (1959), 407.

Selye, H. On the Level of the Organism as a Whole. (Russian translation, 1972)

Selye, H. and G.Heuser. Fourth Annual Report on Stress. — Montreal, 1954.

Serdyuchenko, I.Ya. Conditioned-Reflex Sinocarotid Reactions of the Cardiovascular and Respiratory Systems. — Proceedings of the Conference on Relationships between Different Systems of the Body in Normal and Pathological States, pp.643—648, Ivanovo, 1962. (Russian)

Sergeeva, I.V. Changes in Drinking Excitability of the Feeding Center in Functional Disorders of Higher Nervous Activity. — Trudy Inst. Fiziol. im. I.P.Pavlova, Vol.7 (1958), 496—503. (Russian)

S e r g e e v a , I.V. The Blood Count and Certain Autonomic Functions in Dogs with an Experimental Neurosis Following Anemia of Toxic Origin. — Proceedings of the Conference on the Physiology and Pathology of Corticovisceral Relationships and the Physiological Systems of the Body, Vol.2, pp.259—263. Ivanovo, 1965. (Russian)

S e r g e e v a , I.V. The Importance of Preliminary Trauma in the Primary Lesion of the Vascular System in Experimental Neurosis. — In: Kortikal'nye regulyatsii vnutrennikh organov, pp.135—141. Moscow—Leningrad, 1966. (Russian)

S e r g e e v a , I.V. Changes in the Content of Biologically Active Substances in the Blood of Dogs in the Normal State and with Experimental Neurosis. — In: Gormonal'noe zveno kortiko-vistseral'nykh vzaimootnoshenii, pp.147—157. Leningrad, 1969. (Russian)

S e r g i e v s k i i , M.V. Respiratory Regulation by the Cerebral Cortex. Ser. III, No.54. — Moscow, "Znanie," 1955. (Russian)

S e v e r ' y a n o v a , L.A. The Role of the Hypophysis in the Pathogenesis of Experimental Neurogenic Hypertension. — Author's Summary of Thesis. Leningrad, 1965. (Russian)

S h e r r i n g t o n , C.S. The Integrative Action of the Nervous System. 2nd edition.—Cambridge Univ.Press. 1947.

S i m o n o v , P.V. Three Phases in the Reaction of the Organism to Increasing Stimulus. — Moscow, 1962. (Russian)

S i m o n y a n , K.S. The Importance of Interoception from the Digestive Tract in Surgical Practice. — In: Vzaimodeistvie organov pishchevaritel'noi sistemy, pp.120—125. Leningrad, 1968. (Russian)

S i t d i k o v a , V.V. The Role of the Hippocampus in the Structure and Function of the Visceral Analyzers. — Author's Summary of Thesis. Leningrad, 1970. (Russian)

S m i r n o v , V.M. Neuropsychological Aspects of Studying Emotional and Motive Behavior in Man. — Proceedings of the All-Union Symposium on the Structural, Functional and Neurochemical Mechanisms of the Emotions, pp.95—98. Leningrad, 1971. (Russian)

S ö d e r b e r g , U. Neurophysiological Aspects of Stress. — In: Emotional Stress. pp.97—108. Basel, 1967.

S o l d a t e n k o v , P.F. The Cortical Regulation of Certain Physiological Processes in Ruminants. — Trudy Tomsk. Gos. Univ., Vol.143, biol. ser., pp.135—145. Tomsk, 1956. (Russian)

S o l o v ' e v , A.V. New Data on the Secretory Activity of the Stomach and Pancreas. — Leningrad, 1959. (Russian)

S o l o v ' e v , A.V. The Regulatory Mechanisms of Digestive Activity. — In: Kortiko-vistseral'nye vzaimootnosheniya v fiziologii, biologii i meditsine, pp.160—166. Leningrad, 1971. (Russian)

S o s e n k o v , V.A. Interoceptive Conditioned Reflexes in Decorticate Cats. — Proceedings of the Conference on Problems of the Physiology and Pathology of Corticovisceral Relationships and Physiological Systems of the Body, Vol.2, pp.304—308. Ivanovo, 1965. (Russian)

S o t n i c h e n k o , T.S. The Subsidiary Pathways of Visceral Signals to the Cortex. — Proceedings of the Ninth All-Union Scientific Conference on Problems of Corticovisceral Physiology, pp.201—202. Baku, 1971. (Russian)

S p e r a n s k a y a , E.N. The Physiology of the Autonomic Nervous System. — Moscow—Leningrad, 1961. (Russian)

S p e r a n s k i i , A.D. Elements of the Structure of the Theory of Medicine. — Moscow, 1935. (Russian)

S t a r t s e v , V.G. Experimental Models of Human Neurogenic Disorders in Monkeys. — Moscow, 1971. (Russian)

S t e p a n o v , P.N. The Etiology of Peptic Ulcer. — Trudy Smolensk. Med. Inst. Voprosy Fiziol. i Patol. Pishchevarit. Trakta 34, No.2 (1970), 78—85. (Russian)

S t e p h e n s , W. The Oedipus Complex. Cross-Cultural Evidence. — New York, 1962.

S t i e v e , H. Der Einfluss des Nervensystems auf Bau und Tätigkeit der Geschlechtsorgane. — Stuttgart, 1952.

S t ö h r , Ph. Jr. Mikroskopische Anatomie des vegetativen Nervensystems. — Handbuch der mikroskopischen Anatomie des Menschen, Vol.5. Berlin, 1957.

S t o y a n o v s k i i , S.V., R.M. S t u p n i t s k i i , and N.F. K i s l e n k o . Cortical Influences on the Respiratory Exchange, Permeability and Synthetizing Activity of the Mammary Gland. — Proceedings of the Ninth All-Union Conference on Corticovisceral Physiology, pp.203—204. Baku, 1971. (Russian)

S t r a z h e s k o , N.D. The Pathogenesis of Peptic Ulcer. — Trudy XIII Vses. s"ezda terapevtov, pp.51—60. Leningrad, 1949. (Russian)

S u d a k o v , K.V. The Pacemaker Mechanism of Food Motivation. — XI s"ezd Vses. fiziol. obshch. im. I.P.Pavlova, Vol.1. Abstracts of Reports on the Symposium, pp.187—192. Leningrad, 1970. (Russian)

S u l t a n o v , F.F. The Role of the Cerebral Cortex in Changes of Vascular-Tissue Permeability in Hyperthermia. — Eighth Conference on Corticovisceral Relationships in Physiology, Medicine and Biology, Vol.1, p.141. Synopses of Reports. Leningrad, 1967. (Russian)

Suplyakov, N.T. The Bioelectrical Activity of Some Cortical and Subcortical Formations in Psychogenic Stress. — Proceedings of the Ninth All-Union Conference on Problems of Corticovisceral Physiology, pp.206—208. Baku, 1971. (Russian)

Surikov, M.P. Present Concepts of the Mechanism of Hormone Activity. — Proceedings of the Fourth Conference of the West Siberian Society of Physiologists, Biochemists and Pharmacologists, Vol.2, pp.677—679. Krasnoyarsk, 1969. (Russian)

Suvorov, N.F. Central Mechanisms of Vascular Disorders. — Leningrad, 1967. (Russian)

Suvorov, N.F. The Role of Cortical and Subcortical Structures of the Human Brain in the Mechanism of Experimental Angioneurosis and Hypertension. — In: Kortiko-vistseral'nye vzaimootnosheniya v fiziologii, biologii i meditsine, pp.167—175. Leningrad, 1971. (Russian)

Suvorov, N.F. and L.K.Danilova. A Study of the Mechanism of Neurotic Disorders of Higher Nervous Activity. — Synopses of Reports to the 21st Conference on Higher Nervous Activity, p.285. Moscow—Leningrad, 1966. (Russian)

Syrenskii, V.I. The Self-Regularory Mechanisms of the Human Brain. — Leningrad, 1970. (Russian)

Szentagothai,J., B.Flerko, B.Mess, and B.Halasz. Hypothalamic Control of the Anterior Pituitary. — Budapest, Akademizi Kiado, 1965.

Talan, M.I. The Mode of Influence of the Cerebellum on Certain Autonomic Functions in Cats. — Author's Summary of Thesis. Leningrad, 1970. (Russian)

Tashchenov, K.T. The Activity of the Digestive Glands in Lactating Animals. — Author's Summary of Thesis. Alma-Ata, 1969. (Russian)

Teleshevskaya, M.E. Mental Trauma and Endocrine Disorders. — Proceedings of the Republican Conference on the Physiology, Biochemistry and Pathology of the Endocrine System, pp.260—262. Kiev, 1969. (Russian)

Teplov, S.I. The Nervous and Hormonal Control of the Coronary Circulation. — Leningrad, 1962. (Russian)

Teregulov, A.G. and K.A.Mayanskaya. Reciprocal Pathological Interoception and Disorders of the Digestive Organs. — Proceedings of the Conference on the Functional Relationships between Various Systems of the Body in Normal and Pathological States, pp.307—312. Ivanovo, 1962. (Russian)

Tobias, J.M. A Chemically-Specific Molecular Mechanism Underlying Excitation in Nerve: a Hypothesis. — Nature, Vol.203 (1964), 13.

Tolmasskaya, E.S. The Nervous Mechanisms Coordinating the Somatic and Visceral Activity of the Body. — Moscow, 1964. (Russian)

Tonkikh, A.V. The Hypothalamic-Pituitary Region and the Control of Physiological Activity in the Body. — Moscow—Leningrad, 1968. (Russian)

Tsvetkova, G.M. Morphological Changes in the Nervous System and Heart of Dogs with Experimental Coronary Insufficiency. — Proceedings of the Ninth All-Union Conference on Corticovisceral Physiology, pp.234—235. Baku, 1971. (Russian)

Tuge, H., Hui V.Chang, V.Kanayama, and N.Horikiri. A Study of the Function of the Reticular Formation of the Brain Stem by Means of Motor Conditioned Reflexes. — International Symposium on Corticovisceral Physiology and Pathology. Synopses of Reports, Berlin, 1964. (Russian translation)

Turpaev, T.M. The Mediator Activity of Acetylcholine and the Nature of the Choline Receptor. — Moscow, 1962. (Russian)

Ukhtomskii, A.A. Dominance. — Leningrad, 1966. (Russian)

Ul'yanycheva-Yudintseva, M.F. Corticovisceral Parallels in Clinical and Laboratory Examinations for Chronic Gastritis in Older Children. — Synopses of Reports to the Eighth Conference on Corticovisceral Relationships in Physiology, Medicine and Biology, pp.150—151. Leningrad, 1967. (Russian)

Umbach, W. Autonomic and Emotional Reactions to the Irritation or Removal of Specific Regions of the Human Brain. — Synopses of Reports to the Internat. Symposium on Corticovisceral Physiology and Pathology, pp.108—109. Berlin, 1964.

Usievich, M.A. The Physiology of Higher Nervous Activity. — Moscow, 1953. (Russian)

Uspenskii, Yu.N., V.I.Savchuk, A.Ya.Rappaport, and Yu.A.Tirkel'taub. Conditioned Reflex Study of the Action of Psychotropic Substances. — Moscow, 1964. (Russian)

Vainshtein, I.I. Electroencephalographic Manifestations and Autonomic Function in Dogs during Various Emotional Reactions Caused by Direct Stimulation of the "Emotional Centers" of the Hypothalamus. — Proceedings of the All-Union Symposium on the Structural, Functional and Neurochemical Mechanisms of the Emotions, pp.126—129. Leningrad, 1971. (Russian)

Val'dman, A.V. Aspects of the Study of Emotional Behavior by Experiments on Animals. — Proceedings of the All-Union Symposium on the Structural, Functional and Neurochemical Mechanisms of the Emotions, pp.9—23. Leningrad, 1971. (Russian)

Valueva, M.N. The Voluntary Regulation of Autonomic Functions. — Moscow, 1967. (Russian)

Varbanova, A. Interoceptive Signals. — Sofia, 1967. (Bulgarian)

Vartapetov, B.A., A.I.Gladkova, K.M.Kalmykova, E.S.Kuz'menko, A.I.Molodtsova-Larina, and A.D.Sudakova. The Effect of Hormonal Disorders on Neurovisceral Relationships. — In: Gormonal'noe zveno kortiko-vistseral'nykh vzaimootnoshenii, pp.46—53. Leningrad, 1969. (Russian)

Vasilevskaya, N.E. The Function and Structure of the Viscerochemical Analyzers. — Author's Summary of Thesis. Leningrad, 1967. (Russian)

Vedyaev, F.P. The Functional and Neurochemical Characteristics of Emotional Reactions of Limbic Origin. — Proceedings of the All-Union Symposium on the Structural, Functional and Neurochemical Mechanisms of the Emotions, pp.130—133. Leningrad, 1971. (Russian)

Vein, A.M. Waking and Sleep. — Moscow, 1970. (Russian)

Vilyavin, G.D. and A.I.Nazarenko. The Etiological Basis of Conservative and Surgical Treatment in Peptic Ulcer. — Moscow, 1966. (Russian)

Viklyaev, Yu.I. and T.A.Klygul'. The Effect of Tranquilizers on Various Types of Emotional Reactions Accompanying Certain Forms of Behavior of Animals when Subjected to Experimental Procedures. — Proceedings of the All-Union Symposium on the Structural, Functional and Neurochemical Mechanisms of the Emotions, pp.152—156. Leningrad, 1971. (Russian)

Vogralik, V. The Role of Hypothalamus in Human Pathology. — Meditsinskaya Gazeta, No.42 (1965), 3. (Russian)

Voitkevich, A.A. Hypothalamic-Hypophyseal Regulation of Thyroid Activity. — XI s"ezd Vses. fiziol. obshch. im. I.P.Pavlova, Vol.1, pp.306—311. Reviews and Reports to the Symposium. Leningrad,1970. (Russian)

Voitkevich, A.A. and G.A.Tkacheva. The Enzymatic Basis of the Stimulatory Effect of Adrenocorticotrophic Hormone (ACTH) on the Adrenocortical Cell. — In: Fiziologiya, biokhimiya i patologiya endokrinnoi sistemy. Proceedings of the Republican Conference, pp.169—171. Kiev, 1969. (Russian)

Völgyesi, F.A. Second International Congress of Psychosomatic Medicine, Paris, July 5—8, 1963. — Zhurn. Nevropatol. i Psikhiatr. 64, No.6 (1964), 950. (Russian translation)

Volokhov, A.A. The Ontogenetic Role of the Higher Divisions of the Brain in the Correlation of Autonomic and Somatic Conditioned Reactions. — International Symposium on Corticovisceral Physiology and Pathology, pp.41—42. Synopses of Reports. Berlin, 1964. (Russian)

Volynskii, Z.M. Corticovisceral Relationships in Cardiovascular Pathology. — In: Kortiko-vistseral'nye vzaimootnosheniya v fiziologii, biologii i meditsine, pp.70—75. Leningrad, 1971. (Russian)

Voronin, L.G. Lectures on the Physiology of Higher Nervous Activity. — Moscow, 1965. (Russian)

Voronin, L.G. and R.A.Danilova. Chain Reflexes on the Direct Application of Ribonuclease to the Brain of Rats. — Synopses of Reports to the 21st Conference on Problems of Higher Nervous Activity. Summaries and Abstracts of Reports, p.82. Moscow—Leningrad, 1966. (Russian)

Voznesenskii, B.B. The Significance of the Functional State and Typological Characteristics of the Nervous System in the Effects Produced by the Application of Hormone Preparations. — Reports to the Conference on Corticovisceral Relationships and Hormonal Regulation, pp.47—52, Kharkov, 1963. (Russian)

Vvedenskii, N.E. Excitation, Inhibition and Anesthesia. — In: I.M.Sechenov, I.P.Pavlov, and N.E.Vvedenskii. Fiziologiya nervnoi sistemy. Izbran. Trudy, Vol.2, pp.314—412. Moscow, 1901, 1952. (Russian)

Weitbrecht, H.J. Kritik der Psychosomatik. — Stuttgart, 1955.

Wells, H. Pavlov and Freud. 2 Vols. — NW Intl. Pub. Co., 1956.

Wells, H. The Failure of Psychoanalysis. From Freud to Fromm. — NW Intl. Pub. Co., 1956.

Wittkower, E.D. Twenty Years of North American Psychosomatic Medicine. — Psychosom. Med. 22, No.46 (1960), 308.

Wittkower, E.D. and L.Solyam. Conceptional Models of Mental and Physical Influences on Psycho-Physiological Disorders. — Synopses of Reports to the International Symposium on Corticovisceral Physiology and Pathology, pp.37—38. Berlin. 1964.

Wooldridge, D.E. The Machinery of the Brain. — New York, McGraw-Hill, 1963.

Yakovleva, V.V. and B.I. Stozharov. The Type of Nervous System and Conditioned Reflex Activity in Patients with Hypertension. — In: Raboty leningradskikh vrachei v gody Otechestvennoi voiny, , No.8, p.73. Leningrad, 1946. (Russian)

Yakovleva, E.A. Experimental Neurosis. — Moscow, 1967. (Russian)

Yaroslavtseva, N.A. The Role of Meso-Diencephalic Structures in the Regulation of Cerebrocortical Activity and the Vascular Reactions of the Body. — Synopses of Reports to the 21st Conference on Higher Nervous Activity, p.340. Moscow—Leningrad, 1966. (Russian)

Yuldasheva, M.Kh. Experimental Findings Concerning Functional and Morphological Changes in the Stomach in Gastric Ulceration. — Author's Summary of Thesis. Tashkent, 1966. (Russian)

Zaitseva, E.I. The Clinical Importance of the Functional Relationships of the Stomach, Intestine and Pancreas. — In: Voprosy patologii pecheni i podzheludochnoi zhelezy, pp.186—198. Smolensk, 1969. (Russian)

Zaitseva, E.I. The Pathogenesis of Peptic Ulcer in the Light of Clinical Findings. The Question of Peptic Ulceration and Anacid States. — Opening paper to the Conference of Therapeutists, pp.12—15. Smolensk, 1971. (Russian)

Zakharzhevskii, V.B. The Part Played by Cortical Mechanisms in the Regulation of the Coronary Circulation in Dogs. — In: Kortikal'nye mekhanizmy regulyatsii deyatel'nosti vnutrennikh organov, pp.59—71, Moscow—Leningrad, 1966a. (Russian)

Zakharzhevskii, V.B. The Effect on the Coronary Circulation in Dogs with Experimental Neurosis. — In: Kortikal'nye mekhanizmy regulyatsii deyatel'nosti vnutrennikh organov, pp.72—83. Moscow—Leningrad, 1966b. (Russian)

Zakharzhevskii, V.B. and V.Yu. Ermolaeva. The Characteristics of Afferent Impulses in the Stomach Innervation at Various Stages of Experimental Acute Gastritis. — Proceedings of the Conference on the Physiology and Pathology of Corticovisceral Relationships and the Physiological Systems of the Body, Vol.1, pp.399—402. Ivanovo, 1965. (Russian)

Zambrzhitskii, I.A. The Limbic Region of the Brain. — Moscow, 1972. (Russian)

Zhemkova, Z.P., A.A. Manina, and G.N. Orlova. Histochemical Changes in the Brain Cells of Rats with Various Functional and Organic Disorders. — Ezhegodn. Inst. Eksper. Med., pp.380—385. Leningrad, 1956. (Russian)

Zhgenti, A.D. The Mechanism of the Therapeutic Action of Mineral Water from Borzhomi in Diseases of the Stomach. — Tbilisi, 1956. (Russian)

Zhmakin, I.K. The Effect of Excision of the Cerebral Cortex on the Respiratory Exchange in Dogs. — Opening Papers and Abstracts of Reports of the 16th Conference on Higher Nervous Activity, pp.86—87. Moscow—Leningrad, 1953. (Russian)

Zhukova, E.A. Clinical Forms of Thyrotoxicosis with Neurotic and Neurosislike Manifestations. — In: Fiziologiya, biokhimiya i patologiya endokrinnoi sistemy. Proceedings of the Republican Conference, pp.127—128. Kiev, 1969. (Russian)

Zilov, V.G. The Possible Mechanism of the Cortical Control of Visceral Functions. — Proceedings of the Ninth All-Union Conference on Corticovisceral Physiology, pp.92—93. Baku, 1971. (Russian)

Zubkov, A.A. and F.I. Furdui. Cortical-Reticular-Thyroidin Relationships and the Mechanism of Production of Neurogenic Thyrotoxicosis. — Proceedings of the Conference on the Physiology and Pathology of Corticovisceral Relationships and Physiological Systems of the Body, Vol.1, pp.406—409. Ivanovo, 1965. (Russian)

Zvorykin, V.N. Fractional Irradiation with Relatively Small Doses of Ionizing Radiation and Functional State of the Stomach. — Author's Summary of Thesis. Leningrad, 1968. (Russian)

SUPPLEMENT

Andreeva-Galanina, E.P., S.V. Alekseev, A.V. Kadyskin, and G.A. Suvorov. Noise and Disease Caused by Noise. — Leningrad, 1972. (Russian)

Clegg, R.C. and A.G. Clegg. Hormones, Cells and the Organism. The Role of Hormones in Mammals. Moscow, 1971. (Russian translation)

Dolin, A.O. and S.A. Dolina. The Pathology of Higher Nervous Activity. — Moscow, 1972. (Russian)

Eccles, J.C. The Physiology of the Synapses. — Berlin, Springer. 1964.

Firsov, L.A. Memory in Anthropoids. — Leningrad, 1972. (Russian)

Gorchakova, L.A. Materials for a Study of the Conditions which Affect Chemoreception in the Uterus. — Author's Summary of Thesis. Rostov-on-Don, 1972. (Russian)

Il'yuchenok, R.Yu. The Pharmacology of Behavior and Memory. — Novosibirsk, 1972. (Russian)

Il'yuchenok, R.Yu. and M.A.Gilinskii. The Structure and Mediators of Reticular-Cortical Relationships. — Leningrad, 1971. (Russian)

Iontov, A.S., V.A.Otellin, E.E.Granstrem, and F.N.Makarov. Histological Studies of the Connections of the Central Nervous System Connections. — Leningrad, 1971. (Russian)

Ivanov-Muromskii, K.A. The Self-Regulation of the Brain. — Moscow, 1971. (Russian)

Kolosov, N.G. The Autonomic Ganglion. — Leningrad, 1972. (Russian)

Kostenetskaya, N.A. Conditioned Reflex Regulation of the Tone of the Cerebral Cortex. — Leningrad, 1965. (Russian)

Megrabyan, A.A. General Psychopathology. — Moscow, 1972. (Russian)

Missiuro, W. Emotional Stress, Fatigue and Working Capacity. — 15th Intern. Congress of Occupational Health, Vienna, Symposium on Higher Nervous Activity and Occupational Health. Abstracts, pp.34—35. Prague, 1966.

Naumenko, E.V. Central Regulation of the Pituitary-Adrenal Complex. — Leningrad, 1971. (Russian)

Petrakov, B.D. Mental Disorders in Certain Countries during the Present Century. — Moscow, 1972. (Russian)

Puchkova, S.A. The Striopallidal System and its Cortical Connections in Man. — Author's Summary of Thesis. Moscow, 1968. (Russian)

Selye, H. Adaptive Steroids: their Development and Perspectives. — Zhum. Patofiziol. i Eksper. Terapii 15, No.2 (1972), 3—18. (Russian translation)

Shevchenko, Yu.G. The Development of the Human Cerebral Cortex in the Light of Onto- and Phylogenetic Considerations.— Moscow, 1972. (Russian)

Sokolov, E.N. The Mechanisms of Memory. — Moscow, 1969. (Russian)

Sudakov, K.V. Biological Motivations. — Moscow, 1971. (Russian)